Italian gardens vary widely according to their historical date and geographic location. This collection approaches Italian gardens of all periods, from the middle ages to modern times, and it ranges widely throughout the peninsula, from Genoa to Sicily, the Veneto to Liguria, and Ferrara to Florence.

The authors are a distinguished group of Italian, American, English and German scholars, with different backgrounds in art history, literature, architecture, planning, and cultural history. The explorations of the subject from these different perspectives illuminate not only their own disciplines, but are concerned to make many fresh connections between garden art and the politics of nationalism, between the art of gardens and urban infrastructure, between cultural movements like freemasonry and site planning, between design and planting materials. The book offers therefore a narrative of the garden by selecting ten high points of its history, which are introduced with a consideration by the volume editor of the fresh challenges to contemporary Italian garden history.

CAMBRIDGE STUDIES IN ITALIAN HISTORY AND CULTURE

THE ITALIAN GARDEN

CAMBRIDGE STUDIES IN ITALIAN HISTORY AND CULTURE

Edited by GIORGIO CHITTOLINI, Università degli Studi, Milan
CESARE MOZZARELLI, Università Cattolica del Sacro Cuore, Milan
ROBERT ORESKO, Institute of Historical Research, University of London
and GEOFFREY SYMCOX, University of California, Los Angeles

This series comprises monographs and a variety of collaborative volumes, including translated works, which will concentrate on the period of Italian history from late medieval times up to the Risorgimento. The editors aim to stimulate scholarly debate over a range of issues which have not hitherto received, in English, the attention they deserve. As it develops, the series will emphasise the interest and vigour of current international debates on this central period of Italian history and the persistent influence of Italian culture on the rest of Europe.

Titles in the series

Other titles are in preparation

THE ITALIAN GARDEN

ART, DESIGN AND CULTURE

EDITED BY

JOHN DIXON HUNT
University of Pennsylvania

CAMBRIDGE
UNIVERSITY PRESS

Published by the Press Syndicate of the University of Cambridge
The Pitt Building, Trumpington Street, Cambridge CB2 1RP
40 West 20th Street, New York, NY 10011-4211, USA
10 Stamford Road, Oakleigh, Melbourne 3166, Australia

© Cambridge University Press 1996

First published 1996

Printed in Great Britain at the University Press, Cambridge

A catalogue record for this book is available from the British Library

Library of Congress cataloguing in publication data applied for

ISBN 0 521 44353 9 hardback

CONTENTS

═══════════

ILLUSTRATIONS

CONTRIBUTORS

MARGHERITA AZZI VISENTINI is Professor of the History of Architecture at Milan Polytechnic. Her interests include Palladio and English Palladianism, and the architecture of villas and gardens, with special regard to the Veneto. She is the author of *Palladio in America e l'architettura della villa* (Milan, 1976); *L'Orto Botanico di Padova e il giardino del Rinascimento* (Milan, 1984); *Il giardino veneto tra Sette e Ottocento e le sue fonti* (Milan, 1988); *La villa in Italia: Quattro e Cinquecento* (Milan, 1995). She edited *Il giardino veneto dal tardo medioevo al novecento* (Milan, 1988).

ANNALISA MANIGLIO CALCAGNO trained as an architect at Rome University. She is Pro-Rector of Genoa University and Professor of Architecture, having created the first postgraduate school of landscape architecture in Italy. She has published *L'architettura del paesaggio. Evoluzione storica* (1983) as well as other books and many articles.

MALCOLM CAMPBELL is Class of 1965 Professor of The History of Art at the University of Pennsylvania, and the author of books on Pietro da Cortona and Piranesi, together with many articles on Italian Renaissance and Baroque art and architecture. He has held fellowships from the Guggenheim Foundation, NEH and ACLS and at Villa I Tatti, and been visiting professor at the American Academy in Rome. He has curated exhibitions in Florence, Rome, Venice and London.

RAYMOND GASTIL is executive director of the Van Alen Institute: Projects in Public Architecture, in New York. He recently directed the transit-oriented design project at Regional Plan Association, where he co-authored the *Third Regional Plan* (1996), *Redesigning the Suburbs: Turning Sprawl into Centers* (1994), and 'Visual Simulations: The Future of the Tri-State Region,' in *The New City*, II: *The American City* (1994). In addition, he co-authored *Modern Classicism* and has contributed numerous articles to architecture and design journals, and given lectures, led design studios, and juried projects at a range of architecture, planning, and landscape programmes, including Columbia University and the University of Pennsylvania.

JOHN DIXON HUNT is Professor of Landscape Architecture at the University of Pennsylvania and the editor of the new Penn Studies in Landscape Architecture which begins publishing in late 1996. He is working on a history of the garden in the city of Venice.

IRIS LAUTERBACH studied the history of art and romance philology at Pavia, Paris and Mainz, where she took her Ph.D. in 1985. She has held posts at the Staatliche Museen Preussischer Kulturbesitz, Berlin, Freiburg University, the Hertziana Library, Rome, and (since 1991) the Zentralinstitut für Kunstgeschichte, Munich.

GIOVANNI LEONI teaches architectural history in the Faculty of Architecture at Bari. He took his Ph.D. at the Architectural Institute of the University of Venice with a dissertation on gardens of Ferrara, on which topic he has already published an essay in a volume by various authors, *Fiori e giardini estensi a Ferrara* (Rome, 1992).

GIANNI PIRRONE was Professor of Architecture from 1964 and Professor of Garden Architecture from 1984 in the Faculty of Architecture at Palermo University. From 1990 to 1995 he headed Palermo's school for garden architecture and landscape. He has edited many studies in these disciplines.

LUCIA BATTAGLIA RICCI is Professor of Italian Literature at the Terza Università di Roma, where she specialises in medieval literature and the connections between it and the visual arts during the thirteenth and fourteenth centuries. Her publications include *Dante e la tradizione medievale* (1983), *Palazzo Vecchio e dintorni* (1990), *Parole e immagini nella letteratura italiana mediaevale* (1994) and several articles.

ALESSANDRO TOSI, who gained his Ph.D. in Art History, is the author of several essays on the relationship between art and science. He holds a research post at the Istituto e Museo di Storia della Scienza, Florence.

D.R. EDWARD WRIGHT is an Associate Professor of Art at the University of South Florida in Tampa. His work has appeared in the *Journal of the Warburg and Courtauld Institutes, The Burlington Magazine,* and the *Journal of Aesthetics and Art Criticism.* He was one of the contributors to an international symposium of the Boboli Garden held in Florence in 1989. He is currently completing a major study of L. B. Alberti's *De Pictura.*

MAKING AND WRITING THE ITALIAN GARDEN

JOHN DIXON HUNT

The twentieth-century English reader and amateur has always been well served by publications on Italian gardens. A glance at some of these books can identify the main elements of a modern concern with Italian gardens. To begin in 1903, Edith Wharton's *Italian Villas and their Gardens* sought to identify an ideal scenery that was at once social and spiritual; her impressionistic word-pictures reflected a long ekphrastic tradition in viewing gardens, yet her publishers buttressed those endeavours with photographs and 'evocative' modern paintings by Maxfield Parrish. *Italian Gardens of the Renaissance* (1925), by G. A. Jellicoe and J. C. Shepherd, brought into play sober architectural analysis, along with surveys, elevations and stolid photographic documentation. Georgina Masson's *Italian Gardens* (1961) probably introduced more armchair and later actual travellers to the pleasures and significance of her subject than any other author; there has been little to compare with her learned, intimate and enthusiastic experience of the gardens she rediscovered, researched, described and photographed herself. Most recently and following in an American academic tradition of scholarship in this field (where the names of David R. Coffin and Elisabeth B. MacDougall are clearly prominent) has come Claudia Lazzaro's *The Italian Renaissance Garden* (1990); here conventions of art history collaborate with the publishing resources (including the work of a distinguished professional photographer) that so many books on gardens now seem to elicit.

A study of Lazzaro's documentation will reveal how far research on Italian gardens has come during the twentieth century. And notably it discloses the ever increasing contribution of Italian scholars to their own garden history, the beginnings of which may be dated to Luigi Dami's book, *Il giardino italiano* (1924) and the 1931 *Catalogo della Mostra del Giardino Italiano*, held in Florence.

The advance in Italian garden history studies is not simply the huge increase in both its participants and in the documentation that now exists to sustain their description and analysis, but in positioning garden enthusiasm firmly in academic territory; the two are, of course, closely connected. Though there are many students of gardens and gardening who decry 'academic' approaches, the territory of garden history has been much augmented and refined precisely by archival research and conceptual inquiry, both of which are pursued (though not exclusively) in the modern academy. These chapters also draw (though again not exclusively) upon the academic study of gardens. And they demonstrate the range, variety and versatility of approaches that characterise scholarly garden history now – this volume's necessarily composite structure making more visible than books by single authors the essential polysemy that lies at the heart of garden-making and thus of writing about gardens.

None of the authors here was specifically invited to address the historiography of gardens. Yet inevitably this theme shows through almost all of their chapters or is even addressed directly in passing. Garden history is interdisciplinary and international; the borders of its contributing disciplines are porous, and its specialists, wherever they start (architecture or landscape architecture, literary, economic or art history, urban studies or medicine), learn to transgress the traditional boundaries of study. The sites of gardens – though inevitably grounded in one place – attract designers and craftsmen, involve plant materials and borrow stylistic modes from a much wider world. And when the object of study is also a territory like Italy, subdivided until very late in its history by many authorities and jurisdictions and subjected to an exceptional variety of foreign influences, the study of its gardens takes on a virtually international scope. Add finally that the Italian Renaissance garden has proved the *fons et origo* of the landscape architecture of all other western nations, then the internationalism of its students (including contributors to this volume) is not surprising.

Certain other historiographical concerns recur through these chapters in large part owing to the kinds of questions that contributors choose to pose. The origins of the garden – upon which the first and penultimate chapters especially focus, befitting international medievalism on the one hand and Sicilian multiculturalism on the other – is a topic that has elicited excellent work elsewhere from Robin Osborne and Massimo Venturi Ferriolo.[1] Any search for garden origins, as those two scholars have shown, must mingle regard for etymology and acute interrogation of all sorts of texts (not simply literary ones) with more conventional archaeological inquiry. And the scrutiny of texts requires a sophisticated response to different rhetorical conventions – estate inventories, for example, do not rely upon the same linguistic registers as do love poems, yet neither is necessarily to be privileged over the other as evidence in garden history.

The possible sources for garden history are as unpredictable as infinite, especially if we know how to make them yield their material. I was once told by an eminent Italian archivist that the city archives held nothing that pertained to garden history; yet a

[1] Osborne, 'Classical Greek gardens: between farm and paradise', *Garden History. Issues, Approaches, Methods*, ed. John Dixon Hunt (Washington, D.C., 1992), pp. 373–91; and Ferriolo, *Nel grembo della vita* (Milan, 1989) and his 'Homer's garden', *Journal of Garden History*, 9 (1989), pp. 86–94.

cursory viewing even of the documents already photographed revealed dozens of legal papers (wills, property conveyances) with garden plans drawn into them. If readers of this volume review the kind of materials referenced by the authors they will find – just to start with – that garden-making and garden experience make their presence felt through a whole spectrum of social and cultural history: instructional manuals for hunting, pharmaceutical and medical treatises, agriculture practice and theory, the records of what we today call public works administration, military logistics, free-masonry, museology, political journalism, not to mention Petrarch's garden notes, Claude Lorrain's paintings and Goethe's journal.

If the study of origins of gardens requires an adequate dialogue between written records of all sorts and surviving artifacts, gardens themselves generally deserve to be studied at the intersection between physical place and metaphysical idea. This is only in part a reworking of the old formula about form and function; a garden's functions may not only involve the growing of food, social uses, political prestige and power; we must study how the physical facts of a garden intersect with a whole gamut of less tangible but no less instrumental concerns. We learn about these often through accounts – visual as well as verbal (paintings, say, as well as poems) – of the contemporary experiences of gardens. Mental archetypes and rhetorical conventions may frustrate our using texts to establish exactly what a garden was like on the ground; but they yield much enlightenment as to how gardens were considered, which in turn fruitfully conditions how we examine all sorts of evidence about them. Rhetorical topoi can, in fact, connect with topography, as the gardenist term topiary and its etymology may remind us.

Historiography also raises questions of presentation. The tone and mode of the contributors here will probably yield few surprises: exposition, documentation (in even its most residual form, inventory), argumentation. *The Italian Garden* does not participate in any experimental mingling of history with fiction, as did *Reading the French Garden* by Denise and Jean-Pierre Le Dantec (its original French title, *Le roman du jardin français*, stresses the authors' imaginative enterprise more clearly).[2] Yet careful consideration of some chapters here will suggest that garden history, because relatively new and still searching for its proper modes, does in fact lend itself necessarily to less conventional approaches. The slippage from geomorphological or territorial analysis to symbolic frameworks, from health to hermeneutics, or conversely from poetic trope to practical treatise is crucial and endemic to the subject. So many gardens survive only in fragments of evidence, a fistful of sometimes tangible and physical clues, of hints sometimes shadowy and allusive, that a collage approach may best give access to them. Thus more than one chapter here deliberately builds up its narrative of gardens through a careful montage of fragments, the shards of many cultures, many viewpoints.

A model for this syncretic approach was suggested in the mid-sixteenth century by

---

[2] The English translation by Jessica Levine was published by the MIT Press in 1990; the original French edition by Plon in 1987.

two Italian humanists writing about the newly flourishing garden art. Both Bartolomeo Taegio, whose treatise on villa life is discussed in the chapter by Iris Lauterbach in this volume, and Jacopo Bonfadio[3] called gardens a 'third nature'. This coinage – for they were both conscious of it as a neologism – probably refers to a phrase of Cicero's in his *De natura deorum* by which he designates the cultural landscape of fields, roads, harbours and so on; his 'alteram naturam' or second nature of course presupposes a first (the territory of the gods, the world unmediated by humans).

Taegio and Bonfadio were concerned to situate the newly revived art of fine gardening not only in the almost obligatory classical and mythical traditions, but within a cultural history that interpreted gardens as the culmination (third) of a series of human interventions in the land. For them garden art was derived from agrarian practice – as many modern Italian gardening terms continue to affirm – and its achievements were best seen in relation to the contexts out of which they had grown (second and first natures). It is not, certainly, a startlingly original concept: Petrarch had clearly anticipated the idea of a series of interventions in the land, regarding gardens as the culminating treatment of a territory. But the idea of *terza natura* can help us to study gardens as the outgrowth of a complicated relationship with the social, political and cultural fabric, the other natures. This is particularly useful when gardens are within the 'second nature' of urban developments, as is the case with a surprising number in the following chapters. It also distracts us from any tendency to adjudicate gardens as affirmations of *either* art *or* nature, a sterile option that settled like a blight over Europe after the 'invention' of the English landscape garden.

The history of gardens is ultimately a question of what meanings we look for. As one of the most complex and valued of human creations – like men and women, gardens are a mix of nature and culture – gardens mean many things to many people at any one time and place, just as they generally have been created (compiled is almost a better word) by collective endeavour. Gardens are rarely – like a sonnet or a miniature – the work of one person, and therefore they conserve the traces of multiple motives and ambitions and effects.

It is the historian's business to relate these many motives and meanings both to each other and back to the physical site. Evidently, therefore, there are manifold ways in which that relation will be executed, ways that are best determined by the place and date of the object to be studied. And in the elaborate patchwork that was the Italian peninsula before (and maybe even since) its unification, gardens were eloquent about their specific locality. Yet they were also hugely attentive to their specific moment in the *longue durée* of gardening in the Italian peninsula, what northern Europeans called the 'garden of the world'.

---

[3] I have discussed Bonfadio and his famous letter on the scenery of the Italian lakes in an essay, 'Paragone in paradise: translating the garden', to appear in the yearbook, *Comparative Criticism*, 18 (1996). For an account of the continuing aptness of the idea of three natures see my 'Il giardino europeo barocco: più barocco del barocco', in *Il Giardino delle Muse. Arti e artifici nel barocco europeo*, ed. M. A. Giusti and A. Tagliolini (Florence, 1995), pp. 5–17.

Hence our decision to explore the current state of Italian garden history via chapters that focus for the most part upon one time and place and also upon different kinds of place at different times – public and private, urban and suburban, palace, villa-farm and cottage. There were inevitably many more moments, many more modes, and even many more territories that could be represented: Italy is, after all, a world of gardens.

CHAPTER I

GARDENS IN ITALIAN LITERATURE DURING THE THIRTEENTH AND FOURTEENTH CENTURIES

LUCIA BATTAGLIA RICCI[*]

… in veritate / io sanza me grand'ora dimorai / in non provata mai felicitate.

Dreamt of or real, evoked by the magic of literary writing or evocatively depicted by painters and miniaturists, gardens invaded the artistic and literary imagination between the thirteenth and fourteenth centuries, as well as becoming increasingly commonplace inside the turreted cities. This was not, however, a univocal or easily classified cultural phenomenon: even in medieval times the garden preserved that polysemy derived from having been 'germinated' in the most ancient civilisations and having passed through virtually the entire history of western man.[1] Nourished by biblical culture and patristic interpretations, classical texts and Romance literature, able to measure up to both the present and the past, and to influence it by suggesting (or imposing) precise formal models, this genuine symbolic commonplace of western culture lent itself to the assumption of sometimes opposing connotations and attributes that cannot be resolved, neither diachronically nor, generally speaking, with reference to the writer's or artist's taste: in fact, the same author sometimes uses drastically different, not to say decidedly antithetical, variations. If anything, it is dominated by stimuli of an ideological character or the specific conventions of individual genres.

Maria Corti recently wrote that 'in the universe of artistic invention … a fact presupposes a long history and the long history requires that fact.'[2] It is impossible to understand the individual occurrences of the garden topos in Italian literature between the thirteenth and fourteenth centuries without 'presupposing' its millenary history: but this diachronous perspective also confirms that the medieval segment of its history contains remarkably innovative 'developments', occasioned by both great literary

---

[*]Translated by Lucinda Byatt.

[1] For a reconstruction of the origins of the idea of the garden see M. Venturi Ferriolo, *Nel grembo della vita* (Milan, 1989), with earlier bibliography. Essential reading for the period in question is G. Venturi, '"Picta poësis": ricerche sulla poesia e il giardino dalle origini al Seicento', *Storia d'Italia, Annali* (Turin, 1982), vol.v, pp. 663ff.

[2] M. Corti, *Percorsi dell'invenzione. Il linguaggio poetico e Dante* (Turin, 1993), p. 22.

figures and anonymous intellectuals, which subsequently exerted a significant effect on its millenary history. An attempt to reconstruct these 'developments' – or at least those which appear to be most culturally relevant – may therefore enable us to acquire a fuller understanding of the polyhedric nature of the topos in question and the segment of cultural history thus implicated.

First, it is worth drawing attention to a methodological point. In this study it did not seem appropriate to respect the traditional boundaries between disciplines, in a period marked by such strong ties between art and literature. On the one hand, it was intellectuals and men of letters who planned the figurative works and wrote their accompanying texts, in the same way as artists focused in iconographical terms on significant segments of the imaginary world and guided the reading of the books they illustrated. On the other, the limits between the various Romance literatures were extremely 'mobile' owing to the widespread use of multilingualism and the diffusion of translations and vernacular editions; so the decision to restrict the study to the literary output in vernacular Italian during the thirteenth and fourteenth centuries would mean omitting vital information for the reconstruction of the mental library of the individuals who composed the literary texts and those who utilised them. For this reason, my analysis starts with the works of international culture which were widely represented in libraries belonging to Italian courtly and bourgeois elites, and it takes account of contemporary figurative tradition as it appeared in both monumental and book form.

THE 'COURTLY' GARDEN: A PLACE OF DELIGHT AND LOVE

The *Triumph of Death* in the Campo Santo in Pisa, painted some time around the 1340s, contains a scene which we must suppose was extremely common for the period: a happy gathering of youths in a garden occupied in forms of entertainment typical of courtly life: amorous meetings, playing and listening to music, falconry, pleasant discourse.[3] The image marvellously sums up a series of motifs made widespread by books popular with Romance culture which had become the ideal reference models for the everyday life of the rising classes: first and foremost, the *Roman de la Rose*, started by Guillaume de Lorris around 1230 and completed several decades later by Jean de Meun, with its famous and unusually lengthy description of Deduit's garden.[4] This later served to codify – at both a literary and figurative level, given that the work was probably conceived from the outset as a book *à figures* and characterised by a normally illustrated manuscript tradition[5] – not only the structure and vegetable, animal, human and architectural elements of the courtly garden, but also its function as the 'appointed

---

[3] For a full description of the fresco and the problems concerning its dating and interpretation, see L. Battaglia Ricci, *Ragionare nel giardino. Boccaccio e il ciclo pittorico del 'Trionfo della Morte'* (Rome, 1987).   [4] Lines 629ff.

[5] G. Contini, 'Un nodo della cultura medievale: la serie "Roman de la rose" – "Fiore" – "Divina Commedia"', in idem, *Un'idea di Dante. Saggi danteschi* (Turin, 1976), pp. 274–9. See also J. V. Fleming, *The 'Roman de la Rose'. A Study in Allegory and Iconography*, (Princeton, 1969), p.112, as well as his contribution to *Mediaeval Gardens*, ed. Elisabeth B. MacDougall, Dunbarton Oaks Colloquium on the History of Language Architecture, IX (Washington, D.C., 1986).

setting' for amorous encounters. In the *Roman* the garden, a square area protected by high walls, is a real *hortus conclusus* which the young visitor, the protagonist of the oneiric episode narrated in the book, expressly identifies with earthly paradise; moreover, the narrator carefully describes its various components: the flower garden, the grove, the fountain protected by the tree, the rose garden. Here, among the plants, water and animals, we find the happy band of Deduit's young friends intent on courtly pastimes and here, at the beginning of May, the Dreamer experiences an allegorical love affair in which the components of the garden play an essential role: the fountain – which represents the eyes of the woman he loves – and obviously the rose – which represents the woman, or, according to C. S. Lewis, the woman's love.[6] Another prime model constituted the landscapes described by Andreas Capellanus as the appointed settings for the 'apparitions' of the court of love: the 'locus amoenus et delectabilis . . . herbosus et nemoris undique vallatus arboribus' across whose meadows the dead souls processed in the wake of the God of Love;[7] and, above all, the 'garden of love', the delightful place inhabited by the court of love full of wonderful lawns – 'undique . . . omnium generum pomiferis et odoriferis circumclusus arboribus', distinguished by the presence of a 'mirae altitudinis arbor universorum abundanter proferens fructus' and a spring which welled out of the tree's roots.[8] But Guillaume's invention must have been decisive, in view of the work's remarkable success, in the codification of the topical scenario of amorous adventures and pleasant episodes of communal life at court during medieval times and in the Romance era. Therefore, in addition to models taken from reality, a high wall or a more or less dense circuit of trees ('signs' of its separation from the world), a flower-strewn lawn and birdsong ('signs' of its *amoenitas*), a fountain and a tree ('signs', together with the wall, of its edenic nature) were sufficient to evoke this garden formed through the cooperation of rhetorical conventions and mental archetypes from widely varying cultural areas.[9] We are dealing with a system which was codified to such an extent that often, metonymically, a single element was sufficient to evoke it.

[6] C. S. Lewis, *The Allegory of Love. A Study in Medieval Tradition* (New York, 1958); Ital. trans.: *L'allegoria d'amore. Saggio sulla tradizione medievale* (Turin, 1969), p. 112.

[7] A. Cappellano, *De Amore*, ed. G. Ruffini (Milan, 1980), pp. 83–9.

[8] Ibid., pp. 89ff. For a recent definition of the 'garden of love' see P. Trannoy, 'Le jardin d'amour dans le "De Amore" d'André Le Chapelain', in *Vergers et jardins dans l'Univers Medieval* (Senefiance n.28) (Aix-en-Provence, 1990), pp. 373–88.

[9] The courtly garden emerged from the coalescence of two biblical models: that of the Garden of Eden described in the book of Genesis (2, 8–15), with exegetical and descriptive integrations, in particular the apocryphal Apocalypse of Saint Paul, known in medieval times as *Visio Pauli* (see P. Orvieto, 'Boccaccio o l'allegoria d'amore', *Interpres*, 2 (1979), pp. 62–3), and the mystical model evoked in *Canticus canticorum* using the classical topos of the *locus amoenus* (there is an extensive bibliography on this, but I only cite those works which have made an effective contribution to this chapter: F. Faral, *Recherches sur les sources latines des contes et romans courtois* (Paris, 1913); E. R. Curtius, *Letteratura europea e medioevo latino*, ed. R. Antonelli (Florence, 1992), pp. 207–26; Trans. of *European Literature and the Latin Middle Age* (1953); D. Thoss, *Studien zum locus amoenus im Mittelalter* (Vienna-Stuttgart), 1972, etc.), which was widespread also in medieval rhetoric (E. Faral, *Les arts poètiques du XIIe et du XIIIe siècles* (Paris, 1958), pp. 148ff, p. 152 etc.), and the eastern-style model of the Roman garden (see P. Grimal, *Les jardins romains* (Paris, 1969), pp. 6ff). The real gardens adjoining palaces and monastic gardens also played an active role as not merely mental referents: see the various studies on this aspect in *Vergers et jardins, passim*.

The chivalrous romances written in French during the twelfth and thirteenth centuries and avidly read by Italian readers from all social backgrounds are witness to the remarkable success of this 'complex' topos; a decisive role in the latter's formation was certainly played by the singular convergence of indications given by treatise writers and commentators on ancient texts with the text and mystical exegesis of *Canticus canticorum*. In the wake of the 'interpretatio per etymologiam' it was agreed to identify the *locus amoenus* as the place destined – and indeed propitious – for love,[10] and this coalesced with the *Canticus*, which addressed an evocative series of pregnant images to a lay audience, ranging from the image of the garden as the *hortus conclusus* to the identification of the woman with the garden and its various components.[11] The chivalrous romances thus contributed to assigning the garden a precise role within this system of appointed 'places' which is the hallmark of this literary genre and rotates around the topical opposition of court vs. forest.[12] Here, more often than not the garden was the place appointed for amorous encounters. At the court of Cornwall Tristan and Isolde met in the garden outside King Mark's palace;[13] Guinevere first kissed Lancelot under the trees 'on the lawn with shrubs' – which the author retrospectively calls a 'garden'.[14] It was in the garden which Morgana ordered to be planted outside the room in which Lancelot was imprisoned that, at the beginning of May, in the midst of the luxuriant new growth of flowers and greenery and to the sound of birdsong, the Knight saw the rosebud which he fully identified with Guinevere and, making a superhuman effort, succeeded in picking and so freeing himself.[15] Likewise, in a splendid garden-cum-earthly paradise of a magical nature a woman dreamt that she could keep the man she loved within her power by confining him to a golden segregation which, for him, was a painful separation from the world of the court and adventure.[16] In the same way, the 'wise damsel's abode' became a gilded prison: the beautiful palace surrounded by gardens with 'many wonderful rivers to fish and many water meadows with animals for hunting', built in the desert as a place destined for love, was also used by Tristan and Isolde in *Tristano Riccardiano*, a version of

[10] 'Amoena loca dicta: quod amorem praestant jocunda viridia', in Papias, *Elementarium doctrinae rudimentum*, cited by D'Arco S. Avalle, *Ai luoghi di delizia pieni. Saggio sulla lirica italiana del XIII secolo* (Milan-Naples, 1977), p.109, to which readers are referred. Other equally famous classic gardens of love are present: Tibullus, *Elegiae*, I, iii, 59–64 and Claudianus, *Epithalamium de Nuptiis Honorii et Mariae*, pp. 49ff.

[11] This marks the start of the association, both metaphorical and not, of the woman-garden (woman-fountain, woman-wall, woman-flower and the like) destined to play such an important role in poetry during the early centuries. One need only reflect on Cavalcanti's well-known *incipit*: *Avete 'n vo' li fior' e la verdura*. On the *Cantico* see Venturi Ferriolo, *Nel grembo, passim*; on the *Cantico* and the early lyrics, Avalle, *Ai luoghi*, pp. 109ff.

[12] E. Köhler, *L'avventura cavalleresca. Ideale e realtà nei poemi della Tavola Rotonda* (Bologna, 1985), *passim*. Trans. of *Ideal und Wirklichkeit in der höfischen Epik* (Tubingen, 1956).

[13] On the structures and typical settings of the court of King Mark, see V. Bertolucci, 'La corte e le sue immagini nel "Tristan" di Béroul', in idem, *Morfologie del testo medievale* (Bologna, 1989), p. 22. The motif spread from literary works to figurative art and even to the so-called minor arts, for example, the casket in the Bargello Museum, Florence (Carrand Collection, no. 123).   [14] *Lancelot*, ed. A. Micha (Paris-Geneva, 1978-83), vol. VIII, p. 119.

[15] On the rose–Guinevere exchange and the entire episode of Lancelot as Morgana's prisoner (*Lancelot*, ed. Micha, vol.V, pp. 60–1), see Bertolucci, 'Amor dipinto. Icone della rivelazione amorosa nel "Lancelot en prose"', in *Morfologie*, pp. 35ff.

[16] Chretien de Troyes, *Eréc e Enide*, in *Romanzi*, ed. C. Pellegrini (Florence, 1962), pp. 93ff.

the well-known French romance in Tuscan vernacular.[17] This culminated in the significant process documented by Boccaccio whereby the translation of the *Chastelaine de Vergy* into Tuscan vernacular – a romance in which the garden once again served as the place set aside for the amorous encounters of a couple fated to meet a tragic end – was re-entitled the *Dama del Verzù*: the 'Lady of the Garden'.[18]

Having been transmitted by both the *Roman de la Rose* and the chivalrous romances with their figurative appendages, the springtime image of a garden,[19] understood as the specialised setting for amorous encounters and, more generally, for the happy gatherings of young people – an image which was inevitably closely related to Provençal lyrics – became one of the most fertile and idealised commonplaces of early Italian literature. It was the image used by Monte Andrea to express his wish:

> Ch'io nel giardino
> aulente e fino
> dalo matino
> istesse dal'un chanto
> (laov'è quello dolze fiore,
> fresco ed amoroso,
> ch'a tutora per amore
> a me fa stare gioioso)![20]

It was the image chosen by the Compiuta Donzella when she compared her sad personal state to the collective joy of falling in love in springtime:

> A la stagion che 'l mondo foglia e fiora
> acresce gioia a tut[t]i fin'amanti:
> vanno insieme a li giardini alora
> che gli auscelletti fanno dolci canti;
> la franca gente tutta s'innamora.[21]

It was the image evoked by Paolo Lanfranchi from Pistoia in one of his 'noble and gentle imaginings', when he dreamt that he found himself with his lady

> in un giardin, baciar e abraciare,
> remos[s]a ciascun altra villania.[22]

Finally, Lapo Gianni depicted gardens as part of the enchanted landscape of a *plazer*, together with his beloved and the delightful appendages of courtly life:[23]

---

[17] *Tristano Riccardiano*, critical edition by E.G. Parodi, ed. M-J. Heijkant (Parma, 1991), fos. LXXXIII–LXXXVI.

[18] Boccaccio refers to 'cantare' in the conclusion of the third day of the *Decameron*. The text of the novella can now be read in *La Castellana di Vergy*, ed. G. Angeli (Rome, 1991).

[19] On the springtime connotation of the 'weather' in the garden, see Venturi, '"Picta poësis"', p. 668.

[20] *Oj dolze Amore*, in Avalle, *Ai luoghi*, pp. 205–8.

[21] *Poeti del duecento*, ed. G. Contini (Milan-Naples, 1960) vol. I, p. 434. [22] Ibid., p. 354.

[23] The sonnet *Di giugno* by Folgore de San Gimignano is similar (in *Poeti del duecento*, vol. II, p. 411): see Venturi, '"Picta poësis"', p. 682, note 39.

Amor, eo chero mia donna in domìno,
l'Arno balsamo fino,
le mura di Firenze inargentate,
le rughe di cristallo lastricate,
fortezze alt'e merlate . . .
e l'aira temperata verno e state;
e mille donne e donzelle adornate . . .
e giardin' fruttuosi di gran giro,
con grande uccellagione,
pien' di condotti d'acqua e cacciagione . . .
sonar viole, chitarre e canzone . . .
giovane, sana, allegra e secura
fosse mia vita fin che 'l mondo dura.[24]

C. S. Lewis wrote that 'life and letters are inextricably mixed':[25] it is difficult to ascertain to what extent the garden described by French allegorical and chivalrous romances depended on real examples and to what extent it was modelled by the literary garden; or whether reality, the imaginary world and theoretical elaboration collaborated in forming the stereotype which is so accurately described in the *Roman de la Rose*.[26] As far as Italy is concerned, there is no doubt that, in parallel with rising living standards and the broadening of cultural horizons, the emerging classes adopted 'courtly' models of behaviour and culture based on books, so much so that, for example, it is well known that a company of knights who called themselves the 'Knights of the Round Table' existed in Pisa during this period.[27] In particular, the awareness of the 'courtly' value of the garden is borne out by a passage from Matazone da Caligano's *Detto*, a Lombard text probably dating from the late fourteenth century, in which a knight justifies his own social superiority by recounting the 'myth of the floral birth of the knight',[28] thus continuing to draw on the most outmoded commonplaces of Romance culture:[29]

... del mese de mayo,
quando el tempo è gayo,
un matin me levay,
in un zardin intray.
Guardà' per lo zardin,

---

[24] *Poeti del duecento*, vol. II, p. 603. It is also worth mentioning that some poets considered the component elements of the courtly garden as the mental – and rhetorical – referents for organising a love song. Hence, in the song 'Gioiosamente canto' by Guido delle Colonne: 'Ben passa rose e fiore/la vostra fresca cera ... Come fontana piena, /che spande tutta quanta, così lo meo cor canta ... E più c'augello in fronda – so' gioioso ... (*Poeti del duecento*, vol. I, pp. 99–101).

[25] Lewis, *The Allegory of Love*, p. 22.

[26] For a description of the historical models involved (or implied: i.e. the gardens in monastic cloisters and the garden at court), see *Vergers et jardins, passim*.

[27] On the entire question and for its relative bibliography, see Battaglia Ricci, *Ragionare nel giardino*, pp. 138ff.

[28] Contini in the foreword to *Poeti del duecento*, p. 789.

[29] On the association between the knight and the garden, see also Giacomino da Verona, 'De Jerusalem celesti', in *Poeti del duecento*, vol. I, pp. 117ff, *passim*: 'Lasù è sempre virdi li broli e li vercer/en li quali se deporta li sancti caveler...'

soto un verde pin
li era una fontanela; . . .
guardà per lo verzero,
soto un verde pomero
lì era dove [= due] flore
de diverso colore,
l'una blanca e l'altro vermelio,
zoè la roxa e lo zilio.
Non so per quen raxon
la rosa con el zilion
alor s'aprosimò
e insema se conseyò;
e a lo departire
sì ne vite insire
un cavaler adorno . . .
Vestito era de seta
fresca e colorita . . .
soto à un dester,
in pugno un sparaver,
brachi in cadena
e livrer[i] demena [= conduce][30]

The image of the elegantly dressed knight astride his horse holding a falcon in his hand is no more 'realistic' than that which follows it in which the knight is surrounded by the usual personifications of Virtue: if anything, this is an extremely conventional image which corresponds to a genuine iconographical topos used to indicate the 'courteousness' of the person shown. This is confirmed by the illustrations in Ms. Lat. 5232 in the Vatican Library in which the anonymous Venetian illustrator resorted to this iconographical convention to portray Raimon de Miraval, a 'troubadour' who was 'considered a sort of arbiter of courteousness' at the time, depicting him in the guise of an elegantly dressed knight, seated on horseback and holding a falcon in his fist.[31]

The artist who painted the splendid image of the gathering in the garden on the walls of the Campo Santo in Pisa, which served as the starting point for this discussion, also drew on this system of topoi. Like the figurative series of which it forms part, the painting was completed between the third and fourth decade of the fourteenth century during one of the city's periods of greatest splendour under the Signoria of Fazio della Gherardesca; then aspirations to a more refined way of life, more open to aesthetic enjoyment, had caused the city's leading families to make radical changes in their everyday life, moving from narrow tower-like houses to palaces characterised by the presence of real or painted gardens.[32]

In the Pisan fresco the garden is synthetically represented by a green lawn separated

---

[30] *Poeti del duecento*, vol. I, pp. 796–8.
[31] See M. L. Meneghetti, *Il pubblico dei trovatori. Ricezione e riuso dei testi lirici cortesi fino al XIV secolo* (Modena, 1984), p. 338, from which the above citation is taken.   [32] My *Ragionare nel giardino* is briefly summarised here. See also note 3.

from the rest of the world by a grove of brilliant orange trees and 'furnished' with a stone bench with a chequered ornamentation. A fascinating and extremely elegant group of seven women and three men appear in poses which recall scenes and illustrations from 'courtly' books: young lovers, knights with falcons, ladies with little dogs, musicians.[33] Although representing the sum of topical figures, this image was innovative in that it was given renewed actuality by the careful reproduction of detail, including physiognomy: this search for 'realism' substantiates the age-old popular tradition that the youths in the fresco are portraits of well-known figures of the local *jeunesse dorée*, as well as historical figures living in the city or who had recently visited it. In the eyes of the 'gentle' public to whom the fresco was addressed,[34] the image was intended to represent a nostalgic re-evocation of an idealised world, but also a sort of realistic *tranche de vie* in which they could 'see themselves' and learn correct models of behaviour.

The unusual association suggested between this image and that of Death, which, ignoring the imploring entreaties of the poor and sick –

> Poi che prosperitade ci à llasciati,
> O Morte, medicina d'ongni pena,
> Dè vienci a dare omai l'ultima cena –

heads towards the happy gathering, declaring that

> I' non son brama – [che] di spegner [la] vita;
> Ma chi mi chiama – le più volte schifo,
> Giungnendo spesso chi mi torcie il grifo,

implies a complete reversal of the positive meaning which literary tradition attributes to the image: in this complex composition of words and images, the figurative text informs the reader that the happy group in the garden will be the privileged victims of the terrible huntress and that they will be condemned to hell precisely because they are immersed in such refined, gratifying and hedonistic self-pleasure.[35] This image must

---

[33] These were such conventional iconographical motifs during this period that they appeared on everyday objects such as caskets (see note 13) and combs: see the comb belonging to the Carrand Collection, Bargello (no.139c).

[34] As is explicitly affirmed in the epigraph *Nota, gentile huomo*, now illegible but published together with others in the cycle at the end of the last century by S. Morpurgo, 'Le epigrafi volgari in rima del "Trionfo della Morte", del "Giudizio universale e Inferno", e degli "Anacoreti" nel Camposanto di Pisa', *L'Arte*, 2 (1899), pp. 51–87: 'Nota qui . . . che di' che se' gentile: / Poi che dio [vole] che sia comunale / Lo nascere e 'l morire ad ogni gente, / Non haver dumque l'altra gente a vile, / Ché come l'altri così tu se' mortale . . .' (p. 61).

[35] This is the meaning attributed to the images by the written appendages: see, for example, the epigraph *Della Morte, corpo*, originally 'hung' under the group of young people: 'O anima, perché perché non pensi / Che Morte ti torrà quel vestimento / In che tu senti corporal dilecto / Per la vertù de' suoi cinque sensi, / col quale haverai eternal tormento / Se qui lo lassi con mortal dilecto?' K. Clark, in *Landscape into Art* (London, 1976), p. 3, reported that 'St Anselm, writing at the beginning of the twelfth century, maintained that things were harmful in proportion to the number of senses which they delighted, and therefore rated it dangerous to sit in a garden where there are roses to satisfy the senses of sight and smell, and songs and stories to please the ears.' I have not been able to identify this passage but it appears to be a valuable indication of an ideological attitude which was forced to coexist during the period in question with the lay celebration of the garden and which was fully aware of the meaning of the scene portrayed by the fresco.

have provoked a violent effect of estrangement in fourteenth-century viewers and, above all, in the 'gentle' public who formed the fresco's implicit audience: in this scene the viewers witnessed the demonisation not only of a commonplace feature of their culture, but one of the ideals of their own lifestyle. For them this image, a sort of snapshot in which they could readily 'see' themselves, therefore became – not least owing to its evocative beauty – a chilling document on the true moral standing of that type of life and its related eschatological outcome.

This extremely distressing illustrated sermon composed by the anonymous *auctor intellectualis* for exhibition in the place where the city came face to face with death owes most of its persuasive force to this 'estranged' reproposal of commonplace cultural data and widely accepted certainties. The fresco polemically attacks not only the garden, the symbol of a courtly way of life which may be confused with the eternal nostalgic longing for the lost Eden, but also both the idea of love spread by the chivalrous romances and by Capellanus' treatise and profane and instrumental music. In their place, the fresco proposes the ascetic-penitential way of life as a positive model of behaviour: the desert, a hostile environment inhabited by hermits and animals and dotted with small chapels, is presented as the true earthly paradise, a place which is not subject to the threat of the terrible enemy and guarantor of eternity.

Such sophisticated restructuring of these cultural topoi was certainly closely linked to the ideology of the *auctor intellectualis*. He was probably a Dominican living in the nearby convent of Santa Caterina where, nourished on a diet of literature, he sought to edify those who thought it possible to recreate an earthly paradise of delight by recomposing lay cultural and behavioural models in compliance with Catholic moral theology and by celebrating the penitential life modelled along the lines of the *Vitae Patrum*, while at the same time condemning social life, an offshoot of culture and literary civilisation.[36] The latter might also have conditioned the *auctor intellectualis* in a more immediate and direct manner: in fact, there are close intertextual relations between some parts of the fresco, including the epigraphical series, and the song *O morte, della vita privatrice* by Lapo Gianni. Like the figurative text, the *stilnovo* poet also affirmed that Death 'devours all ages' and brings the world's 'great figures' to hell.

---

[36] Whereas literary tradition has mingled heterogeneous cultural and ideological data to produce a form (and an idea) of the garden which readily adapts to biblical culture, monastic tradition and lay, not to say pagan, culture, religious culture usually distinguishes between the garden of the soul or the Church and the garden of earthly delights: by way of example it will suffice to cite two passages from the *Lettere* of Saint Catherine of Siena, who in a letter to Pope Urban V used the following phrase to express the degradation of those who should be an example of virtue within the church: 'abbondano li vizii, e singolarmente in coloro che sono posti nel giardino della santa Chiesa come fiori odoriferi acciocché gittino odere di virtù'; on the other hand, in the *Dialogo*, she wrote, '[agli uomini di mondo] addiviene come de l'uomo che è in uno giardino: che *in esso giardino, poiché v'ha diletto, si riposa con la sua operazione*' (taken from *Scrittori di religione del Trecento. Testi originali*, ed. Don G. de Luca (reprint, Turin, 1977), respectively pp. 117 and 157: (my italics). Moreover, according to Cavalca, who might be the *auctor intellectualis* of the fresco cycle in Pisa (see C. Frugoni, 'Altri luoghi, cercando il paradiso (Il ciclo di Buffalmacco nel Camposanto di Pisa e la committenza domenicana)', in *Annali della Scuola Normale Superiore di Pisa*, 18 (1988), 4, pp. 1557ff), the garden seen as a *locus amoenus* was the typical setting for lechery (see 'Vita di san Paolo', in D. Cavalca, *Cinque vite di eremiti*, ed. C. Delcorno (Venice, 1992), p. 86); Abelard expressed a similar opinion (see below).

Death, he stated, 'still ... takes pleasure in selecting the best / and the most honourable', and picks on young couples, but above all:

> Morte, sempre dai miseri chiamata,
> e da' ricchi schifata come vile
> troppo se'n tua potenza signorile,
> non provedenza umile,
> quando ci togli un om fresco e giulivo,

concluding, in an envoi which serves as a genuine 'counter-melody' to the fresco:

> Canzon, gira'ne a que' che sono in vita
> di gentil core e di gran nobilitate:
> di' che mantengan lor prosperitate
> e sempre si rimembrin de la Morte
> in contrastarla forte;
> e di' che, se visibil la vedranno,
> che faccian la vendetta che dovranno.[37]

This abundance of common topical, figurative and stylistic elements justifies the suspicion that the two works are bound together by a precise link in terms of subject-matter and imagery, in spite of the fact that they are completely antiphrastic from an ideological point of view. This idea is further substantiated if, in addition to the song, we consider the *plazer* mentioned earlier: the celebration in dream form of an imaginative place created by the enchanted transposition of everyday reality into a setting which is both an earthly paradise and a Golden Age, a place in which to spend eternal youth:

> Giovane sana allegrae secura
> fosse mia vita fin che 'l mondo dura.

If read immediately after this conclusion the opening of the song acquires greater pregnancy, giving the clear impression that the two texts were constructed to form an organically structured whole whose continuity is guaranteed by the lexical repetition of the term 'vita'. But the manuscript tradition precludes any evaluation of the accuracy of this impression and, likewise, uncertainties regarding the biography of the *stilnovo* poet and, more importantly, those concerning the dating of the song, rule out any conclusive affirmation that the *auctor* of the fresco was in any 'debt' to the poet.[38]

But even if it is not possible to identify the exact relationship of who owed whom what in textual terms, the thematic and formal affinities, together with the differences that separate them from an ideological point of view, serve as a valuable clue to the

---

[37] *Poeti del duecento*, vol. II, pp. 594–7.

[38] On the manuscript tradition see the *Nota al testo* in Contini, *'Un' idea di Dante*. The only fixed point of reference in Lapo Gianni's biography is that he is known to have been alive in 1328; however, the exact date of his death varies according to the identification proposed. If he is identified with a certain 'ser Lapo Gianni da Feraglia', he may have survived until 1336, a time when the fresco was certainly at an advanced stage of elaboration, if not already completed.

existence of a precise and culturally significant 'debate' on these topics at this moment in time: a debate which also included other voices and from which the garden was to emerge with renewed 'semantic' content.

THE GARDENS OF GIOVANNI BOCCACCIO

The powerful voice of Giovanni Boccaccio, whose works abound with the splendid image of a shady garden replete with flowers, water, trees and animals, also made itself heard in this 'debate'. This image is in fact a recurrent topos in his works, almost an obsessive fancy, a compulsory place for his writing, which he adapts to a multitude of different meanings. By following the variegated nature, structure and use of his 'gardens' it is possible to reconstruct virtually the entire spectrum of meanings and functions represented by this topos in fourteenth-century literature.

The novellas in the *Decameron* are full of gardens: in the majority of cases, these are still the appointed settings for amorous encounters. However, they, too, are subject—like so many other popular themes in medieval literature—to constant 'transformation' in the multiform variety of Boccaccio's works. They range from the idealised and 'courtly' tone of the novella about Andreuola, whose loved one dies dramatically in the garden of their happy amorous encounters and over whose corpse she scatters the customary, mythical roses,[39] to the 'realistic' tale of Simona and Pasquino, two members of the Florentine populace whose encounters in a garden lead to their death;[40] from the parodical rewriting of the most famous themes of courtly romance (in this case the theme of Arthur who hid up a pine-tree to spy on Guinevere and Lancelot as they met in the flower garden) in the novella of Egano, who, having taken up a position under the pine-tree in his garden to simulate an amorous encounter, is soundly beaten by his wife's lover,[41] to the carnevalesque abasement of Masetto, the dumb gardener at a convent whose 'beautiful garden' is the setting for Boccaccio's most classic of love-affairs;[42] or finally the fabulous invention through which a splendid winter garden appears in a frozen city in northern Italy as a gift and token of courtly love.[43]

We need only compare two 'rewritings' of a theme which 'responds to the canons of contemporary amorous and chivalrous romances'[44] to witness the diverse uses made of the topos. First, Iphigenia contemplated by Cimone:

> Thus he happened one day . . . into a clearing hemmed in by tall trees, with a beautiful cool spring in one corner of it; fast asleep beside it on the green meadow grass he saw the

---

[39] *Decameron*, IV, 6. All excerpts from the *Decameron* are taken from Giovanni Boccaccio, *The Decameron*, trans. by Guido Waldman (Oxford, 1993).   [40] *Dec.*, IV, 7.

[41] *Dec.*, VII, 7. The choice of the tree is not accidental: this was the tree which was consecrated to literature by both the Arthurian romances and the *Roman de la Rose*. On the parody implied in Boccaccio's rewriting of the theme of Tristan see M. Picone, 'Il rendez-vous sotto il pino (*Decameron*, VII, 7)', in *Studi e problemi di critica testuale*, 22 (1982), pp. 71ff.

[42] *Dec.*, III, 1.   [43] *Dec.*, X, 5. This novella was previously included in *Filocolo*, IV, 31.

[44] Taken from V. Branca's commentary on the *Decameron* (Turin, 1980), p. 595.

most gorgeous young woman; she was wearing such a sheer dress, it barely concealed her milk-white flesh . . .[45]

– then Masetto 'contemplated' by the nuns and abbess of the convent:

> Now one day . . . two of the nuns – mere youngsters – who were walking in the garden came over to him as he feigned sleep and took a good look at him . . . Last of all the abbess . . . happened upon Masetto as she was walking . . . through the garden one very sultry day; he was stretched out, fast asleep, in the shade of an almond tree . . . Now a puff of wind happened to have plucked up the front of his smock, leaving him totally exposed . . .[46].

If the sight of Masetto asleep – or feigning sleep – triggered off a genuine spate of illicit couplings, only partially stemmed by the false miracle of his regained speech, Iphigenia asleep roused the 'amorous and redeeming enchantment of Cimone'[47] and offered Boccaccio an opportunity to celebrate the 'great theme of beauty and love as the catalysing forces of every good disposition'.[48] The topical setting of the garden could therefore form part of semantically different, if not – as in this case – antiphrastic contexts. This explains why in the absence of explicit signals it may sometimes prove ambiguous. This is the case of the garden described by Salimbene in his *Cronica*,[49] whose negative connotation is based exclusively on the presence of exotic animals, such as leopards, with known allegorical associations, and the express condemnation of profane music in the Book of Job which Salimbene recalls a few lines further on.[50]

In Boccaccio's works, however, even if the topos is used in a joking and abasing manner, it never conveys negative connotations and the positive, nobilitating and 'courtly' significance of the garden predominates throughout. On the contrary, his works reveal both an innovative coherence, a consolidation into genuine systems of images and motifs taken from a variety of sources, and the introduction of new meanings; together they constitute a single signification capable of expressing a much more complex content, so much so that we can perhaps talk of the development of a genuine personal topic. It is only possible to give a rapid overview of these systems here.

As was seen earlier, Boccaccio offers two variants of the stereotype derived from 'love poetry and romance prose' (young lovers in a garden):[51] the simple and

---

[45] *Dec.*, v, 1.   [46] *Dec.*, III, 1.   [47] V. Branca, *Boccaccio medievale* (Florence, 6th ed., 1986), p. 117.   [48] Ibid., p. 112.

[49] 'cum essem cum eo . . . in civitate Pisana . . . occurrit nobis quedam curtis, quam ambo pariter sumus ingressi. In qua erat vitis frondosa desuper extensa per totum, cuius viriditas delectabilis ad videndum et umbra nichilominus ad quiescendum suavis. Ibi erant leopardi et aliae bestie ultramarine quam plures . . . Erant etiam ibi puelle et pueri in etate ydonea, quas pulchritudo vestium et facierum . . . faciebat amabiles. Et habebant in manibus . . . viellas et cytaras . . . in quibus modulos faciebant dulcissimos et gestus representabant ydoneos . . . (*Cronica*, ed. G. Scalia (Bari, 1966), p. 61).

[50] Job 21. Salimbene's description is closely dependent on the medieval symbology and topos: for leopards one need look no further than the first canto of the *Divine Comedy*. On the 'non-realistic' presence of animals and plants in medieval gardens see Curtius, *Letteratura europea*, pp. 208–9. Generally speaking, the passage 'sets the scene' for the seductive effect of the garden: the care with which Salimbene describes these 'effects' on the different senses and the use of the animal symbol of lust leads us to believe that we are still within the ideological area of monastic influence (see note 35).

[51] Or in a space that could be likened to it: on the difficulty of distinguishing between the garden-paradise and the *locus amoenus*, see Venturi, '"Picta poësis"', p. 678.

straightforward adoption of the 'courtly' model for his characters, irrespective of whether they are noble, bourgeois or populace, characters from the middle ages or from the classical world;[52] and his parodical 'estrangement' which is reserved for those novellas which justify disruption of this type.

The 'court of love' variation[53] is grafted onto this stereotype to create the image of the happy gathering of youths who, seated in a circle on a flower-dotted lawn inside a real garden or in a *locus amoenus* modelled on Capellanus' 'garden of love', dedicate themselves to more or less 'festeggevole ragionare' during the hottest hours of the day under the shade of green branches. This motif, to which Boccaccio rapidly alludes in one of the *Rime*:

> Intorn' ad una fonte, in un pratello
> di verdi erbette pieno e di bei fiori,
> sedean tre angiolette, i loro amori
> forse narrando . . .[54]

reappears in *Filocolo, Ameto* and the *Decameron*, altered on each occasion by the inclusion of details conveying new meanings, thus confirming the garden's status as one of the most pregnant symbolic settings in Boccaccio's vernacular writing.

In *Filocolo*, composed in Naples in around 1336, the garden is a *hortus conclusus* which the protagonist first enters and where he is then invited to join the celebrations of the happy young band, before listening to their 'questioni d'amore' while sitting on a lawn decked with flowers.[55] The merry group of nymphs meets in a similar setting, albeit not in a garden, to tell Ameto their love stories.[56] This experience might be described as a wholly mental and sentimental 'adventure' in which the nymphs guide the protagonist, through their beauty, songs and, above all, their tales, causing his radical transformation from an ignorant, savage man subject to the most earthly passions into a lover conscious of the most profound meanings which sublimate the amorous experience: an 'adventure' which may also be interpreted as an image of the 'emergence and evolution of human civilisation through the intellectual illumination of Eros'.[57] More recent interpretations tend to emphasise that it is precisely this use of the Romance topos of the 'garden of love', understood as a complex of polysemantic signs which Boccaccio interpreted from an orphic-Christian point of view and 'refashioned into a new

---

[52] Also in the *Teseida*, gardens and pleasant groves are the typical setting for 'l'idillio amoroso' (see G. Barberi Squarotti, 'Le figure dell'Eden', in idem, *Fine dell'idillio* (Genoa, 1978), p. 239).

[53] For the essential bibliography on the 'courts of love' see P. Remy, 'Le "cours d'amour": légende et réalité', in *Revue de l'Université de Bruxelles*, 7 (1954–5), pp. 179–97 and M.R. Jung, *Etudes sur le poème allégorique en France au Moyen Age* (Berne, 1971), pp. 129–226. The experience of court life in Naples at the court of King Robert was crucial for Boccaccio: on this aspect see F. Sabatini, *Napoli angoina. Cultura e società* (Naples, 1975), and G. Padoan, 'Mondo aristocratico e mondo comunale nell'ideologia e nell'arte di G. Boccaccio', in *Il Boccaccio, le Muse, il Parnaso e l'Arno* (Florence, 1978), pp. 8–9.

[54] *Rime*, I, 1ff.

[55] *Filocolo*, IV, 14ff.: on this episode see L. Surdich, *La cornice d'amore. Studi su Boccaccio* (Pisa, 1987), pp. 13–75, with earlier bibliography.

[56] *Comedia delle ninfe fiorentine (Am)* (Milan, 1964), vol. XV, 2ff; cf. Surdich, *La cornice d'amore*, pp. 119–54.

[57] S. Battaglia, 'Schemi lirici nell'arte del Boccaccio', in *Archivum Romanicum*, 19 (1935), p. 69.

aggregate', which generates the complex allegorical nature of *Ameto*; likewise in the *Caccia di Diana* and the *Amorosa visione*, the 'garden of love' topos is interwoven with the equally topical and complex theme of the journey/pilgrimage to narrate the 'palingenesis and restoration provoked by love', thus inventing a 'macrogenre' which would later enjoy considerable success with the followers of Ficino and Poliziano in neoplatonic Florence.[58] There is no doubt that in these texts the topos was adapted to indicate stages in the transformation process of man provoked by the redeeming function of that love which, as seen above, was closely linked to the courtly garden. On the other hand, it is difficult to ascertain whether Boccaccio consciously resorted to an organic allegorical filigree of a neoplatonic–orphic nature in the construction of his numerous gardens. The complex polygenesis of the garden image which he inherited from literature and contemporary culture involved, as has been seen, the biblical model of the Garden of Eden, inevitably backed by a vast patristic exegesis, which coexisted more or less pacifically with the *locus amoenus* popular with classical tradition and medieval dogmatic or formal teaching, the 'lay' paradise of Capellanus' court of love and the hyper-metaphorised and glossed *hortus conclusus* from *Cantico dei cantici*, the descriptions of gardens drawn from classical texts and Latin erotic poetry, the allegory of love assigned to the tale-cum-description of Deduit's garden (but also that sort of iconographical and symbolic counter-melody represented by Jean Meun's supernatural park),[59] the precepts in treatises (both ancient and modern) dedicated to the art of gardens and the daily practice of *ars hortulorum* in lay, seigneurial and bourgeois, and religious settings,[60] as well as a mental encyclopedia which inevitably tended to interpret every sign, including plants and beasts, in allegorical terms. All these were more than sufficient to account for the polysemous nature of the garden in question and to justify our difficulty in understanding and rigidly cataloguing the passages involved. The 'medieval' aspect of this Boccaccio is borne out, in my opinion, by a passage from the *Vita di Dante* in which Boccaccio, having spoken 'of the laurels granted to poets' goes on to explain the 'origin of this custom'.

> Sono alcuni li quali credono, percioché sanno Danne amata da Febo e in lauro convertita, essendo Febo e il primo autore e fautore de' poeti stato e similmente triunfatore, per amore a quelle frondi portato, di quelle le sue cetere e i triunfi aver

---

[58] Readers are referred to the work by Paolo Orvieto, who has written copiously on the complex allegorical significance of these interpretations.

[59] *Roman de la Rose*, 20237–588. On this see R. Louis, *Le roman de la Rose. Essai d'interpretation de l'allegorisme erotique* (Paris, 1974) and A. Strubel, 'L'allegorisation du verger courtois', *Vergers et jardins*, pp. 329–42, with bibliography.

[60] See Pliny's *Historia naturalis*. (On the possible influence of Pliny on Boccaccio see L. Bek, 'Ut ars natura. Le ville di Plinio e il concetto del giardino nel Rinascimento', in *Annalecta Romana instituti Danici*, 7 (1971), pp. 109–56; M. Massaglia, 'Il giardino di Pomena nell' ''Ameto'' di Boccaccio', *Studi sul Boccaccio*, 15 (1985-6), especially pp. 239ff.) Other essential works include Pietro de Crescenzi's treatise on agriculture and those on the properties of plants: *De proprietatibus rerum* by Bartolomeo Anglico, or Alberto Magno's essential *De vegetabilis* for the part concerning *De his quae per cultum domesticantur in agro hortolano*. On the significance of plants, above all herbs, in medieval gardens, see G. Sodigne-Costes, 'Les simples et les jardins', *Vergers et jardins*, pp. 329–42, and K. Clark, *Il paesaggio nel arte* (Milan, 1962). Ital.trans. of *Landscape into Art* (see note 35), pp. 8–26.

coronati; e quinci essere stato preso esemplo dagli uomini . . . E certo tale opinione non mi spiace, né nego così poter essere stato; ma tuttavia me muove altra ragione, la quale è questa. Secondo che vogliono coloro, li quali le virtù delle piante ovvero la loro natura investigarono, il lauro tra l'altre più sue proprietà n'ha tre laudevoli e notevoli molto: la prima si è, come noi veggiamo, che mai egli non perde né verdezza, né fronda; la seconda si è, che non si truova questo albore mai essere stato fulminato, il che di niuno altro leggiamo essere avvenuto; la terza, che egli è odifero molto, sì come noi sentiamo: le quali tre proprietà estimarono gli antichi inventori di questo onore convenirsi con le virtuose opere de' poeti e de' vittoriosi imperadori . . .[61]

The passage continues with a description of the analogies between the plant's 'properties' and the actions of poets and emperors. But what is more interesting is that it reveals Boccaccio's particular attention to all studies dedicated to the properties of plants, as well as his competence in this subject. This was reinforced by the cultural choice between a highly popularised classical myth and the 'scientific' treatises on botany which allowed him to draw on a symbolism which was firmly anchored to reality, and could also be verified. In this context it is worth noting the annotations, 'sì come noi veggiamo', 'sì come sentiamo', etc., which I believe enable us to acquire a fuller understanding of the instruments with which Boccaccio constructed his gardens.

One need only think of the poisonous sage in Simona and Pasquino's garden, compared to Andreuola's roses: inevitably, the couple who adopt a courtly way of behaviour spend part of the time in the garden picking roses; by contrast, the presence of the deadly sage is surprising. According to medieval culture, *salvia salvatrix*, together with rue and hyssop, was a guarantor of the eternal vitality and protection from death symbolised by the garden. The community refuses to believe Simona, not least on account of their common experience: her declarations are in fact contrary to the very foundations of popular botanical symbology, summed up in the famous adage of the Salerno school of medicine: 'Cum moriatur homo cui salvia crescit in horto?'[62] And in order to resolve the case the judge has to discover the real 'culprit' hidden under the innocent bush.

The same attention to precise botanical information is also evident in the *Comedia delle ninfe fiorentine* in the description of that extraordinary herbal which is Pomena's garden. Among the trees, shrubs, flowers, aromatic and medicinal herbs, vegetables, pulses, kitchen garden plants and fodder there was not a single empty space; no vegetable was missing, except for 'the arid fescue grass and entangling couch grass' which had obviously been eliminated since no corner of the kitchen garden was 'poorly filled'. The author lists and describes over forty vegetables with painstaking accuracy:

la calda salvia con copioso cesto in palida fronda . . . con strette foglie il ramerino utile a mille cose . . . [la] frigida ruta . . . [l']alta senape, del naso nimica e utile a purgarsi la testa . . . il serpillo, occupante la terra con sottilissime braccia . . . abondevoli viti . . .

[61] *Vita di Dante*, ed. D. Guerri (Bari, 1918), pp. 44–5.   [62] Cited in Sodigne-Costes, *Les simples*, p. 338.

spessissimi gelsomini ... pungenti rosai ... Narciso ... Adone ... l'amata Clizia dal
Sole ... lo sventurato Iacinto ... la non pieghevole Danne ... molti meranci carichi a
un'ora di fiori e di verdi frutti e di dorati ... le piacevoli castagne difese da aspra veste ...
varie biade ... già biancheggianti ... un olmo altissimo, congiunto con l'amichevole
ellere e con l'usate viti ... gli alti papaveri utili a' sonni ... i leggeri fagioli ... i rotondi
ceci ... l'incensi ... il lazzo sorbo ... il fronzuto corbezzolo ... le cipolle coperte da
molte vesti ... i capituti porri ... e petronciani violati con molti altri semi, de' quali la
terra vie più s'abbellia.

Here Boccaccio combines material from a variety of sources. In the first place, he
obviously borrows from literary works:[63] Ovid's *Metamorphoses* is extensively plun-
dered and Boccaccio takes most of the botanical repertoire – and corresponding
mythological onomatology – as well as the figure and, in part, the story of Pom-
ena/Pomona from this source;[64] but neither Dante of the 'bitter berries'[65] nor the
Moretum from the *Appendix Vergiliana*[66] are lacking, nor works from medieval
allegorical and philosophical literature, such as Bernardo Silvestre's *De mundi Universi-
tate*.[67] Boccaccio must also have used encyclopedias[68] and/or books dedicated to
describing the properties of plants, if we are to believe his express declaration in the
passage from the *Vita di Dante*, as well as treatises on *ars hortulorum*, in particular that by
Piero de' Crescenzi to which Gianni Venturi repeatedly draws attention, also in
relation to Pomena's garden.[69] It is also possible that his imagination was influenced by
real images: either illustrations of the works themselves or direct experience.[70] A clue to
this co-presence might be identified in the difference between Boccaccio's 'onions
dressed in many clothes' and the 'caepa rubens' in *Moretum*.

This unique blend of literature, 'scientific' knowledge and direct experience
contributed to creating an absolutely original herbal which, while not excluding
inevitable symbolic meanings,[71] is certainly capable of incredibly 'realistic' reproductions of the plant world. Even the 'oranges laden at the same time with flowers and
green and golden fruits', which usually fulfil a manifestly symbolic function in garden

---

[63] In complete conformity with medieval rhetoric: 'le immagini relative al paesaggio della poesia medievale debbono essere intese nel quadro di una solida tradizione letteraria' (Curtius, *Letteratura europea*, p. 209).

[64] *Metamorphoses*, XIV. On Boccaccio's debt to Ovid see the comment by A. E. Quaglio in *Com. delle ninfe* and G. Velli, 'Cultura e "imitatio" nel primo Boccaccio', in *Annali della Scuola Normale Superiore di Pisa*, 37 (1968), pp. 65–93.

[65] *Inferno*, XV, 65. The expression used by Boccaccio to describe the immense variety and richness of colour of the flowers covering the lawn also relates back to Dante: 'and the place is painted with so many colours that not even Minerva's cloth or Turkish fabrics contained so many', which blends the passage from *Inferno*: 'and both flanks were painted arabesques and curlicues: / the Turks and Tartars never made a fabric / with richer colours intricately woven, / nor were such complex webs spun by Arachne' (*Inf.*, XVII, 15–18) with that from Eden: 'A lady all alone, who wandered there / singing and plucking flower on floweret gay, / With which her path was painted everywhere' (*Purgatorio*, XXVIII, 40–2). All English translations of Dante's *Divine Comedy* are taken from Dante Aligheri, *The Divine Comedy*, trans. by Mark Musa (Indiana, 1971). [66] Velli, 'Cultura e "imitatio"', pp. 66ff. [67] Surdich, *La cornice d'amore*, p. 141.

[68] Isidore of Seville discussed *De herbis aromaticis sive communis* in Book XVII of his *Etymologie*: see comment by A.E. Quaglio in *Comedia*. [69] Venturi, '"Picta poësis"', pp. 678–9.

[70] Illustrated herbals must have been relatively widespread in the period in question: see a preliminary survey in *Piante e fiori nelle miniature laurenziane (sec. VI–XVIII)*. Catalogue ed. G. Moggi and M. Tesi (Florence, 1986) and *La scuola medica salernitana* (Naples, 1988). [71] On this aspect see, in particular, Massaglia, 'Il giardino di Pomena'.

literature as genuine connotations of a paradisiacal reality,[72] belong in Boccaccio to an imagined botany: only if based on an objective fact[73] were they used to symbolise or evoke the vegetation of lost Eden.

But the description as a whole gives the impression that the important symbols here are not the individual plants, but rather the entire garden and its history, namely the tendentially infinite but carefully selected, organised and protected herb collection[74] that the garden contains. The 'container' of this collection is in fact far from being irrelevant. The garden is structured like that in the *Roman de la Rose*: square in shape and cut off from the world by high walls, its extensive inner area is divided up and organised by 'flat' paths leading to the various parts, while in the centre we find the usual lawn carpeted with flowers and the inevitable fountain. But there are major differences: there are no animals or happy gathering of youths or loving couples in Pomena's garden; it does indeed contain roses, lilies, pine-trees and, in general, the flowers and plants popular with literary culture, but medicinal herbs, kitchen vegetables and fodder are also grown. This is no garden of love, and Boccaccio takes pains to describe and underline the gardener's precise manual and rationalising role in relation to nature: the elimination of weeds, the need to pay attention to wind exposure and the correct grouping of different plants, the rules of the art of topiary, the rationalisation of space and ornamentation, culminating in the 'conversion' of the courtly garden's mythical

[72] 'the natural cycle of the seasons . . . is suspended: in this eternal springtime, the trees "[hanno] i vecchi fructi e i nuovi et i fiori ancora"': from G. Mazzotta, 'The "Decameron": the Literal and the Allegorical', in *Italian Quarterly*, 18 (1975), p.54. The motif is a favourite one in literary writing and garden literature, appearing as early as Homer and continuing up to Milton (see R. Assunto, *Ontologia e teleologia del giardino* (Milan, 1988), pp. 43ff, which identifies this passage with the sign of an 'absolute garden'). It is worth pointing out, however, that while Boccaccio identifies the botanical species of the plant to which he attributes these characteristics, in Alcinous' garden Homer indifferently describes all the trees as producing fruits which 'never wither' (trans. by E. Villa, cited by Assunto, p. 45). Likewise the trees carrying 'Blossoms and Fruits at once' in Milton's *Paradise Lost* (IV, 142–56) are never identified in botanical terms even if they are laden down with golden fruits and are certainly dependent on a *ver perpetuum* in the Edenic myth, perhaps contaminated by the mythical golden apples of the Hesperides (see Assunto, *Ontologia*, pp. 45ff, with bibliography).

[73] F. Chiappelli, 'Note su un'immagine e su un motivo del Boccaccio in Tasso', in *Studi tassiani*, 11 (1961), p. 106, attributes this annotation to the experience Boccaccio must have acquired of the 'aranceti partenopei'. In 'Cultura e "imitatio"' Velli affirms that this is 'abstractly possible. But what really counts . . . is the overall effect of a precious and sophisticated arabesque . . . The realistic aspect, if it exists, is softened and neutralised by imagination which is constantly fed by bookish arguments' (p. 73). But the aforesaid passage from *Vita di Dante* expresses a botanical symbolism which, for Boccaccio, was closely dependent on reality (a term which is understood to mean that which is documented by books and subject to personal verification). The overall organisation of the garden, the attention paid to the rules of *ars hortolorum* (see below) shows that this passage is not intended to be read as, or solely as, a 'precious arabesque'. The simultaneous presence of both these components in Boccaccio's writing is amply borne out in the *Decameron*, whose novellas without doubt originate from the rewriting (and contamination) of themes popular with the bookish tradition but which certainly do not fail to measure up to reality: an example of this is the alleys and characteristic glimpses of Naples in the novella on Andreuccio da Perugia.

[74] The garden in fact contains 'all' the plants, not only those known to the writer, whereas Boccaccio, concerned with the potentially endless expansion of the catalogue, comments: 'io non ne saprei nominare tante che tutte quivi non siano, e molte di più'; but it does not include those which damage crops: in particular, couch grass and fescue grass. In addition, there are no empty or poorly 'filled' spaces and the plants are grouped together according to precise criteria which Pomena explains to Adiona and the latter to Ameto. On the 'mirabile ordine' of this collection and its meaning, see Surdich, *La cornice d'amore*, pp. 142–3.

'fountain made from carved white marble' into an irrigation system regulated by Pomena. The garden model elaborated by French literature thus becomes the structural container of a real botanical garden in which Pomena guarantees, with her 'usual care', the survival of a primordial Eden-like state: a naturalness which was shattered by the 'dissolute epochs' that followed the Golden Age and which she – with her skill – 'must' conserve.[75] The description of Pomena's garden, the celebration of a perfect state of nature on which it is possible – indeed necessary – to model human experience, so much so that Adiona uses it to 'correct' the vices of the dissolute Dioneo,[76] is also, inevitably, the celebration of the garden as the result of man's rationalising activities aimed at the recreation of his own earthly paradise: a place in which it is possible to restore, albeit 'artificially', that edenic balance between man and nature which was characteristic of the Golden Age.

Drawing extensively on popular literary conventions, including the topos of the *locus amoenus* as the setting for love, in the last cantos of *Purgatorio* Dante 'limits' himself to describing earthly paradise by suggesting corresponding analogies between the Garden of Eden in the history of biblical man and the Golden Age in the history of classical man[77] in order to underline its unattainable and impracticable nature for mankind after the fall.[78] In the *Comedia delle ninfe fiorentine*, on the contrary, Boccaccio used the garden model elaborated from Romance culture to construct a genuine 'surrogate' of earthly paradise: an 'artificial space' in which 'the prosperous and happy state of nature during the Golden Age'[79] was able to survive for Iron Age generations owing to Pomena's miraculous care.[80]

Even man is allowed to reproduce an Eden of this sort for his own use alongside his own residence. We need only refer to the garden described in the introduction to the third day of the *Decameron* – a real milestone in Boccaccio's meditations on the garden – in which the author freely combines details gathered from Deduit's garden[81]

---

[75] *Com. delle ninfe*, XXVI, 66: 'Da tutte queste cose . . . nacquero i diluvi e le varie mutazioni delle umane forme; laonde io, bisognevole alle età dissolute, cominciai ad avere sollicita cura de' miei giardini.'

[76] *Com. delle ninfe*, XXVI, 89–91.

[77] There is a vast bibliography on the celestial and earthly paradises which abound in medieval literary and figurative culture and are often closely linked to real gardens: a useful starting point, above all for the relationship between the two topoi during this period, is Venturi, '"Picta poësis"', *passim*.

[78] Ulysses, who succeeded with his own strength in reaching the mountain of Purgatory on whose peak Dante places his Eden, was shipwrecked; and Dante, who was allowed to reach the long-sought peak through divine intervention, was then violently rebuked by 'his' Beatrice: 'How hast thou deigned to climb the hill? Didst thou not know that man is happy here?' (*Purg.*, XXX, 74–5).

[79] Barberi Squarotti, 'Le figure dell'Eden', p. 279.

[80] A garden disguised as paradise (of an Islamic type) was built by Veglio della Montagna so as to be able to dispose at will of the 'assassins', as Marco Polo reports in his *Milione*: 'Lo Veglio . . . avea fatto fare tra due montagne in una valle lo più bel giardino e 'l più grande del mondo. Quivi avea tutti frutti e li più begli palagi del mondo, tutti dipinti ad oro e a besti' e a uccelli; quivi era condotti: per tale venia acqua e per tale mèle e per tale vino; quivi era donzelli e donzelle, li più begli del mondo, che meglio sapeano cantare e sonare e ballare. E faceva lo Veglio credere a costoro che quello era lo paradiso' (chap. 40, ed. V. Bertolucci Pizzorusso (Milan, 1975). See on this subject, Venturi, '"Picta poësis"', p. 672.

[81] E. G. Kern, 'The Gardens in the "Decameron" cornice', in *Publications of the Modern Language Association of America*, 66 (1951), pp. 505–23.

and Pomona's kitchen garden, and even elements taken from real life:[82] the enclosure protected by the outer wall, the rationally laid-out space intersected by paths across the garden, 'straight as an arrow and covered over by trellised vines', the white and crimson rose bushes which, together with the jasmine, granted solace from the sun's rays, the orderly presence of every possible 'laudable' plant, the flower-covered lawn – now innovatively 'surrounded by orange and other citrus trees with the most luscious foliage' decked with old and new fruit and blossom – and, standing in the centre of both the lawn and the garden, the white marble fountain with 'superbly sculpted reliefs' which spontaneously provided water for the garden, a large number of animals and, everywhere, an intoxicating fragrance. In order to confirm the significance of this garden Boccaccio draws attention to the fact that, on finding themselves surrounded by this charming setting for the first time, the members of the happy group unanimously exclaim that, 'were it possible to build a heaven on earth, they would be at a loss to know how else to embody it but as this garden, nor could they imagine a single thing that might enhance its splendour'.[83]

Having fled from Florence to escape the raging plague and corrupted way of life, the ten young people spend their time in this garden-paradise playing, singing and telling tales: they therefore appear to attain a sort of immortality:

> They all wore oak-leaf garlands and carried fragrant herbs or flowers, and whoever had met them on the way could have reached only one conclusion: 'Death will never get the better of these folk, or if it does, they'll die happy.'[84]

The garden in the *Decameron* therefore becomes 'an oasis which not only protects but also gives a kind of invulnerability'.[85] And the merry dances, the songs, the serene conversations within the garden built by man in imitation of earthly paradise are in violent opposition to the macabre scenes of death described in the introduction to the first day. For the first time Boccaccio's gardens are, one might say, besieged by the shadow of death which they victoriously oppose. It is impossible not to think of the Pisan *Triumph of Death*. This reference is all the more legitimate if we remember that the 'happy group in the garden' / 'triumph of death' association, which, at the time of the *Decameron*, represented the radical renewal of a motif which had already been the subject of numerous rewritings by Boccaccio and which had been expressed in iconographical terms, perhaps by Buffalmacco,[86] on the walls of the Pisan cemetery during the 1330s and 1340s, represented a real iconographical and ideological 'innovation'.

---

[82] On the relationship created between gardens and the Florentine landscape, see the comments by Branca in *Decameron*.
[83] *Dec.*, III, Intr.   [84] *Dec.*, IX, Intr.
[85] L. M. Muto, 'La novella portante del "Decameron". La parabola del piacere', in *Genèse, codification et rayonnement d'un genre médiéval. La Nouvelle.* Actes du Colloque International de Monréal (14-16 October 1982) (Montreal, 1983), p. 150.
[86] This attribution, suggested by L. Bellosi (*Buffalmacco e il 'Trionfo della Morte'* (Turin, 1974)), is not unquestioningly supported by all historians of figurative art.

Other innovations which are apparent in this rewriting of the 'happy group in the garden' motif confirm that the author had established a precise intersystemic relationship with the painting. This was especially true of the two major formal variants involving the size and composition of the group and the structural details of the garden, aspects which contrasted with both the merry group described in *Filocolo* and the group of nymphs who sing their love to Ameto in the *Comedia delle ninfe fiorentine*. In the *Decameron* the happy group, consisting of seven women and three men, whose elegant members belonged to the best Florentine families, dedicates itself to music, singing and story-telling on the lawn, which is literally 'enclosed' by a 'trellis' of citrus fruit trees.

Taken as a whole, the innovations introduced by Boccaccio to the garden topic he had elaborated over the course of the years – and their overall meaning – amply demonstrate, I believe, that during the period spent on the new book of novellas the Florentine writer was competing against what must have represented the most recent and provocatory *mise en page* of the image to which he was so attached, and that in writing this book he intended to play an active part in the debate on the ethical, existential and ideological implications of the topos.[87]

The formal affinities which link the *Decameron* to the fresco emphasise their evident contrast in terms of meaning. In the *Triumph* the happy group represents Death's privileged victims. On the contrary, in Boccaccio's garden, a place in which, as was seen above, Eden is positively recreated by human reason, the group of people who have taken refuge there to escape from the death raging through Florence and corrupting the rules of society, not only do not die but, by adopting the very models of life attacked by the anonymous *auctor* of the *Triumph* and thereby enabling 'the palingenesis of the world . . . following the apocalyptical downfall'[88] provoked by the plague, appear destined to become 'immortal', as far as it is within mankind's capacity to do so.

While the anonymous *auctor* contrasted Deduit's garden, the product of medieval literary and artistic culture, with the desert of ascetic and penitential life depicted in the adjacent fresco dedicated to the hermitage, repeatedly citing the most representative literary text of the culture of penitence, the *Vitae Patrum*, of which a vernacular version had recently been edited by the Dominican Cavalca, Boccaccio responded by celebrating the very same topical literary setting (it is important not to forget that the primary structural model for the garden in the *Decameron* was still the *Roman de la Rose*), enriching it with all the 'additions' and nuances of meaning which he had elaborated over the years, and at the same time celebrating that form of literature of which it can truly be said 'we were *reading* one day *for pleasure*': the 'pleasant discourses' that can save us from death and offer *solacium* to the tribulations of human life, as Boccaccio expressly

---

[87] For a more detailed analysis of the problem, see Battaglia Ricci, *Ragionare nel giardino*, above all pp. 162ff.

[88] The excerpt is taken from G. Barberi Squarotti, 'La "cornice" del "Decameron" o il mito di Robinson', in *Il potere della parola. Studi sul 'Decameron'* (Naples, 1983), pp. 5ff: a fundamental study for an understanding of the relationship between the garden in *Decameron* and the Edenic archetype.

declared in presenting the 'Book of Prince Galehaut' to his favoured readers, women in love.[89]

Thus, the group's invulnerability, its potential immortality, can only be interpreted as a conscious and controversial reversal of the message that the *auctor intellectualis* had expressed in the fresco. For Boccaccio, in fact, the theme of gardens represented a valuable occasion for a discussion on the types, functions and recipients of literature. In response to those who criticised the book because its author had 'used too much licence in writing these novellas', Boccaccio was anxious to justify his approach by invoking the specificity of this literary genre, which differed from both scholastic and philosophical writings and from religious texts:

> It is perfectly obvious, furthermore, that these discussions were not held in church . . .
> Nor were they held in the Philosophy Schools . . . nor were the participants clergymen
> or philosophers. The discourses were held in gardens, places devoted to pleasure, and
> the participants were young people, though not immature nor readily influenced by
> stories; and the times were such that no offence was given by people . . . who went
> about with a pair of breeches wrapped about their heads as a precaution.[90]

GARDENS AND POETRY: BOCCACCIO, PETRARCH AND DANTE

As well as being the emblematic image of an existential ideal, the merry gathering in the garden ('in a place of solace'; in Deduit's garden), singing 'popular songs' 'for *their own* delight' and telling 'pleasant and sad love stories and other fortunate episodes',[91] became for Boccaccio an image capable of representing the activity of literary writing itself. Contrary to 'preaching in the churches' and the 'serious disputes in the schools', it became the most luminous and controversial metaphor possible to express his idea of literature. A metaphor which was in fact not wholly inappropriate given that when the group, protected by the walls of the *hortus conclusus* from widespread death, pain and moral abjection, sat in a circle on the lawn and 'conversed' of the infinite sad and joyful cases of human life, it symbolically reproduced the very act of literary communication and its fruition.

Real everyday experiences, like those acquired, and already idealised, at the court of Naples, might have influenced the writer's imagination by attributing unusual meanings to one of the most conventional images elaborated by courtly literature. In the extraordinary autobiographical passage which brings the *Comedia delle ninfe fiorentine* to an end, Giovanni Boccaccio had in fact already 'charged' this motif with a precise meta-literary function. By doing so he transformed the *locus amoenus* into a genuine spatial and figurative hypostasis of the poet's creative activity, a splendid

---

[89] In the *Proemio* he explicitly attributes to pleasant and comforting 'conversation' the power of warding off death: 'In this unhappy state I derived so much refreshment from pleasant conversation with friends and their admirable support, I cannot doubt but that if I'm still alive it is thanks to them.' On this topic, and for an analysis of the relationships between Boccaccio in *Decameron*, the penitential-ascetic culture celebrated by the *auctor* of the *Triumph* and Dante in his *Divine Comedy*, readers are again referred to my *Ragionare nel giardino*.   [90] *Dec.*, author's Afterword.   [91] See *Proemio*.

representation of the aesthetic, consolatory and didactic function of poetry and the fantastic dimension of poetic invention, now seen as 'separate' and antithetical realities to the bitter, harsh necessities of daily life, represented in Florence, not just symbolically, by the 'dark and silent house' and the 'cold, rough and miserly old man' which await the writer in the evening when the nymphs stop singing. In conclusion, passing abruptly from a third-person narrative to one in the first person, the author portrays himself in the setting which serves as the background to the episodes narrated in the book, sharing the metaphorical space of the literary garden with the characters he has invented, representing the creative 'act' and its fruition in concrete terms and explicitly conveying the effect of ecstatic estrangement.

> Fra la fronzuta e nova primavera,
> in loco spesso d'erbette e di fiori,
> da folti rami chiuso, posto m'era
> ad ascoltare i lieti e vaghi amori,
> nascostamente, delle ninfe belle,
>
> . . .
>
> Li quali udendo e rimirando quelle
> negli occhi belle e nelle facce chiare
>
> . . .
>
> sentendo appresso il lor dolce cantare
>
> . . .
>
> sì dolcemente nell'anima mea
> Amor si risvegliò . . .
> . . . che in veritate
> io sanza me grand'ora dimorai
> in non provata mai felicitate . . .

Petrarch, to whom the topos of the courtly garden is essentially foreign,[92] also sees the garden as a space connected to poetic activity. He does not think of it, however, as a mental or symbolic place, but rather a real space within the picturesque landscape of Vaucluse which he describes at length in the *Epystolae*:[93] a 'saxose rigidus telluris agellus' snatched from the nymphs of the Sorga river who engaged him in a 'bellum de finibus ingens'.[94] This was an *hortus* which was *conclusus* after a fashion,[95] built – and repeatedly

---

[92] This may perhaps be a vague reminiscence of that system glimpsed in the landscape described by the anti-*plazer*, *Né per sereno ciel ir vaghe stelle*: 'né tra chiare fontane et verdi prati / dolce cantare honeste donne e belle' (*Rerum vulgarium fragmenta*, CCCXII, 7–8). The expression of a generally late gothic character, they also formed the background for Laura's appearance; the latter was also described in a style halfway between 'stilnovistico' and 'courtly' which Petrarch appears to have shared with Boccaccio: 'in the midst of flowers and grass', amidst 'clear, cool sweet water', amongst 'shady groves' or under 'tender green foliage'. M. Santagata (*Per moderne carte. La biblioteca volgare di Petrarca* (Bologna, 1990), pp. 262ff) believes that Petrarch derived the style from Boccaccio, rather than shared it with him.

[93] There are also scattered references in the *Familiari* and in *De vita solitaria*. On the 'garden' in Petrarch and the early bibliography: Venturi, '"Picta poësis"', p. 682ff. The text of the *Epystolae* cited here is in F. Petrarch, *Rime, Trionfi e poesie latine*, ed. by F. Neri, G. Martellotti, E. Bianchi and N. Sapegno (Milan-Naples, 1951), pp. 706ff.

[94] The two excerpts are taken from *Ep. Ad Iohannem de Columna* (III, 1), 8 and 1.

[95] *Ad Guillelmum Veronensem* (III, 3), 7–13.

repaired – by himself, moving rocks with the help of more or less professional labour,[96] and subject to the inclemency of the weather and the changing seasons; it consisted of a well-built open space and a lawn whose imported turf was covered with flowers in spring, where the poet planted laurels, chosen in this instance for their capacity to ward off the devastating fury of lightning.[97] This corner of the landscape was 'reorganised' through the rational intervention of Petrarch the man[98] who, in the Sorga valley, his longed-for retreat and the setting for an idealised solitary life, created a space for poetry for himself and populated it with divinities from classical mythology.[99]

The 'agellus' snatched from the nymphs is, he wrote, a place dedicated to the poet's ideal conversation with the muses:

> ... hic sepe precanti
> antiquos renovare modos, contingere lauros,
> nectere sera manu, sacra renovare choreas
> permissum ...[100]

This is his personal Helicon, whence he addressed notes to his friends:

> Hoc Helicone meo circumviridantibus herbis
> fontis et ad ripam queruli sub rupe silenti
> atque inter geminas properatum perlege lauros;
> quas tibi, sacrata forsan sessure sub umbra,
> dum serere, heu quotiens suspirans 'crescite' dixi.[101]

None the less, the memory of the cultural topos of the '*loca amoena* viridia que solum praestant Amorem' also hovers over Petrarch's *hortus* – for the most part modelled on the Horatian celebration of the small allotment which allows a life set apart from the city hubbub, pleased with 'exigui fines ... agelli / angustamque domum et dulces ... libellos', and encourages poetry;[102] a celebration inevitably

---

[96] Together with Petrarch himself, paid workers and friends of the poet took part in the enterprise: for example, Guglielmo da Verona, about whom the poet wrote: 'Hic te mecum convulsa revolvere saxa / non puduit campumque satis laxare malignum', Ibid., 5–6.   [97] *Ad Iohannem de Columna* (I, 10), 116–22.
[98] 'Natura cedenti operi': *Ad Guillelmum Veronensem* (V, 8).   [99] On this see Venturi '"Picta poësis"', pp. 685ff.
[100] *Ad Iohannem de Columna* (III, 1), 78–81.
[101] *Ad Franciscum priorem Sanctorum Apostolorum de Florentia* (III, 33), 19–23.
[102] Horace, *Satires*, II, 6, 60–3, Petrarch, *Ad Iacobum de Columna* (I, 6), 7–8. In *Epistles*, I, 16, 1ff, Horace also gives a comprehensive description of the *ager* adjoining the Sabine villa and its 'latebrae dulces et ... amoenae'. Petrarch drew on many classical authors, ranging from Cicero to Virgil and Horace, not to mention Homer, for his celebration of solitary and pleasant places which encourage literary *inventio* ('nusquam felicius quam in silvis ac in montibus ingenium experiar nusquam michi paratius et magnifici sensus occurrant ... et equa conceptibus verba respondeant': *De vita solitaria*, I, 7). From Horace in particular he derived both the radical opposition between the city and the countryside which characterises all the first part of *De vita solitaria* before reappearing in the *Canzoniere* as the historical-symbolic variant of Avignon/Vaucluse (see M. Santagata, *Petrarca e i Colonna* (Lucca, 1988), pp. 100ff; *I frammenti dell'anima* (Bologna, 1992), pp. 170ff, with earlier bibliography), and the dominant idea of the particular relationship between a pleasant and solitary landscape and poetic *inventio*: 'silvis et locis virentibus ... nichil est Musis amicius'; Petrarch, *De vita sol.*, I, 7; Horace, *Ep.*, II, 2, 77: 'Scriptorum chorus omnis amat nemus et fugit urbem' and above all the apparition of the inspiring muses in the typical landscape of a pleasant wooded retreat: *Carmina*, III, 4, 5ff: 'Auditis, an me ludit amabilis / Insania? Audire et videor pios / errare [inferred subject: Calliope invoked in the preceding strophe] per lucos, amoenae / Quos et aquae subeunt et aurae'. On Horace's 'garden', see Grimal, *Les jardins romains*, pp. 347–96: 'son jardin, a lui seul, lui inspire des poems' (p. 396).

contaminated by evocations of bucolic poetry.[103] In a letter to Lelio, Petrarch in fact complains that the *ortulus* awakes in him *exstinctum ignem* and the *dulcia preteriti suspiria vite*, encouraged by the charm of the place, pleasant rests on the green banks, the ripple of the water and the nymphs' songs. Not even Petrarch could resist the dangerous seduction of the garden which Abelard had already warned against in his *Historia Calamitatum*;[104] and the mythological youth armed with flames and fiery darts also flew lightly about in his kitchen garden.[105] The small *hortus*, together with the wider space, namely his beloved Vaucluse, of which it was, one might say, the ideal centre, therefore serves as the appointed setting for the memories and ghosts of love and as a place of poetry.

Compared to these models, Petrarch paid unusual attention to the 'manual tasks' and 'technical expertise' required to keep the *hortus* (both that in Vaucluse and those which many years later he would find himself tending in Milan and Arquà). These manual tasks and skills required his personal involvement and he accurately described them, initially in the limited notes inserted in the *Epystolae* and later on the blank pages of his beloved antique codices.[106]

The author's artistic output in general still contains, in my opinion, clear-cut traces of the everyday practice of *ars hortulorum* – probably elaborated in close connection

[103] Symptomatic of this are the 'promises' to Giovanni Colonna (*Ep.*, III, 1) to convince him to visit him in his retreat: 'Nos tibi multiloquos, si fert ea cura, libellos / Musarumque choros domitisque insistere Nimphis; / nos tibi pampineos colles gravidosque racemos, / denique mellifluas ficus undamque recentem / gurgite de medio offerimus cantusque volucrum / innumeros montisque sinus curvosque recessus / et nemorum gelidas udis in vallibus umbras' (106–12). The non-opposition between garden, a space which is structured and composed by man's labour according to a precise mental project (in particular, Petrarch's gardens were characterised by the presence of laurel, closely linked to the subject-matter of his poetry) and the *locus amoenus* must have facilitated exchanges between the characteristic motifs of the two symbolic areas. While the place inhabited by the muses was the poet's own garden snatched from the nymphs, the whole of Vaucluse was a place of poetry: 'saepe montanum carmen quasi hedum e toto grege letissum atque lectissimum vidi et, nitore insito admonitus originis, dixi mecum: "Gramen alpinum sapis, ex alto venis"' (*De vita sol.*, I, 7) or 'qui non palazzi, non theatro o loggia, ma 'n lor vece un abete, un faggio, un pino, / tra l'erba verde e 'l bel monte vicino, / onde si scende poetando et poggia . . .' (*Rerum vulgarium fragmenta*, X, 5–8). This was based both on his own experience in real life and on the adoption of cultural and behavioural models which are explicitly set out in *De vita solitaria*: Cicero, who 'ad tractatum legum civilium accessurus frondosas quercus et delectabiles secessus . . . et procerissimas populos et concentum avium et strepitum fluviorum . . . queret', and Virgil who, 'suum Alexim . . . pastorio carmine laudaturus "inter densas umbrosa cacumina fagos" assidue veniens, solus in montibus et silvis id faceret' (*De vita sol.*, II, 7).

[104] 'Multi philosophorum reliquerunt frequentias urbium et ortulos suburbanos, ubi ager irriguus et arborum come et susurrus avium, fontis speculum, rivus murmurans, et multe oculorum aurium illecebre, ne per luxum et abundantiam copiarum anime fortitudo molleresceret et ejus pudicitia stupraret' (ed. by J. Monfrin (Paris, 1959), lines 1060–75).

[105] *Ad Lelium suum*, I, 8, 49.

[106] In Vatican Ms. 2193 Petrarch described his actual experience of gardening in a series of curious technical notes. These have been published on several occasions, most recently by M. Miglio, Appendix to 'Immagine e racconto. Note sul giardino in qualche manoscritto italiano (XII–XIV secolo)', in *Il giardino storico italiano. Problemi di indagine. Fonti letterarie e storiche* (Florence, 1981), pp. 290–3; this work also includes interesting information on the use of the literary garden in political public relations. As P. De Nolhac wrote in 'Pétrarque et son jardin d'après ses notes inédites', *Giornale storico della Letteratura Italiana*, 9 (1887), pp. 404–14: 'C'est sans doute la présence de Palladius dans le manuscrit qui a engagé Pétrarque à confier à ce volume les principaux souvenirs des ses expériences de jardinier' (p. 407), and, on the other hand, 'Les *Géorgiques* ont grande autorité pour le jardinier-humaniste': so much so that in a footnote Petrarch recalls having used an unusual transplanting technique in which he did not place much confidence because 'omnia sunt contra doctrinam Maronis' (p. 290).

with the great classical models, Palladio's *De agricoltura* and Virgil's *Georgics*, which offered him a description of the *ars topiaria* with which old *Corycius* tended the 'pauca ... iugera iuri' which he had transformed into a luxuriant garden,[107] as well as, in more general terms, basic agricultural guidelines – together with the symbolic meanings of varying cultural origin linked to the semantic area of the *hortus*. Moreover, through a singular form of osmosis, the literary celebration of the mythical aggregate of a rhetorical and cultural matrix, 'Laura/lauro: amore/poesia', not only implies the real practice of planting laurels in one's own garden, perhaps in the company of other garden-loving and laurel-loving poets,[108] but also the plant's botanical 'properties' and the memory of the biblical archetype which are successfully combined in the text with the myth of Daphne. Thus, in a reflection of the violence and absurdity of Laura's death, in the 'Canzone delle visioni' it is precisely, and incredibly, a laurel – a plant of such beauty that it appeared to be 'one of the trees ... of paradise' – that is struck down by lightning.[109]

Petrarch also derived his metaphors for poetic activity from gardening techniques, since, as a poet, he also became an infertile and parched *hortus* now that he was no longer irrigated by the spring which gushed forth from Parnassus:

> S'i' fussi stato fermo a la spelunca
> là dove Apollo diventò profeta,
> Fiorenza avria forse oggi il suo poeta,
> non pur Verona et Manta et Arunca;
> ma perché 'l mio terren più non s'ingiunca
> de l'humor di quel sasso, altro pianeta
> conven ch'i' segua, et del mio campo mieta
> lappole et stecchi co la falce adunca.
> L'oliva è secca, et è rivolta altrove
> l'acqua che di Parnaso si deriva,
> per cui in alcun tempo ella fioriva.
> Così sventura over colpa mi priva
> d'ogni buon fructo, se l'etterno Giove
> de la sua grazia sopra me non piove.[110]

And in the *Canzoniere*, as well as being a consolatory retreat from the trials of love, the *ortulus* in Vaucluse continues to be the physical setting for poetic inspiration:

> Non Tesin, Po, Varo ...
> ... non edra, abete, pin, faggio o genebro

---

[107] *Georgics*, IV, 125–48.

[108] From the notes to the Vatican ms. cited in n. 106 we learn that Petrarch repeatedly planted laurels also in his gardens in Milan and Arquà. In particular, in the note dated 26 March 1359 he describes having planted five laurels 'in orto Sancte Valerie Mediolani', and hopes that these 'sacri arbuscelli' thrive, not least because 'insignis vir dompnus Joannes Boccacci de Certaldo, ipsis amicissimus et mihi ... sationj interfuit' (p. 292).

[109] *Rer. vulg. fr.*, CCCXXIII. See also XXIV and, on the mythical and edenic character of evergreen laurel, XXX, LX, etc.

[110] CLXVI.

poria 'l foco allentar che 'l cor tristo ange,
quant' un bel rio ch'ad ognor meco piange,
co l'arboscel che 'n rime orno et celebro.

. . .

Così cresca il bel lauro in fresca riva,
e chi 'l piantò pensier' leggiadri et alti
ne la dolce ombra al suon de l'acque scriva.[111]

The particular affinity which links the images evoked here to those painted in real life by Simone Martini on the frontispiece of a Virgil manuscript owned by the Ambrosiana Library[112] seems to confirm that it was Petrarch who suggested both the concept and the details of the illustration to the painter, and that it is to him (a poet-cum-gardener and grower of laurels) that we owe the elaboration of this variant of the topos. Through a singular projection of the image elaborated by the poet to portray himself in the act of poetic creation ('chi l' piantò pensier' leggiadri et alti / ne la dolce ombra al suon de l'acque scriva'), the Virgil portrayed by Simone in the act of composing is seated on the lawn in the shade of a tree[113] within a space enclosed by other trees, whereas the fruits of his writing are translated into three realistic but also emblematic figures: a shepherd herding his flock, a peasant cutting the briars with a curved scythe, and a soldier. The presence of these portraits in miniature detracts from the belief that the background is merely an evocation of the bucolic landscape: those trees can only represent the muses' grove, or rather, the Petrarchesque reinterpretation of the classic 'garden of poetry'.[114]

In his lyrical works Dante appears to establish a complex relationship with the topos of the *locus amoenus* popular with Romance culture, consisting of more or less violent contortions or sublime rewritings. Only in the song *Al poco giorno* does Dante use a traditional 'beautiful grass lawn . . . enclosed by very high hills' as the background to the desire for love, but solely to emphasise the opposition between the poet's desire and the harsh reality of his love for the woman Petra. In the poems dedicated to her Dante

---

[111] CXLVIII.

[112] Ms. Ambrosiano, previously A.49 inf., now Sala del Prefetto 10/27. On this see the recent study by M. Ciccuto, 'Circostanze francesi del "Virgilio" Ambrosiano', in idem, *Figure di Petrarca, Giotto, Simone Martini, Franco Bolognese* (Naples, 1991), pp. 79–109, with earlier bibliography. On the importance of the 'mirabile rapporto' established between the two at Avignon during this epoch and on the influence of Martini and Petrarch's lesson on the 'manifest tendency to rediscover the wonders of nature, paying fond attention to rural life with accurate portrayals of plants and animals, trees and meadows', which characterised several famous paintings such as the frescoes in the papal chambers of the Guardaroba, see E. Castelnuovo, *Un pittore alla corte di Avignone. Matteo Giovannetti e la pittura in Provenza nel secolo XIV* (Turin, 1962), pp. 41ff. The ability to observe nature carefully, coupled, as in Petrarch's case, with a detailed knowledge of classical culture, must have been decisive for this purpose. (On the subject of the small birds praised in his verse, M. Santagata, *Petrarca e i Colonna*, p. 99, wrote that Petrarch 'alternated a mythographer's memory with the careful eye of the ornithologist'). In fact, 'technical' texts such as the *Georgics* had taught Petrarch to spy – like a poet-gardener – on the significant variety of the natural world.

[113] The entirely Petrarchan motif of the poet sitting in the shade of the laurel planted in his own garden is contaminated here by the stylistic element 'lentus in umbra' used by Virgil in his bucolic works to evoke 'the idyllic condition of the poet in harmony with nature' which was also dear to the bucolic Petrarch (Ciccuto, *Circostanze francesi*, p. 92).

[114] On the 'garden of poesy' in Roman culture see Grimal, *Les jardins romains*, pp. 362ff.

usually employs the traditional *locus amoenus* antiphrastically to 'construct' landscapes which express his dysphoria:

> Passato hanno lor termine le fronde
> che trasse fuor la vertù d'Arïete
> per adornare il mondo, e morta è l'erba
> . . .
> . . . morti li fioretti per le piagge.[115]

Likewise in *Fiore* – if we accept its attribution to Dante – the protagonist falls in love with the flower grown in the 'garden of Pleasure', but 'during the month of January, not May'.[116]

Likewise, the commonplace metaphor of the woman-flower, whose origin, it is worth underlining, can be traced back to the *Cantico dei cantici*, perhaps through the Rose of the *roman* of that name and chivalrous literature itself, and which can be found throughout the works of the early 'canzonieri' and mystical writers, was destined to be radically 'contorted' and presented in an erotic sense in *Fiore*:

> Sì ch'io allora il fior tutto sfogl[i]ai,
> E la semenza ch'i' avea portata,
> Quand'eb[b]i arato, sì·lla seminai.
> La semenza del fior v'era cascata:
> Amendue insieme sì·lle mescolai,
> Che molta di buon'erba n'è po' nata.[117]

Again, in a mystical sense in the *Divine comedy*, Bernardo's last prayer to the Virgin rephrases the analogy between the bride and the *hortus conclusus* in *Cantico dei cantici*[118] by making paradise-the mystical rose 'germinate' from the Virgin's womb-God's garden:[119]

> Nel ventre tuo si raccese l'amore,
> per lo cui caldo ne l'etterna pace
> così è germinato questo fiore.[120]

Dante therefore blends together traditional materials to construct 'his' earthly paradise, creating a place set apart and 'enclosed' by a wall of fire, watered by perennial fountains,

---

[115] *Io son venuto al punto de la rota*, 40ff.   [116] *Fiore*, I, 4 and III, 1.   [117] *Fiore*, CCXXX, 9–14.

[118] It seems likely that this was derived from the Bernardian texts, or those which Dante believed to be such; see also the *De laude Mariae Virginis* published in Migne's *Patrologia Latina* (CLXXXII, cols. 1142–7), in which Bernardo calls the Virgin Mary 'paradisus omnium deliciarum', 'Virga Iesse, per quam in ramo convalescit quod perierat in radice' and, on the subject of the expression 'fructus ventris tui' in the Ave Maria, notes: 'huius fructus odore homo de terra ad patriam trahit . . . In hoc fructu ventris tui amplectitur anima, quia lignum vite de paradiso in convallem transportatum . . . immo quasi lignum vitae, Verbum Patris in utero tuo.' See also Venturi Ferriolo, *Nel grembo*, pp. 109–10.

[119] Avalle, *Ai luoghi*, p. 10, observes the tendency in lyric poetry 'to identify the inside of a flourishing *orto* with the woman herself'. In other instances the Empyrean is the 'garden bright / shone on by Christ, and flowering in his rays' (*Paradiso*, XXIII, 71–2; XXXI, 97; XXXII, 39).

[120] *Par.*, XXXIII, 7–9. On the other hand, in *Par.*, XXIII, 73ff the celestial rose is the Virgin Mary, she 'wherein God's Word was dight / with Flesh'.

endowed with eternal springtime, a deep and dense forest, and lawns dotted with flowers on which, as might be expected, 'beautiful' women 'in love' come to dance;[121] here Dante himself again experienced the burning desire of the flames of love.[122] But the symbolic pregnancy of Dante's writing completely transformed the meaning and function of this setting which became the core of the character's cathartic experience and the place in which the contemporary history he represents comes face to face with the eternal history of the Church, thus investing the unusual traveller with prophetic and quasi-messianic functions.[123] Even classical history is invoked in the opening to Matelda which – perhaps in the wake of *Ovidio moralizzato* – identifies precise analogies between the biblical Eden and the Golden Age dreamt of by classical poets. The sort of short-circuit which Matelda establishes between Eden and Parnassus is of particular importance:

> Quelli ch' anticamente poetaro
> l'età de l'oro e suo stato felice
> forse in Parnaso esto loco sognaro (*Purgatory*, XXVIII, 139-41).

According to the majority of commentators, the passage should be interpreted as 'gli antichi poeti "sognarono" l'Eden stando in Parnaso' (namely: while writing poetry they had an intuitive and fantastic awareness of the divine garden created for Adam), but others interpret it as: 'the ancient poets imagined Eden as being on Parnassus'. However, the tercet describes an evocative similarity between two symbolic settings of literary culture, perhaps acting as a catalyst for the various analogous relations established by writers in fourteenth-century Italy between the garden and poetry, Eden and Parnassus. This complex metaphorical and symbolic area, in which the garden represented the appointed place for poetry, Parnassus the garden, and the poets 'cultivators' of Parnassus, was destined to be used once again, at the end of the century, by Franco Sacchetti when he lamented poetry's silence following the death of the three crowns:

> Secche eran l'erbe, gli albuscelli e' fiori,
> e spersi i dolci frutti del Parnaso,
> e d'Elicona era rotto ogni vaso,
> che dava l'acque a chi disiava honori;
> e, morti i fiorentini coltivatori,
> sul monte alcun non era più rimaso.[124]

---

[121] *Purg.*, XXVIII, 34–46 and XXIX, 1ff. [122] *Purg.*, XXX, 34–48.

[123] There is a vast bibliography on these cantos of the *Comedy*. The most recent works are: P. Sabatino, *L'Eden della nuova poesia. Saggi sulla 'Divina Commedia'* (Florence, 1991), pp. 45–124; and R. Migliorini Fissi, 'L'ingresso di Dante nell'Eden', in *Studi danteschi* 58 (1986), pp. 1–47, with earlier bibliography. On the theme discussed here readers are referred to G. Venturi, 'Eden e giardino della Divina Commedia', *Rassegna della Letteratura italiana*, 46 (1992), pp. 7–16.

[124] *Libro delle rime*, ed. F. Ageno (Florence, 1990), CCXVI, 1ff.

CHAPTER 2

SOME MEDICI GARDENS OF THE FLORENTINE RENAISSANCE: AN ESSAY IN POST-AESTHETIC INTERPRETATION

D. R. EDWARD WRIGHT

Dedicated to my mentor and friend David R. Coffin

The history of landscape architecture has traditionally been studied by art historians, professional designers and genteel amateurs, all of whom share an orientation toward the formal analysis of aesthetic artifacts. Garden histories normally organise the material according to the broad stylistic categories of art history. In the case of Italian Renaissance gardens, whenever social history enters the discussion it tends to be anecdotal rather than explanatory – as if human use of planned environments was a mere afterthought to an essentially artistic endeavour – and is often referred to the reductively elementary motive of 'pleasure', in a not infrequently romantic rhetoric of horticultural delights and wonders. Certain writers avoid the topic of landscape/nature altogether in limiting description to the culturally more refined, but in the end non-essential roles of sculptural adornment/art, thereby shifting attention from the equally significant relationship between usage and patterns of structuration. Furthermore, the secondary literature exhibits a penchant for documentation, visual and verbal, at the expense of interpretation. Given this focus on the artistic subject and aesthetic intentionality, conjoined with a monolithic view of causality based on a tactful 'empirical' methodology, such studies are informed by the increasingly unsatisfactory modernist outlook currently under fire from scholars influenced by critical theory of continental origin. To put it differently, the literature on Italian gardens is characterised by a hierarchised opposition of Art versus Nature which needs to be deconstructed.

The foregoing situation is complicated by the unavoidable format requirements of the printed book, the illustrations of which turn gardens and parks into static, two-dimensional framed pictures that dramatically distort one's experience in phenomenological terms. Indeed, photographs and diagrams have become a distinctive sign system which effectively reconstitutes Renaissance landscape environments as objects of the aesthetic gaze, distancing the viewing subject to an external Archimedean point from which gardens appear as problems in design, decoration, iconography and classical influence. Without the possibility of direct experience as an internally placed consumer of the multi-layered sensations chosen among the variety of natural phenomena in connection with particular human needs, one cannot make sense of many structures and details in any but a purely visual manner. The rectilinear format of the printed page seems to encourage the illustration of geometrically distinctive sectors of Italian gardens as somehow typical of the Renaissance style, thus undermining the potential study of cross-cultural links determined by common patterns of use, and of casually organised features, which in certain instances are interpreted as a (dubious) historical precedent for the more 'natural' eighteenth-century English manner.

The purpose of this chapter will be to re-study a group of well-known sixteenth-century gardens from the perspective of the user rather than the designer, examining conventions of utilisation and functional requirements in relation to physical infra-structure, with the aim of establishing protocols of interpretation that are not misleadingly skewed toward the discursive categories of formal/visual analysis. It is hoped that such an approach will result in an expanded discourse that will open the way to alternative, non-stylistic models of historical comparison and typological categorisation. We shall try to make sense of these gardens and parks in terms of conventional distinctions made in ancient, medieval and Renaissance writing on matters of health, agriculture and social practice. This is not intended so much to replace visual/aesthetic readings as to integrate them into a different discourse where that seems appropriate.

Perhaps the most frequent excuse for excursions to gardens in the countryside noted in treatises and private correspondence is medical hygiene, the preservation of health and the prevention of disease. As Petrus Crescentius remarked a propos of *viridaria*, 'they preserve bodily health'.[1] One fundamental mode of prophylaxis was the breathing of pure air: 'Air is a cause of great moment in producing [melancholy] or any other disease, being that it is still taken into our bodies by respiration, and our more inner parts.'[2] The most beneficial climate was to be found outside the urban confines: 'It is the privilege of those who stay at country houses to live in better health, with less illness, which does not turn out thus in cities, where, since the dwellings are high, the rooms bleak, and the streets dark, the air gets infected more rapidly, and people fall ill frequently.'[3] Corruption of the air in Florence – believed to result from putrefaction under dark damp conditions that released tiny particles to create a miasma potentially aspirable into the lungs – came from a variety of insanitary practices, including the disposal of raw sewage in the open ditches formerly along the present Via de' Fossi, the employment of human urine in the wool manufacturing process, and the dumping of dead animals and butchers' refuse to be picked clean by scavenging birds on a barren

---

[1] Petrus Crescentius, *Opus ruralium commodorum* (Basel, 1548), p. 377.
[2] R. Burton, *The Anatomy of Melancholy*, I, sec. 2, subsec. v.
[3] Antonio Guevara, *Il dispregio della corte, e lode della villa* (Florence, 1601), p. 55.

strip of land called Sardigna, by the Arno.[4] To counteract the effects of putrid air, one would have to seek out regions of cool, dry atmosphere swept by gentle, temperate breezes, which could disperse pestiferous particles, of open sunlight for its drying effect, and pleasant smelling plantations whose scent could forestall the inhalation of air-borne miasma.[5] Such conditions would obtain 'below the base of some forested mountain where the farmlands are rich and arable (*dolci et tractabili*)' away from the sea or any kind of standing water.[6] To the north-west of Florence, the foothills of Monte Morello offered ideal atmospheric conditions since the well-forested mountain was believed to block the dampish winds emanating out of the west, and had long been a place of healthful resort when the Medici acquired there the Villa of Castello (fig. 2.1). The villa's main garden occupied a position to the north of the palace, which served as a shield against the 'south winds [which] are always harmful'.[7] Because of Castello's location 'in the most agreeable and temperate air under these our [Florentine] skies',[8] Duke Cosimo I de' Medici frequented his villa regularly at times of illness, presumably because contemporary medical opinion recommended country air to hasten the recovery process: 'The duke my lord ate this morning with a good appetite and says that the air here [at Castello] has been quite restorative, and he is much reassured.'[9] Beneficial fragrances were given off by typically suggested plantings of cedars, cypresses, orange, lemon and olive trees. The cedar, lemon and orange trees were set into raised planting beds along the side walls of the main garden, where the fragile growth of the citrus could be protected from harmful winds and strollers could breathe in their fragrances enhanced by the warmth of the sunlight playing off the light-coloured walls. The raised beds probably facilitated the care and constant watering of the citrus trees, which do not have very extensive root systems. Agricultural theorists also advised the planting of flowers in these beds.

By way of contrast, the centre of the main garden at Castello was occupied by a circular stand of cypress trees interlaced with laurel and myrtle, surrounded by an outer ring of boxwood hedge and rose bushes. To the shade and fragrant effluvia of these plantings was added the coolness of falling water created by a central fountain designed to augment the exposure of water surface to air by the superposition of the increasingly large round basins downward along the supporting spindle. The garden may, therefore, be read in terms of a peripheral/central polarity founded in the opposition between open-sunny-warm and enclosed-shady-cool, a syntax connected to specific patterns of usage, that is, physical exercise/sedentary amusement.

[4] The late fifteenth-century 'Chain Map' of Florence (see G. C. Argan, *The Renaissance City* (New York, 1969), fig. 38) depicts the 'Sardigna'.

[5] G. Saminiati, *Dell'edificar delle case e palazzi in villa, e dell'ordinar dei giardini e orti*, text in Isa Bella Barsali, *La villa a Lucca* (Rome, 1964), pp. 233-4 and 239. Cf. L. B. Alberti, *Della famiglia* (Turin, 1969), p. 240, and Tommaso del Garbo, *Consiglio contro la pistolenza (1348)* (Bologna, 1866), pp. 13 and 20.

[6] Petrus Crescentius, *Trattato della agricoltura* (Venice, 1511), p. 8, and Alberti, *Della famiglia*, p. 240. See also Folgore da San Gimignano, *Sonetti* (Milan, 1965), p. 53.   [7] Saminiati, *Dell'edificar della case*, p. 239.

[8] Niccolo Martelli, *Dal primo e dal secondo libro delle lettere* (Lanciano, 1916), p. 21.

[9] Archivio di Stato di Firenze, Mediceo del Principato (henceforth ASF, MDP), 1171, insert 1, p. 88: 'Il Duca mio Signore ha mangiato questa mattina con buon gusto, et dice haver preso gran recreatione di questo aere, et molto si conforta.'

Moderate physical exercise went hand in hand with clean air as a hygienic necessity. Alberti, for example, warns against the ill effects of indolence: 'Through inactivity the veins fill up with phlegm, becoming water-logged and flaccid, and the stomach becomes finicky, the nerves dull and the whole body sluggish and drowsy; and furthermore with undue laziness the mind gets clouded and dim, and every spiritual force becomes stagnant and feeble.'[10] Exercise prior to eating was a fundamental stimulus of digestion: 'Let not the sun go down behind the hill, without having gone out ... take before meals a little exercise to tire you, without causing you to sweat ... For your food has no help from nature, and even as embers die out if they are not stirred, so the food in your stomach is frozen, for lack of exercise of your person,' advised one doctor.[11]

Since the time of Hippocrates walking had been especially preferred for its physical effects, and the recommended site needed to have an incline, to be exposed to open air and sunshine rather than under the cover of shade, and better a straight than a winding path.[12] In accordance with these medical guidelines, the main garden at Castello slopes upward to the north, and is criss-crossed by an intersecting series of straight walkways. The physical challenge to anyone who ascends its approximately 100 metre length is quite sufficient (at least in my case) to stimulate the circulation and open pores to release insalubrious excess humours. Duke Cosimo I, during recurring bouts with fever, diarrhoea and blood in the stool, regularly took his constitutional stroll in the garden before the noon-day meal: 'His Excellency was about in the garden this morning and then ate with wondrous appetite and yesterday evening he could not get enough to eat and as we got up from supper said I'm still hungry.'[13] As laid out in the sixteenth century, each of these paths offered a perspectival vista through regularly spaced olive trees – regularly spaced to offer equal exposure to sun and air in the interests of identical development of foliage and fruit – toward a sculptural climax, a point of visual interest as the goal of pedestrian traffic. However, the evergreen bower (laberinto) in the centre interrupted these pathways to become an independent focal point. Functioning as a stopping place, it was furnished with stone seating around the fountain where the family might enjoy sedentary pleasures over longish stretches of time. Ducal correspondence reveals that it was used in the afternoons, that is, following the mid-day meal, during the hottest part of the day: 'The duke has felt well all day today [2 Nov. 1544], and this afternoon was in the garden for more than an hour'[14] with his two children Francesco and

[10] Alberti, *Della famiglia*, p. 58.

[11] Francesco Datini's physician quoted in English by Iris Origo, *The Merchant of Prato* (Harmondsworth, 1963), p. 309.

[12] Celsus, *De medicina*, I, 2. A sloping garden site was also important for drainage; see Varro, *De re rustica*, I, vi, 6.

[13] ASF, MDP, 1170, ins. 6, p. 322: 'Sua Excellenza è stata stamani nel giardino e poi desinato con una fame mirabile e hiersera, non si posseva satiarsi e quando si levò da cena disse ancora ho fame.' Cf. ibid., ins. 3, p. 135.

[14] ASF, MDP, 1171, ins. 3, p. 147: 'Il Duca tutto di hoggi e stato bene, e questa sera è stato nel giardino più d'un hora, dove il Nano havendo teso i panioni a quelli bossi del laberinto di fuora, et havendo messo li appresso la sua civetta ha preso sei o otto uccellini con piacer' di Sua Excellenza, ma molto maggior delli Signori Don Francesco et Dona Maria.'

Fig. 2.1 (above) Giusto Utens. *The villa of Castello*, 1599. (right) Schematic indication of structural features (D. R. E. Wright)

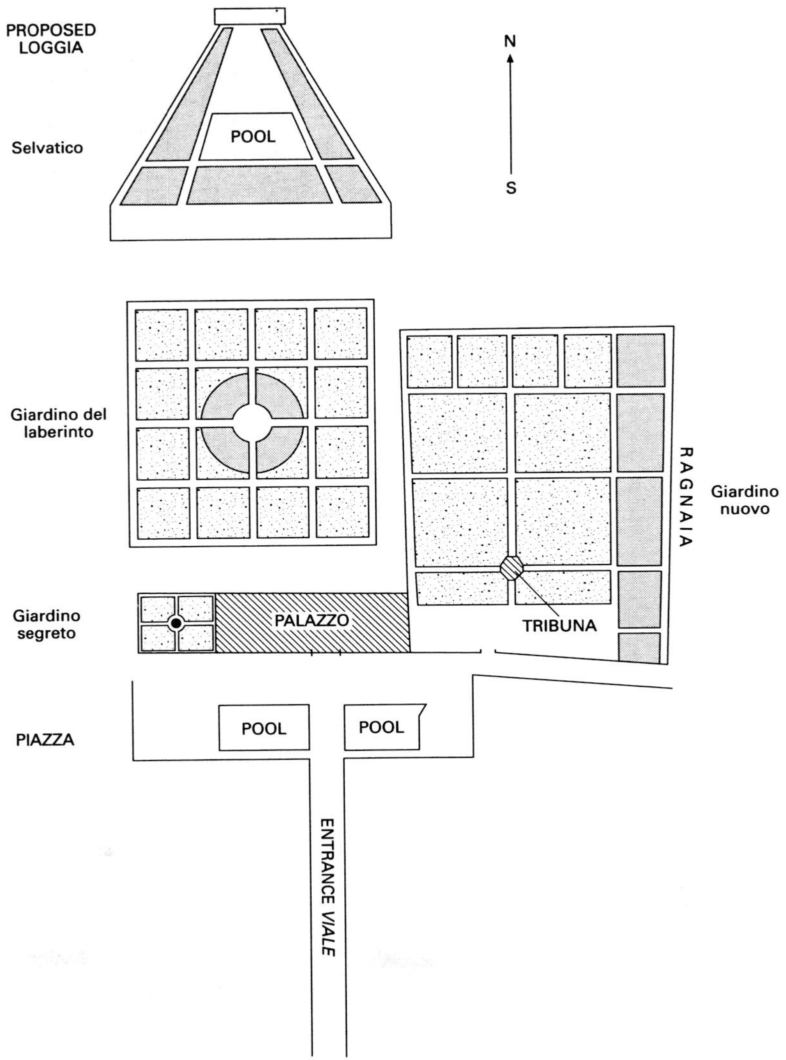

Diagram labels:

N ← S

PROPOSED LOGGIA

Selvatico

POOL

Giardino del laberinto

Giardino nuovo

RAGNAIA

TRIBUNA

PALAZZO

Giardino segreto

POOL

POOL

ENTRANCE *VIALE*

PIAZZA

Maria watching the court dwarf fowl for songbirds in the boxwood hedge surrounding the circular *laberinto*.

Doctors and laymen alike knew the salubrious nature of pleasurable diversion owing to the close interconnection between mental state and physical health, a basic principle which had been forgotten until recently in modern medical science: 'touching accidents or motions of the minde, I will only say that mirth is a great preserver of health, and sadnesse a very plague thereunto. The bodie followes the temper of the mind, as the temper of the mind followes that of the body.'[15] Even as late as 1871, the restorative value of a cheerful disposition could become the main theme of an American physician in a publication entitled *Fun Better than Physic or, Everybody's Life-preserver.*[16] Both strong passions and intense rational thought were believed to distemper the four humours, leading to a variety of illnesses. Several modes of symptomatic therapy might bring them back into harmonious balance, including soothing sounds operative directly on the emotions (music, falling water, birdsong), as well as pleasant amusements acting on the imagination (light conversation, storytelling, social games, laughter-provoking sports) to set the animal spirits in agreeable motion. The Castello *laberinto* thus offered the sound of falling water, berry-producing evergreens that attracted small songbirds, and the fun of fowling with a decoy.

Thus, the main garden at Castello is patterned according to an opposition between an enclosed shelter for mental recreation at the centre and exposed pathways for physical exercise around the periphery, a syntax repeated throughout garden history and having a long association with royalty. The shelter might take the form of a sacred tree in the ancient Near East (e.g. the Garden of Eden); a vine-covered kiosk, as in some Persian gardens; a rustic pavilion as at Henry I's garden at Woodstock; a vine-laden pergola as in Petrus Crescentius' 'royal garden'; or a hill with a wooded labyrinth and fountain as in Antonfrancesco Doni's account of *Villa civile, da Re, da Duce, et da potente signore.*[17] It is difficult to say whether the ancient Near Eastern symbolism of the centre of the garden, the *axis mundi* (consisting of a little hill with water emerging at its peak to divide into four channels moving toward the points of the compass as emblem of kingly dominion and symbolising the major rivers of the world) remained familiar over the centuries. If it did, perhaps from ideas about the Garden of Eden at the exact centre of the Earth, it would explain the choice of a Venus-Florence fountain figure for the centrepiece of the main garden at Castello, proclaiming from its elevated station the supremacy of Medici-ruled Florence over the rest of Tuscany.[18]

The so-called *Giardino segreto* adjoining the west side of the palace at Castello must be distinguished from the main garden described above, despite an obvious visual similarity

---

[15] Fynes Moryson, *Itinerary*, III (Glasgow and New York, 1908), p. 394.

[16] W. W. Hall, *Fun Better than Physic* (Springfield, Mass. and Philadelphia), 1871.

[17] On Woodstock see W.H. Matthews, *Mazes and Labyrinths* (London, 1922), p. 165. See also Petrus Crescentius, *Opus*, p. 380, and Antonfrancesco Doni, *Le ville* (1566) (Modena, 1969), p. 34.

[18] On the *axis mundi* see Mircea Eliade, *The Sacred and the Profane* (New York, 1959), pp. 33, 35–47, 52–4. See also James Ackerman, *The Architecture of Michelangelo* (New York, 1961), vol. I, pp. 71–4.

in design (the quartered square). The term *segreto* indicates a private space for the patron, distinct from the public main garden with its elaborate programme of political iconography. Because the Giardino segreto, more properly called an *orto* in accordance with Italian usage in agricultural writings, was planted with medicinal and culinary herbs and flowers requiring specially treated, fine topsoil, it had to be located in the level plain (*la pianura*) to keep heavy rains from washing away the soil.[19] And since total exposure to light and air was essential to plant growth, trees were eliminated altogether, or else confined to the edges to give shade to seated or strolling observers. Shade could also be provided in the form of circumambient *loggie*. Water, employed here solely for agricultural purposes – herbs had to be watered by hand from buckets twice a day in the hot season – came from standing sources such as cisterns, wells, or, as at Castello, an ornamental stone *vasca*, rather than overflowing fountains. *Orti* were intended for quiet personal diversion such as reading, playing a musical instrument, or intimate conversation rather than for any kind of bodily exercise. Consequently, its olfactory delights apart, it would have been experienced in a visual manner, for the 'refreshment' of the eye. Two medical issues seem to be involved here, one the optical benefit of seeing green plants, the other nerve stimulation accruing from visual variety (in the diversity of flowers and planting bed designs).[20] Vitruvius reported that green plants tend to thin the air, helping to improve vision by the evaporation (?) of thick humour from the eyes. The colour green was also said, according to the English traveller Fynes Moryson, to comfort the eyes, perhaps in the sense of being restful. Secondly, the stimuli related to visual variety constituted a mild form of exercise resulting from the activation of the optic nerve and a consequent exhilaration of the animal spirits within the nerve sheath. For these reasons Petrus Crescentius insists that in the *hortus* 'there should be a large variety of medicinal and aromatic herbs, since they not only delight the olfactory sense with their smells, but also the flowers in their diversity refresh the sight, among which rue is to be mixed in in several places for the beauty of greenness ...'[21] As a result of its space limitations, the *orto* had to be viewed from within at points along its four walls, in contrast with the considerably larger and taller *giardino*, visible 'in perspective' only from the elevated distance point of a palace window: 'let the garden be placed on the North side near the patron's residence, so that it can be enjoyed easily from the windows in the perspective manner ...'[22] In Renaissance treatises this visual enjoyment of *giardini* is always treated as a secondary consequence of the ordered patterns resulting from agricultural necessity and considerations of use.

[19] Gian Vettorio Soderini, *Il trattato della cultura degli orti e giardini* (Bologna, 1903), pp. 8 and 11. Compare Agostino Gallo, *Le tredici giornate della vera agricoltura e de' piaceri della villa* (Venice, 1566), p. 142.

[20] Gallo, *Le tredici giornate*, p. 143. For a contemporary assessment of the need for visual refreshment in Renaissance gardens see the letter of Lorenzo Valla quoted in D. R. Coffin, *Gardens and Gardening in Papal Rome* (Princeton, 1991), p. 6.

[21] Crescentius, *Opus*, p. 378. See also Vitruvius, *De architectura*, v, ix, 5. Moryson, *Itinerary*, p. 391. Compare Hippocrates, *Regimen*, II, lxi (Loeb edition, vol. IV, p. 349).

[22] Gallo, *Le tredici giornate*, p. 142. Cf. Crescentius, *Opus*, p. 379: 'et ipsius fenestrae ad viridarii temperatum habebunt aspectum, non fervore solis infectum.'

The medical requirement of visual stimulation was also to be satisfied at Castello from a loggia planned at the highest, northernmost point of the garden enclosure, the top of the wooded Selvatico, 'which . . . overlooked in the middle of the palace, the gardens, the fountains, and all the plain below and around [the villa] . . . and all the surroundings for many miles'.[23] The variety associated with far-reaching vistas made the 'borrowed landscape' or 'scenic refreshment' a fundamental therapeutic feature in the planning of villas, baths and health spas from ancient Rome through the nineteenth century. The aforesaid loggia, apparently left unbuilt by Cosimo I de' Medici,[24] would have doubled as an observation point for the small game hunts staged in the Selvatico adjacent to the north end of the main garden. One of the several wooded hunting/fowling enclosures clustered around the Giardino del laberinto, its siting was determined by the necessity of separating the evergreen plantations, with their deep, extended root systems, from interfering with the more fragile domestic trees found in *giardini*; by the fact that the forest trees (*selvatichi*) need no special care or watering; and by the need to screen the main garden from harmful winds. Agricultural writers advised the placement of *selvatichi* along the axis of the palace to facilitate the viewing of game animals from an indoor vantage point.[25] The limited modes of hunting cultivated in these middling garden groves (derived from the ancient Roman *leporarium*) possessed only entertainment value since they were treated as spectator sports, to be enjoyed by patron and guests from the protective cover of a pavilion or loggia. The prey, predominantly water birds and small game (hares, rabbits, deer, ducks, heron) were selected for their physically unthreatening nature, and, moreover, were not hunted by the patron and guests, but by paid professionals with their hounds, which performed the actual kill (*piccola caccia forzata*). Its function as a form of theatrical entertainment following an outdoor banquet in a garden enclosure is noted by ancient, medieval and Renaissance authors such as Varro, Giovanni da Prato and Antonfrancesco Doni; and other sources confirm that this tradition was observed in Florence.[26] The therapeutic value of this sporting display had advocates in Boccaccio, the physician Tommaso del Garbo, and the villa writer Giuseppe Falcone, who gleefully described what fun it was to watch a poor frightened rabbit desperately trying to dodge pursuing hounds, and its violent bloody extinction in canine jaws.[27] Accommodation for these events consisted of a covered shelter for the pre-hunt banquet, perched on an elevated site for the viewing of the post-prandial hunt display. Thus, one

---

[23] Vasari-Milanesi, VI, p. 76.

[24] 'Ora [15 Oct. 1559] soli ci basta servir il salvatico, ne volgliamo per ora far loggia o altro,' rescript of Cosimo I de' Medici published in Giorgio Vasari, *Literarischer Nachlass*, vol. I, ed. K. Frey (Munich, 1923), p. 521.

[25] Columella, *De re rustica*, IX, praef.; Crescentius, *Opus*, pp. 379–80.

[26] Varro, *De re rustica*, III, xiii, 3; Giovanni da Prato, *Il Paradiso degli Alberti* (Bologna, 1867), vol. III, p. 15; Doni, *Le ville*, p. 42. See also F. C. Giacometti, *Storia della caccia* (Milan, 1964), p. 156; and Florence, Uffizi, *Feste e apparati Medicei da Cosimo I e Cosimo II* (Florence, 1969), pp. 96–101.

[27] G. Falcone, *La nuova, vaga et dilettevole villa* (Brescia, 1602), p. 222 (chapter entitled 'Caccia de' lepri: Elevatione de' spiriti, e scacciamento dell' otio dannoso'). Boccaccio, *Decamerone*, proemio: 'se alcuna malinconia o gravezza di pensieri gli afflige, hanno molti modi da alleggiare o da passar quello; per ciò che a loro, volendo essi, non manca . . . uccellare, cacciare, pescare.' Tommaso del Garbo, *Consiglio*, p. 40.

would have to interpret the open meadow depicted in the Utens lunette of Castello within the Selvatico adjoining the spot where the dining loggia was to have been constructed as a stage for the allegorical performances which sometimes preceded the actual hunt, as well as for the concluding massacre by the hounds. Evergreen trees normally planted in garden wildernesses (firs, cypresses, oaks, and holm oaks at Castello) not only produced fruit essential for the nourishment of birds and small game, but also created a leafy canopy to help conceal the animals from hovering birds of prey. By night, these trees might serve as a fowling grove *per andare a frugnuolo*, a specialised lantern employed to blind nesting blackbirds, thrush, wood pigeons, etc. for the prowling trapper.[28]

An analogous syntax (stationary observers/performance space for hunters) obtained in the Giardino nuovo at Castello, located to the east of the main garden and occupying a similar amount of land surface. Two-thirds of the space was taken up by square planting beds, and the eastern third by a lengthy strip of evergreens running north and south. The latter contained two distinct types of fowling grove, a *frasconaia* at the north end and a *ragnaia* to the south, and the whole was planted with laurels and tine trees, the berries of which attract songbirds. A *frasconaia* normally consisted of a circular or square clearing from which all vegetation had been removed. To one side would stand a blind covered with ivy or something similar, and the enclosing trees might be tines, and myrtle with the addition of boxwood and rosemary. At the centre of the cleared ground the fowler would place two nets stretched over rectangular frames leaning together in the form of a pup tent and concealed by branches (*frasche*). Decoy birds tied to the *frasche* lured finches under the nets, which could be collapsed over them by means of a cord controlled by the fowler. This activity would have to be observed from close up, apparently from stone seats under the trees at the edge of the clearing. A *ragnaia*, often conjoined with a *frasconaia*, was an evergreen grove parted by a wide central *viale* enshrouded by a series of fine nets hung from a framework of poles and preceded by an entrance tunnel formed by interlacing top-branches, and was intended for the capture of garden warblers. Part of the fun of warbler netting was watching their flight as they swooped downward and into the tunnel to land in the nets. For which reason, G. V. Soderini urged, 'to either side it is a good idea to have some shelters of greenery, with foliage-covered seats round about, for viewing the casting [of the nets]'.[29] This would seem to be the purpose of the wooden garden pavilion (*tribuna*) set, in the Giardino nuovo at Castello, on a line of sight along the east-west axis of the *ragnaia*. The planting beds amid which the pavilion sits would probably have contained the usual fruit trees, figs, grapevines, etc. recommended for enticing songbirds into gardens.

---

[28] Gian Vettorio Soderini, *Trattato degli arbori* (Bologna, 1904), p. 288.

[29] Ibid., pp. 303ff and 288ff. On the stone seating see Agnolo Firenzuola, 'I ragionamenti', in *Prose scelte* (Florence, 1895), p. 73: 'trees, making a wreath around the lawn . . . certain stones, which . . . had been placed at the foot of those trees to form seats'.

Yet another sort of 'theatrical space', one that more closely resembled an empty stage because used for courtly performances not involving the rustic habitats of animals of prey, was the piazza, or *prato*, before the principal entrance to the palace of the villa. As at Castello, the piazza would have a rectangular shape, and be entered from a formal, tree-lined *viale* leading in from the main gate to the villa complex. Although possibly a modified version of the *aia* or wheat-threshing floor found in front of Tuscan farm houses, in terms of function its primary antecedent was the jousting meadow typically sited before medieval castles in such a way that noblewomen could observe the festivities from the safety of windows or balconies. In Renaissance writings, the piazza was treated as a royal or aristocratic appurtenance:

> In our Country House (for a Gentleman) . . . let us imitate the Prince's Palace. Before the Door let there be a large open Space (big enough to receive the train of an ambassador, or any other great man, whether they come in Coaches, in Barks, or on horseback), and for the Exercizes either of Chariot or Horse racing . . .[30]

Antonfrancesco Doni imagines a royal villa with a loggia overlooking the piazza from the palace, where guests could watch festivals and games such as horse races, tilting matches, soccer games, or wrestling displays (*lotta*) by the local farmboys.[31] The famous Utens lunette of Castello depicts a tilting match unfolding on the piazza, while a manuscript collection of projected (but never executed) sketches of Florentine *vedute* bears this indication for the drawing of Castello: 'Upon the piazza or lawn before the Palace is to be depicted a peasant dance, and also Gentlefolk there to watch, all in the clothing usually worn in the country.'[32] Activities such as solemn entry processions, jousts, dances, and displays of athletic prowess had a largely ceremonial value associated with princely status, and were demanded by courtly etiquette as well as Florentine social custom.[33] The Florentines had a long-standing tradition of entertaining both fellow citizens and visiting dignitaries during the *villegiature* seasons, and during the state visits by *personaggi* invited by the commune. During the republican era, the Florentine Signoria assumed the diplomatic and financial responsibilities of state-sponsored entertainment, a duty which Duke Cosimo I de' Medici inherited along with the reins of government. He exercised it with punctilio especially with regard to envoys of the Emperor Charles V, whose favour was essential to the stability of his regime. The duke constantly kept in mind the political repercussions of his treatment of these envoys when he entertained them at his villas.[34]

---

[30] L. B. Alberti, *On the Art of Building in Ten Books* (London, 1965), pp. 104 and 185. See also, for example, Wolfram von Eschenbach, *Parzival* (New York, 1961), pp. 89 and 95, 124–5, 284 and 287–8.

[31] Doni, *Le ville* pp. 32 and 42.

[32] Florence, Biblioteca Nazionale Centrale (henceforth BNC), Fondo Palatino, Ms. 1181, 'Progetto e schizzi per una raccolta di vedute della città di Firenze,' pp. 100ᵛ–101: 'Sopra la piazza, o prato avanti il Palazzo retragginsi un ballo de' contadini e contadine, et che di Gentil huomini e Gentildonne chi son' a vedere, tutti nell' habiti che soglino portarsi in villa.'

[33] Scipione Ammirato, 'Della hospitalità,' in *Opuscoli* (Florence, 1583), p. 51.

[34] On the use of Castello by the Medici to entertain agents of the emperor see D. R. E. Wright, 'The Medici villa at Olmo a Castello', Ph.D. thesis, Princeton, 1976, p. 57.

The formal piazza at Castello is organised on two cross axes with respect to the honorific viewing point from the balcony over the main portal of the palace. The dominant line of sight extends straight out along the entrance *viale*, allowing a head-on view of courtly processions coming into the villa. The east–west cross axis parallel with the palace façade offers a side view of tilting lists and horse races, for reasons of both visibility and safety for spectators. It is precisely this structure (with one modification) which formed the organising principle of the garden theatre laid out under Cosimo I in the Boboli Garden behind his secondary residence in Florence, the Palazzo Pitti.

The Pitti Palace, purchased by the Medici in 1549 as a semi-official residence, was an urban retreat from the cramped living quarters of the seat of government in the Palazzo Vecchio. Whereas the ceremonial space for the latter, the stone-paved Piazza della Signoria, was accessible to the general public, the *teatro* at the Pitti stood apart from urban thoroughfares within an extensive walled garden enclosure behind the palace (figs. 6.2 and 6.3). Evidence indicates that only members of the ducal court, their guests, and the cream of Florentine society ever gained entry to staged festivities. Serving mainly for ceremonial displays of equitation, the Boboli theatre was designed as a level rectangular lawn bordered by evergreens, entered at its far end from a long *viale* descending the hillside along a line of sight from the windows at the rear of the palace. The inspiration for the creation of this new kind of performance space must have been the similar shift in papal Roman from the theatrical arena of the Piazza San Pietro to the more protected and aesthetically pleasing venue of Bramante's Belvedere Court. At the Boboli, however, for Bramante's elaborate multi-storied architectural enclosure were substituted rows of trees, planted in the form of an ancient hippodrome on the slopes surrounding the grassy meadow.[35] The Medici's sylvan version of a garden circus might have been modelled after Virgil's description of the site of Aeneas' funeral games for Anchises ('a grassy field, bordered with curving hills covered with trees, where in the middle of the valley was a *teatri circus*'),[36] which included an equestrian event known as the *Ludas Troiae*; others have mentioned Pliny the Younger's hippodrome garden at his Tuscan villa as a possible precedent. But it is always important, in the study of Italian landscape environments, to pay attention to the purely practical motives, such as those suggested by Vitruvius:

> [In the theatre] citizens with their wives and children remain seated in their enjoyment; their bodies motionless with pleasure have the pores opened. On these the breath of the wind falls, and if it comes from marshy districts or other infected quarters, it will pour harmful spirits into the system. If, therefore, special care is taken in choosing a site, infection will be avoided.[37]

It makes as much sense to attribute the preference for an evergreen enclosure around the Boboli theatre to health considerations of air quality as to a revivalist aesthetic.

---

[35] D. R. E. Wright, 'The Boboli Garden in the evolution of European garden design . . . ,' in *Boboli '90: Atti del Convegno Internazionale* (Florence, 1991), vol. I, p. 315.

[36] Virgil, *Aeneid*, v, pp. 287–9.

[37] Vitruvius, *De architectura*, v, iv, 1, trans. by F. Granger (Cambridge, Mass. and London, 1965), vol. I, p. 178.

Fig. 2.2 Stephano della Bella. Engraving of the Boboli amphitheatre during the marriage
festivities of 1637

In Italian travel literature, the Boboli theatre came to be celebrated for its aristocratic
displays of *opere cavalleresche* (fig. 2.2).[38] It is well known that Cosimo I de' Medici took a
great interest in fine horses and horsemanship. Furthermore, his wife, Eleonora da
Toledo, came from a region of Spain (Castile) noted for its superb riding horses, and for
knightly exercises on horseback. During her father's tenure as viceroy of Naples, a
Neapolitan nobleman named Federico Grisone opened the first modern riding
academy, where young nobles went to acquire equestrian skills. The school rapidly
gained an international reputation.[39] Grisone explains in his *Ordini de Cavalcare* (1550)
that the best method of teaching a horse to stop and advance, to turn, and especially to
perform jumping movements was to lead him to a hill, preferably having some kind of
enclosed passageway, and make him advance two paces and stop repeatedly, 'all the
length of the hill downwards'.[40] This, then, is one possible function for the main *viale*
descending the hillside into the Boboli theatre – it would also explain the need for two
fountains, one at the very top of the *viale* and a second at the bottom in the centre of the

[38] Galeazzo Gualdo Priorato, *Relatione della città di Fiorenza, e del Gran Ducato di Toscana* (Cologne, 1668), pp. 7–8.

[39] Hans Handler, *The Spanish Riding School: Four Centuries of Classic Horsemanship* (New York, St Louis, San Francisco, Mexico and Toronto, 1972), p. 58.

[40] Grisone, trans. by Thomas Blundeville as *The Arte of Ryding and Breakynge Greate Horses* (London, 1560), chap. 2, unpaginated.

rectangular meadow. Its alignment on the line of sight from the rear of the Pitti Palace would have permitted the ducal family to observe, from indoors, their horse trainers at work. Secondly, this descending passageway could have accommodated the kind of formal entry procession which normally opened ceremonial pageants or equestrian ballets. The horsemen might have ridden up the hill along the paths through the evergreens and converged toward the central axis at several points in the ascent. The entering riders would thus have been facing the assembled dignitaries, who sat on platforms just behind the palace, a fine point of etiquette in any type of honorific ceremonial, past or present. This advance in the direction of the principal spectators continued as the riders spread out into the theatre proper, a fact which explains the elongation of its rectangular shape along the sight-line extending from the rear façade of the palace toward the *viale*. In stately equestrian ballets, as distinct from the fast-moving jousts and horse races that are potentially dangerous to spectators in the path of contestants, some carousel formations where the performers line up in short rows to canter simultaneously toward the viewing stand demanded this extra length to accommodate both their forward progress and turns back around into the centre of the field. As depicted in contemporary illustrations, certain ballets centred around an allegorical float encircled by rings or detached files of prancing horsemen accompanying its advance in the direction of the grand ducal party. Other typical carousel figures involving rotary motion about a fixed centre (spokes of a wheel, concentric circles, four-leaf clover, etc.) could, by contrast, be accomplished within the confines of a square.[41] Thus, it was the etiquette of formal ceremony which dictated the spatial organisation of the Boboli *teatro*, as was the case for the entrance-way and piazza before the Medici villa at Castello.

From the instrumental perspective adopted in this chapter an exclusively stylistic comparison between the landscaping at Castello and the Boboli would be otiose. Castello was, for its part, a typical Italian, private working farm where certain plots in the vicinity of the house were adapted for the use of the owner in accordance with medical theories as to the proper means of preserving and restoring health, since rural habitation had long been deemed superior to urban existence at least with regard to mental and physical well-being. As such, the Castello estate, its plantings, its various functional elements and their spatial organisation on the land cannot be interpreted as in any way exemplary of the Renaissance approach to gardening. This kind of villa, form and function, had a long tradition that can be traced in agricultural writings from ancient Rome, the middle ages, through the sixteenth century and beyond. The conventional health guidelines include, first and foremost, purified air, then moderate physical exercise, visual stimulation resulting from variety, and several types of mood-altering sedentary amusements such as spectator hunting-sports. Whenever visual aesthetics based on geometric regularity came up in discussion – normally only as a passing

---

[41] An engraving of equestrian formations performed at the Boboli is illustrated in *Boboli '90*, fig. 138. See also Georgina Masson, *Italian Gardens* (London, 1966), p. 87; and F. Gurrieri and J. Chatfield, *Boboli Gardens* (Florence, 1972), fig. 7.

reference – they were treated as an ancillary consequence of fundamental agricultural or other commonsense considerations. Varro, for instance, noted in an aside that formal arrangements of plantings which created a beautiful appearance ('quae specie fiant venustiora') maximised agricultural productivity, and thus profitability, but with the added benefit of making the land more saleable, because buyers tended to prefer plots that were attractive rather than unsightly.[42] And, from the viewpoint of the sixteenth-century Medici patron with a mother in failing health, an often pregnant wife who suffered terribly from morning sickness, dynastically important offspring to raise in a salubrious environment, and his own problems with recurring bouts of fever and bowel disorders, one would not spend vast sums on a country estate just to appreciate nature for its own sake, or, in its artificially reorganised form, to take pleasure in culturally refined aesthetic experiences. In effect, the visual refinements at Castello (as a 'villa da mostra') had to do with the social and political need to impress tourists, passers-by, and visiting dignitaries with symbols of princely status – this preferably when the family and court were not in residence. Nature and culture could, and occasionally did, collide, as instanced by the turmoil that arose when Duchess Eleonora learned that the entire farm profits from Castello were being consumed by the showy but expensive revamping of the gardens undertaken by the sculptor Niccolo Tribolo.[43] With the passing of time Castello functioned mainly as a health spa for Medici youngsters, and as a tourist attraction on the Florentine itinerary. The Boboli Garden, on the other hand, is a more representative Renaissance type, reflecting the sixteenth-century transformation of knightly combat into less dangerous theatrical spectacles, including the noble art of manège in equestrian ballets, and the displacement of the events from the public venue of urban *piazze* to the socially more exclusive confines of a princely residential complex, such as the Belvedere Court in Rome. For, as Baldassare Castiglione cautioned, a courtier engaging in knightly exercises on horseback 'must carefully consider in whose presence he is seen and of what sort the company is, for it would not be seemly for a gentleman to honour a rustic festival with his presence, where the spectators and the company are of low degree.'[44] To this elitist motive for the creation of the Boboli theatre, we might add that of the personal safety of the ducal family, who in the public *piazze* (and in the distant countryside) were more difficult to protect from potential assassins. In fact, Bramante's garden court provided another safety precedent for the Medici duke in the form of raised corridors leading from the Vatican Palace to the Villa Belvedere, which must have inspired the erection of Vasari's Corridore from the Palazzo Vecchio to the Pitti. Renaissance etiquette aside, the general form of the tree-lined Boboli amphitheatre is more obviously traceable to classical inspiration, both textual (Virgil, Pliny the Younger) and archaeological (the remains of Nero's garden

---

[42] Varro, *De re rustica*, I, iv, 2 and vii, 1–3.

[43] Wright, 'The Medici villa', pp. 34–5. The payments for the Castello garden did not come exclusively from the farm accounts. Cosimo I seems to have been a genius at the creative financing of his building projects.

[44] Baldassare Castiglione, *The Courtier*, trans. by L. E. Opdycke (New York, 1929), p. 83.

circuses near the Vatican). However, visual aesthetics can have played only a minimal role in the planning of the Boboli, since without the equestrian actors it left the impression of a mere empty stage with bland evergreen sets. Indeed, as both Margherita Azzi Visentini and Charles Avery have pointed out, the Boboli Garden made hardly any impression at all on sixteenth- and early seventeenth-century tourists: 'a big garden' or 'a great and brave garden.'[45] This type of outdoor space acquired visual interest only with the addition of elaborate parterres in the French manner, as at the Jardin du Luxembourg in Paris or the Villa Garzoni at Collodi.

The Medici villa at Pratolino belongs neither to a timeless Mediterranean tradition like Castello, nor to a specifically Renaissance phenomenon like the Boboli. As an enclosed hunting park, its particular form and function relate to medieval customs which had died out by the seventeenth century. Large wild game hunting on horseback had its origins in the ancient Near East, and throughout its history had been viewed as a kind of peace-time practice for war. Early on it assumed two distinct aspects, one as a healthful physical sport on unenclosed land, and another as a much tamer princely diversion within the sanctuary of a walled precinct. This dichotomy will be important for the purposes of interpreting Renaissance parks such as Pratolino.

Xenophon's biography of Cyrus of Persia expresses this as an antithesis between the physical challenges that were hazarded by hardy warriors in confrontation with perilous terrain and savage beasts (lions, leopards, boars), and the relative security of gentler animals (deer, gazelles, wild sheep, wild asses) chased inside the controlled confines of a man-made environment. Approaching manhood, Cyrus became impatient with the second of these:

> To me at least, it seems just like hunting animals that were tied up. For, in the first place, they were in a small space; besides they were very lean and mangy; and one of them was lame and another maimed. But the animals out on the mountain and the plain – how fine they looked, and large and sleek! And the deer leaped up skyward as if on wings and the boars came charging at one, as they say brave men do in battle.[46]

Over this polarity Roman property law regarding wild animals laid a juridical distinction. In the codes of Gaius and Justinian, wild creatures, because not previously owned by anyone, became the property of the person who captured them, even on someone else's land, and remained so as long as they were in that individual's keeping. If the animal escaped, or merely wandered away from its regular feeding site, the first capture rule still prevailed. However, land owners were entitled to prevent others from hunting or fowling on their estates if they could catch the perpetrator at it and warn him off.[47] So, when the Romans under Hellenistic influence began stocking and breeding game animals in rural farms, due to the demand for exotic foods at lavish banquets, the park evolved into just one more showy

[45] *Boboli '90*, pp. 131–54.

[46] Xenophon, *Cyropaedia*, trans. by W. Miller (London and New York, 1925), vol. I, pp. 39, 49–51 and 55.

[47] Gaius, *Institutes*, II, 66–8; Justinian, *Institutes*, II, tit. i, 12–16.

appurtenance amid the tasteless luxury of pretentious villa complexes. The indolent owner could hire professional hunters and fowlers 'so that the sight of [game] being hunted within an enclosure might delight [his] eyes'.[48] In the discourse of moralists such as Seneca, an effete lifestyle became the subject of a nature/culture contrast aimed at condemning the Romans for abandoning their manly martial past for an effeminate present, in which animals and humans were slain 'not in anger or through fear, but just to make a show'.[49] In some instances, the game were turned into something resembling trained pets which could be summoned at the sound of a horn for the amusement of the *al fresco* diners.[50]

During the Carolingian era the Roman code was overridden by feudal lords, once more dedicated to serious hunting pursuits, through the creation of the royal forest preserve. The 'forest', merely a legal fiction for a specific territory over which the ruler retained exclusive hunting rights relative to certain types of prey, could embrace not only woods, but farms and rural villages, in addition to private estates. All things being equal, the peasantry might be able to pasture pigs in wooded areas of the reserve or gather firewood and brush, and could occasionally gain fowling privileges. Under optimal conditions, private estate owners had licence to fowl and to engage in the chase for less desirable prey within the boundaries of their property.[51] The royal 'forests', however, generated great animosity in local populations, a problem some-times resolved by the creation of walled-in parks to prevent foraging game animals and mounted hunters from destroying farm cultivations, and peasants and outlaws from poaching.[52] The upshot was an eventual polarisation between the hunt in open forest, which had perforce to be only a short expedition, through unfamiliar territory exposed to unforeseeable perils, and the greater ease of a park and lodge where the lord could vacation in comfort and safety for extended periods. In the wake of the arrival of Eastern luxuries in Europe, some park enclosures became the loci of experiments in the exotic, from the importation of leopards as hunting animals by the Visconti to the wondrous waterworks and amazing hydraulic toys of Hesdin. By the Renaissance, it seems possible to speak of a contrast between the hunt as a physical sport involving the direct participation of the nobility, and the hunt as a type of mental recreation staged by professionals for dignitaries who, for one reason or another, might wish to limit exertions to the most pleasurable and ceremonial aspects, such as the boisterous outdoor banquets, the exciting *coup de grace*, and the feudal rite of the division of the kill.

Sixteenth-century Medici hunting legislation offers a typically feudal motive for their erection of hunting parks in Tuscany:

[48] Columella, *De re rustica*, IX, praef., and i, 1.   [49] Seneca, *Epistulae morales*, XC, 45, and LI.

[50] Varro, *De re rustica*, III, xiii.

[51] B. H. Slicher van Bath, *Storia agraria dell' Europe occidentale (500-1850)* (Turin, 1972), pp. 100–2.

[52] M. Borsa, *La caccia nel Milanese* (Milan, n. d.), pp. 80–7, 207ff and 236. G. Duby, *L'economia rurale nell' Europa medievale* (Bari, 1970), vol. I, 245; D. M. Stenton, *English Society in the Middle Ages* (London, 1971), pp. 102 and 106–7.

especially in assuring that the farmlands and orchards of our subjects be free of the kind of damage which, as a result of the proximity of woods and brush, almost irreparably they suffer from stags, boar, fallow-deer, and such like animals; and that from the hunting reserve for these animals, permitted to the Prince for his pleasure and recreation, there ensue no damage in the properties adjacent thereunto, but that it be licit to capture and kill them there, their [Grand Ducal] Highnesses have . . . caused to be built the Royal Park with a walled precinct of more than 20 miles [circumference] with its cataracts, gates, houses, and other things requisite for keeping the said animals enclosed therein . . .[53]

These public notices may also have served a propaganda function, helping to divert public attention from potentially embarrassing fears of the court for the safety of the ducal family when hunting or fishing in undefended regions of Florentine territory:

Here it was rumoured yesterday evening that his Excellency and Madama were going to Pistoia this morning and this afternoon to Igno, to stay the night and tomorrow fish for trout. This did not please me, because staying for two nights and one day in the woods and in alien, even enemy territory did not for the most part seem particularly safe to me.[54]

These fears only worsened under the severe and reclusive Francesco de' Medici, who kept himself and his Venetian mistress Bianca Cappello under heavy guard. Furthermore, as Galluzzi points out, Francesco's construction of an enclosed park at Pratolino only aggravated problems with local farmers as a result of the demands of forced labor and the requisitioning of their farm animals, which diverted them from their normal cultivations.[55] The park of the villa at Pratolino stood within an extensive hunting reserve known as 'La Bandita di Pratolino, podesteria di Fiesole', the regulations regarding which Francesco and his father published on 22 September 1568, apparently just a few months prior to the first land purchases for the new estate. When the *banda* was renewed on 15 April 1581 the government exempted fowling for songbirds in privately owned blinds (*ragnaie, paretai, boschetti*), prohibiting only the taking of partridge and pheasant, which the grand dukes regularly reserved for their own sport, along with the hart, roe-buck, wild boar and hare.[56] Archival accounts and contemporary descriptions[57] indicate the game stocked at Pratolino included hart,

[53] ASF, Collezione Bandi e leggi: Caccia e pesca, I, n°. 33, p. 39: 'particolarmente in provedere che i Beni di di [*sic*] essi [sudditi] coltivati, e fruttiferi venghino liberi da quei danni, che per la vicinanza ai Boschi, e Macchie, quasi irreparabilmente, sentivano da Cervi, Porci, Daini, e altri simili animali, e che dalla riserva della Caccia di detti animali, permessa al Principe per suo gusto, e recreazione, non segua ne' beni ad essa adiacenti alcun danno, ma sia lecito pigliarveli e ammazzarveli, hanno le Altezze loro . . . fatta fabricare il Bar[c]o Reale con ricinto di muro di più di 20 miglia con sue cataratte, e cancelli, case, a altre cose necessarie a tenervi racchiusi detti animali . . .'

[54] ASF, MDP, 1170, ins. 1, p. 42: 'Qui si vociferava hiersera che Sua Eccellenza et Madama andavano stamani a Pistoia et stasera a Igno, per starvi stanotte et domani pescare alle truote. Il che a me non piaceva, perche lo stare due notti e un giorno ne' boschi e in paesi strani e di inimici per la maggior parte non mi pareva ben sicura.'

[55] R. Galluzzi, *Istoria del granducato di Toscana* (Capolago, 1841), vol. I, p. 170.

[56] ASF, Collezione Bandi e leggi: Caccia e pesca, I, n°. 18.

[57] Cesare Agolanti, *La descrizione di Pratolino*, Ms. in Florence, BNC, Fondo Magliabecchiano, Cl. VII, 8, pp. 44ᵛ–55 and 57. ASF, Guardaroba, 136, p. 327ᵛ.

roe-buck, boar, hare, partridge, rock-partridge and pheasant along with domestic farm animals such as rabbits, turtle-doves, ducks and geese. In addition, there were gazelle imported from Alexandria, and ostriches, bald coot, guinea fowl (*augelli d'India*) and 'il gentil Cecera'. The requisite constructions and other provisions for the shelter, raising and nourishment of game are described in treatises on agriculture.

First is the stone perimeter wall, considered preferable to wooden fences, which allowed hares to escape and vermin a way in. Pratolino is divided into an upper and a lower park (fig. 2.3) by an east–west wall, astride which sits the palace, on a raised platform, dominating the central north–south axis. The main entrance to the estate lay just to the west of the house and took arriving guests onto an extensive *prato* adjoining the north façade. The lower park, which is the object of the present discussion, could be entered directly from the *prato* via gates located on either side of the platform, and from the south side of the palace by means of stairways leading down from a grassy terrace into the main north–south *viale* descending through the woods. Another entrance to the lower park was available in the south-east corner adjacent to a house labelled on an eighteenth-century plan 'Casa per il Fontaniere'.

A second requirement was a supply of running water, either from an existing stream or created artificially by the construction of mortar-lined pools. Two serpentining cataracts, consisting of a series of irregularly shaped walled pools with sluice gates emptying the flow into successive basins, descended through the park close to the east and west walls. Besides walls and running water, game animals also needed trees that furnished regular nourishment, especially the several varieties of acorn-producing oak. Not surprisingly, Pratolino was planted with oaks, turkey-oaks, holm-oaks, beech trees and firs.[58] But 'at the season of the year when the wood did not provide food', says Columella, confined game, especially the smaller types like hares, had to be hand fed on grains and leafy green vegetables, strewn 'in small open spaces [*parvulis areolis*] made at different intervals apart'.[59] This seems a likely interpretation for the eight circular clearings depicted in the Utens painting of Pratolino in the north-west reaches of the lower park. Their vicinity to the palace would have allowed the court to observe the feeding, possibly while dining on the terrace overlooking the woods.

A major consideration in the interpretation of the structure of Pratolino's lower park is the particular form of the hunt it could accommodate. The most ancient, physically demanding and dangerous was the *caccia chiusa*, in which the game was pursued by spear-bearing horsemen into an open field previously cordoned off by long rope nets (substituted much later by canvas), where the cornered beasts were speared by men on foot, and mounted. Originating in Assyria and Persia, the *caccia chiusa* was depicted in Roman hunt mosaics, it was later introduced into medieval Europe by Charlemagne, and under the designation *caccia alla francese* became popular in Renaissance Rome. Its decline after the death of Pope Leo X occasioned the publication of Domenico

---

[58] Agolanti, *Pratolino*, p. 57. [59] Columella, *De re rustica*, IX, i, 8.

Boccamazza's *Le caccie di Roma* (1548).[60] The less strenuous, more ritualised *caccia forzata* (described above) was more of a spectator sport, often conducted in parks for patrons unwilling or unable to participate actively. A twelfth-century abbot of Bury St Edmunds is said to have 'enclosed many parks, which he replenished with beasts of chase, keeping a huntsman with dogs; and upon the visit of any person of quality, sat with his monks in some walk of the wood, and sometimes saw the coursing of the dogs; but I never saw him take part in the sport.'[61] Franco Giacometti has said that the *caccia forzata* was taken up again in Italy around 1300.[62] Cesare Agolanti's passing reference to techniques of the chase at Pratolino ('a caccia vanno, usan cani, usan lacci, inganni, e reti')[63] not only corresponds to those that the Medici arrogated to themselves in Tuscan forest reserves, but also to the several methods described in Gaston de Foix's influential *Livre de chasse* and understood as appropriate either to open territory or an enclosed park.

The conventions of hunting with hounds, nets, rope-snares, and traps had an elaborate protocol requiring numerous paid professionals for what was, in effect, a lavish spectacle staged for the amusement of princes and their guests. Deer hunting had several distinct phases:

> The night before the Lord or the Master of the Game will go to the wood, he must cause to come before him all the hunters and the helps, the grooms and the pages, and shall assign to each of them their quests in a certain place, and separate the one from the others, and the one should not come into the quest of the other, nor do him annoyance or hinder him . . . and should assign them the place where the gathering should be made, at the most ease of them all, and the nearest to their quests.[64]

The most logical site for such a public assembly at Pratolino would be the Prato dell' Appennino before the north façade of the palace, accessible from the main entrance to the villa to the west and from the countryside to the east, and closest to various outbuildings having living quarters on their upper floor (it is not visible in Utens's view, being hidden by the palace). At dawn the next day, 'if the hunting shall be in a park all men should remain at the park gate . . . till the king comes'. At Pratolino this would have meant the entrance at the south-east corner of the lower park, near the Casa per il Fontaniere. Meanwhile, a scouting party would enter with bloodhounds held to leash to track down the deer in their lairs, to take foot-print measurements and spoor samples, set the 'stable' (a relay of yeomen with greyhounds spaced out at intervals around the sector where the deer had been discovered); and also to 'Make fair

[60] David R. Coffin, *The Villa in the Life of Renaissance Rome* (Princeton, 1979), p. 125.
[61] Jocelin of Brakelond quoted in J. and F. Gies, *Life in a Medieval Castle* (New York, Hagerstown, San Francisco and London, 1979), p. 140.   [62] Giacometti, *Storia della caccia*, pp. 80–3.
[63] Agolanti, *Pratolino*, p. 57.
[64] English translation of Gaston de Foix known as *The Master of the Game*, ed. Wm A. and F. Baillie-Grohman (New York, 1909), p. 163.

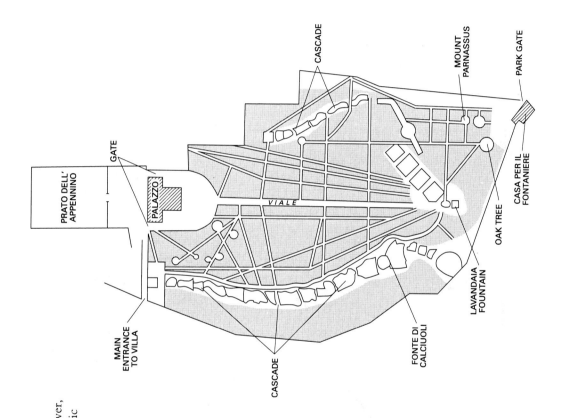

Fig. 2.3 (above) Giusto Utens.
Pratolino, 1599, showing the lower,
southern sector. *Right:* Schematic
indication of structural features
(D.R.E. Wright)

PRATO DELL'
APPENNINO

GATE

PALAZZO

MAIN
ENTRANCE
TO VILLA

VIALE

CASCADE

CASCADE

MOUNT
PARNASSUS

PARK GATE

CASA PER IL
FONTANIERE

OAK TREE

LAVANDAIA
FOUNTAIN

FONTE DI
CALCIUOLI

CASCADE

lodges of green boughs at the tryste to keep the King and Queen and ladies and gentlewomen and also the greyhounds from the sun and bad weather.'[65]

These preparations once completed, the Master of the Game would conduct the royal party into the park to the place of the hunt gathering and breakfast. The obvious site for a ceremonial entry from the palace would be the long Stradone leading thence along the central axis down to an open lawn surrounding a large basin with seating accommodation ('intorno alla detta vasca vi sono de' sederi')[66] adjacent to the Fountain of Washerwoman (Lavandaia) at its south end.

> The place where the gathering shall be made should be in a fair mead well green, where fair trees grow all about, the one far from the other, and a clear well or beside some running brook. And it is called gathering because all the men and the hounds for hunting gather thither, for all they that go to the quest should all come again in a certain place that I have spoken of. And also they that come from home, and all the officers that come from home should bring thither all that they need, everyone in his office . . . and should lay the towels and board clothes all about on the green grass, and set divers meats upon a great platter after the lord's power. And some should eat sitting, and some standing, and some leaning upon their elbows, some should drink [wine], some laugh, some jangle, some joke and some play . . . and when men be set at tables ere they eat then should come the lymerers and their grooms with the lymerers the which have been questing, and everyone shall say his report to the lord of what they have done and found and lay the fumes [spoor] before the lord he that hath found and then the Lord or Master of the hunting by the counsel of them all shall choose which they will move and run and which shall be the greatest hart and the highest deer. And when they have eaten, the lord shall devise where the relays shall go . . . and then shall every man speed him to his place, and all haste them to go to the finding.[67]

The Lavandaia Fountain would have furnished an appropriately named spot for the servants to rinse the breakfast dishes, a hygienic necessity that is illustrated, for example, in a fifteenth-century French painting of a hunt banquet now in the Louvre.[68] The Washerwoman statue, depicted wringing a piece of cloth, was also a comic but learned reference to Bianca Cappello as Diana-Luna, patron goddess of the chase.[69] The statue

[65] Ibid., pp. 188–90.
[66] Bernardo Sansone Sgrilli, *Descrizione della regia villa, fontane, e fabbriche di Pratolino* (Florence, 1742), p. 22.
[67] *The Master of the Game*, pp. 163–4.
[68] The French hunt painting is illustrated in Francois Boucher, *20,000 Years of Fashion* (New York, n.d.), p. 211.
[69] At the north end of the Stradone at Pratolino, in a grotto between the stairs, sat a statue of the River Mugnone, which in Medici iconography was associated with Fiesole (depicted as a standing female crowned with a crescent moon in allusion to the heraldic emblem of that city). Boccaccio, in his *Ninfale fiesolano*, explained the origin of the crescent moon emblem as a remembrance of Fiesole's ancient worship of Diana. Now, in Arab-influenced astrological illustrations Luna was represented as a washerwoman wringing out a cloth, e.g. Andola de Negro, *Introductorius ad iudicia strologiae*, London, BM, MS. Add. 23770, p. 37ᵛ (on this manuscript see Fritz Saxl, *A Heritage of Images* (Harmondsworth, 1970), pp. 35–6). This interpretation of the Lavandaia at Pratolino as Diana-Luna appears to be corroborated by Cesare Agolanti's remark that the fountain was dedicated to the daughter of Atlas (presumably the Phaesyle named by Hesiod) who gave her name to the city (Fiesole) founded by her father. Since the Moon, like Galatea, who appears as the centrepiece of the grottoes under the house at Pratolino, was closely associated with whiteness in the mythographic tradition, the comic reference to Bianca Capello becomes obvious. Agolanti *Pratolino*, p. 46; and Hesiod, *The Astronomy*, frag. 2.

of the pissing putto beside the Lavandaia seems equally in the jocular spirit of the hunt assembly.

As the hunt started, the lord and his party would be conducted to their sheltered bower within the previously encircled sector of the wood. Once in place, he would sound his hunting horn, the signal to unleash the dogs. The object was to course the deer on horseback and on foot toward the princely group, to wound it and bring it to bay, then corner it until the lord could be brought close to administer the *coup de grace*. These activities allow us to interpret the *viottole* fanning outward to the north-east and north-west from the lawn at the Lavandaia. The east-west *viottole* that intersect the foregoing would have functioned as subsidiary boundaries along which the 'stable' would be stationed to complete the encirclement of prey. Giusto Utens' painting of Pratolino depicts some forty-five or fifty white herms throughout the park, whose location at the intersections and terminal points of *viottole* suggests an interpretation as precursors of our modern traffic signs, that is, to control equestrian circulation and prevent collisions among the relays racing after the deer. The circumstances of the hunt also suggest a further meaning of the artificial cascades at Pratolino:

> When [the hart] is weary and hot, then he goeth to yield, and soileth to some great river (or a brook, pond, ditch or moat). And some time he foils down in the water half a mile or more ere he comes to land on any side. And that he doeth for two reasons, the one is to make himself cold, and for to refresh himself of the great heat he hath, the other is that the hounds and the hunter may not come after him nor see his fues [spoor] in the water, as they do on the land.[70]

As evidenced by the Unicorn tapestries in the Cloisters, and a letter of Lodovico il Moro, deer were often brought to bay, wounded and killed in the water:

> After a good while realizing he was still being pursued [the deer] returned to the water in the ditch, where I pierced him in the side with an arrow. Afterwards wounded by one of these pensioners with a spear and then brought down by the dogs, he received so many wounds when the hunting party descended into the ditch that he was quickly dispatched.[71]

The western cascade at Pratolino was provided, at the third pool from the bottom, with a double stairway of forty steps having a grotto with spring-fed fountain halfway down. The name of this fountain, 'Fonte di Calciuoli',[72] implies that this could be the point where spear-bearers stood to wound or kill the prey in the water (the word *calcio* means the foot of a lance in older Italian).

The closing ritual of the hunt was the *curée*, during which the carcasses (now gathered up and transported through the park on carts) were ceremonially skinned, the

---

[70] *The Master of the Game*, pp. 32–3, 39, 43, 44–5.

[71] Borsa, *La caccia*, p. 172. James Rorimer, *The Unicorn Tapestries at the Cloisters* (New York, 1962), fig. 10.

[72] ASF, Miscellanea Medicea, 55, Report of Fernando Tacca on the state of Pratolino (1657), item n°. 36: 'Per ristaurare il Vivaio sotto i Calciolo, che non tiene, e fare i balustri, lo sdrucciola, e le scale 40. Va male ogni cosa, se non si rasetta.' Sgrilli, *Descrizione*, map of Pratolino, n°. 23, 'Fone di Calcuioli [*sic*]'.

neck, bowels and liver cut up, the entrails displayed on the hide, and then tossed to the ravenous hounds after they were made to bay for their reward. Next, when the lord had chosen the best venison for his larder, the Master of the Game distributed the rest in accordance with the claims of the huntsmen who had made kills, the hounds were leashed and returned to the kennels, and the carcasses were removed from the park.[73]

> And this done the Master of the Game ought to speak to the officers that all the hunters' suppers be well ordained, and they drink not ale . . . but wine that night for the good and great labour that they have had for the Lord's game and disport, and for the exploit and making of the hounds. And also that they may the more merrily and gladly tell what each of them hath done all the day and which hounds have best run and boldest.[74]

Where, at Pratolino, the *curée* would have occurred is hard to determine, although it necessitated a spot that could accommodate the grand duke, numerous hunters and dogs, as well as the display of the game 'in a row, all the heads one way – and every deer's feet to the other's back . . . harts . . . laid in two or three rows (by themselves) and the rascal in the same way by themselves',[75] and a source of water for the cleansing of the digestive organs. The largest open area in the lower park was a *prato* just inside the entrance gate in the south-east corner, near the house of the *fontaniere*. Its proximity to the park gate would have facilitated the speedy withdrawal of the malodorous corpses.

Convention did not demand that the lord stay to the very end of the *curée*, which could be left in the charge of the Master of the Game, thus liberating the noble party to go off to the post-hunt supper *al fresco*. One can imagine this taking place at Pratolino within the branches of the nearby giant oak, fitted out with spiral stairs and a dining platform with table in its crotch. From this elevated station the ladies could hear, but not necessarily smell the messy *curée*. The shaded lawn just below with stone seating around its perimeter would have suited the presumably less elaborate supper for members of the court and the merry-making hunters and yeomen. The adjoining Mount Parnassus complete with a water organ would have furnished the dinner music.

The second most popular game animal was the hare, 'a good little beast, and much good sport and liking is the hunting of her, more than that of any other beast that any man knoweth, if he were not so little.'[76] Of the several recommended methods, one was the *caccia forzata*, demanding dogs with sufficient stamina to course their prey over long straight stretches and the agility to keep up with its frequent abrupt shifts of direction before they could catch and kill it. More suited to the amusement of stationary spectators was the method of nets and snares: 'They slay them also with small pockets, nets, with hare pipes, and with long nets, and with small cords that men cast where they make their breaking of small twigs when they go to their pastures.'[77] In some of the circular clearings in the Pratolino park mentioned above as hand-feeding stations for hares, Giusto Utens has added eight little dabs of white paint, apparently

---

[73] *The Master of the Game*, pp. 175–9, 186, 197 and 208–9.
[74] Ibid., p. 180.   [75] Ibid., p. 193.   [76] Ibid., p. 14.   [77] Ibid., p. 22.

one on each side of the *viottole* entering therein. These white dabs may be interpreted as stone (?) blocks or seats for those observing the netting or snaring sport.

To summarise, whatever the precise historical details respecting its utilisation, the park at Pratolino should be understood as having a structural logic of its own, one quite different from the aestheticised informality of the eighteenth-century English country estate to which it is often compared. Its central axis relates to ritualised entries much like the entrance *viale* at Castello or the *viottolone* at the Boboli. From the bottom of the park this formality is destabilised in conformity with the rather more unpredictable movements of game animals fleeing human pursuers. By contrast, the logic of the English gentleman's park is founded on the more casual, and cadenced errancy of the meditative stroller in search of 'natural' scenic effects planned in conformity with philosophically defined norms (the Beautiful, the Picturesque).

In the earlier European tradition, Art, conceived as a goal-directed know-how, was continuous with Nature, indeed a teleological extension of it. With the rise of modern epistemology know-how became intellectualised as a mathematically modelled knowing-that, as a conceptual abstraction of the rational subject and thus the antithesis of mere Nature, which now had to be rethought and redesigned by the professionally trained landscape architect. The modern science of aesthetics grew from Cartesian seed. The British 'taste', ushered in in tandem with an empiricist epistemology, simply stood Le Nôtre on his head through its attempts to conceal Art and make it look 'natural'. The Kantian compromise refined this modernist dichotomy from a mentalist perspective, and it has continued to shape our attitudes, as typified in the bibliographic problem of how to classify landscape architecture texts, under Fine Art or Agriculture. My point is that the know-how (*ars/technê*) which underlies the structuration of Florentine Renaissance gardens was a matter of skills accumulated, handed down, and enlarged over many generations through a continuing intimacy with natural materials. As such it is incommensurate with a modernist notion of landscape Art, founded in a subject-centred epistemology and confined to issues of style and aesthetic intentionality. Renaissance gardens were for the most part a collaborative effort among patrons and technicians: gardeners, estate managers, building contractors, hydraulic engineers, game-keepers and fountain sculptors. Niccolò Tribolo was first hired at Castello only to design and make the fountains. Besides it hardly took an artistic genius to come up with the quartered square plan of the Giardino del laberinto at Castello or the rectangular lawn bordered by evergreens at the Boboli. Consequently, there may be some benefit in approaching Renaissance gardens and parks as works of Nature – the nature of plants, air and water, the nature of human health in relationship to physical and mental environs, the nature of animals, their habits and habitats, and of human Convention, timeless or topical.

CHAPTER 3

CHRIST THE GARDENER AND THE CHAIN OF SYMBOLS: THE GARDENS AROUND THE WALLS OF SIXTEENTH-CENTURY FERRARA

G. LEONI[*]

For most of the sixteenth century Ferrara was encircled by a chain of gardens laid out beside the city walls. These gardens around the walls – which were effectively the main ducal gardens in sixteenth-century Ferrara – mark the stages of a long itinerary over land and water by which the duke could leave the castle, reach the city walls and make a complete circuit around the city without either having to enter it or leave its bounds. While remaining unseen and protected, he could, if he wished, control the surrounding territory, the walls and the city itself, obtaining access to each if required. Each garden had different, unique characteristics, but this sequence of spaces was linked by the itinerary and the walls, thus creating a complex, partly natural and partly artificial 'structure', which was perceived, utilised and maintained as a single unit. The subject of this chapter is therefore this vast circular garden which, owing to its location between the city and its territory, became the allocated setting for the search for and representation of many equilibria necessary to the city's existence: that between artifice and nature, between war and peace, between health and disease (figs. 3.1 and 3.2).

A detailed description of the individual gardens would occupy this entire chapter.[1] A number of special features will be analysed later, but first of all it is worth rapidly outlining the main stages of the itinerary. The duke left the castle, heading north, and commenced his 'walk' by entering the Pavilion Garden which owed its name to the presence of a marble building topped by a large gilded copper sphere. The first part of

---

[*]Translated by Lucinda Byatt.

[1] There are two descriptions of the full itinerary around the walls and gardens, written shortly after their destruction: M.A. Guarini, *Compendio historico dell'origine, accrescimento e prerogative delle Chiese e Luoghi Pii della città e Diocesi di Ferrara* (Ferrara, 1621), pp. 3–7, 131, 187–90, 200–1, 295; A. Penna, *Descrittione della porta di San Benedetto della città di Ferrara, dè luoghi delitiosi, che erano attorno le mura di essa, e del ressiduo dè Giardini Ducali* (Padua, 1671). For a rather more detailed description than that given in the present chapter, made through the integration of bibliographical and documentary sources, we refer readers to: G. Leoni, 'La città salvata dai giardini. I benefici del verde nella Ferrara del XVI secolo', in *Fiori e giardini estensi a Ferrara* (Rome, 1992), pp. 14–27; and, for those who wish to examine the transcription of archive documents: G. Leoni, 'I giardini delle mura di Ferrara (1490-1598)', typescript deposited in the National Libraries in Rome and Florence, 1989. For a concise bibliography of works relating to Ferrara's wall gardens, see p. 92.

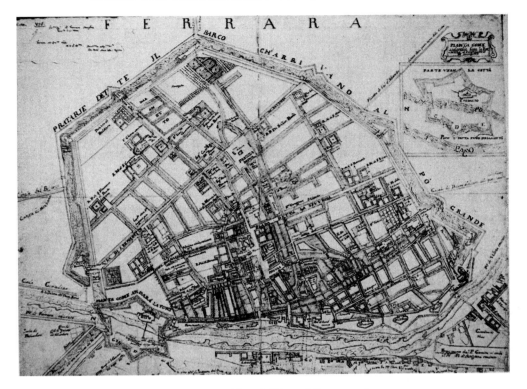

Fig. 3.1 G. B. Aleotti. Plan of Ferrara, 1605

the itinerary followed the line of what used to be the old north-facing walls prior to Ercole's expansion of the city in the late fifteenth century (fig. 3.4). It is immediately clear that we are not moving through the city's street plan: the *contrade* 'della rosa', 'delle stalle ducali' and 'di S. Gabriele' are all avoided by means of a vaulted underground passage allowing pedestrians and carriages to travel towards the bastion of S. Benedetto, around which lies the second group of gardens. On the left, heading towards the walls, we find La Castellina, a building 'constructed with a number of fortress-like elements' and equipped with a genuine thermal structure for which water from the Po was duly heated by a 'stove'. Following the curve of the walls we head north to reach the Ragnaia, on the slope of the embankment, a dense scrub of oak trees followed by a grove of citrus fruit trees enclosed, along the sides at right angles to the walls, by two painted and decorated loggias with marble Ionic columns. From here steps lead up to a balcony overlooking the large marble basin used as a fish-pond. For a short tract this forms the city's outermost boundary and doubles as an irrigation reservoir for the surrounding gardens; the short northern side is bordered by the bastion of S. Benedetto and the walls of the street named after it, completely overgrown with pomegranate bushes. Looking down from the Giardini della Castellina you can see the island known as Belvedere not far off, lying between the Po di Ferrara and the Po di S. Giacomo. To

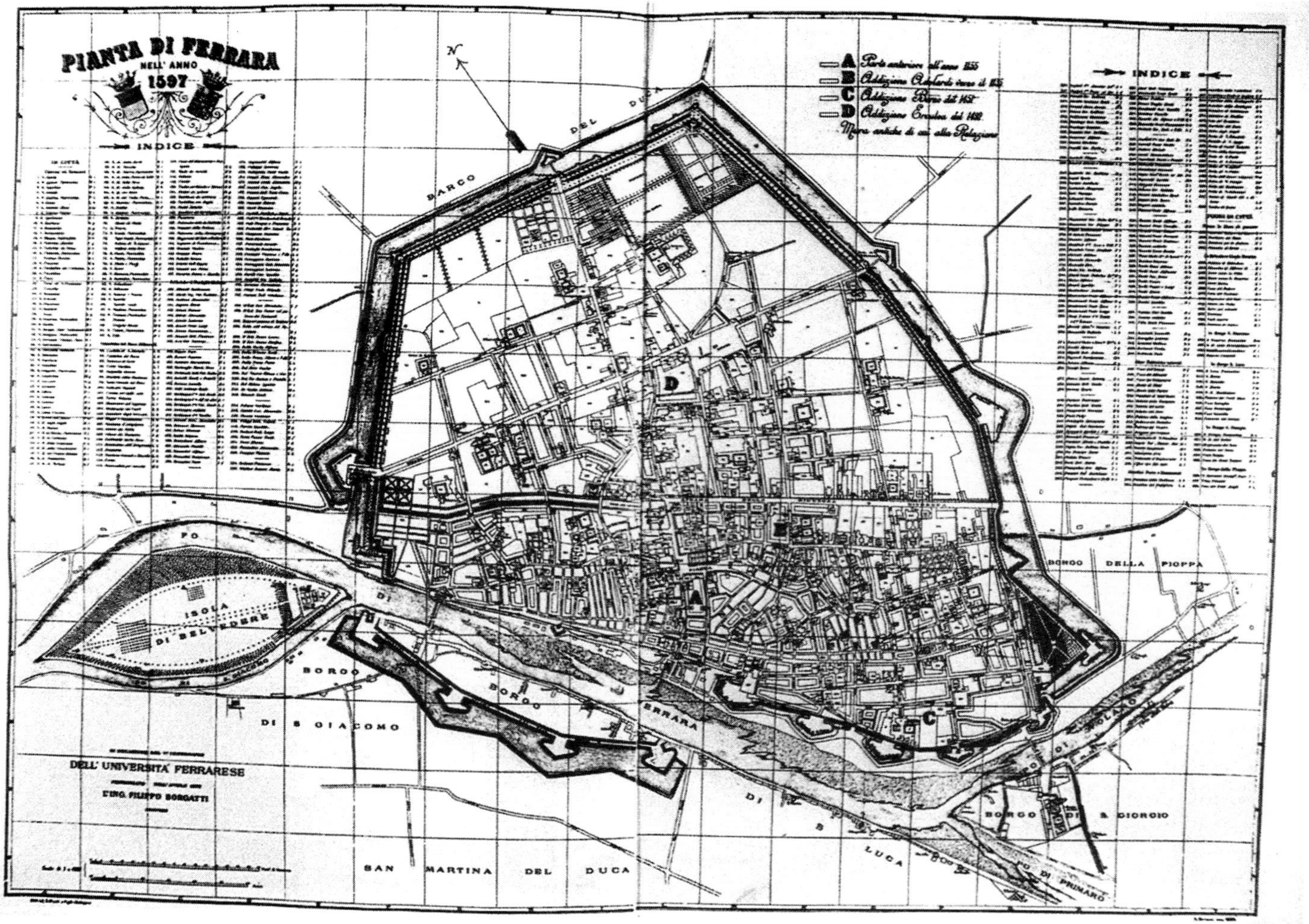

Fig. 3.2 F. Borgatti. Plan of Ferrara, 1597

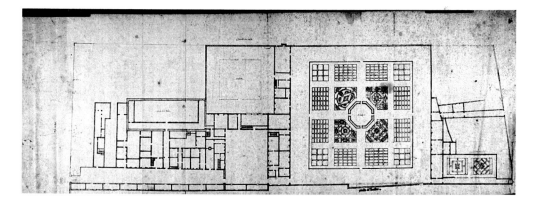

Fig. 3.3 The Pavilion Garden

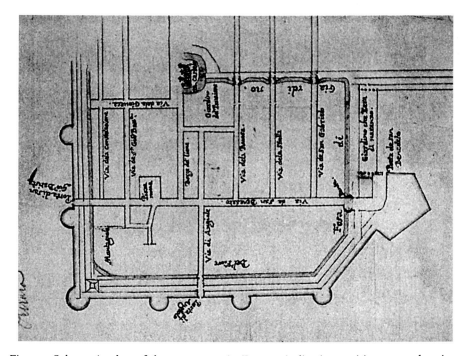

Fig. 3.4 Schematic plan of the *terra nuova* in Ferrara, indicating an itinerary and various stopping places along the garden route

reach it you must leave the path along the wall gardens and be ferried across the Po – a very short crossing. The island's position in the river, one of the decisive elements for the defence and definition of the city, makes the Belvedere an integral part of the garden chain. In fact, bearing in mind the literary tradition which immediately grew up around the island, it can be said that it represents the single most important element. Of all the literary images it has inspired, the most well known is certainly that of the 'happiest island' evoked by Ariosto in *Orlando Furioso*.[2]

Returning to the walls and continuing along the path until we reach the Porta degli Angeli (fig. 3.5), we find another group of gardens consisting – in this order – of the kitchen gardens and the Belfiore, Barchetto and Montagnola complex. Gardens, vineyards, groves, orchards, fish-ponds: this sequence of spaces was originally linked to the ancient residence of Belfiore but was completely transformed, in terms of its meaning and role within the city context, from the moment they became part of this itinerary. A little further on, partly sunk into the embankment, lies the building which, owing to its shape, was known as the Rotonda. The building is entered from the sunken area which at this point separates the walls themselves from the embankment; it is a cool place and therefore used above all during summer. Leaving the city through the Porta degli Angeli – accessible only with the duke's permission – we enter that area of the Barco which lay outside the city walls after Ercole's expansion. Of all the areas we have rapidly passed through, the Barco is perhaps that which is furthest from the usual image of the garden. Enclosed by walls which follow those of the city for a short stretch, the Barco covers a large and mostly unbuilt area; its complex structure comprises a number of heterogeneous elements: a large farm for breeding domestic animals, arable land, hunting grounds strictly reserved for the duke, the falconry, but also a number of structures more appropriate to a proper garden, such as the peacock enclosure and the labyrinth for horse races. Past the Belfiore complex, we return to the itinerary along the walls and head for the last stage: the gardens on the Mountain of Saint George. The most striking feature here is an artificially constructed earth mound covered with woody scrub and, on the side facing the city, with low vines. Vine-trellised paths lead up to an open space on the summit but, on the south-facing slope, it is also possible to go inside the Mountain into a 'grotto' adorned with paintings and mosaics. To the south beyond the Mountain lies a wide clearing containing a building whose outer walls are embellished with paintings by Girolamo da Carpi and Garofalo. Lastly, a thick wood lying between the clearing and the city encloses a labyrinth and a fountain.

Two important questions arise: who built this 'structure' and when? Once again we are obliged to be more concise than an adequate reply would merit. After verifying the documents, the way in which the place was created dispels any tendency to attribute the work to a single author. The wall gardens in fact owe their layout not to a single project realised in a linear sequence, but rather to a series of overlapping and interwoven strategies implemented by a multiplicity of 'players' rather than a single designer. A military technician created an empty space alongside the walls or a ditch for strategic or defensive purposes. The ditch was utilised by a fisherman who, without jeopardising its possible use as a defensive element, transformed it into a fish-pond. Likewise, an area of empty ground required for fortification was taken over by a

---

[2] L. Ariosto, *Orlando Furioso* (1532), XLIII, pp. 56–9 (Guido Waldman, Orlando Furioso. A New Prose Translation (Oxford, 1974), p. 515).

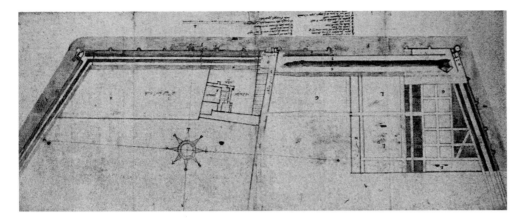

Fig. 3.5 Schematic plan of the gardens near the Porta degli Angeli, Ferrara

gardener who created a *parterre* with box hedges, for example, whereas another area may have been given to a herbalist who turned it into a herb garden, or to a kitchen gardener who used it for agricultural purposes. Later, an architect (who might also have been a military technician, as in the case of Aleotti) was invited to design ornamental elements such as a 'casino' or fountain with water jets. Thus, the ducal gardens around the city walls, an area which was by definition multiform and composite, took shape following a multiplicity of decisions taken within the context of a relative and well-defined sphere of autonomy. But the heterogeneous origin of this concatenation of spaces never ceased to possess a global identity based on the precise awareness, by ducal power, of the need to locate some functions in the border area between the city and its outlying territory.

The manner of their creation obviously also complicates the question of dating the gardens, a close analysis of which would lead us into a labyrinth of dates and events. However, seen as an element in the city's definition and defence, the garden circuit around the walls has a precise chronological dimension which can be summarised in general terms. The germinal phase coincides with the decision taken by Ercole I in 1490 to push the city's boundaries northwards. The areas in which the gardens were later created only began to take shape, however, during the fortification works carried out by Alfonso I in the early 1520s. On the other hand, the decline of the gardens was chronologically more compact, even in the case of those not involved in episodes of active destruction, like the Castellina and Belvedere gardens: there was a general and extremely rapid decline – which to a certain extent is implicit in the very nature of the garden – after the Este court left Ferrara following the city's devolution to the Papal States.

It could be said that the notional beginning and the effective end of the history of the wall gardens were marked by two decisive military episodes, two affronts to the power of the Este and their ability to protect the city.

The first episode occurred in the context of the war against Venice in 1482. The Barco, previously used as the ceremonial entrance into the city, became the target for constant raids and attacks by the Venetian troops under the command of the Sanseverino. The killing of the peacocks, the capture of the deer, which were then sent to Venice, and other significant actions culminated in the abduction of the statue of Niccolò, an offence which stung so deeply that it was recalled in *Orlando Furioso*.[3] To his amazement Ercole realised that Ferrara could be defended but not protected, that the city walls represented the bounds beyond which nothing was safe. This realisation led to the conception of a major defence programme which was at the same time a project for peace: the construction of a new city boundary capable of guaranteeing Ferrara's safety and also representing a clear statement of that guarantee to both the city and the territory. It was this peace programme which we find already fully elaborated in the report on the frontiers of the state of Ferrara presented by Pellegrino Prisciani to the Venetian Signoria in 1485.[4] The first tangible sign was the excavation, commenced in August 1492, of the new city moat to the north of Ferrara, followed by the start of a whole series of urban transformations generally known as the 'addizione erculea'.

The second episode, which marked the start of the rapid decline of the wall gardens, coincided with the end of the Este family's rule in Ferrara. When Cesare disbanded all the troops stationed in Ferrara so as not to impede the negotiations underway in Faenza between the duchess of Urbino and Cardinal Aldobrandini, some companies engaged in acts of vandalism specifically aimed at destroying the wall gardens.[5]

Between these two episodes we find the image of a safe and protected city which is accurately described in the 'Discorso sopra la fortificazione di Ferrara' sent to Alfonso II on 22 August 1588 by Giulio Tieni, his military adviser.[6] There emerges the image of a defensive ring consisting of the actual walls themselves, but including also areas of open ground modelled into different shapes by groves or other vegetation, as well as by a complex system of natural and controlled waterways, including an entire stretch of the river Po. It was precisely this defence system based on the use of extensive embankments which required the presence, alongside the walls, if not of gardens, then

---

[3] *Orlando Furioso*, III, 46. For an account of the Venetian forays into the Barco between November 1482 and March 1483, see the anonymous: 'Diario ferrarese dall'anno 1409 sino al 1502' (1467?-1502), ed. by G. Pardi, *Rerum Italicarum Scriptores*, vol. XXIV, part VII, 1 (Bologna, 1934); U. Caleffini, 'Cronica di Ferrara (1471-96)', Biblioteca Vaticana, Mss. Chigi I.I.4; B. Zambotti, 'Diario ferrarese dall'anno 1476 sino al 1504', ed. G. Pardi, *Rerum Italicarum Scriptores*, XXIV, part VII, 2.

[4] P. Prisciani, 'Oratione recitata in presenza del Serenissimo Duca e della Illustrissima Signoria di Venezia dimostrativa dei veri confini del Ducato ferrarese dalla parte del dominio veneto (1485)', Archivio di Stato di Modena, Mss. Biblioteca, 135, pp. 60ff.

[5] 'On leaving they not only confined themselves to military insults, since many of them stole from houses, others ran into the duke's parks and slaughtered the animals who sheltered there owing to the beauty and delight of those enclosed areas, others went not only to the Belvedere, but to the Mountain of Saint George and the Mount, where they not only cut the vines, but also the trees, oranges and citrus fruits which were sheltered at this time of year, it being winter, inside planks covered with tiles. Not satisfied with this, they then killed the peacocks of which there were a great number; and passing into the Garden of the Pavilion, they uprooted the flowers and from this day on the city, which had previously been the pride of Lombardy and the compendium of all the beauties and delights in Italy, was left disfigured and damaged' (A. Faustini, *Aggiunta alle historie del signor Gasparo Sardi*, p. 133; see Appendix, p. 92).

[6] G. Tieni, 'Discorso sopra la fortificazione di Ferrara', Archivio di Stato di Modena, Archivio militare estense, b. 246.

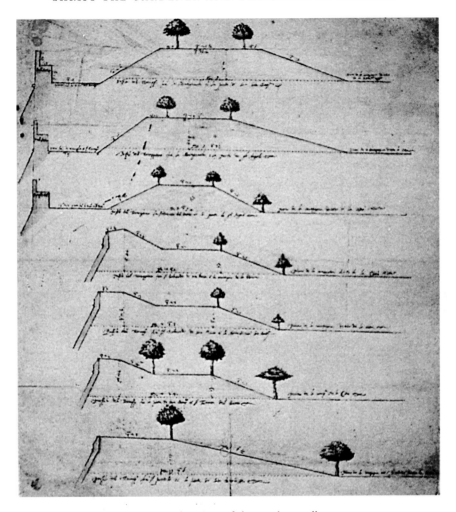

Fig. 3.6 Section drawing of the garden wall terraces

at least of a series of elements which could be usefully organised like a garden. Large areas of land had to be left empty of buildings and modelled according to specific gradients. Trees were required so that their roots would reinforce and stabilise the mounds of earth. Open areas covered with sparse vegetation were required so as not to hinder the movement of troops and machinery in the event of war. Water was required to be channelled through the moat system. In the case of Ferrara, each of these elements formed part of the city's defence strategy and, at the same time, could be used as part of a garden. There was therefore a genuine and original structural interpenetration of the gardens and the city walls.

The gardens also fulfilled a strategic function given that, if necessary, they could be used to enter or leave the city unseen, or as a genuine escape route; they could also be used with the necessary discretion to welcome illustrious guests travelling incognito or, on the other hand, to stage a magnificent reception for particularly important visitors.

The neutral area of the gardens was therefore the ideal place for controlling any dangers threatening the city and to defend it, as Alberti suggested, from the enemy both without and within. In fact, it is precisely in this treatise – whose influence on the milieu surrounding Ercole during the 1490s is well known – that Alberti suggested the idea of a neutral ring set between the city and its territory, an image which was underlined by the extreme solution of a double city wall.[7] The solution adopted in Ferrara was certainly not as drastic, but it is worth adding that Alberti identified it as being appropriate to the 'town of a tyrant'. While the duke of Ferrara did not need to live in a fortress, 'neque in urbe neque ex urbe', he did not abandon the idea of stationing well-armed military garrisons precisely in the gardens, on the boundary between the city and the outlying territory.

The importance of the gardens in terms of the city's defence extended far beyond a purely war-time and strategic function. In many ways the gardens round the walls represented the conformation which vitally important defensive elements assumed in peace time. The peaceful conformation of the defensive enclosure was an index of the city's security. The decision to construct a place of peace beside the walls, on the very site where any battle to gain control of the city would be waged, offered a guarantee of security. The fact that the duke was allowed to walk around with his court in the proximity of the city boundary, indulging in his own pastimes, meant that the city was a safe place. Thus, the area in which the gardens were created became the setting in which both citizens and foreign visitors could appreciate the equilibrium achieved between war and peace.[8]

And equilibrium was indeed the right term because the situation could also be interpreted in a very different light. The duke could only afford to maintain his idleness and slacken the defences beside the city walls if here he was most closely guarded against every possible external or internal attack. In other words, the gardens could only exist provided they were fortified.

The wall gardens in Ferrara were therefore the complete embodiment of an idea which had already been fully expressed in one of the classic works of garden literature. In Xenophon's *Oeconomicus* the well-founded legitimacy of Cyrus, king of the Persians, whom all willingly obey and no one wishes to betray, is explicitly related to the assiduity with which military exercises were combined with care for his 'paradises', namely his luxuriant gardens.[9]

---

[7] L. B. Alberti, *De re aedificatoria* (1452), v, 1: 'a circle within a circle'; this and subsequent excerpts are taken from L. B. Alberti, *On the Art of Building in Ten Books*, trans. by J. Rykwert, N. Leach and R. Tavernor (Cambridge, Mass., 1988), p. 118.

[8] It is worth recalling that Ariosto links the image of the happy island constructed at Belvedere with the duke's capacity to protect and defend the city. He writes that the transformation of that place would 'be owed to the diligent efforts of one who, combining knowledge and power with purpose, would so endow the city with dykes and walls that it would stand secure against the world without invoking outside help': *Orlando Furioso*, XLIII, 59.

[9] Xenophon, *Oeconomicus*, IV, 25. The topic of the relations between garden and the city's military defence is certainly one which requires further study. To cite another example close to sixteenth-century Ferrara in both geographical and chronological terms, it is worth remembering 'Ioannis Francisci Pici Mirandulanae Insulae Suae Descriptio' (1524)',

Over and above the resolution of its defensive problems, the wall gardens represented a much more important triumph in terms of the city's existence: namely, a triumph over Ferrara's unfortunate natural surroundings. The gardens brought inside a ring which linked the city to its surrounding territory all the landscape elements of open ground, water, fresh air, diverse types of flora and fauna. At the same time these elements were manipulated and subjected to every possible form of artifice: 'unnatural' climates were created, the ground was shaped into improbable forms, the waters of the Po were channelled using complex hydraulic systems, and the choice of plants and animals was often decisively exotic. If we compare the features of the ducal gardens with the natural characteristics of the area surrounding Ferrara, it is clear how, on the one hand, they represent a compendium of local elements and, on the other, an ideal completion in order to remedy the climatic and geographical drawbacks of the city's natural site. In view of the strongly neoplatonic culture of Renaissance Ferrara, it is impossible not to recognise, in this purification of nature, the idea of the platonic myth of the true earth.[10] But there are also other references. A *regio* conforming to the precepts laid down by Vitruvius and Alberti was in fact created between the city and the countryside and Ferrara finally found itself immersed in a generous nature: ventilation controlled by hills and forests, running water, high ground, a balance between sun and shade – together with the added advantage of its unique location. The gardens became a sort of laboratory for research into the right balance between the eminently artificial city environment and the conditions of an area in which agricultural requirements imposed the need to comply with the characteristics of the natural environment. Nothing could better define the physical limit of the city than this magical ring in which nature was supremely virtuous as a result of the major effort made to rectify it.[11]

The court benefited in numerous ways from the green ring encircling Ferrara. Above all, in a city which was particularly sensitive to bodily matters the idea of the garden as a place of healing inevitably assumed considerable importance. We need only glance through a work such as Antonio Musa Brasavola's *Examen omnium simplicium medicamentorum* to get a clear idea of the programme to bring to Ferrara all the natural substances required by medicine; moreover, as Brasavola himself admitted, this was a

Modena, Biblioteca estense, Ms. Alpha.H.1.10.(1), in which, after describing the defensive advantages offered by the small island which served as the garrison for the castle of Mirandola, the author added: 'Atque huic, atque illi est Insula praesidio. / Verum hae sunt artes cum bellica munera fervent, / Cum tuba pugnaces excit ad arma viros. / At cum se pexos olea redimita capillos, / Pax offert niveo laeta per arva pede; / Tum sunt quae blando recreent praecordia visu: / Longus ager, multis consitus arboribus. / Porticus et varios porrecta sedilia in usus / Et subjecta oculis optima quaeque tuis.'

[10] Plato, *Phaedo*, 109d-111c. For a general study of Platonism in Ferrara the reference standard continues to be E. Garin, *Motivi della cultura filosofica ferrarese nel Rinascimento, Belfagor* (1956), pp. 612–34.

[11] The enormous commitment required to preserve this quintessence of pleasant nature, to prevent this propitious support of life at court and in the city from disappearing, is accurately documented by a series of registers kept by the *Camera ducale* (Archivio di Stato di Modena, *Camera ducale, Computeristeria, Mandati in volume*). For the decade from 1587 to 1598 we have a record of all payments relating to the wall gardens, made at less than daily intervals and accompanied by detailed notes regarding the motive for payment as well as the recipient.

programme which was personally followed with great interest by Alfonso I up until his death.[12]

However, the gardens were not only visited in the emergency of an illness, but, on the contrary, were a place in which individual imbalances, which could provoke the degeneration of body and mind, could be combatted every day. The complete and virtuous nature created around the city's boundaries offered all the benefits outlined by Marsilio Ficino in *De vita*. The pursuit of physical health and individual harmony in fact presupposes harmony with the heavenly bodies, and is facilitated by a natural, perfectly balanced setting in which, as in paradise, 'nullum inesse … elementalis qualititas excessum'.[13] Bearing in mind that Ficino's recommendations are above all addressed to those born under Saturn, it was certainly no coincidence that the planet's baneful influence dominated the unlucky horoscope of Alfonso I, during whose reign work was started on the majority of the wall gardens.[14]

The well-being of the prince and the court only represents one aspect of the more general state of health of the entire city, and the city's body required specific treatment. As is clearly pointed out in *Picatrix*, there are no general expedients in the search for an equilibrium between earthly and heavenly things,

> et eciam scire oportet civitates et climata eo quod planetarum potencie diversificatur in eis. Hoc autem apparet in rebus nascentibus in aliquo ipsorum climatum que nullo modo possunt in altero reperiri, quemadmodum sunt minere, lapides, metalla, arbores et plante, e eciam aliqua hominum accidencia que in uno loco specialiter reperiuntur, omnibus aliis locis carentibus.[15]

---

[12] A. Brasavola detto Musa, *Examen omnium simplicium medicamentorum, quorum in officinis usus est*, apud Ioannem et Franciscum Frellaeos (Lugduni, 1537). The benefits deriving from the execution of this programme are set out in detail by some members of the Brasavola dynasty (including Antonio himself) in 'Consilia medica', a collection of manuscript annotations relating to cures provided for members of the court (Modena, Biblioteca estense, Mss. Lat. Alpha. J.4.4).

[13] M. Ficino, 'De vita coelitus comparanda', XIX, in *De vita* (1439), republished in *Opera* (Basileae, 1576), pp. 493ff: 'there is indeed no excess of an elemental quality in the heavens'. Eng. trans. by C. V. Kaske and J. R. Clark in Marsilio Ficino, *Three Books on Life. A Critical Edition and Translation* (New York, 1989), p. 346. On Ficino's direct and substantial influence on the cultural sphere in Ferrara, see Garin, *Motivi della cultura*.

[14] As Gasparo Sardi recalls in his *Historie ferraresi*: 'Cominciarono nel principio del suo stato li travagli, ne quali lungamente visse, et sempre con grandissima sua gloria sostenne, et vinse; come havea, nascendo lui, dimostrato con le stelle in cielo, apparendo quando egli nacque Giove insieme co Pesci, et essendo Saturno nel sesto luoco (case dicono quelle, che di questa scienza ragionano) chiamato Fortuna trista; Marte pianeta malvagio nell'ottavo luoco, anco egli rio e tristo, onde vengano i danni, et ogni male, et perciò è detto luoco di Morte, et Epicataphora, per la simiglianza ch'l sonno tiene con la morte; Saturno pigro, et maligno dimostrò l'infirmità ch'egli ebbe, et lo stato, che quasi tutto levato gli fu dal Papa; Marte gli affanni, l'angustie, l'insidie, i tradimenti, et perigli che patì, et dove incorse, ma funne liberato per lo favore di Giove con i Pesci benigno, et gentile, che anco dimostrò lo stato, et imperio che haver divea, l'ingegno altissimo, la fede, l'amicitia, che intieramente serbò, et le vittorie, che rapportar dovea de suoi nimici: ove sempre si fe maggior la dignità, et gloria sua, come giudicarono i dotti Astrologhi... Et il Duca, cui non havevano molto piacciuto gli Studij, *diedesi a piaceri honesti et dilettosi di bellissimi giardini, di vaghe pitture, et di molti lavori di mano*': G. Sardi, *Historie ferraresi* (Ferrara, 1556), pp. 331–2, my italics.

[15] *Picatrix. The Latin Version of the Ghayat Al-Hakim*, ed. D. Pingree (London, 1986), vol. III, pp. 3, 26; and see also vol. III, pp. 7, 8. Studies on the Schifanoia painting cycle, too numerous to set out here, have clearly evidenced, from the Warburg studies onwards, the enormous influence exercised by *Picatrix* on culture in Renaissance Ferrara.

As Luca Gaurico recalls, the expansion and rebuilding of Ferrara without doubt provided an opportunity, according to a custom that was far from eccentric at the time, to improve the astrological prospects of the city which during the same period also passed from the ascendancy of Capricorn to that of Virgo.[16] But the siting of the gardens around Ferrara, the construction of this magical ring, suggests an astrological programme whose scope extended well beyond this period of rebuilding and included a genuine redefinition of the site on which the city stood.

The idea of setting court and city life against a backdrop of improved and virtuous nature was only new to Ferrara in terms of its practical realisation. A programme of this type had already been fully elaborated in a figurative tradition whose greatest and most outstanding expression was obviously the Schifanoia cycle. The botanical and zoological accuracy with which a plan for the recomposition of the natural environment was formulated at Schifanoia, and the interpenetration between the real landscape of the Po river valley and the imaginary landscape – two aspects which are repeatedly highlighted by the critics – point to Schifanoia as the figurative expression of the programme which was subsequently implemented in the circle of gardens.[17] The degree of concordance, regarding both single elements and their composition, is striking: the same essences, the same fruits, the same fauna, the same activities, as well as entire parallel passages, such as the artificial mountain with narrow passages leading inside it illustrated in the upper fascia of the month of March. This was by no means an isolated example (one need only recall the background to *San Giorgio e il Drago* by Cosmé Tura (Fig. 3.7)); but it is impossible not to compare it to the Mountain of Saint George, about which more will be said later, only a few metres away from the room in Schifanoia. However, given that a detailed comparison lies outside the scope of this chapter, we will restrict ourselves to proposing a simplified hypothesis.

It is difficult to imagine that the example of Schifanoia (fig. 3.8) can have failed to influence the programme which, during the early decades of the sixteenth century, resulted in the construction of the actual garden spaces described above. Certainly, it may be supposed that these analogies owe more to common reference to an ideal landscape elaborated by the culture of Ferrara during this period, or at all events forming part of it, than to direct influence. However, this does not detract from the interest of the analogy, but on the contrary gives it added emphasis: in sixteenth-century Ferrara, namely in the same place and during the same historical period, we would appear to have two complete formulations of an ideal landscape, one expressed in figurative terms of outstanding quality and the other actually constructed. An ideal which was initially enclosed within the magical space of the Sala dei Mesi and later recreated to form a none the less magical ring around the entire city, protecting and defending it. A magical ring. Numerous studies have focused attention on the significance of the Schifanoia cycle, not as a generic

[16] L. Gaurico, *Operum omnium*, 3 books in 2 volumes (Basle, 1590), vol. II, pp. 1723–4.

[17] *Atlante di Schifanoia*, ed. R. Varese (Modena, 1989) is extremely useful for an accurate comparison between the nature portrayed in Schifanoia and that expertly constructed around the edge of the city.

Fig. 3.7 Cosmé Tura. Organ case in Ferrara cathedral showing St George and the dragon
(1469)

programme to engender harmony between the natural setting, man's actions and the
positions of the planets, but as a talisman elaborated for a specific geographical, historical
and social situation.[18] It is in this light that we should therefore once again reinterpret the
gardens: not only as a defensive structure, not only as virtuous and healing nature, but also
as a magical ring of images and symbols which encircled and protected Ferrara, a genuine
talisman on an urban scale.

[18] See E. Battisti' 'Tre osservazioni generali', *Atlante*, pp. 21–3, for a recent and authoritative reconfirmation of this
interpretation.

Fig. 3.8 Detail of a fresco in the Palazzo Schifanoia

The first question we should accordingly ask is: why use a garden as a talisman, or, in other words, as an object with which to attract divine goodwill? First, because the garden is the ideal setting in which to conform the human spirit to celestial things. As was mentioned earlier, this idea was fully expressed by Ficino: 'Per res igitur temperatas vita permanens in spiritu recreatur. Spiritus per temperata coelestibus conformatur.'[19] But green is the temperate colour par excellence, above all owing to its special relationship with light and its ability to balance black against white. Likewise, the

---

[19] Ficino, *De vita longa*, XIV, in *De vita*: 'through tempered things the spirit is conformed to celestial things' (Eng. trans., p. 206).

virtues of water, another essential component of the garden, are founded on its relationship with light and sight: 'radius quidam est in quadam oculorum aqua naturaliter nobis accensus ac temperatum lumen in aqua quodammodo resistente requirit.'[20] Water, green hills, airy places, trees and grasses, which are likened to the world's hair – all these elements do not exist on their own but form part of the life of the whole and amidst them quivers and throbs the very spirit of the world: 'Item frequenti quodam usu plantarum similiterque viventium, potes e mundi spiritu plurimum haurire.'[21] A predisposition to welcome the spirit of the world was, to use Ficino's words again, merely the first step to capturing the stars and benefiting from them. This could be achieved by imitating celestial things and, after repeatedly emphasising this point, Ficino tackles what was for him a delicate issue, namely the question of the talisman. Without doubt, in fact, according to the hermetic tradition the elements making up the garden represent the essential basis for all magical practice and for the construction of images and talismen. This is confirmed by the *Corpus hermeticum*: 'Et horum, o Trismegiste, deorum, qui terreni habentur, cuiusmodi est qualitas? – Constat, o Asclepi, de herbis, de lapidibus et de aromatibus divinitatis naturalem vim in se habentibus.'[22] But the concept is also clearly expressed in *Picatrix*:

> Et similiter elixir idem in alchimia facit quia leviter convertit corpora de una natura in aliam nobiliorem. . . Et elixir esse non potest noisi compositum ex animalibus, arboribus et vegetabilibus, et de mineris pro una parcium composicionis quemadmodum dicunt qui dicunt quod assimilatur mundo, et mundus est compositus ex rebus illis quas diximus.[23]

The properties of the simple elements which composed the purified nature recreated around Ferrara were therefore increased and the benefits they offered were enhanced if they were organised so as to form figures and images.

Defining the ring of gardens around the walls as a 'talisman' is clearly extending this concept, given that we are not dealing with a small image to be used in magical practices but rather with a large urban construction. And yet this extension appears to be legitimate and is backed by precise references which were indisputably present in the culture of Ferrara at the time. Ficino again writes: 'Stellae nanque fixae si solae spectent, proportionem humanam, idest unius hominis, nimis exsuperant. Proportionem vero cum civitatibus moderatiorem habent.'[24] The idea of surrounding the city with a ring

---

[20] *Ibid*: 'a certain ray kindled by nature in the water of the eyes and it requires a tempered light in water somehow opposing it' (Eng. trans., p. 204).

[21] M. Ficino, *De vita coelitus comparanda*, XI in *De vita*: 'by a frequent use of plants and a similar use of living things, you can draw the most from the Spirit of the World' (Eng. trans., p. 290).

[22] *Corpus hermeticum*, ed. A. D. Nock trans. by A.-J. Festugière (Paris, 1945), vol. II, parts XIII–XVIII, *Asclepius*, p. 349.

[23] *Picatrix*, I, 2, I.

[24] Ficino, *De vita coelitus comparanda*, VII in *De vita*: 'For indeed if the fixed stars alone are in the aspect with her, they excessively overcome the human proportion, I mean, that of one individual; but fixed stars are more commensurate with cities' (Eng. trans., p. 276).

of propitiatory images appears in the passage from *Picatrix*, made famous by Frances Yates, which describes the city of Adocentyn built by Hermes in Egypt.[25]

The four animal figures standing over the doorways to defend the ideal Egyptian city can hardly fail to evoke the apocalyptic vision of the four living creatures[26] which was consolidated by a strong figurative tradition present on the façades of romanesque and gothic cathedrals.[27] Again in the Book of Revelations, the walls of the celestial city adorned with all kinds of precious gems[28] conjure up the image of a city protected by talismans. But there are also other references belonging to a more specifically Hebraic-Christian rather than hermetic tradition. One example, for instance, is the fall of the idols described in the apocryphal Armenian Gospel of the Infancy:

> They arrived in the city of Mesrin, which was inhabited by a large multitude of people. It was a very large city surrounded by high walls. The quarter of the city they entered contained magical statues and every time an enemy threatened to attack or damage the land, all these statues cried out in unison and their cry could be heard throughout the city. And anyone who heard the voice of all these statues recognised it and understood that the country was threatened by some danger. Over the first gate in the walls stood two iron eagles, with copper talons, a male and a female, one on the right and the other on the left. Over the second gate were two animals of prey fashioned in clay and terracotta: on one side a bear and on the other a lion, together with other ferocious beasts made of stone or wood. Above the third gate was a bronze horse, and astride the bronze horse sat the statue of a king, also in bronze, holding a bronze eagle in his hand.[29]

The idea of surrounding and protecting the city with sacred images can be interpreted as a specific instance of the broader tradition which attributes sacred value to the city walls, a tradition which can be backed by numerous canonical references from the

---

[25] 'Iste vero fuit qui orientalem Egipti edificavit civitatem cuius longitudo duodecim miliariorum consistebat, in qua quidem construxit castrum quod in quatuor eius partibus quatuor habebat portas. In porta vero orientis formam aquile posuit, in porta vero occidentis formam tauri, in meridionali vero formam leonis, et in septentrionali conis formam construxit. In eas quidem spirituales spiritus fecit intrare qui voces proiciendo loquebantur; nec aliquis ipsius portas valebat intrare nisi eorum mandato. Ibique quasdam arbores plantavit, in quarum medio magna consistebat arbor que generacionem fructuum omnium apportabat. In summitate vero ipsius castri quandam turrium edificari fecit, que triginta cubitorum longitudinem attingebat, in cuius summitate pomum ordinavit rotundum, cuius color qualibet die usque ad septem dies mutabatur. In fine vero septem dierum priorem quem habueret recipiebat colorem. Illa autem civitas quotidie ipsius mali cooperiebatur colore, et sic civitas predicta qualibet die refulgebat colore. In turris quidem circuitu abundans erat aqua, in qua quidem plurima genera piscium permanebant. In circuitu vero civitatis ymagines diversas et quarumlibet manerierum ordinavit, quarum virtute virtuosi efficiebantur habitantes ibidem et a turpitudine malisque languoribus nitidi. Predicta vero civitas Adocentyn vocabatur. Hi autem in antiquorum scienciis, earum profunditatibus et secretis atque in astronomie sciencia erant edocti' (*Picatrix*, IV, 3, 1); see also F. A. Yates, *Giordano Bruno and the Hermetic Tradition* (London, 1964).

[26] Rev. 4, 6–7.

[27] See E. Mâle, *L'art religieux du XIII siècle en France. Etude sur l'iconographie du Moyen Age et sur ses sources d'inspiration* (Paris, 1922).

[28] Rev. 21, 18–21.

[29] Armenian Infancy Gospel, xv, 6. Excerpts from the apocryphal gospels are taken from B. H. Cowper, *The Apocryphal Gospels and other Documents relating to the History of Christ* (Edinburgh and London, 3rd ed., 1870), and M. R. James, *The Apocryphal New Testament* (Oxford, 1924, 1966). There is no English translation of the Amenian Infancy Gospel, except for a brief resumé in James, pp. 83–4; also see J.K. Elliott, *The Apocryphal New Testament* (Oxford, 1993), pp. 118–119.

scriptures[30] but which also appears, as is well known, in Vitruvius[31] and is extensively recalled and reiterated by Alberti himself.[32]

Alberti goes further to identify a precise and original link between defensive structure and sacrificial rite. The concept is expressed particularly clearly in the passage describing the fortress (*arx*), an element which, as mentioned earlier, is located, like the gardens of Ferrara, 'neque in urbe neque ex urbe'. The fortress, Alberti writes, in ancient times was built to protect the sacred objects from contamination, 'archanumque illic fieri quoddam solitum per virgines sacrificium occultum longeque a vulgi notitia remotissimum.'[33] The wall gardens of Ferrara were also the site of propitiatory sacrifices and, what was more, themselves represented a sacrificial offering to legitimise the city's existence and attract the goodwill of the stars or a divinity. The next step is to identify the divinity to whom these sacrifices were addressed.

We have cited references belonging to two different traditions: hermetic and Hebraic-Christian. The question now arises as to whether the sacrifice celebrated on the walls of Ferrara did not pay homage to different divinities belonging to different religious systems. The desire to serve two religions, on the one hand the Christian faith and on the other ancient Egyptian rites, was certainly typical of Renaissance culture in Ferrara and would require a lengthy digression. For the sake of economy let us take a single episode from *Gerusalemme liberata*.[34] The protagonists of this passage are Aladine and the magician Ismeno, a frequenter of demons who 'a Christian once, Macon he now adores, / Nor could he quite his wonted faith forsake, / But in his wicked arts both oft implores / Help from the Lord, and aide from Pluto blake.' By confusing the two laws, Ismeno urges Aladine to steal the image of the Virgin from the Christian temple and performs his ancient magical rites in front of the 'consecrated image'. As Ismeno promises, his intention is to use the image of the Madonna's face to make the city impregnable: 'Which then I will enchant in wondrous sort, / That while the image in the church doth stay, / No strength of armes shall win this noble fort, / Or shake this puissant wall, such passing might / Haue spels and charmes, if they be said aright.' Therefore, in complete continuity with the tradition referred to earlier, we again find the idea that it is possible to protect and safeguard the city through the use of sacred images. Thereby, however, running the risk of transforming the use of images into a blasphemous practice. In *Gerusalemme* Christianity wins the day; at dawn on the day after its abduction, the profaned image has already mysteriously disappeared from the magician's cave.

---

[30] 'Make the round of Zion in procession, / count the number of her towers, / take good note of her ramparts, / pass her palaces in review, / that you may tell generations yet to come: / Such is God, our God for ever and ever; / he shall be our guide eternally' (Ps. 48, 13–15).

[31] Vitruvius, *De architectura*, IV, 5.

[32] Alberti, *De re aedificatoria*, IV, 3 and VII, 1.

[33] Ibid., V, 3: 'a certain arcane and secret sacrifice was performed there by virgins, away from the eyes of the crowd' (Eng. trans., p. 276).

[34] T. Tasso, *Gerusalemme liberata*, II, 1ff. The English translation is taken from *Godfrey of Bulloigne. A Critical Edition of Edward Fairfax's Translation of Tasso's 'Gerusalemme Liberata'*, ed. K. M. Lea and T. M. Gang (Oxford, 1981), p. 117.

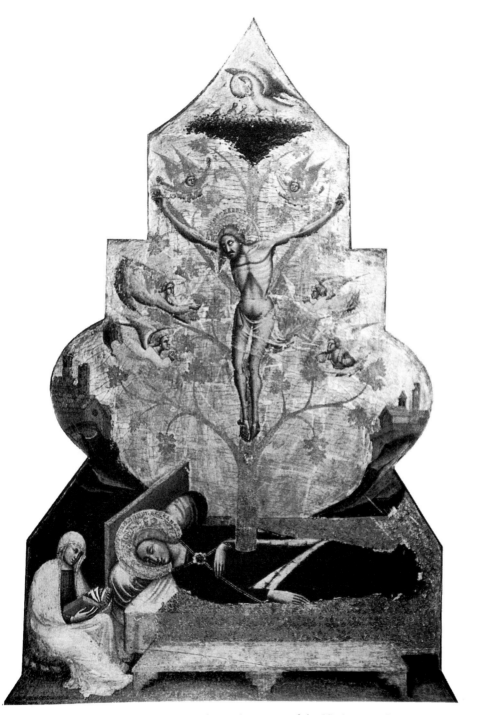

Fig. 3.9 Simone de' Crocifissi. *The Dream of the Virgin*, c. 1360

However, the use of images still implies the risk of idolatry, and precisely in this context the garden offers a further guarantee: the idea of Christ the gardener and healer. Although the apocalyptic description of the heavenly city includes, again in affinity with the Egyptian city of Adocentyn and its vegetation, a tree whose leaves 'serve for the healing of the nations,'[35] and although, in the Gospel according to John, the resurrected Christ appears for the first time to Mary in the guise of a gardener,[36] the idea of Christ the gardener and healer is only fully developed in the Apocrypha. Among a number of examples is the episode in the Gospel of Pseudo-Matthew in which the palm was given renewed life so as to shade Mary or, again from the same source, the episode in which James was healed by Jesus in the kitchen garden.[37] The figure of Christ the gardener portrayed by John is paralleled by the passage in the Gospel of Peter which describes how Joseph, having been handed Christ's body, 'wrapped him in linen and brought him unto his own sepulchre, which is called the Garden of Joseph.'[38] In the Gospel of Nicodemus Jesus is explicitly accused of dealing with demons and practising black magic. Invoking the god Asclepius, Pilate defends him and affirms that healing the sick is not devilry but on the contrary divine work, even if he is then obliged to yield to popular condemnation and decrees that he shall be crucified in the garden in which he was arrested. And again in this evangelical version, Mary asks that Christ's body be buried in a garden.[39] The Acts of Pilate are dominated by the idea of Christ the healer; if not appreciated as a god, it is clear that he should at least have been appreciated as a doctor.[40] In the medieval *Vindicta salvatoris*, Titus, ill and wounded, addresses Nathan saying: 'If ever thou canst find any thing, whether of drugs or of herbs, which can heal the wound which I have in my face, as thou seest, so that I may become well . . . I will bestow upon thee many benefits.' But Nathan replies: 'I am not aware, nor do I know of such things as thou sayest to me. But if thou hadst been in time past in Jerusalem, thou wouldst have found there a chosen prophet whose name was Emanuel.' Titus then curses Tiberius for having given Judaea laws which enabled Christ, his possible healer, to be killed. But as soon as he declares his allegiance to the Lord and evokes his image, he is magically cured and with him all the other invalids present. Later, in the same way, the image of Christ's face impressed on a cloth of gold wrapped in Velosianus' mantle instantly heals Emperor Tiberius and every other sick person present.[41]

The key event in the confrontation between ancient magic and Christianity is of course the visit of the Magi to the newborn Christ. In *De vita* Ficino strategically recalls the episode and interprets it as an act of submission by ancient magic, and hence its legitimisation:

---

[35] Rev. 22, 1–2.   [36] John 20, 13–18.   [37] Gospel of Pseudo-Matthew, XX –XXI and XLI.

[38] Gospel of Peter, VI, 23–4.

[39] Gospel of Nicodemus, or Acts of Pilate (Greek text A), I; IX, 5; XI.

[40] Letter of Tiberius to Pilate.

[41] Vindicta salvatoris (The Revenging of the Saviour) in C. Tischendorf, *Evangelia Apocrypha* (Leipzig, 1852).

Magi stellarum observatores ad Christum vitae ducem stella duce venerunt, pretiosum vitae thesaurum offerentes, aurum, thus et myrrham, tria dona pro tribus planetarum dominis stellarum domino dedicantes. Aurum quidem pro temperamento iovis maxime omnium temperamentum. Thus autem pro Sole praecipue Phoebeo, calore simul odoreque flagrans. Myrrham denique firmantem corpus atque conservantem pro Saturno, omnium firmissimo planetarum.[42]

Ficino appears to wish to introduce the Magi above all as representatives of a Greek-Latin pantheon; in doing so he may have been motivated by prudence, since the idea of a partial continuity between Greek religious culture and Christianity was certainly already an orthodox position fully accepted by patristic and medieval tradition. He was well aware, however, that the Magi really represented another much more ancient culture with radically different implications in terms of the revival of magical practices.[43] In fact he explicitly referred to this culture when he returned to the subject of the Magi's visit in the Apologia addressed to his friends Pietro Neri, Pietro Guicciardini and Pietro Soderini.[44] In an explicit reference to the history of the Chaldaeans, the Persians and the Egyptians, Ficino points to the parallelism between the priesthood and medicine, attributing to Christ 'vitae largitor', with the mandate to heal with herbs and stones.[45] Taking care to condemn in no uncertain terms all profane magic involving demonic dealings, he wonders, on the other hand, why the word magician is so feared when in the Gospels it is accepted as being equivalent to others such as wise man or priest. 'Quidnam profitetur Magus ille venerator Christi primus? Si cupis audire, quasi quidam agricola est, certe quidam mundicola est. Nec propterea mundum hic adorat, quemadmodum nec agricol terram, sed sicut agricola humani victus gratia ad aerem temperat agrum, sic ille

---

[42] Ficino, De vita longa, XIX, in De vita: 'The Magi, observers of the stars, came to Christ, the guide of life, under the guidance of a star; they offered a precious treasury of life – gold, frankincense, myrrh; they dedicated three gifts representing the lords of the planets to the Lord of the stars: gold, that is, representing the temperedness of Jupiter, because gold is the most tempered substance of all; frankincense for the Sun, because it especially glows with Phoebean heat as well as odour; and finally myrrh, which firms up the body and preserves it, for Saturn the most stable of all planets' (Eng. trans., p. 228).

[43] In the canonical gospels the Magi are only described as coming generically from the East (Matt. 2), but the apocryphal gospels are more explicit. In the Armenian Infancy Gospel, for example, after the annunciation to Mary, the angel journeyed 'to the land of the Persians to warn the Magi kings that they should come to adore the newborn child' (V, 10). The Magi who arrived at the time of Christ's birth were Melqon, king of the Persians, Gaspar, king of India and Balthasar, king of Arabia. They presented themselves as the custodians and bearers of a very ancient evidence, of divine origin and indeed paradisiacal provenance: 'The evidence that we possess comes neither from man nor from any other living creature. It is a divine order, concerning a promise that the Lord made to the sons of men, which we have conserved until this day . . . When Adam was forced to leave Paradise, and Cain killed Abel, the Lord God gave Adam Seth, as the son of his consolation, and with him this written document, closed and sealed by the hands of God' (XI). This secret message, whose existence was widely accredited in gnostic circles, heralded the Saviour's coming. The custody of this message by the Magi forms a link of continuity between Christianity and the magical-sapiential tradition of Indian, Arabian and Persian origin.

[44] 'Apologia quaedam, in qua de megicina, astrologia, vita mundi, item de Magis, qui Christum statim natum salutaverunt' (1489, 15 September), appendix to De vita: 'An Apologia Dealing with Medicine, Astrology, the Life of the World, and the Magi who greeted the Christ Child at his birth' (Eng. trans., pp. 394–401).

[45] At the opposite extreme, in a passage which was conclusive and in some ways summed up the cultural developments in Renaissance Ferrara, Pirro Ligorio confirms the possible continuity and consistency between magical practice and theology (cf. Pirro Ligorio, 'Magia', in Delle antichità di Pyrrho Ligorio, XI, fos. 17–17 bis, Archivio di Stato di Torino, Corte, Biblioteca antica).

sapiens, ille sacerdos gratia salutis humanae inferiora mundi ad superiora contemperat.'[46] Ancient magic thus pays homage to the new neonate *magus* and completes a historical circle by handing him the evidence of a wisdom which he and his Father had originally created. Only through death does Christ attain his full power, thus becoming the greatest magician and healer. The Christian idea of the garden as a place of healing was in fact conceived in relation to Christ's death. To return to John's words: 'Now in the place where he was crucified there was a garden, and in the garden a new tomb where no one had ever been laid.' This is immediately followed by Christ's apparition to Mary in the guise of a gardener or caretaker. Eliade has reconstructed the numerous Christian accounts of officinal herbs growing at the foot of the Cross nurtured by Christ's blood.[47] At the cosmic moment of the crucifixion, Christ, immolated in the centre of the world, takes on the suffering of the whole of creation and heals it, generating a mystic solidarity between man and plants. But as Eliade usefully remarks, creation through self-sacrifice is the basis for all building rites by virtue of the conviction that no artificial and constructed object will be animated without sacrifice. This is what Peter means when he says that Christ shall be the 'cornerstone'.[48]

The garden as the place of Christ's sacrifice, as the place of redemption and healing, thus also becomes the setting for the legitimacy of man's work, namely the transformation of nature through artifice. In other words, the image of Christ's sacrifice guarantees the legitimacy of the works skilfully constructed by man and the most correct frame for this image is the garden, a place that is always the fruit of a creation which is partly human – in that it is an artificial space – and partly divine – in that it is a natural space. But this co-presence of man and god in an artificial construction created by man is also the essence of the talisman, a celestial figure made with earthly materials in order to attract divine benevolence to man's works. As was affirmed earlier – and this serves to further clarify the meaning of that affirmation – the garden is the most propitious place for the construction of talismen. In the clash, or encounter, between talisman and the image of Christ's sacrifice we are again faced with the problem of referring to more than one religion.

Although committed to his project for the integration of the ancient genealogy of wise men and Christianity, Ficino tackles the problem of images with extreme caution and his reference to Plotinus' *Enneads* almost appears to be in self-

---

[46] *Apologia*: 'For what does that Magus, the first adorer of Christ, profess? If you wish to hear: on the analogy of a farmer, he is a cultivator of the world. Nor does he on that account worship the world, just as a farmer does not worship the earth; but just as a farmer for the sake of human sustenance tempers his field to the air, so that wise man, that priest, for the sake of human welfare tempers the lower parts of the world to the upper parts' (Eng. trans., p. 396).

[47] Eliade Mircea, 'Ierburile de sub croce...' *Rivista Fundatiilor Regale*, 6 (11) (1939), pp. 353–69.

[48] 'So come to him, our living Stone – the stone rejected by men but choice and precious in the sight of God. Come and let yourselves be built, as living stones, into a spiritual temple; become a holy priesthood, to offer spiritual sacrifices acceptable to God through Jesus Christ. For it stands written: "I lay in Zion a choice corner-stone of great worth. The man who has faith in it will not be put to shame"' (1 Pet. 2, 4–7).

Fig. 3.10 Benvenuto Tisi dello Garofalo, *The Old and New Testaments*, 1523

defence.[49] But, if we attempt to see through his prudence, we find he was unmistakably attracted by the mercurial ability to compose statues using herbs, trees, stones or aromatic substances, namely elements that encompass divine strength. The fact that Ficino does not tackle the problem of the images simply as a commentator on Plotinus' text is demonstrated by the multitude of sources he can cite on this subject: Ptolemy and Haly, the doctor Hahamet, Serapione, Trismegistos, the Magi followers of Zoroaster, the Egyptians, the Chaldaeans, the Jews, Giamblico, Porphyry, Albertus Magnus, Pietro d'Abano, to list them in the chance order in which they are mentioned. And while Ficino initially refers to the doubts expressed on this subject by Thomas Aquinas, 'our guide in theology', he does not refrain from citing a passage from *De fato* in which Thomas affirms that clothes and other products of human art are attributed

[49] When asking Pietro Guicciardini for a defence of *De vita coelitus comparanda*, a work in which he dealt with the problem of images, Ficino wrote: 'curiosis ingeniis respondeto magiam vel imagines non probari quidem a Marsilio, sed narrari, Plotinum ipsum interpretante': 'and reply to intellectual busybodies that Marsilio is not approving magic and images but recounting them in the course of an interpretation of Plotinus' (Eng. trans., *Apologia*, p. 396). The work by Plotinus commented on by Ficino was *Enneads*, III, 11.

Fig. 3.11 Benvenuto Tisi dello Garofalo. *Christ in the Garden of Gethsemane*

certain qualities by the stars.[50] The creation of 'extraordinarily beautiful and almost celestial' things can therefore only take place with the help of heaven and the product of this creation must necessarily embody virtues of considerable efficacy. However, leaving aside Ficino's scarcely convincing doubts regarding the use of images for therapeutic purposes and in the search for an equilibrium with the stars, he continued to be fascinated by the image as a possible point of contact between God and man. But in order for this contact to occur, the image must be *offered* by man to God. This is an explicit reference to the idea of the levitical sacrifice: 'Exploratu quoque dignissimum est Hebraicum illud, in mactandis animalibus rebusque nostris sacrificio dissipandis, mala coelitus imminentia a nobis ad nostra deflecti. Sed haec Pico nostro exploranda relinquimus.'[51] Here again the *exemplum* Ficino evokes is that of Christ's sacrifice. This is stated with utmost clarity in the digression on the cross, the matrix of space, whose long tradition is outlined by Ficino but whose power, he affirms, has always been seen as a portent of the power received from Christ.[52]

---

[50] Ficino, *De vita coelitus*, xxv in *De vita*. The reference to Thomas Aquinas is 'D. Thomae Aquinatis doctoris Angelici', *Opuscola omnia* (Venice, 1587), pp. 360–5.

[51] *De vita coelitus*, xxii in *De vita*: 'It would be very worthwhile to explore that Hebrew notion, namely that in the ritual slaughter of animals and in the scattering of our possessions as a sacrifice, the evils menacing us from the heavens are deflected from us to our possessions. But we leave these things for our friend Pico to explore' (Eng. trans., p. 368).

[52] Ibid., xviii.

Here, therefore, is a theory on the virtue of the image in which Christ's sacrifice is evoked to avert the risk of being accused of idolatry. Ficino was obviously well acquainted with scriptural tradition relating to the dangers of idolatry and, as will be seen shortly, so was the cultural milieu of Ferrara at the time the gardens around the walls were designed and constructed. This is not the place for a detailed discussion of such a complex and tricky problem. It is worth recalling, however, that the first, inevitable reference is the passage relating to the construction of the golden calf in Exodus.[53] This biblical passage clearly outlines the contrast between an idolatrous religion which requires an image, a representation of the divinity to which it can pay homage, and, the written laws of which Moses is the spokesman and whose tablets he shatters in front of the idolaters. In this case Moses' reaction is, after the pulverisation of the idol, a brutal reference to the levitical sacrifice: 'Arm yourselves, each of you, with his sword. Go through the camp from gate to gate and back again. Each of you kill his brother, his friend, his neighbour.' From a Christian and New Testament point of view, the real vanquisher of idolatry is Christ who does not counter the idols with written laws but combats them with their own weapons and overpowers them by offering the visible image of his own sacrifice.[54] The proposal in a Christian context of the reuse of the image as an object of veneration, and therefore also any hypothesis of continuity with magical and hermetic traditions, is countered by the scriptural condemnation, forcefully underlined by Augustine;[55] but the same works offer an instrument to restitute the votive use of the image while maintaining the substance of an ancient tradition. The instrument in question is in fact the icon of Christ born, dead and resurrected. In other words, in order to comply with Christian precepts, the use of the image must not depart from the icon of the crucified Christ and its redeeming virtues.

This affirmation is inevitably true of the large 'talisman' into which the city of Ferrara was set. Reduced to extremely simple terms, the problem can be summarised as follows: could a culture like that of Ferrara between the fifteenth and sixteenth centuries, imbued with hermetism and references to astrological culture, perhaps have surrounded the city with a magical ring of places and propitiatory images without guarding itself against the risk of being accused of idolatry? Certainly not. The wall gardens therefore cannot be other, as we will shortly see, than a reference to the figure of Christ. A reference which naturally does not exclude, but on the contrary legitimises and acquiesces in the reiteration of a pre-Christian tradition of hermetic origin, such as that outlined in *Picatrix*.

Before going on to analyse some of the places belonging to the wall gardens in the

---

[53] Exod. 32.

[54] Numerous scriptural passages mention Christ destroying idols. Among others, see: 1 Cor. 10 (to which we will return shortly); Zech. 12, 2; Isa. 19, 1; Jer. 16, 20; Acts 17, 15–29; Rom. 1, 21–5. Among the apocryphal gospels: Pseudo-Matthew XXII ff; (Greek text A) XVI, 7.

[55] Augustine, *De Civitate Dei*, VIII. In her study of Giordano Bruno, Yates underlined the important role played by Augustine's and Lactantius' opinions of idolatry in relation to Renaissance attitudes towards hermeticism.

terms outlined above, we must first draw a last conclusion of a more general kind. If these gardens cannot be separated from Christ's image, and if moreover the garden must be interpreted as an analogy of Christ, given that it is a place characterised by the co-presence of man and God, clearly the customary topos of the Garden of Eden is not sufficient to explain its significance. This is no longer a garden inhabited by Adam since the gardener here is, to use a term popular with medieval culture, the New Adam, the redeemer who was sacrificed in the place where Adam was first created then buried, he who was crucified on a cross made from the tree of good and evil.[56] First of all, this results in a substantial transformation of the temporal dimension of the garden which, instead of being a place outside time, is transformed into a space in eternity, understood as the triple dimension of the origin, history and final conclusion. Secondly, the garden is transformed from a place of complete naturalness into the emblem of mankind's redeemed work. Not only is artifice not excluded, but on the contrary it is fully justified and legitimised.

The shift from the origins to the centre of history, the transformation of the edenic landscape into a Christological landscape, is decisive for the conception of the garden as a place of healing, namely that which Eden is not and cannot be. A passage from the Gospel of Nicodemus expresses this concept inherent in Christian doctrine with particular clarity:

> And Seth said: Ye prophets and patriarchs, hearken: My father Adam, the first created, laid him down on a time to die, and sent me to make supplication unto God hard by the gate of paradise, that he would lead me by his angel unto the tree of mercy, and I should take the oil and anoint my father, and he should arise from his sickness. Which also I did; and after my prayer an angel of the Lord came and said unto me: What asketh thou, Seth? askest thou for the oil that raiseth up the sick, or for the tree that floweth with that oil, for the sickness of thy father? this cannot be found at this time. Depart therefore and say unto thy father, that after there are accomplished from the creation of the world five thousand five hundred years, then shall the only-begotten Son of God become man and come down upon the earth, and he shall anoint him with that oil, and he shall arise: and with water and the Holy Ghost shall he wash him and them that come out of him. And then shall he be healed of every disease: but now it is not possible that this should come to pass.[57]

The concept is still valid even if the term healing is used, as it has been up to now, in its widest sense to mean both the healing of the body and a programme conceived to protect a city. The wall gardens have the ability to protect Ferrara owing to the fact that they are a place of sacrifice and offering. Christ's uncalled for and voluntary sacrifice serves as a model for the enormous and 'superfluous' effort made to maintain the gardens, an effort which far exceeds the need to meet practical requirements and culminates, through the suspension of all commitments to government and the city's

---

[56] For an overview of this subject see Mâle, *L'art religieux*, in particular: *Livre IV. Le miroir historique*.
[57] Gospel of Nicodemus. Descent into hell (Greek text), III (XIX).

defence, in the creation of a place of quietness. In this case the essence of the garden is the *offering*, the offering of a 'useless' place which, precisely for this reason, is supremely useful to the maintenance of the city's *equilibria*. As a useless offering the wall gardens adorn the city in the most profound sense of the term: as the pure expression and image of legitimised order.[58]

Given that the gardens around the walls of Ferrara form an extremely complex structure made up of numerous elements, we must limit ourselves to a few samples, drawing attention to a few particularly strong and explicit images in the light of what has been said up to now. If space permitted, it would also be equally interesting to make a detailed analysis of all the individual elements, namely those that, to use an expression in line with the general meaning of the programme of which they form part, we might call the 'medicinal plants' used to compose the great 'talisman' protecting the city.

The first element worth considering is, inevitably, that which characterises the ring of gardens and makes their very existence possible, namely the stretch of the river Po which flows beside Ferrara. Pellegrino Prisciani dedicated a number of pages to the Po in his *Historie Ferrariae*,[59] but it is worth focusing on two particular passages. In the first,[60] 'in order to establish the real history of the Po' and its name, Prisciani recounts the myth of Eridanus, 'also known as Phaëton the son of the Egyptian Sun God', who, 'together with many of his companions and the Nile pilot boarded ship and with the help of the winds reached the gulf which they call Ligure', whence he journeyed up the Po. He then fell into the river and was drowned, an episode which led to 'the Po being called Eridanus: the same Eridanus which the Egyptians, in memory of their lost fellow-countryman, included among the heavenly images. Some therefore believe that this episode gave rise to the legend according to which Phaëton was struck down by a thunderbolt and thrown into the Po.'

---

[58] There is no room here to digress on such a complex theme as the profound and original relationship between ornament and order. So as not to move away from the historical context and the specific problem with which we are dealing, it is worth remembering that the idea of the ornament as a supreme but superfluous effort is also expressed by Alberti. An example is given in the passage which describes the two temples built out of gold by Osyris, one dedicated to celestial Jove, and the other to royal Jove, where it is suggested that an entire and vast wall should be constructed using a single stone, especially 'if the stone comes from abroad, and has been conveyed along a difficult route': *De re aedificatoria*, VI, 5 (Eng. trans., p. 163). There is a tendency to create an ornament for the purpose of arousing admiration, and this is best situated in a setting like that of the wall gardens. 'There may be different attractions all around, such as promontories, rocks, heights, chasms, grottoes, springs, and other reasons making it attractive to build there rather than anywhere else': *De re aedificatoria*, VI, 4 (Eng. trans., p. 160). Alberti also maintained that through the use of such marvellous ornaments or 'magical figures' the place or building could acquire extraordinary virtues, as in the case of the four gold birds on the roof of the royal basilica of Babylon which had the 'power to reconcile the mind of the crowd to the heart of the king', or the terrible statue on the temple of Pellene (ibid.). It should be said that Alberti immediately disassociates himself from this form of argument ('Sed dicta haec sint anima gratia': 'But these anecdotes are included for entertainment', Eng. trans., p. 162), but returns to them so often that they appear anything but marginal in the context of his treatise.

[59] P. Prisciani, *Historie Ferrariae*, 15th-16th century, Archivio di Stato di Modena, Mss. Biblioteca, nos. 98 and 129-37. For obvious chronological reasons, Prisciani cannot have taken part in the realisation of the ring of gardens around the walls of Ferrara. As is well known and has already been mentioned, however, he played an important role in the elaboration of the city's programme of redefinition and defence of which the gardens represent a logical and immediate consequence.

[60] Ibid., Ms. no. 129, fol. 27.

Fig. 3.12 P. Prisciani, folio from *Historie Ferrariae*

To support this tale Prisciani cites numerous sources,[61] one of which is particularly significant owing to the manner with which it is presented, in a linguistically involuted style, almost as if wishing to dismiss but at the same time highlight its importance: 'We will silently pass over the fact that Plato in *Timaeus* deduced that this is not merely a tale but expresses a genuine reality in the heavenly orbits and deviations which occur during the world's long passage.' This reference to Plato's narration of the Phaëton myth[62] is used by Prisciani as a means of introducing, in a cryptic and extremely prudent fashion, a number of decisive elements with which to conclude and emphasise his description of the Po. First of all, far from being a simple reference to Greek mythology, this passage indirectly but none the less explicitly evokes a much more ancient culture of Egyptian descent. Or rather, it describes how knowledge was handed down from the Egyptian priests, the depositaries of the most ancient traditions, to the Greek Solon who was regarded by the priests themselves as the representative of a childlike people, ignorant of all genuinely ancient knowledge. Prisciani certainly sees himself as the last heir of the knowledge transmitted by the Egyptian priests to Solon. But if we continue with Plato's text we find the explanation of the myth of Phaëton. Phaëton's unruly course reflects a deviation of the heavenly bodies in orbit around the earth, and therefore an imbalance between celestial and earthly matters; this imbalance leads to catastrophes, droughts or floods, which in Egypt are countered and rendered innocuous by the beneficial action of the Nile. According to the priests, the possibility of safeguarding a genuinely ancient knowledge derives from this action. By avoiding the catastrophe of a clash between heaven and earth the Nile also prevents the destruction of knowledge. By recalling Plato's interpretation of the myth of Phaëton and connecting it to the myth of the Po, Prisciani intends to draw a parallel between the Nile and the river flowing beside Ferrara, attributing to the latter the same power of preserving the equilibrium between Ferrara and the heavenly bodies and thus creating the necessary conditions for inheriting, preserving and transmitting this ancient knowledge. On the other hand, together with an explicit reference to the Nile, Prisciani could have found the idea of bringing water, a temperate element, to the city in a work which was more directly connected to the magical hermetic tradition. In fact, in *Picatrix* we find the story of Behentater, king of India, and the city of Menif which he built. In addition to building 'domum totam ymaginibus circumvolutam, que vero ymagines ab omnibus languoribus curabant, abantur ex ea',

> preterea fecit . . . vas terreum quod implevit aqua, ex quo totus exercitus bibebat, nec aqua minuebatur ex eo. . . Preterea hoc modo facta fuit pila quam fecit Acaym rex Indie

---

[61] He does not cite Pliny (*Naturalis historia*, III, 117ff), with whose works he was well acquainted, perhaps because he thought it was an implicit and too obvious reference. Instead he recalls Polybius and his refusal to give credit to the myth of Phaëton. He then cites Boccaccio (with particular reference to his treatise on classical mythology entitled *De geneaologis deorum gentilium*), Paolo da Perugia (probably with the mythological collection entitled *Collectiones* in mind), Leonzio, who by affinity may be supposed to be the Leonzio Pilato summoned by Boccaccio to the 'Studio fiorentino' in 1360, Sicardo's *Cronica universalis* and other medieval sources, including Jacopo da Varagine.

[62] Plato, *Timaeus*, 21e–22e.

in porta civitatis Nube, que ex marmore nigro fuit facta et erat tota aqua repleta. Et quantumcumque ab ea auferebatur ea minime deficiebat; et erat hoc propter quod humiditates aeris virtute magisterii quo fuit facta attrahebat. Hoc vero opus contruxit ad populi restauracionem propter distanciam euisdem civitatis a flumine Nili et eius propinquitatem mari salso.[63]

However, these references to Greek and hermetic traditions are not sufficient and, as can be inferred from the caution with which Prisciani introduces them, also involve a risk in terms of Christian orthodoxy.[64] The second passage from *Historie Ferrariae* to which it is worth drawing attention in fact contains the necessary corrections and completion.[65] This time Prisciani explicitly refers to Pliny's passage dedicated to the Po, but this is only an expedient to cite the classical text in a discourse of a completely different nature. Pliny in fact merely affirms that, during its course, the Po flows through an underground stretch and then resurfaces further on. Prisciani's account of how the Po once completely dried up close to a cave and then reappeared almost miraculously *in the same place* has very different implications: 'Iterum exoritur / aqua ipsa ibi mirabiliter scaturiens.' On the one hand, the drought episode is an implicit reference to the myth of Phaëton and, on the other, the idea of death and resurrection is an explicit and direct Christological reference, a fact which is borne out by the terminology used throughout the passage. Any possible doubts are dispelled by the image Prisciani uses to illustrate the text: the river 'dies and is resurrected' beside a cave excavated in a mountain. The fact that the image of a cave excavated in a mountain is a precise evangelical reference to Christ's death and resurrection is all too obvious. However, we find this very same image, no longer drawn but actually built, set into the ring of gardens around the walls: namely, the Mountain of Saint George. The inclusion of a cross in the far right-hand corner of Prisciani's drawing only serves to underline the significance of the tale, should this still be necessary (fig. 3.12).

Before moving on to the Mountain of Saint George, it is worth pausing for a moment to examine the Belvedere island which rises above the waters of the Po. Of all the wall gardens this is the place which has inspired the richest literary output. Traditionally, it is one of the most outstanding examples of edenic gardens, but other scenes with considerable emblematic impact which were carefully constructed on the island evoke other meanings. For example, there can be little doubt about the interpretation of the wood growing out of the bare ground containing four benches and an enormous rock out of which spurts a jet of water. In the first place the image contains a precise reference to Revelations, which is somewhat out of place in the supposedly celestial nature of the setting. 'The first [angel] blew his trumpet; and there

[63] *Picatrix*, IV, 5.

[64] The letter to Eleonora d'Aragona dated 26 October 1487, published and made famous by A. Warburg (*Gesammelte Schriften. . .*, vol. II, pp. 480–81), is a good example of the prudence with which Prisciani refers to the magical tradition as well as his awareness and fear of being accused of idolatry. On this, and also for a general overview of Prisciani, see A. Rotondò, 'Pellegrino Prisciani', in *Rinascimento*, 9 (1960), pp. 69–110.

[65] Prisciani, *Historie Ferrariae*, Ms. no. 129, fol.17v.

came hail and fire mingled with blood, and this was hurled upon the earth. A third of the earth was burnt, a third of the trees were burnt, all the green grass was burnt.'[66] In the light of what has been said, it comes as no surprise to find that this passage from Revelations is immediately followed by a condemnation of idolatry: 'The rest of mankind who survived these plagues did not abjure the gods their hands had fashioned, nor cease their worship of devils and of idols made from gold, silver, bronze, stone and wood, which cannot see or hear or walk.' Clearly, the rock which spouts water close to the four benches is a reproduction of the rock which Moses struck causing water to spring forth.[67] In Paul's reinterpretation in his first Letter to the Corinthians, the rock personifies Christ. And Paul also includes a warning against idolatry, thus confirming the apocalyptic message:

> I mean, they all drank from the supernatural rock that accompanied their travels – and that rock was Christ. And yet, most of them were not accepted by God, *for the desert was strewn with their corpses*. These events happened as symbols to warn us not to set our desires on evil things, as they did. Do not be idolaters, like some of them; as Scripture has it, *'the people sat down to feast and rose up to revel'* ... So then, dear friends, shun idolatry.[68]

Lastly, it should be noted that Augustine uses the same combination of citations against idolatry in a passage in *De civitate dei*.[69] This is therefore a concrete example of how the image of Christ is evoked within the gardens to counteract the revival of a magical hermetic tradition and to ward off the risk of idolatry.

The image created by the Mountain of Saint George is even more explicit. Explicit, but still ambivalent. On the one hand, the cave is a clear evocation of the figure of Christ, his resurrection and also his birth which, according to an Oriental apocryphal tradition which appears to have been particularly popular in Ferrara, took place in a cave.[70] An illustration of Christ's birth in a grotto or cave can in fact be found in *Presepe* by Garofalo (fig. 3.13),[71] a painter who, as was seen earlier, collaborated artistically in the realisation of the Mountain of Saint George complex. On the other hand, however, the cave is the typical setting for the exercise of magic, indeed it is almost the tangible embodiment of magical practice, as is clear from Pirro Ligorio's definition of magic, to cite a source close to the city of Ferrara. He writes that 'Magicians all over the world practised [their arts] in dens, in the Earth's secret lairs, in sanctuaries under Caves.'[72]

Within the space of a few lines it is obviously not possible to examine in detail the numerous scriptural definitions of the mount or the links through which, in New Testament terms, it is virtually identified with the figure of Christ. However, the

---

[66] Rev. 8, 7.
[67] Exod. 17, 5–6. See also, in the Armenian Infancy Gospel (XVII, 4) the episode in which Jesus makes water spout from a cliff by touching it with a rod.   [68] 1 Cor. 10, 4.   [69] Augustine, *De Civitate Dei*, 8.24.
[70] On the tradition of Christ's birth in a cave rather than in a stable, see Pseudo-Matthew, XIII, 2 and XVIII, 1; Armenian Infancy Gospel, VIII, 5.
[71] Garofalo (Benvenuto Tisi), *Presepe* (first decade of 16th century, Pinacoteca di Ferrara).
[72] P. Ligorio, 'Magia'.

Fig. 3.13 Benvenuto Tisi dello Garofalo. *Nativity*, c. 1510

mountain and cave are an almost overly explicit reference to the figurative tradition
generated by the legend of Saint George, as is openly confirmed by the fact that the
garden in Ferrara is dedicated to the saint. And, according to the description in
Revelations, the dragon's prime adversary is naturally Christ. In this instance the
dragon appeared in the heavens 'and with his tail he swept down a third of the stars . . .
and flung them to the earth,'[73] an act which certainly recalls the deviation of the
heavenly bodies provoked by Phaëton–Eridanus and offset by the Po–Nile. But in
other biblical passages the dragons, which first attack man and then bow down before
Jesus, emerge from a cave. A prime example occurs in the Gospel of Pseudo-Matthew
whose extensive influence on medieval literary and artistic culture is well known.[74] If

[73] Rev. 12, 4.

[74] 'And when they had come to a certain cave and wished to rest in it, the blessed Mary came down from the beast, and sat and
     held the child Jesus in her lap. Now there were with Joseph three youths, and with Mary a certain damsel, who went on
     their way at the same time; and behold there suddenly came out of the cave many dragons, seeing which the youths cried
     out through excessive fear. Then Jesus, descending from his mother's lap, stood on his feet before the dragons, and they
     adored Jesus and then departed from them' (Pseudo-Matthew, XVIII, 1).

we then turn to the version of Saint George's exploits as narrated by Jacopo da Varagine in *The Golden Legend*, a text which was also influenced by the evangelical version of the Gospel of Pseudo-Matthew, we can see how the topic is linked to the questions acknowledged by the wall gardens of Ferrara: the 'pestilential dragon' presses as far as the city walls, threatening it and contaminating the air with its breath; its defeat by Saint George, perhaps armed with a cross and certainly in the name of Christ, causes a spring to well up whose water heals the sick; immediately after defeating the dragon, Saint George pledges himself to the struggle against idolatry.[75] And a number of dragons, albeit willing to bow down to the Saint George–Christ figure evoked by the setting, certainly inhabited not only the grottoes but also the high areas inside the wall gardens around Ferrara, which were likewise used as the setting for non-orthodox magical practices. We need only recall, for example, the procedure described in *Picatrix* for the purpose of attracting the king's goodwill: 'Postea accipe ymaginem et predictam suffumigacionem et unum thuribulum, et supra altum montem ascendas, a quo illam civitatem videre possis.'[76] In the same work we also find the description of a place in which: 'invenitur absinthium, in qua est mons in cuius cacumine emanatur aqua ipsius montis partes decurrens, et antequam planiciem circa ipsum monte attingat coagulatur et in alumen album convertitur'.[77] The mount in the Belvedere garden was constructed in precisely the same way: a hill out of whose summit rose a jet of water which was ducted through small terracotta channels as it ran down the slopes to reach level ground. Certainly this is a surprisingly detailed reference, but the image of the channels containing the water gushing from a single spring on the hilltop can hardly fail to remind us of the water which Jesus channelled into small pools and made clear:

> This little child Jesus when he was five years old was playing at the ford of a brook: and he gathered together the waters that flowed there into pools, and made them straightway clean ... But the son of Annas the scribe was standing there with Joseph; and he took a branch of willow and dispersed the waters which Jesus had gathered together. And when Jesus saw what was done, he was wroth and said unto him: O evil, ungodly and foolish one, what hurt did the pools and the waters do thee? behold, now also thou shalt be withered like a tree, and shalt not bear leaves, neither root, nor fruit. And straightway that lad withered up wholly ...[78]

This image of Christ engaged in the construction of channels to control and purify the waters, Christ the Lord of Fertility, Christ the gardener, may serve as a resonant conclusion to this search for the literary and iconographical references necessary to explain the images which surrounded Ferrara and encircled it with a chain of propitious symbols.

---

[75] See Jacopo da Varagine, *Legenda aurea*, for the tale relating to St. George, Eng. trans., *The Golden Legend* (Manchester, 1878). [76] *Picatrix*, III, 10, 14 [77] Ibid., III, 26.

[78] This excerpt is taken from the Gospel of Thomas (Greek text A), II–III, K, but ther are other versions of the same episode.

APPENDIX

The following is a concise bibliography of works in chronological order, relating to Ferrara's wall gardens: L. Carbone, 'De amoenitate, utilitate, magnificentia Herculei Barchi (1475-76)', Biblioteca Vaticana, Mss. Lat. 8761, fos. 1–24, or Mss. Lat. 8618, fos. 165–82, quoted in A. Lazzari, *Il 'Barco' di Lodovico Carbone* (Ferrara, 1919); G.C. Bordoni (or G.C. Scaligero), 'Julii Caesaris Bordoni Elysium Atestinum ad divam Isabellam Estensem Mantuae Marchionissam', (1519-1520?), Biblioteca Comunale di Ferrara, Mss. II.154, quoted in H.F. Longianesi, 'Commentariolum de Julii Caesaris Bordonii Elyso', in *Raccolta ferrarese di opuscoli* (Venice, 1780), vol. v, p. 192; S. Balbo, *Pulcher visus. Locus Illustriss. Ducis Ferrariae*, c. 1530, quoted in S. Ferraguti, *Per laurea in legge di Alberto Zaina* (Ferrara, n.d. [1879]); A. Steuco da Gubbio, *Cosmopoeia*, Sebastianum Gryphium (Lugduni, 1535); Giovanni di Santafoca, *Cronaca* (1536), partial transcription in P. L. Bagatin, *La tarsia rinascimentale a Ferrara. Il coro di S. Andrea* (Florence, 1991), pp. 105–6; P. Giovio, *De vita et rebus Alfonsi atestini Ferrariae principis* (Florence, 1550). Trans. by G. B. Gelli as *La Vita di Alfonso da Este Duca di Ferrara* (Venice, n.d.); C. Calcagnini, *Carminum Libri* III, in G. B. Pigna, *Carminum Lib. quatuor, ad Alphonsum Ferrariae principem*, ex officina erasmiana Vincentii Valgrisii (Venice, 1553); G. B. Giraldi, *Ab epistolis de Ferraria et Atestinis Principibus Commentariolum*, ex L. G. Gyraldi Epitome Deductum, per Franciscum Rubeum, Ferrariae MDLVI, Ital. trans. in G. B. Giraldi, *Commentario delle cose di Ferrara et dè Principi da Este* (Venice, n.d. [1598?]); G. Sardi, *Historie ferraresi* (Ferrara, 1556); L. Alberti, *Descrittione di tutta Italia* (Venice, 1568); O. Della Rena, 'Relazione dello Stato di Ferrara', 1589, Biblioteca Comunale di Ferrara, Mss., quoted in G. Agnelli, 'Relazione dello stato di Ferrara di Orazio della Rena (1589)', *Atti e Mem. della Dep. Ferr. di St. Patria* (1896), vol. VIII, pp. 255–322; A. Faustini, *Aggiunta alle Historie del signor Gasparo Sardi nuovamente composte dal sig. dott. Agostino Faustini ferrarese. Libro primo*, in *Libro delle Historie ferraresi del sig. Gasparo Sardi*, (Ferrara, 1646); L. Schrader, *Ferrariae Urbis descriptio, et monumenta*, in Graevius, *Tesaruus antiquitatum et historiarum Italiae* (Lugduni Batavorum, 1722), vol. VII, p. 1. G. A. Scalabrini, *Memorie istoriche delle Chiese di Ferrara e dei suoi Borghi* (Ferrara, 1773); A. Frizzi, *Memorie per la storia di Ferrara*, with additions and notes by C. Laderchi, 5 vols. (Ferrara, 1847-48; 1st ed., 1790); A. F. Trotti, 'Le delizie di Belvedere illustrate', in *Atti e Mem. della Dep. Ferr. di St. Patria* (1889), vol. II, pp. 1–32; A. Solerti, 'Ferrara e i luoghi di delizia degli Estensi,' in *Ferrara e la Corte Estense nella seconda metà del secolo decimosesto* (Città di Castello, 1891); F. Borgatti, 'La pianta di Ferrara nel 1597', in Atti e Mem. della Dep. Ferr. di St. Patria (1895), vol. VII, pp. 7–27; P. Sella, 'Inventario testamentario dei beni di Alfonso II d'Este', in *Atti e Mem. della Dep. Ferr. di St. Patria* (1931), vol. XXVIII, pp. 131–395; G. Pazzi, *Il 'Belvedere' ferrarese nei versi di Ariosto e di Balbo* (Rome, 1933); G. Pazzi, *Le delizie estensi e lo Ariosto* (Pescara, 1993); J. F. C. Richards, 'The "Elysium" of Julius Caesar Bordonius (Scaliger)', *Studies in the Renaissance*, 9 (1962), pp. 195–217; L. Chiappini, *Gli Estensi* (Milan, 1967); G. Venturi, "Picta poësis": ricerche sulla poesia e il giardino dalle origini al Seicento,' in *Storia d'Italia. Annali, 5. Il Paesaggio* (Turin, 1978 *et seq.*). Over and above any bibliographical references the basis for any research on this topic is the wealth of documentation preserved in the Modena State Archives.

CHAPTER 4

THE GARDENS OF VILLAS IN THE VENETO FROM THE FIFTEENTH TO THE EIGHTEENTH CENTURIES

MARGHERITA AZZI VISENTINI[*]

The so-called 'civiltà delle ville venete' represents a unique phenomenon within the context of the history of the villa in Italy.[1] The time span is an extremely long one, stretching from the period immediately following Venetian occupation of the mainland at the beginning of the fifteenth century to the decline of the Serenissima at the end of the eighteenth century, and even beyond. The area over which these villas spread was likewise extremely far-reaching: it involved almost the entire area under Venetian rule, stretching from the Adriatic coast and the Po to the Alpine foothills, from the Isonzo to the Mincio, and included a few thousand examples. As a result, the typology of the villas was also extremely varied. This was dictated both by the differing environmental settings in which the villas were located and the specific function which they were expected to fulfil. In fact, and herein lies a partial explanation of the phenomenon, villas in the Veneto were not merely used to escape from urban *negotia*, taking refuge in rural *otia*, as was most often the case in other regions of the peninsula, in accordance with the ideology of villa life which had spread throughout Italy following the rediscovery of the ancient world; they were also called upon to comply with a specific policy of agricultural exploitation of the Po river plain. Therefore, they were

---

[*]Translated by Lucinda Byatt.

[1] There is a vast bibliography on villas in the Veneto: there follow a few relatively recent works with extensive bibliographies. For details of studies prior to 1969 prompted by renewed interest following the travelling exhibition organised by Giuseppe Mazzotti in 1952, see L. Puppi, 'Rassegna degli studi sulle ville venete (1952-1969)', *L'Arte*, 7–8 (1969), pp. 215–6.

    B. Brunelli and A. Callegari, *Ville del Brenta e degli Euganei* (Milan, 1931); G. Mazzotti (ed.), *Le ville venete*, Exhibition catalogue (Treviso, 1953); G. Mazzotti, *Ville venete* (Rome, 1963); J. Ackerman, *Palladio's Villas* (New York, 1967); A. Alpago Novello, *Le ville della provincia di Belluno* (Milan, 1968); G. G. Zorzi, *Le ville e i teatri di Andrea Palladio* (Venice, 1969); A. Canova, *Ville del Polesine* (Rovigo, 1971); R. Cevese, *Ville della provincia di Vicenza* (Milan, 1980); C. Semenzato, *Le ville del Polesine* (Vicenza, 1975); G. F. Viviani (ed.), *La villa nel veronese* (Verona, 1975); G. Venturini, *Il Terraglio e le sue ville* (Mogliano Veneto, 1977); G. B. Tiozzo, *Il Palladio e le ville fluviale* (Venice, 1981); C. B. Tiozzo, *Le ville del Brenta* (Lizza Fusina, 1982); G. F. Viviani, *Ville della Valpolicella* (Verona, 1983); M. Muraro, *Civiltà delle ville venete* (Udine, 1986); E. Bassi, *Ville della provincia di Venezia* (Milan, 1987); J. Ackerman, 'Palladio's villas and their predecessor', in idem, *The Villa. Form and Ideology of Country Houses* (Princeton, N.J., 1990), pp. 89–107; D. Battilotti, *Le ville di Palladio* (Milan, 1990); P. Holberton, *Palladio's Villas* (London, 1990); M. Azzi Visentini, *La villa in Italia: Quattro e Cinquecento* (Milan, 1995), pp. 221–94, with bibliography.

not located solely in pleasant sites on high ground which were particularly attractive from the landscape point of view that thereby make short stays as pleasing as possible, as happened in Tuscany, Lazio, Liguria and other parts of Italy famous for their *villeggiature*. On the contrary, given the socio-economic reasons underlying the extraordinary abundance of villas within Venetian territory, in many cases they were perforce located in areas of limited attraction, such as the flat, monotonous stretches of the tidewater land south of Padua, most of which was originally marshy and malaria-ridden. Although these areas were drained by major land-reclamation operations carried out as part of a complex programme to exploit uncultivated ground, they still suffered from considerable humidity and were enshrouded in mist for most of the year.[2]

In addition to the quantity and quality of the villas, of which only a limited number have survived with gardens in a reasonable state of preservation, it is worth drawing attention to the wealth of both manuscript and printed, iconographic and literary documentation on this subject, which has been considerably added to by research carried out during the past few years.[3] A number of recent studies have highlighted the different features of the gardens belonging to Veneto villas and readers are referred to these for a more detailed analysis.[4]

All this has persuaded me to attempt a new type of approach to the topic, which for obvious reasons cannot be used for villas in other areas of Italy, namely an approach based on the relationship between the structure of the garden and that of the site on which the villa was built. Critics have always insisted on the harmonious relationship which grew up during Renaissance and Baroque Italy between the villa – the term is used here in its traditional context to mean the entire complex of which the palace, or 'Master's residence', and garden form part – and the nature which surrounded it. In

[2] On the question of land reclamation, see A. Ventura, 'Considerazioni sull'agricoltura veneta e sulla accumulazione originaria del capitale nei secoli XVI e XVII', *Studi Storici* 9 (1968), pp. 674–722; V. Fontana, 'Alvise Cornaro e la terra', in L. Puppi (ed.), *Alvise Cornaro e il suo tempo*, Exhibition catalogue (Padua, 1980), pp. 120–8; D. Cosgrove, 'The geometry of landscape: practical and spectacular arts in sixteenth-century Venetian land territories', in *The Iconography of Landscape*, ed. D. Cosgrove and S. Daniels (Cambridge and New York, 1988), pp. 254–76.

[3] B. Aikema, 'A French Garden and the Venetian Tradition', *Arte Veneta*, 34 (1980), pp. 127–37; M. Azzi Visentini, 'Note sul giardino veneto: aggiunte e precisazioni', *Arte Veneta*, 37 (1983), pp. 77–89; idem, 'Descrizioni di giardini e di ville del Veneto', *Libro e incisione a Venezia e nel Veneto nei secoli XVII e XVIII* (Vicenza, 1988), pp. 61–80; idem, 'Fonti per lo studio dei giardini', in *Paradisi ritrovati*, ed. M. P. Cunico and D. Luciani (Milan, 1991), pp. 15–32; idem, '"Et in Arcadia ego" Innovazioni e tradizione nel giardino veneto del Settecento', *I Tiepolo e il Settecento vicentino*, Exhibition catalogue (Milan, 1990), pp. 350–81; idem, 'Francesco Muttoni architetto di giardini: Villa Trissino-Marzotto a Trissino', *Arte Veneta*, 44 (1993), pp. 34–47.

[4] C. E. Pauly, *Der venezianische Lustgarten* (Strassburg, 1916); L. Puppi, 'The villa garden of the Veneto from the fifteenth to the eighteenth century', in *The Italian Garden*, ed. D. Coffin (Washington, D.C., 1972), pp. 83–114; C. A. Ruffo, 'I giardini delle ville', in Viviani, *La villa nel veronese* pp. 185–210; L. Puppi, 'L'ambiente, il paesaggio, il territorio', *Storia dell'arte italiana*, IV: *Ricerche spaziali e tecnologiche* (Turin, 1980), pp. 43–99; M. Azzi Visentini, *L'Orto Botanico di Padova e il giardino del Rinascimento* (Milan, 1984), pp. 149–241; idem, 'Per un profilo del giardino a Venezia e nel Veneto', *Comunità*, 187 (Nov. 1985), pp. 258–93; M. Azzi Visentini (ed.), *Il giardino veneto dal tardo medioevo al novecento* (Milan, 1988); A. Conforti Calcagni, 'Giardini di città e di villa: dalla simbologia medioevale alla razionalità illuministica', in *L'architettura a Verona nell'età della Serenissima (sec. XV - sec. XVIII)*, ed. P. Brugnoli and A. Sandrini (Verona, 1988), 2 vols., I, pp. 347–413; F. Venuto, *Giardini del Friuli Venezia-Giulia. Arte e storia* (Pordenone, 1991); *Giardini di Vicenza* (Vicenza, 1993).

many cases the view which could be enjoyed from the villa represented its true *raison d'être* (one need only think of the fifteenth-century Medici villa at Fiesole or the villas in Frascati). As will be seen later, special care was dedicated to the environmental location of these country residences within the territory of the Serenissima, a fact which is only partly explained by the Venetians' sensitivity to nature and the landscape, amply demonstrated by sixteenth-century painting. In the text of their treatises on the villa, architects such as Palladio and Scamozzi – the first of whom was, generally speaking, more sparing in terms of the information he included – focused particular attention on the site in which the complex was located; they dwelled with evident satisfaction on the description of the 'beautiful views' which could be admired from inside the building or from its immediate vicinity, irrespective of whether these took the form of a picturesque natural environment or an idyllic rural landscape only marginally touched by human intervention, or were completely artificial, such as an orderly cultivated countryside or even the view of a distant town. By doing so they emphasised the decisive role played by the site in the definition of a project.[5]

While being fully aware of the difficulties of generalisation, in particular because any such attempt will always jeopardise the individuality of the single artistic expression, it seems possible, selecting from the infinite range of possibilities, to identify three basic types among the extremely heterogeneous series of villas referred to above, which corresponded to three distributive and formal schemes in which specific solutions have been adopted in response to specific conditions.

Let us start by taking the most commonplace site. The majority of Veneto villas are located 'on completely flat terrain',[6] standing 'in the centre of the estate', a position whose limited attractions in terms of climate and landscape were not paralleled, at least during the sixteenth century, by the pleasure villas in other parts of Italy. However, such a site was recommended by Palladio and later by Scamozzi in the case of an aristocratic residence which must also serve as the management centre of an agricultural estate, as was the case with the majority of Veneto villas situated on the plain.

These buildings, which were generally unhampered by environmental restrictions, gave the architect complete freedom of expression, allowing him to exercise his art to make up for the drawbacks of the site. The garden played a dual role in these projects in that it was conceived not only to fulfil the traditional function of a place for

[5] A. Palladio, *I quattro libri dell'architettura* (Venezia, 1570), II, pp. 45–78; V. Scamozzi, *L'idea della architettura universale*, 2 vols. (Venice, 1615), vol. I, book III, pp. 266–349. See M. Azzi Visentini, 'Vincenzo Scamozzi e il giardino veneto', in *L'architettura a Roma e in Italia (1580-1621)*, ed. G. Spagnesi, Congress proceedings (Rome, 1989), pp. 243–53, 514–16; Azzi Visentini, '"Et in Arcadia"', p. 359. On relations between the villa and its surroundings, see E. Forssman, '"Del sito da eleggersi per le fabriche di villa". Interpretazione di un testo palladiano', *Bollettino del Centro Internazionale di Studi di Architettura A. Palladio*, 9 (1969), pp. 149–62; G. Suitner Nicolini, 'Per una lettura urbanistica delle ville venete. Proposta di una tipologia territoriale', *Bollettino del Centro Internazionale di Studi di Architettura A. Palladio*, 15 (1973), pp. 447–65; L. Benedetti, 'Giardino, paesaggio, territorio', in Azzi Visentini (ed.), *Il giardino veneto*, pp. 281–301; M. Azzi Visentini, 'Architettura, giardino, paesaggio. Un saggio di lettura: le ville venete', *Il Veltro*, 35 (1991), 1–2. pp. 39–61.

[6] Scamozzi, *L'idea della architettura*, p. 325.

'recreation',[7] as an open-air extension of the palace to which it was directly linked, but also to provide numerous 'beautiful vistas' from within the building, thus compensating for the lack of panorama offered by the flat and monotonous stretches of farmed fields.

The villa was generally located within a rectangular enclosed area, laid out symmetrically to either side of a central axis which ran through the entire complex lengthways like a fish's backbone, from one end to the other, crossing through the centre of the owner's residence, right through the large hall at the core of the building. If the villa did not overlook a road or waterway, the central axis continued on one side along the straight avenue which connected it to the nearest public road, whereas on the opposite side the avenue led into the countryside. There was sometimes also a second axis perpendicular to the first with which it intersected in the centre of the owner's residence, the fulcrum of the whole complex, thus establishing the spatial coordinates governing the entire layout.

Laid out in this manner the villa became part of the rhythmic division of the rural landscape of the Venetian *padanìa*, reinforcing rather than interrupting the reticulated pattern based on the Roman process of *centuriazione*—traces of which, given added emphasis by the typical rows of trees festooned with vines so admired by Montaigne, are still visible today in various areas—and then subsumed into the grid of canals used to channel the slack waters that had invaded most of this region.

Within the villa's boundaries the various elements were laid out according to a pattern which, already established between the fifteenth and sixteenth centuries, became increasingly precise and complex over time: in the centre lay the entry court surrounded by low, symmetrical porticoed buildings containing the working quarters and sometimes flanked by towers used as dovecotes or for other purposes; at the back in the centre stood the owner's residence behind and alongside which lay the gardens, adjoining the *brolo*. The kitchen garden lay close to the working quarters and beyond it were the fields. Later, the chapel, guesthouse and ballroom would be added in separate buildings, while over time the owner's section tended to become increasingly isolated from the working buildings involved in running the estate. We sometimes find a bird-trap at the far end of the garden which was used for shooting tiny birds, a favourite villa pastime during the seventeenth and eighteenth centuries,[8] and which replaced the medieval *barco* used for hunting.

An essential requirement of these villas was that nothing should block the view of the 'palazzo' from the surrounding area and, vice versa, its outlook to the countryside which in some instances was framed by an attractive vista of distant mountains, since the owner's residence provided a clear visual symbol as the hub of the farmland belonging to the family. For this purpose it was recommended that the villa should be built 'on a site elevated at least to eye level by Nature or by Art, a result which can be

---

[7] Ibid., p. 323.   [8] A. Acanti, *Il Roccolo, ditirambo* (Venice, 1754); Azzi Visentini, '"Et in Arcadia"', p. 361.

achieved with Skill: so that passers-by see the plane of the building as the horizon', and likewise that when 'standing in the middle [of the owner's residence] there should be a good view of those passing by and also the trees and flowers, and the other delights of the courtyards and Gardens'.[9] The entire villa therefore, and not only the loggia, a transition stage between interior and exterior, was transformed into a 'theatre' from which to enjoy a view of the surrounding area, a concept which was most fully expressed in Palladio's Rotonda. Two expedients were used to give the owner's residence the necessary pre-eminence in the event that it was sited on the plain. Scamozzi observed that in this case a moderate height would be sufficient since 'insufficient height did not bestow dignity, and too much was inconvenient to climb up and detracted from the convenience of being able to see out'.[10] First, without upsetting the traditional layout of a single floor surmounted by a low attic, the villa was built over a high basement which was also useful as protection against damp. The external central staircase leading directly up to the loggia outside the public rooms emphasised its temple-like character and was sealed off at the top by the pediment, whose pinnacle 'gave added height to the centre in relation to the sides'.[11] The 'majesty' of the building was then further underlined by being positioned on a site which was as open as possible, both at the front on the courtyard side and at the back where the garden appeared like a multicoloured carpet of flowers, so as to 'leave the horizontal view unhindered'.[12]

The layout of the gardens was akin to that of the surrounding area.[13] The ground, which was made to slope slightly and imperceptibly into or away from the centre so as to facilitate water drainage, was divided into even squares by a series of straight parallel paths. The uniform, elongated structure of the service quarters, *barchesse,* greenhouses and so on, the garden's architectural elements, such as pergolas and trellises, as well as an irrigation system in the form of canals and rectangular fish-ponds, all emphasised a linear layout which was only interrupted by the semicircular courtyards and gardens reflecting the low, curving porticoes which occasionally surrounded the main residence.

Within this simple layout the range of ornamental features became increasingly more varied and refined over time in order to match the requirements of the increasingly sophisticated ritual of villa life and entertainment. The garden played a prominent role as the setting for banquets, concerts and various entertainments, as is clearly shown in paintings, drawings and engravings (fig. 4.1).[14] The labyrinths, fish-ponds, loggias, nymphaea, grottoes, aviaries and belvederes which had already been present in the sixteenth century were now joined by theatres of greenery, menageries, small temples, rabbit warrens and diverse pavilions. There was a striking increase in the number of

---

[9] Scamozzi, *L'idea della architettura*, p. 270.   [10] Ibid.   [11] Palladio, *I quattro libri*, p. 48.

[12] Scamozzi, *L'idea della architettura*, p. 280.   [13] Cosgrove, 'The geometry of landscape'.

[14] The villa pastimes which for preference took place in the garden were sport, music, reading and learned conversation, as is borne out by several sixteenth-century fresco cycles and other iconographic evidence. In this context it is worth recalling the painting by Pozzoserrato in the Civic Museum in Treviso. G. Crosato, *Gli affreschi nelle ville venete del Cinquecento* (Treviso, 1962).

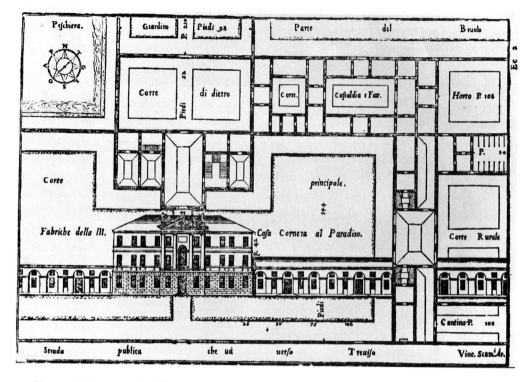

Fig. 4.1 V. Scamozzi, Villa Cornaro, called 'Il Paradiso', at Castelfranco Veneto (Treviso),
from *L'idea della architettura universale* (Venice, 1615)

statues, paralleled by their increasingly varied repertoire, and in the intricacy and
complexity of watercourses. However, because of the nature of the land and the need
to use water to irrigate the fields, we do not find the spectacular water architecture and
sophisticated hydraulic devices in the Veneto gardens which had brought fame to the
gardens of Tivoli, Bagnaia, Frascati and Pratolino. Running water was rarely used. At
most, it lay still in basins and fish-ponds reminiscent of the lagoon environment and
peacefully flowing rivers and canals, above all the Brenta canal which over time had
become a much sought-after site for aristocratic country villas.[15] The still waters
reflected the two features which helped to give the Veneto gardens their unique
character: an abundance of statues and plants in vases. Using the soft, easily worked and

[15] Scamozzi was among the first to recognise that 'of all the roads in Italy (not to mention elsewhere) there is none that can
   equal that from Padua to Lizzafucina, which runs 20 miles or more along the Brenta and is crowded with people and
   merchandise at almost all times of year.' Scamozzi, *L'idea della architettura*, p. 270. The villas along the Brenta were then
   immortalised in paintings by Coronelli, Volkamer and Costa. V. Coronelli, *La Brenta quasi borgo della città di Venezia luogo di
   delizie dei Veneti Patrizi* (Venice, 1711); J.C. Volkamer, *Continuation der Nürnbergischen Hesperidum* (Nuremberg, 1714);
   G. F. Costa, *Delizie del fiume Brenta espresse ne' palazzi e casini sopra le sue sponde*, 2 vols. (Venice, 1750 and 1756); L.
   Magagnato, *Ville del Brenta nelle vedute di Vincenzo Coronelli e Giovan Francesco Costa* (Milan, 1960); L. Puppi, 'Le Esperidi in
   Brenta', *Arte Veneta*, 29 (1975), pp. 212–18; E. Concina, *Ville giardini e paesaggi del Veneto nelle incisioni di Johann Christoph
   Volkamer* (Milan, 1979).

weather-resistant stone from the Berici and Euganean hills, skilful and well-organised workshops (those belonging to the Marinali and Bonazza, near Vicenza, were particularly famous) produced a steady output of items of first-rate artistic quality. From the second half of the seventeenth century onwards statues, which had been present in the gardens since the sixteenth century, became one of the most important forms of ornamentation. They were often the main items in the iconographic programme and were even linked to the paintings which decorated the interior of the owner's residence.[16] Nicolò Beregan's 'philosophic parterre' near Vicenza, described in blank verse by the author-client himself, is highly representative.[17] In some instances, as in the garden at Villa Cordellina in Montecchio, the same artist, namely Giambattista Tiepolo, frescoed the central hall of the villa and provided the drawings for a number of sculptural groups dotted around the garden.[18] In the eighteenth century the traditional repertoire, which included Olympian deities and mythological figures, protagonists from ancient history and allegorical personifications, the senses, the hours of the day, the seasons of the year and the continents, were joined by masked characters from the Commedia dell' Arte, exotic damsels and gallants, dwarfs and arcardian pastoral figures, either alone or grouped together in complex creations of which Marinali's famous *macchina* in the garden of Villa Conti-Lampertico at Montegaldella is an outstanding example.[19] It was precisely this aspect, sculptural decoration – which became the object of a reforming intellectualistic programme in stark contrast to the traditional repertoire – that led to the early development of landscape gardening in the Veneto at the end of the eighteenth century in the wake of the new vogue which had spread from England to France and Germany, as can be seen at Angelo Querini's villa in Altichiero.[20]

---

[16] There is still no detailed study of the plastic decoration of the villa gardens and the programme this expressed. On the sculptors active in the villas, see C. Semenzato, 'Giovanni Bonazza', *Saggi e memorie di storia dell'arte*, 2 (1959), pp. 281–314; idem, *La scultura veneta del Seicento e del Settecento* (Venice, 1966); F. Barbieri, 'Schede varie', in *Pietra di Vicenza*, ed. F. Barbieri and G. Menato (Vicenza, 1970), pp. 9–128; idem, 'Le scene della scultura', in *I Tiepolo*, pp. 226–45.

[17] N. Beregan, 'Dilucidazione del parterre filosofico nella Villa dell'Autore ne' sobborghi di Vicenza detta il Moracchino', in *Poesie diverse di Niccola Beregani* (Padua, 1786), pp. 87–90; M. Azzi Visentini, *Il giardino veneto tra Sette e Ottocento e le sue fonti* (Milan, 1988), pp. 167–70; idem, '"Et in Arcadia"', p. 367.

[18] G. Mariacher, 'Le sculture di Villa Cordellina Lombardi' and L. Puppi, 'Nella luce dell'intelligenza: l'Olimpo di Carlo Cordellina. Nota iconografica', in *I Tiepolo*, pp. 321–3 and 329–31. The name of another Tiepolo, Giandomenico, who was responsible for the frescoes in the *foresteria*, has also been put forward for the dwarfs at Villa Valmarana at San Bastiano. L. Puppi, 'I Tiepolo a Vicenza e le statue dei "nani" a Villa Valmarana a San Bastiano', *Atti dell'Istituto Veneto di Scienze, Lettere e Arti* (1967-8), pp. 243–50; idem, 'I nani della Villa Valmarana ai nani di Vicenza', *Antichità Viva*, 2 (1968), pp. 34ff.

[19] The extraordinary 'engine' or 'obelisk', as Muttoni defined it in a drawing attributed to him (N. Grilli, *Un archivio inedito dell'architetto Francesco Muttoni a Porlezza* (Florence, 1991), p. 156, fig. xv, 135), which was very similar to that commissioned from the Marinali workshop, inserted in the album kept by the Municipal Museum of Bassano del Grappa (Semenzato, *La scultura*, pp. 98, 103, fig. 72; Barbieri, in Barbieri and Menato, *Pietra*, pp. 92–5; Azzi Visentini (ed.), *Il giardino veneto*, pp. 52–5; Barbieri, 'Le scene' in *I Tiepolo*, pp. 233–4), represented the four quarters of the world, associated with the four seasons, a theme which often appeared in the fresco decorations inside villas. Together with the other points mentioned above, Muttoni's interest in the plastic ornamentation of gardens reveals the extremely close links between architecture and sculpture which was seen as a structural element rather than as a purely decorative accessory for gardens.

[20] See Azzi Visentini, *Il giardino veneto tra Sette e Ottocento*, pp. 113–35, and the bibliography listed on pp. 276–7; idem, 'Fermenti innovativi nel giardino veneto del secondo Settecento da Villa Querini a Altichiero a Prato della Valle', in *L'Europa delle corti alla fine dell'antico regime*, ed. C. Mozzarelli and G. Venturi (Rome, 1991), pp. 249–76; on pp. 249–59.

Among the potted plants which, together with the statues, lined the edges of the flowerbeds, pride of place was taken by the citrus fruit trees (fig. 4.8). Having been grown on the Brescia side of Lake Garda since the fourteenth century, where they flourished out of doors and were only protected in the winter by temporary shelters assembled on the spot, they had been introduced in the Veneto in the second half of the sixteenth century, as reported by Scamozzi, and within a short space of time became one of the main garden adornments, as well as a modest source of income. Together with the citrus trees, the simple architectural structures of the conservatories, pergolas for citrus trees and lemon houses were transformed into functional and at the same time decorative elements present in all gardens.[21]

The flowers and scented plants which were most sought after for their beauty and fragrance grew in the flowerbeds closest to the owner's house. A number of documents record the evolution of the design of the *parterres* and the plants they contained: these range from the geometrical plans reproduced in *Hypnerotomachia Poliphili*, the well-known incunabulum published in Venice in 1499, in which marjoram, thyme and other aromatic herbs were grown together with primulas and violets, to the flowerbeds illustrated by Serlio in his *Quarto Libro*, printed in Venice in 1542, which recall those of the Botanical Garden in Padua described by Porro in a guide dated 1591.[22] After the mid-fifteenth century numerous sources supply lists of the plants and flowers in the gardens in Venice and on the mainland.[23] The small volume by the doctor and versatile writer from Verona, Francesco Pona, *Il paradiso de' fiori*, published in Verona in 1622, is particularly valuable on the introduction of exotic plants into the region, in particular the highly prized bulbous plants from the Eastern Mediterranean countries with which Venice had always enjoyed intensive commercial relations, and which, owing to the occupation of Cyprus and other strategic bases, had not been interrupted after the Turkish conquest of Constantinople. Pona was also the author of an accurate description of the Giusti garden in Verona; a number of sketches for flowerbeds included, among other flowering plants, anemones, tulips and hyacinths.[24]

Numerous villas standing on the plain were laid out according to the above scheme. One of these was the fabulous *barco* belonging to Caterina Cornaro at Altivole, which was fully illustrated in two eighteenth-century drawings whose reliability has been

---

[21] In his famous treatise on agriculture, Agostino Gallo from Brescia limits himself to making a few comments on the cultivation of citrus fruits. A. Gallo, *Le vinti giorante dell'agricoltura* (Venice, 1628; 1st ed. 1565); Scamozzi, *L'idea della architettura*, pp. 325–6. Over time, and in parallel with their spread through Lazio and other regions, citrus fruits became increasingly numerous in the Veneto, so much so that Volkamer was persuaded to make the striking association between fruits and Veneto villas in the plates of the second volume of his treatise on citrus fruits. Clarici dedicated a large part of his *Istoria e coltura della piante . . .*, published posthumously in Venice in 1726, to citrus fruits. M. Azzi Visentini, 'Il veneto come giardino delle Esperidi nell'interpretazione di J.C. Volkamer', in *Parchi e Giardini Storici, Parchi Letterari*, III: *Paesaggi e giardini del Mediterraneo* (Pompei, 1993), pp. 13–23; A. Tagliolini and M. Azzi Visentini, eds., *Il giardino delle Esperidi gli agrumi nella storia, nell'arte, nella cultura* (Florence, 1996).

[22] G. Porro, *L'horto de i semplici di Padova* (Venice, 1591); Azzi Visentini, *L'Orto Botanico*, pp. 105–27.

[23] L. Puppi, 'I giardini veneziani del Rinascimento', *Il Veltro*, 22 (3–4) (1978), pp. 279–98; idem, 'Le residenze di Pietro Bembo "in padoana"', *L'Arte* 7–8 (1969), pp. 30–65.

[24] M. Azzi Visentini, 'Il governo del giardino storico: l'apporto delle fonti', in *Il giardino e il tempo*, ed. M. Boriani and L. Scazzosi (Milan, 1992), pp. 83–9; on pp. 85ff.

partially confirmed by recent excavations; the garden is also described in Pietro Bembo's *Asolani*.[25] The front-page illustration of Pietro de' Crescenzi's edition of *Ruralia commodora* published in Venice in 1495 was inspired by the same concept. A layout of this type is also visible at the Villa Castello Giustinian in Roncade, built during the second decade of the sixteenth century: the entrance courtyard was surrounded by elongated rustic buildings which opened onto an inward-facing portico, while the raised palazzo stood in the centre at the back, featuring a double projecting loggia surmounted by a pediment; behind it lay the private walled gardens and beyond them the square *brollo picullo del Castello* surrounded by the *brolo grande*.[26] These earliest complexes were enclosed within high walls with massive corner towers above which only the upper part of the graceful building was visible. In later villas the walled enclosure of feudal origin was replaced by low walls or hedges accompanied by ditches, thus eliminating, at least visually, any interruption between artificial nature in the garden and cultivated nature in the surrounding countryside. Examples of this can be found in Palladio's works: Villa Badoer at Fratta Polesine, Villa Emo at Fanzolo and Villa Cornaro at Piombino Dese, just to mention those laid out along these lines whose 'surroundings', or at least their perimeters, have survived intact.

Gardens laid out in regular squares can be found at the back and, later, at the sides of numerous villas on the plain designed by Scamozzi – for example, Villa Cornaro at Poisuolo di Castelfranco, Villa Badoer at Peraga and Villa Trevisan at San Donà di Piave – and described in detail in his treatise.[27] Within the narrow bounds of the illustrations, he skilfully manages to convey a schematic idea of the complex layout of open spaces and buildings, those areas used by the owner and those set aside for service, all methodically laid out within the orthogonal grid of the villas; he also focuses on their individual component features.

> Behind lies the Garden divided into squares with beautiful plants and herbs, and sweet-smelling flowers; paths run along the walls where you can walk in the shade of the leafy branches. In the centre stands a beautiful fountain spouting water high into the air: and there at the end of the Garden, where the midday sun strikes, you may construct a trellis for citrus fruits or pergola which will serve as the last view of the Garden.[28]

The architect then proceeded to examine all the specific features of the garden, namely the size of the paths and their paving, the hydraulic systems used to guarantee the garden's water supply, including fountains, loggias and grottoes, together with their plastic ornamentation. Special attention was focused on the botanical species which were most suited to the garden's decoration, ranging from potted plants, primarily citrus plants, and the conservatories used to protect them during the colder months, to those species most suitable for 'making trellises, niches, arches, cubes, porticoes, loggias and similar items'. Scamozzi also gave details of such wooden or metal structures, concluding that 'the little we have said of plants will suffice to know how to place them,

[25] L. Puppi, 'Il "barco" di Caterina Cornaro ad Altivole', *Prospettive*, 25 (1962), pp. 52–64.
[26] C. Kolb Lewis, *The Villa Giustinian at Roncade* (New York and London, 1977).
[27] Scamozzi, *L'idea della architettura*, pp. 290–7.   [28] Ibid., p. 271.

and use them for these purposes; since this is the part which falls to the Architect, leaving their care and maintenance to capable Agriculturists'.[29] As well as specifying the limits of their own specific competences, this enlightened observation also underlines the close link between the architecture and design of buildings and that of gardens, understood as two inseparable stages of a single project.

Longhena also used the same layout in the project for Villa da Lezze at Rovarè di San Biagio di Callalta, near Treviso, as can be seen in a drawing kept at the Correr Museum in Venice (fig. 4.2). The oblong site is divided into three strips of equal width by two parallel canals running from one end to the other of the whole estate. The entry piazza, bordered by elongated arcaded buildings housing the domestic and working quarters, lay in front of the main façade of the villa, sited in the appropriate position as described above. Behind and at the sides of the owner's house lay two symmetrical gardens divided into rectangular flowerbeds, with a fountain in the centre and a pergola for citrus trees and lemon-houses along the two sides, while dovecotes were erected at the outside corners. Beyond the gardens lay the long orchard whose trees, planted in a quincuncial arrangement, were surrounded by loggias of greenery. In the centre a tree-lined avenue led out into the countryside from the courtyard, encompassed by a low semicircular wall.[30]

A number of maps from the Fondo Beni Inculti in the Venice State Archive – an incredible mine of information for the study of Veneto villas and, above all, their gardens – illustrate estates whose layout reflects these principles.[31] Their application can be seen in the gardens of Villa Cappello at Cartigliano, Villa Grimani at Martellago, Villa Marcello at Levada, as well as Villa Morosini at Sant'Anna (fig. 4.3), the two Sagredo villas at Marocco and Sarmazza, and Villa Cordellina at Montecchio Maggiore, all dating back to the last decades of the seventeenth century and the first half of the eighteenth.[32] Villa Manin at Passariano, the residence of the last Doge, was also conceived along the same lines: the grandiloquent semicircular porticoes encompassing the entry court were matched by the four-square garden at the rear, admired in 1738 by Maria Amalia of Saxony who left a detailed description. It was later transformed into an English-style park within which some of the numerous eighteenth-century statues were redistributed.[33] It is worth drawing attention to the case of the two Priuli villas at

[29] Ibid., p. 327.

[30] E. Bassi, 'La Villa Lezze', *Critica d'Arte* (1965), pp. 42–53; L. Puppi, G. Romanelli and S. Biadene, *Longhena*, Exhibition catalogue (Milan, 1982), p. 173; Azzi Visentini, '"Et in Arcadia"', p. 352.

[31] M. F. Tiepolo, 'Fonti documentarie sui giardini nell'Archivio di Stato di Venezia fino al 1797'; E. Tonetti, 'I giardini nelle fonte catastali', M. Azzi Visentini, 'Le fonti a stampa', in Azzi Visentini (ed.), *Il giardino veneto*, pp. 328–33, 339–42 and 343–8. See also Azzi Visentini, 'Fonti'.   [32] Azzi Visentini, 'Note' idem (ed.), *Il giardino veneto*, *passim*.

[33] On the description by Maria Amalia of Saxony see Bibl. Ap. Vaticana, Ms. Vat. Lat. 14145, and Azzi Visentini, '"Et in Arcadia"', p. 352. I wish to thank my friend M. Moli Frigola for having brought this manuscript to my attention. F. Venuto, 'La vicenda edilizia del complesso di Passariano', *Arte in Friuli, Arte a Trieste*, 7 (1984), pp. 57–74; idem, 'Il parco di Villa Manin a Passariano tra '700 and '800', in *Parchi e Giardini Storici, Parchi Letterari*, II (Monza, 1992), pp. 234–41; L. Puppi, '"Fortunam Virtus vincere potest". L'Olimpo dei Manin a Passariano', in *La letteratura e i giardini* (Florence, 1987), pp. 395–409.

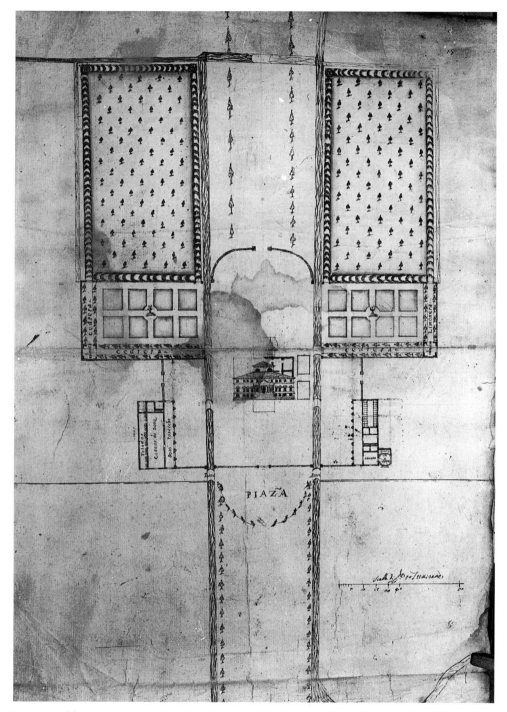

Fig. 4.2 Baldassare Longhena (attrib.). Pen and ink drawing of a project for the Villa da Lezze at Rovarè di San Biagio di Callalta (Treviso)

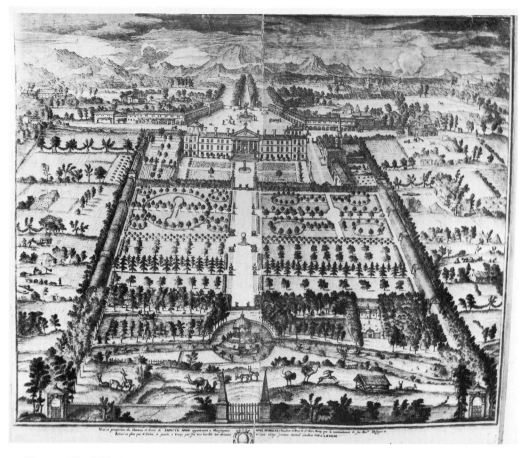

Fig. 4.3 The Villa Morosini at Sant'Anna Morosina (Padua) in a print drawn by N. Cochin
and engraved by Martial Desbois, Venice, 1683

Treville, one of which appears with its garden in a *catastico* dated 1711. The villas rose up
'from the delightful plain' facing one another so that, decorated by 'gardens, fountains,
avenues, covered bowers, pergolas for citrus trees, backdrops and meeting places . . .
they served as a prospect for one another given that there was nothing between them
but a road, thus reciprocally adding to their magnificence and splendour'.[34]

While the overall layout for a villa on the plain remained broadly speaking
unchanged from the sixteenth to the eighteenth century, its dimensions expanded
although even the largest villas never exceeded a total area of 300 by 200 metres, thus
adding more volume to the buildings and space to the gardens. 'The larger and more
spacious the garden, the more respectability it will give to the House,' wrote Scamozzi,
adding, however, the practical observation that their size must never be such 'that it

---

[34] B. Scapinelli, 'Istoria di Castelfranco', Ms. Cicogna 119, Correr Museum Library, Venice (1740), and M. Stocco, *Notizie
storiche del Castello di Treville e delle sue pertinenze: Poisolo – S. Andrea oltre il Musone – Soranza* (Venice, 1910), pp. 33, 35–6.

augments the owner's costs and makes maintenance too laboursome for the Gardener'.[35]

In the *Istoria e coltura delle piante che sono pe'l fiore più ragguardevoli, e più distinte per ornare un giardino in tutto il tempo dell'anno*, published posthumously in 1726, together with an appendix containing an exhaustive *Trattato sugli agrumi*, Paolo Bartolomeo Clarici described, as a model, the garden he had created for Villa Sagredo at Marocco, which was accurately illustrated in the attached engraving by Francesco Zucchi made from the drawing by Giovanni Filippini. 'The delightful garden lies', he explained,

> in the most charming Villa at Marocco, almost beside the sea and only ten miles away from Venice; it is frequented at all times by the Venetian nobility who are attracted, like Foreigners, by the fame of the spot's beauty and amenities. Four wide roads lined with delightful, high trees . . . [which] bring us to the Garden and from there . . . to the Palace. The Garden, which is enclosed by a wall measuring 770 feet long and 450 feet wide, is adorned and decorated by perpetually verdant plants. The entire Garden is divided into four wide squares of the same size, two of which face northwards and between them stands the magnificent Palace; the other two face southwards and, surrounded by green arbours artfully sculpted into beautiful, shady loggias, are proportionately divided into various shapes. Those adjacent to the Palace are however much more magnificently adorned: the northern part houses the buildings used by the Gardeners and Servants, and for other domestic purposes. Among these are the conservatories and pergolas for citrus trees supported by selected marble columns. These squares contain the most noble plants . . . There are also plentiful citrus trees, not only in the pergolas and conservatories, but also planted in enormous pots standing in the Garden. Lastly, there are also marble Statues, whose gigantic forms rise up from prominent bases, and other ornaments worthy of the Magnificence of such a Noble Family,

including 'the beauty of a wooded Theatre, or a wooded Amphitheatre used for games', to which were added 'numerous Statues by Excellent Sculptors standing in the different areas of the Garden which serve to provide a prospect and ornament for any situation'.[36]

Among the rare exceptions for such a type it is worth mentioning the design illustrated in an engraving preserved in the Correr Museum in Venice, which shows a grandiose villa from whose rear garden a series of avenues radiates out into the enormous surrounding 'wood'. This is one of the few Venetian projects to reflect baroque town-planning designs and even the magniloquent conception of the garden formulated by Le Nôtre (fig. 4.4).

One might wonder what influence the garden layout of Venetian villas sited in the plain, which had evolved as early as the sixteenth century, may have had on villas built in similar environmental settings in Italy (for example Lombardy) or in other European countries. In fact, there are striking similarities between Dutch and Veneto gardens.

The introduction of long-trunked trees from the second half of the eighteenth

[35] Scamozzi, *L'idea della architettura*, p. 325.

[36] P. B. Clarici, *Istoria e coltura delle piante, Spiegazione della tavola*; Azzi Visentini, 'Descrizioni', pp. 76–7.

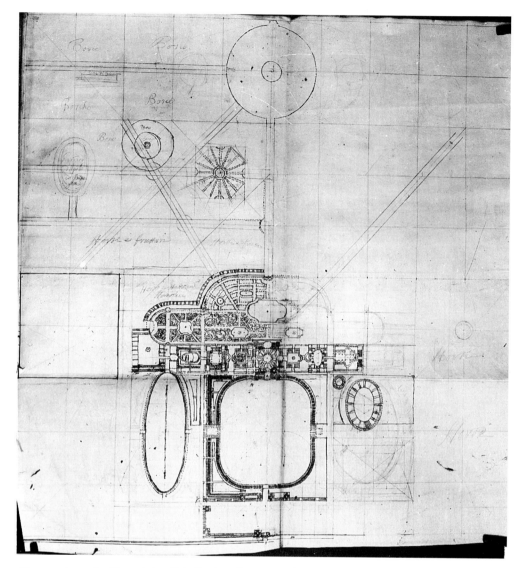

Fig. 4.4 Antonio Gaspari (attrib.). Project for an unidentified villa surrounded by a large park

century onwards, in response to the spreading vogue for the English garden,[37] completely upset the delicate relationship between architecture, garden and landscape which represented, as has been seen, one of the essential characteristics of the Veneto villa.

A second group consists of villas built on hillsides, either halfway up or at the foot of the slope, on a site which sloped more or less steeply into the valley where the

[37] Azzi Visentini, *Il giardino veneto tra Sette e Ottocento*.

Fig. 4.5 Aerial view of the Villa Barbaro, Maser (Treviso)

large, rectangular garden was laid out and traditionally subdivided into squares of equal size. These sites offered a view of the surrounding countryside; the buildings backed onto the high ground and, in some cases, were even set into the hillside, whose dense vegetation framed them and sheltered them from the winds. The Barbaro residence at Maser (fig. 4.5), built shortly after the middle of the sixteenth century, was one of the first Veneto villas whose position reflected that described by the younger Pliny for his villa in Tuscany and recommended by later treatise writers, starting with Leon Battista Alberti. The fifteenth-century Medici villa at Fiesole and that at Castello, whose sixteenth-century renovation shortly preceded the construction of Villa Barbaro, were in fact erected on similar sites. But the model of the villa resting on a hillside, articulated on evenly spaced, sloping terraces succeeding one another along a central axis, is above all typical of early sixteenth-century Rome: starting with Bramante's Belvedere courtyard and Raffaello's project for Villa Madama, the vogue reached its apex in Villa d'Este at Tivoli, Villa Lante at Bagnaia and Villa Aldobrandini at Frascati.[38]

---

[38] Azzi Visentini, *La villa in Italia. Quattro e Cinquecento.*

The influence of classical literature and the first-hand experience of modern buildings, such as the unfinished Villa Madama and the recently completed Villa Giulia, must have been decisive in the choice of both the site and the design of Villa Barbaro, made by the cultured patron who certainly helped Palladio to elaborate the design.[39] The cavea of the ancient theatre planned for Villa Madama, which, having been dug out of the hillside of Monte Mario and framed by the leafy branches of the holm-oaks behind it, was intended to represent the climax of the entire complex, appears to be reflected in the curve of the nymphaneum at Villa Barbaro standing on the slopes of the Asolani Hills (fig. 4.6). The latter also recalled the exedra, originally planned by Bramante, at the far end of the upper terrace of the Belvedere courtyard, as depicted by Serlio, as well as the numerous ancient hemicycles reused in sixteenth-century Rome, such as the one incorporated into the *horti bellaiani* (having previously been part of Diocletian's Baths), which appears in Dupérac's plan of Rome dated 1577.

When Palladio and Daniele Barbaro conceived the layout of the villa at Maser in around 1556, the most famous of the Lazio villas built on a series of sloping terraces – ranging from Villa d'Este to Villa Lante – did not yet exist, and it would be necessary to wait several decades before the Frascati villas were built. Starting with Villa Aldobrandini, villas often included a scenographic elliptical water theatre dug into the hillside at the back of the palace and framed by the dense vegetation behind it, whereas the front view was designed to emphasise the panorama of the surrounding countryside. The private garden behind Villa Barbaro, hemmed in between the hill and the building, the 'infinite stucco and painted ornamentation'[40] which decorated the hemicycle of the nymphaeum, and the prime role of water which, channelled from a nearby spring, gushed from the amphora held up by the river god reclining at the back of the small room 'cut into the hillside'[41] before feeding the numerous fountains in the front garden, are probably all elements taken from Julius III's villa. On the other hand, the river god resting inside the grotto-cum-sanctuary may have been inspired by the similar reuse of antique statues in the Belvedere courtyard. However, contrary to the customary practice in the sixteenth-century gardens of Lazio and Tuscany, in which, in the words of Bandinelli, the 'things which were built' were the 'guide for and more important than those which were planted',[42] the architectural features were limited to the rear garden where the compromise between nature and artifice reached its apex. In the garden in front of the villa, on the other hand, the architect preferred to respect the site's natural disposition, limiting any constructed works to the square, slightly raised terrace in front of the main building 'which juts out by the same amount',[43] usually recognised as an allusion to Pliny's Laurentian villa. The remainder of the garden, lying between the palazzo with its

[39] Azzi Visentini, *L'Orto Botanico* pp. 178–208; idem, 'Daniele Barbaro e l'architettura: la villa di Maser', in *I Barbaro. Una antica famiglia veneziana*, Conference papers (forthcoming).   [40] Palladio, *I quattro libri*, vol. II, p. 51.   [41] Ibid.

[42] As written in letter of 11 Feb. 1551, sent from Florence by Baccio Bandinelli to Jacopo Guidi, re Pitti Palace and Boboli Gardens. See *Raccolta di lettere sulla pittura, scultura ed architettura, scritte da più celebri professori che in dette arti fiorirono dal secolo XV al XVII . . .*, 8 vols. (Milan, 1822; 1st edn Rome, 1754–89), vol. I, letter XXXVIII, pp. 93–4

[43] Palladio, *I quattro libri*, vol. II, p. 51.

Fig. 4.6 The nymphaeum at Villa Barbaro

elongated outbuildings and the road, was laid out in uniform squares on either side of the central axis running from the nymphaeum above, through the palace and garden to the straight avenue which led into the countryside on the far side of the public road; today it is only possible to trace the vague outlines of these squares based on the layout of the numerous pools and fountains.

A similar scheme to that of Villa Barbaro was used a century later for the nearby Villa Rinaldi-Barbini at Caselle d'Asolo. Compared to the former, however, there was a narrower space, on a more steeply inclined slope, between the main building and the road, and it was occupied by the steeply sloping front garden and the raised terrace in front of the villa. Uphill, behind the villa, lay the private garden, which was enclosed by the elliptical nymphaeum containing mythological figures and enlivened by surprising water jets or *giochi d'acqua*.[44]

Over the following centuries many of the villas sited on the sunny slopes of the

[44] The exhibition on Italian gardens organised at Palazzo Vecchio in 1931 is known to have included two drawings by G. B. Polloni dating from 1779 and respectively showing the villa with the front garden and the grotto behind. From my research it appears that these are now lost together with a considerable quantity of material which had already been published or was merely referred to. U. Ojetti (ed.), *Mostra del guardino italiano*, (Florence, 1931), p. 222, notes 13 and 14.

Euganean and Berici hills, which rise abruptly out of the monotonous plain, or along the Alpine foothills stretching from Friuli to Lake Garda, which enclose the Venetian Republic to the north, were laid out as variants of the Villa Barbaro plan. This plan was in fact reflected in the seventeenth-century Villa Allegri, now Arvedi, at Cuzzano di Valpantena, which stands on the eastern slope of a pleasant hill, the last outcrop of the Monti Lessini. Moving up along its central axis we find the deep *brolo* and the short, rectangular garden whose box hedges have been skilfully trimmed over the centuries to form the intricate double-fan design of the *parterre*, a feature which is unrivalled in the Veneto or elsewhere.[45] The garden, which is protected by a high wall along the northern side, forms a terrace, an architectural feature which rises slightly above the surrounding countryside in order to emphasise the distinction between the owners and the country folk. The terrace leads on to the level ground lying in front of the elongated façade of the palace, from whose central block extend low wings surmounted by terraces which culminate in slender dovecote towers; the whole provides a spectacular backdrop, beyond which can be seen the branches of the century-old olive trees growing on the hilltop. On the opposite side is a large sunken courtyard, enclosed to the east by the rear of the palace which surrounds it, forming a U-shape and, to the west, by a hemicycle which culminates in the baroque chapel of S. Carlo built on a platform set into the hillside and reached by an intricate stairway.

This type of villa may be compared to the late seventeenth-century residence at Valsanzibio in the Euganean Hills, belonging to the Barbarigo, a noble Venetian family (fig. 4.7). Sited in a hollow set between two areas of high ground, the villa possesses one of the largest and best conserved Venetian baroque gardens.[46] The façade of the villa was portrayed in an idealised oil painting which not only gives the main block an elegant courtly appearance that it would never have had, but also shows the entrance at the level of the embankment which enclosed the bottom of the garden. As in the villas examined earlier, the main building, its outbuildings and front terrace serve as a backdrop for the garden, which is laid out geometrically on either side of the central axis. The splendid pavilion known as Diana's Bath provides a spectacular opening for the wide watercourse which runs through the lowest part of the garden in a series of pools and fountains unique in the Veneto and reminiscent of the similar *enfilade* at Villa d'Este in Tivoli. On the northern face, looking towards the hill, a straight avenue of cypresses leads out of a semicircular exedra in a continuation of the central axis and makes its way upwards, vaguely recalling, although without the use of water, the solution adopted for a number of villas in the Tusculanum area; a similar feature was also introduced at Ca' Borin in Este at the start of the eighteenth century.

[45] G.C. Becelli, 'La ninfa di Cuzzano', in *Rime nelle nozze del nob. sign. Conte Carlo Allegri et nob. sig. Marchesa Donna Camilla Lucini, raccolte dal Dott. Antonio Mello* (Verona, 1734), pp. III–XIII; V. Fontana, 'Villa Allegri Arvedi, Cuzzano in Valpantena', in Azzi Visentini (ed.), *Il giardino veneto*, pp. 135–7.

[46] L. Puppi, 'The Giardino Barbarigo in Valsanzibio', *Journal of Garden History*, 3(4) (1983), pp. 281–300; idem, ' "Quivi è l'inferno e quivi è il paradiso". Il giardino di villa Barbarigo a Valsanzibio nel Padovano', in *L'architettura dei giardini d'occidente*, ed. M. Mosser and G. Teyssot (Milan, 1990), pp. 181–3.

Fig. 4.7 The Villa Barbarigo, Valsanzibio. A late seventeenth- or early eighteenth-century painting by an unknown artist, recently restored

Muttoni's plans for Villa Fracanzan-Piovene at Orgiano and Villa Zileri dal Verme at Biron di Monteviale show analogous layouts. Both these projects, which were not entirely realised, date back to the early decades of the eighteenth century and included the palace and its outbuildings, the gardens, *broli* and farmyards.[47] Both villas stood at the foot of a slope and the architect endeavoured to use the high ground at the back of the palace for scenographic purposes by constructing a raised terrace from which it was possible to enjoy a view of the surrounding countryside. At Orgiano, Muttoni designed a 'Piazza sive Anfiteatro' facing the northern façade of the patrician's residence. On this side of the building the grand stairway 'resting on two arches' gave direct access from the courtyard to the first floor of the palace. A high, wide platform was dug out of the steep slope facing the stair, in the centre of which it was planned to build the new

[47] Azzi Visentini, '"Et in Arcadia"', pp. 375–7.

PRIMO VIALE DEGL' AGRVMI CON FONTANE E SCHERZI D'ACQVA NEL GIARDINO DELL'ECCELLENTISSIMA CASA BARBARIGO POSTO IN VAL SAN ZIBIO TRA COLLI EVGANEI

Fig. 4.8 Citrus alley, 'Primo viale degl'agrumi con fontane e scherzi d'acqua nel giardino dell' Eccellentissima Casa Barbarigo, posto in Val San Zibio tra Colli Euganei', from D. Rossetti, *Fabriche e giardini dell' Eccellentissima Casa Barbarigo* (Verona, 1702)

church; in his plans the architect specified that it was to be preceded on the sides and at the front by a curved 'walk approximately 8 feet above the road, including the parapet which will be decorated with statues and vases, and the wall above covered by trellises and plants'. The slopes of the hill behind were covered by 'Vignalj'. A simpler variation of the uphill piazza, the elliptical loggia being set into the side of the 'vine-covered hill' behind and the uniform garden in front of the villa (although the basic scheme remains unchanged), can be seen in Plate XXXIII(i) of the file of Muttoni's drawings at the Library of Congress in Washington.[48]

A hanging staircase also connected the *piano nobile* of the palace at Biron to an octagonal 'private garden or belvedere above the hill which was larger, more arbitrary and more suited to the site', as is observed in the illustrative notes to the project. On the flat ground in front of both villas were large square gardens,

---

[48] D. Lewis, 'A New Book of Drawings of Francesco Muttoni', *Arte Veneta*, 30 (1975), pp. 132–46.

geometrically intersected by paths and waterways, which blended into the cultivated landscape around them. The monumental nature of the palace at Orgiano was further emphasised by the gently sloping site, which enabled a terraced solution to be adopted for the front garden. Similar solutions were used at the villas located in the hill areas around Feltre and Belluno. In this context it is particularly worth mentioning Villa Pasole at Pedavena, Villa Bellati at Feltre and Villa Vescovile at Belluno.[49]

The third type of villa consists of those built on prominent sites, for the most part on hilltops: while hills had always been the preferred sites for castles and forts, during the Renaissance they were also used for some central-plan churches built on the outskirts of towns.

Villa dei Vescovi at Luvigliano di Torreglia in the Euganean Hills is one of the oldest examples. Jointly designed by Falconetto and Alvise Cornaro, this square-plan villa translates Sangallo's idea of an ancient extra-urban residence into the Veneto style: this was achieved by setting the building on an imposing *basis villae*, following the Medician example at Poggio a Caiano, and by opening up the *piano nobile* with arcades which ran round the entire façade and rear of the building. This resulted in a complete interpenetration between the building, whose basic *raison d'être* was its panoramic view over the countryside, and the surrounding environment. The latter permeated the very heart of the villa through the loggias at the exact point where the central hall was located, a process which was only partly interrupted by the courtyard built a few decades later by Andrea da Valle.

This was also the position subsequently made famous by Palladio at La Rotonda (fig. 4.9). As the architect himself wrote:

> The site is as pleasant and as delightful as can be found; because it is upon a small hill, and is watered on one side by the Bacchiglione, a navigable river; and on the other, it is encompassed with most pleasant risings, which look like a very great theatre, and are all cultivated, and abound with the most excellent fruits, and most exquisite vines: and therefore, as it enjoys from every part most beautiful views, some of which are limited, some more extended, and others that terminate with the horizon; there are loggias made in the four fronts. . .[50]

The jutting pronaoi at La Rotonda extend into statue-lined stairways which bind the building to the site, on which it appears to rest comfortably. This impression is reinforced by the lower version of the actual dome compared to the higher, rounder version illustrated in the treatise. The staircases and loggias at La Rotonda occupy as much space as the building itself, and these outstanding elements of transition between

---

[49] Alpago Novello, *Le ville*, pp. 130–45, 146–59, 160–73.

[50] Palladio, *I quattro libri*, vol. II, p. 18. On the Rotonda and in particular on the relationship between the building and its surroundings, see R. Assunto, 'La Rotonda e il paesaggio: architettura nella natura e architettura della natura', in *La Rotonda* (Milan, 1988), pp. 8–20.

Fig. 4.9 Aerial view of La Rotonda, Vicenza

interior and exterior, between the villa and the landscape, appear to fulfil the role of the garden, which in this case cannot otherwise have overly preoccupied Palladio. Even if it is unclear how the architect would have planned the access to the villa, the compromise solution adopted by the Capra family and implemented by Scamozzi, namely the entrance ramp bounded by the elongated rustic building which welcomes visitors today and, likewise, the irregularly shaped platform which runs round three sides of La Rotonda, certainly appear to have eluded the architect's control. This therefore accounts for the fact that the varied landscape on all four sides of the villa – on which Palladio intentionally dwells in his description in the *Quattro libri* – was seen as a ready-made garden. As Goethe realised when he visited La Rotonda in September 1786, this predated by almost two centuries the discovery attributed to William Kent that every aspect of nature can be converted into a pleasant garden with the use of a few cunning devices; the same discovery was likewise anticipated by the younger Pliny when he compared the view of the partly cultivated and partly wild countryside spread out like an amphitheatre before his villa in Tuscany to a painted scene.

La Rotonda, together with the unrealised project for Villa Trissino at Meledo, is not the only Palladian creation of this type. Villa Godi at Lonedo was also 'set on a hill with a beautiful view', and the hanging garden which was completed behind the building a few years later was designed with the panorama in mind. It was supported 'by vaults at no

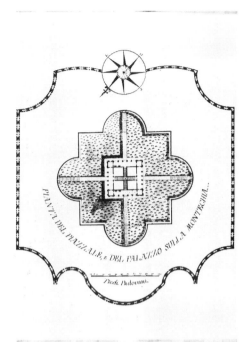

Fig. 4.10 Pietro Fornari. Drawing entitled 'Pianta del piazzale, e del palazzo sulla Montecchia' (plan of the courtyard, and of the palace on the Montecchia), from *Le piante ed i prospetti ed i disegni delle Terre della tenuta della Montecchia del Nob. Sig. Conte Giordano Capodilista*

small expense',[51] and in the centre stood a well and an exedra leading down into the valley below which was accessed by two curved flights of stairs. Palladio's idea was later clearly reflected in Muttoni's plans for the 'hanging courtyard supported by large semicircular walls, somewhat larger than the other hanging courtyard on the eastern side',[52] which was constructed in the early eighteenth century facing the front of the villa.

Villa Emo-Capodilista in Montecchia di Selvazzano, which was designed by the painter Dario Varotari who also painted the major fresco cycle inside the villa, was likewise built on a hilltop in around 1575, perhaps on the site of an old fort. In the case of this 'graceful, four-square and perfectly symmetrical Palace whose four corners faced the four corners of the earth',[53] a fully centralised scheme was used comprising four identical façades opened to the outside by loggias over five supporting arches defined by single bays closed at the corners, thus recalling the *Portikusvilla mit Eckrisaliten* motif (fig. 4.10). It is not known how the space surrounding the villa was originally organised since in the mid-eighteenth century it was enclosed by a wall whose four-foiled shape

[51] Palladio, *I quattro libri*, vol. II, p. 65.

[52] As Francesco Muttoni, the designer, explained in ibid., *Architettura di Andrea Palladio Vicentino con le osservazioni dell'architetto N.N.*, 8 vols. (Venice, 1740-1748). Zorzi, *Le ville*, p. 29.

[53] As Pietro Fornari wrote in a manuscript on the villa dated 1785 belonging to the private archive of the Emo-Capodilista family in Padua (*Le piante ed i prospetti et i disegni delle Terre della tenuta della Montecchia del Nob. Sig. Conte Giordano Capodilista*). See M. Botter, *La Villa Capodilista di Dario Varotari a Montecchia* (Treviso, 1967), pp. 38ff.

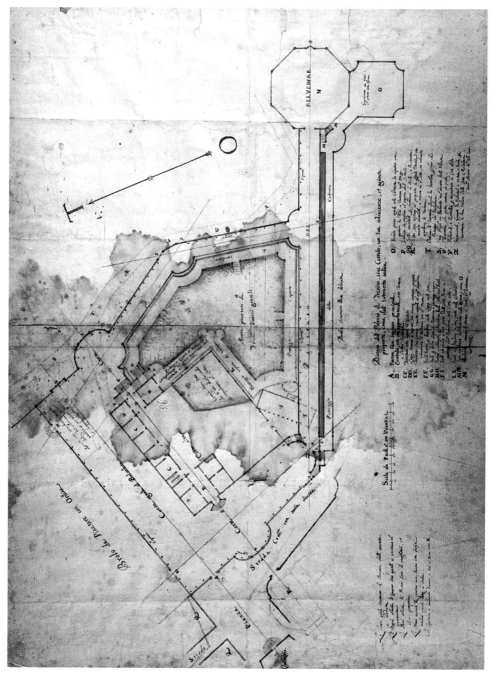

Fig. 4.11 Francesco Muttoni. Project for the reconstruction of the upper villa of Trissino a Trissino (Vicenza), c. 1720

echoed the plan of the building. The four entrances in the centre of each side were emphasised by the same number of semicircular overhangs, whereas 'four flagged paths lead out from each of the [palace's] façades to a gently sloping stone stairway closed by a simple iron gate. The recently built new wall is also pleasantly designed and runs all the way round the palace and quite close to it, thus creating a well adapted and attractive courtyard.' The same eighteenth-century manuscript described the arcadian view from the hilltop over the 'well watered fields which produce a sufficient harvest of fodder and good quality wine, the relatively well grown trees and the terrain which is well divided and exposed, so that its appearance might be likened to a pleasant garden'.[54]

Vincenzo Scamozzi designed central-plan buildings for the Rocca at Lonigo at the request of Vettor Pisani, and for Villa Bardellini at Monfumo. He gives a detailed description of the latter's pleasant position and the spectacular views to be had on all four sides, in which the artificial nature of the garden blended harmoniously with the natural, uncultivated landscape and the well-tilled fields. Again, in both these cases the space set aside for an architectonic garden was relatively small.[55]

The villa built in the late sixteenth century by the Selvatico family on the top of the hill of Saint'Elena in Battaglia also served as a prestigious belvedere. It was constructed on a square platform and was only later linked to the public road below using an architectonic frontal route.

The straight stairways leading up from the road to the seventeenth-century Villa di Rovero in San Zenone degli Ezzelini and to Villa Negri Piovene at Mussolente, which dates back to the second half of the eighteenth century, are reminiscent of the approach to Villa Selvatico. The villas with their small gardens are perched not far from one another on the crests of hills. A position of this type would have tempted any architect operating during the same period in another part of Italy to exploit the natural disposition of the terrain so as to achieve spectacular, sloping terraces linked by complex ramp systems. In a region with a predominantly agricultural economy, such as the Veneto, the costs involved in an operation of this nature, added to the loss of fertile ground for the purpose of achieving supremely artificial results, would certainly have prompted observations similar to those made by Addison in the articles published in *The Spectator* in 1714 that herald Kent's garden.[56]

Let us round off this analysis of those villas built on high ground, conceived in terms of the views offered by the surrounding landscape, with the most daring and original garden project planned in the Veneto during the early eighteenth century, namely that designed by Francesco Muttoni for the Trissino family at Trissino (fig. 4.11). The

[54] This is also written by Fornari. M. Botter, *La Villa Capodilista*, p. 38.

[55] Scamozzi, *L'idea della architettura*, pp. 272–3 and 278–9. A villa with a similar central plan was designed by Scamozzi for an unnamed client on a site along the Brenta canal between Stra and Dolo, idem, pp. 276–7.

[56] J. D. Hunt and P. Willis (eds.), *The Genius of the Place. The English Landscape Garden 1620-1820* (Cambridge, Mass., 1988; 1st edn, 1975), pp. 138–47.

imposing complex occupied the entire south-facing slope of the hill of the same name, and was composed of two villas: the upper one built on the site of the medieval fort belonging to the feudal overlords of the area, the Trissino, who from this high position could easily dominate the Agno valley and part of the adjacent area, and the lower villa built in the eighteenth century for another branch of this noble family from Vicenza. It is worth bearing in mind, however, that in practice this villa represents a compromise, imposed by the unique characteristics of the site, between the villa set into a hillside and that built on a hilltop. By making a few basic alterations Muttoni succeeded in radically altering the structure of the villa while respecting the pre-existing structures as far as possible. His project was only partially realised but can be accurately reconstructed from an outstanding series of autograph drawings.[57] It included the extension of the villa's site to cover the entire hilltop after the crag which loomed over the buildings on the eastern side had been flattened, thus opening up the view of the eastern side of the Agno valley. Owing to these outstanding vistas the complex was transformed into a single, vast belvedere (fig. 4.12) in which the buildings were surrounded by a disorganised but extremely articulate series of terraces and courtyards, well adapted to the site's uneven nature, as well as by covered and open hanging promenades, view points and panoramic belvederes looking down into the valley below; as they wound their way at varying levels around the perimeter of the villa, interconnected by external or hidden stairways, their sole objective appears to be a direct confrontation with the project's real interlocutor: the panorama. As Muttoni clearly explains in his project, the spectacular views in every direction are captured and converge along well-defined visual trajectories which, passing through the buildings, link one end of the varied landscape to the other through the openings in the wall made by the numerous belvederes (fig. 4.13). All the decorative elements, ranging from the infinite statuary (fig. 4.14) and fantastic portals with an oriental air, the cypresses and the citrus trees to the tranquil fish-ponds, all help to achieve the same result: to frame the views, to capture the landscape by reflecting it in the still water surfaces, and to enhance the harmonious symbiosis between man-made product and nature which reaches a zenith in this building.

I have deliberately focused attention on Francesco Muttoni's work. This architect from Ticino was not only one of the most ingenious interpreters of Venetian rococo; he was also in direct contact with many of the erudite British figures who visited Vicenza following the birth of the English neopalladian movement to study Palladio's works during the first half of the eighteenth century. Muttoni drew a series of views of Palladio's buildings for a leading member of this refined cultural milieu, Lord Twisden,[58] and perhaps his greatest work, the general edition of the leading architect's

[57] M. Azzi Visentini, 'Francesco Muttoni architetto di giardini: Villa Trissino a Trissino', *Arte Veneta*, n.s.,1 (1993); Grilli, *Un archivio inedito*, *passim*.

[58] This is a small, incomplete album entitled *Dissegni et annotationi fatte di commissione del Sig.r K.re Tomaso Tuixden [Thomas Twisden] inglese. Da Francesco Muttoni attuale Architetto della Città di Vicenza, in occasione delli Sopralochi, e visite con lui fatte delli*

Fig. 4.12 The upper villa of Trissino a Trissino (Vicenza), showing part of the octagonal
belvedere with the flower beds designed by Francesco Muttoni

works which he completed in collaboration with Giorgio Fossati, may even have been
suggested to him by his Anglo-Saxon patrons.[59] It is well known that during the early
eighteenth century the English neopalladian movement was inseparably linked to the
invention of the irregular, landscape garden – *all'inglese* as it was called on the continent,
in stark contrast to the French *grand siècle* style. In a seminal essay John Dixon Hunt has
argued that, from William Kent onwards, the inventors of the landscape garden were
profoundly influenced by central Italian Renaissance and baroque gardens.[60] We know
that some of these people were regular visitors to the Veneto, whereas a whole host of
Venetian artists worked in England during the first decades of the eighteenth century.
It is worth asking ourselves whether, on the one hand, the exemplary integration

Palazzi, eretti sovra Dissegni ideati dal celebre Andrea Palladio, dating back to the period around 1708, belonging to the Centro
Internazionale di Studi di Architettura A. Palladio at Vicenza. See L. Puppi, 'Alle origini del Neopalladianesimo. Il
contributo comasco di Francesco Muttoni', *Arte Lombarda*, monographic issue, *Civiltà neoclassica nell'attuale territorio della
provincia di Como* (1980), pp. 236–42.

[59] Muttoni, *Architettura di Andrea Palladio vicentino*; Azzi Visentini, *Il giardino veneto*, pp. 7–12.

[60] J. D. Hunt, *Garden and Grove. The Italian Renaissance Garden in the English Imagination (1600-1750)*. (Princeton, N.J., 1986),
pp. 180–222.

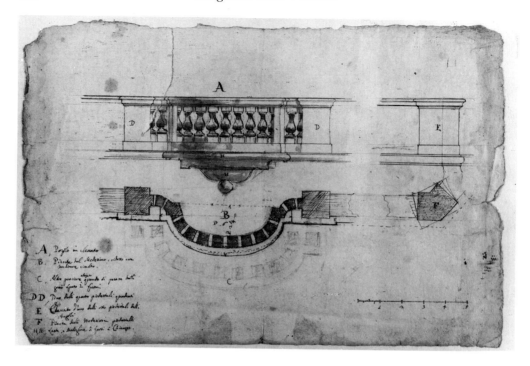

Fig. 4.13 Francesco Muttoni. Project for one of many well sites, or belvederes, of the upper villa of Trissino a Trissino

between art and nature, spontaneity and artifice in the gardens in this part of Italy did not in some way influence the new conception of the open spaces laid out around country residences in Georgian England and, on the other hand, whether these open spaces might not have been influenced by the works of Venetian painters. One need only recall the pre-romantic landscapes painted by Marco Ricci between 1709 and 1710 for Lord Carlisle at Castle Howard.[61] And to the eyes of an English visitor might not La Rotonda have looked like a vast folly picturesquely set in an irregular landscape? This is in fact just what it looks like in an idealised view of Vicenza painted by Zuccarelli for an English client.[62]

In addition to the villas built in settings with well-defined characteristics, which can therefore be classified within the groups outlined above (villas standing on the open plain, on hillsides, at the foot of a hill, or on hilltops), there are numerous other cases in which it was preferred, owing to the site's unique geographical features or the presence

[61] A. Delneri, 'Il soggiorno inglese', in *Marco Ricci e il paesaggio veneto del Settecento*, ed. D. Succi and A. Delneri, Exhibition catalogue (Milan, 1993), pp. 97–112, 192–203.

[62] On the painting by Zuccarelli see M. Magnifico, 'Scuola veneziana', in *Vedute italiane del '700 in collezioni private italiane*, ed. M. Magnifico and M. Utili, Exhibition catalogue (Milan, 1987), pp. 48, 86; Azzi Visentini, *Il giardino veneto tra Sette e Ottocento*, pp. 11, 19.

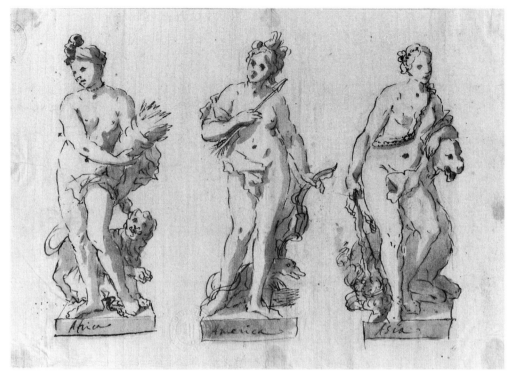

Fig. 4.14 Orazio Marinali et al. Project for a group of garden statues representing Africa, the Americas and Asia. Pen and watercolour drawing from *Album del Marinali*

of important pre-existing works, to search for a highly personalised solution suited to that position alone rather than adapting the site to any pre-established scheme. This prompted the adoption of highly original solutions in which art and nature blended to create a harmonious symbiosis.

A good starting point is the late sixteenth-century villa in Verona belonging to the Giusti family. Despite being an urban residence rather than a country villa, this is in my opinion a prime example of the Veneto approach to the problem. At the rear of the palace lies an Italianate garden, initially on level and then on gently sloping ground, articulated into uniform squares on each side of the straight cypress-lined avenue. This level part of the garden is abruptly interrupted by a spectacularly high cliff rising up several metres. Above it lay a long strip of ground also belonging to the Giusti family. In other regions advantage might have been taken of this considerable difference in height to create architectonic terracing. At Verona it was preferred, however, to leave the cliff in its unspoilt natural state. This provided a deliberate contrast to the artificial features below – the entry portal to the central grotto and the grotto itself which skilfully gave the illusion of an airy loggia – and above – the grotesque mascaron attributed to Ridolfi topped by the belvedere whose panoramic view over the city and surrounding country attracted all visitors passing through Verona. It is worth emphasising that the garden was structured in this fashion precisely on account of the panorama.[63]

At the end of the sixteenth century Vincenzo Scamozzi designed the picturesque pilgrims' way which wound its way up the hillside, visiting six chapels on the way before finally leading to the villa-cum-sanctuary belonging to the Duodo family at Monselice. The villa was flanked by the chapel of S. Giorgio, whose elegance rivalled the nearby aristocratic residence set into the side of Colle di Monselice, and partly encompassed by the ancient walls leading up to the medieval fortress. This complex scenic *machina*, which provided the uphill backdrop for the building resting against the slope of Colle di Monselice, the site of the original family mausoleum culminating in the grotto of S. Francesco where profane and sacred mingled in strange promiscuity, was counterbalanced below by a hanging 'garden with pergolas for citrus trees' overlooking the wide plain (fig. 4.15). The original layout of the slope above the villa was later altered but not radically changed during the eighteenth-century rebuilding. This was directed by Andrea Tirali, who transformed the already tiered slope into a large cavea enclosed by the exedra which framed the sacred grotto, whereas a side stairway led up to the old castle, thus respecting the relationship between constructed and natural elements which had been proposed almost a century and a half earlier. As at Rocca Pisana and numerous other sites, local stone was used to bring the man-made interventions as far as possible into harmony with nature.[64]

Il Cataio is worth mentioning as one of the strangest country residences in the Veneto. Two sides of this odd building back onto the slope of a rocky hilltop and were intentionally designed to look like an imposing fortress as a tribute to the man of arms, Pio Enea I degli Obizzi, who had built a small villa on the same site in the 1570s. His mother, Beatrice Pia, used to assemble a select group of intellectuals in this building whose loggias faced the river. The austere, inward-looking appearance of the castle's façade, characterised by high walls with embrasures and surrounded by sentry-boxes, watch-towers and other military features, was associated with the numerous courtyards and hanging gardens within the complex, and the equally numerous sloping terraces and loggias overlooking the countryside towards the canal. This contrast, which represented the most striking feature of Il Cataio right from the start, became even more marked during the second half of the seventeenth century following the building's enlargement by the then owner, Pio Enea Il degli Obizzi. He constructed new buildings above the villa by excavating building sites out of the hard rock in the hill above, and built several courtyards, including the vast sunken courtyard intended as a setting for special events, tournaments and naumachia. He also augmented the number

[63] M. Azzi Visentini, 'La grotta nel Cinquecento veneto: il giardino Giusti di Verona', *Arte Veneta*, 39 (1985), pp. 55–64; idem, 'Il giardino Giusti di Verona', in *Il giardino come labirinto della storia*, ed. G. Pirrone (Palermo, 1987), pp. 177–81.

[64] L. Puppi and L. Olivato Puppi, 'Scamozziana. Progetti per la "via romana" di Monselice e alcune altre novità grafiche con qualche quesito', *Antichità Viva*, 13 (1974), no. 4, pp. 54–80; V. Fontana, 'Villa Duodo, Monselice', in Azzi Visentini (ed.), *Il giardino veneto*, pp. 123–5.

Fig. 4.15 The Villa Duodo at Monselice. Eighteenth-century print engraved by Giovanni Angeli after a drawing by Francesco Guerra

of sloping terraces facing the canal and, above all, planned the extensive garden which stretched well beyond the side of the castle and was lined with magnificent pergolas used to house the precious citrus fruits in winter. All these features serve to underline the typically Veneto intolerance of any project enclosed within artificially imposed limits; here, these were audaciously broken to allow all the constructed features to blend with the surrounding countryside.[65]

Another example of successful integration, or, better still, successful symbiosis between art and nature, is the eighteenth-century rebuilding of Villa Trento da Schio at Costozza di Longare. The villa's garden, whose sloping, south-facing terraces follow the gradient of the hillside on which they perch, protected by the hill behind, occupies a particularly advantageous position for the cultivation of citrus fruits and other precious essences. The garden was in fact designed like a vast conservatory, embellished by grottoes, statues and stairways, most of which stood along the central axis in order to leave as much space as possible for plants. The main residence, enlarged from an

[65] G. Betussi, *Descrizione del Cataio Luogo del marchese Pio Enea degli Obizi . . . con l'aggiunta del Co. Francesco Berni Delle fabriche, & altre delizie accresciutevi in 18 anni dal Marchese Pio Enea* (Ferrara, 1669); Azzi Visentini, 'Il Cataio, Battaglia', in idem (ed.), *Il giardino veneto*, pp. 114–17.

existing building, lies to one side of the complex and is also divided into a number of different levels. The conservatories above it are approached by the stairway along whose balustrade stand Marinali's magnificent dwarves. Higher up, and again on one side, stands what is referred to as 'Marinali's grotto': this small, odd construction was the artist's house and is partly dug into rock behind, sections of which are very apparent on the wall at the back of the main room, forming a striking contrast with Dorigny's frescoes. In front of the grotto is a hanging garden overlooking the Villa Trento and a wide panorama beyond.[66]

At Villa Verità in San Pietro di Lavagno advantage was taken of the geographical layout of the steeply sloping site to articulate the garden, built in the early seventeenth century, into a series of sloping terraces running from the top to the bottom of the hill. In descending order these consisted of the 'piazza', the 'arena' and the large hanging garden which was on the same level as the ground floor of the villa; it was divided into uniform squares in the Italian style with a pool ornamented with Gerolamo Campagna's famous sculptural group in the centre. Under this was the lower garden onto which opened the large grotto beneath the pool, whose water fed the noisy cascades, a relatively uncommon feature in Veneto gardens, and the fish-pond which doubled as a water reservoir. These elements, connected to one another by scenographic stairways, were aligned along the central axis running down the slope of the hill, exactly as can be seen in numerous gardens in Lazio. The central axis lay at right angles to that of the main residence, whose rear façade bounded one side of the intermediate level of the garden. The intersection of the two axes coincided precisely with Campagna's statue of Hercules and Antaeus. Panoramic views of the fertile estates owned by the noble family from Verona could be enjoyed from the parapets surrounding the garden.[67]

In conclusion, a telling comparison can be drawn between the sixteenth-century Villa Brenzone at Punta San Vigilio, which stood on a promontory overlooking the Verona bank of Lake Garda (fig. 4.16), and the seventeenth-century Villa Borromeo built on a small island in Lake Maggiore. The former provides a clear example of the extreme discretion used in the Veneto in all interventions involving the natural setting, whereas the latter shows how in other, not distant regions of Italy it was preferred to make greater concessions to artifice. The garden at Villa Brenzone lies to the east of the building and consists of a series of separate elements, ideally linked to one another by the humanistic programme inspired by the renaissance of the antique.[68] These elements succeed each other in a paratactical manner, giving added emphasis to the structure of the site and harmoniously encompassing major pre-existing features, ranging from the

[66] Azzi Visentini, 'Villa Trento da Schio, Costozza di Longare', in idem (ed.), *Il giardino veneto*, pp. 142–4.

[67] Azzi Visentini, 'Villa Verità, San Pietro di Lavagno', in idem (ed.), *Il giardino veneto*, pp. 126–8; A. Conforti Calcagno, 'Villa Verità-Fraccaroli al Boschetto di S. Pietro di Lavagno', in *Lavagno. Una comunità e un territorio attraverso i secoli*, ed. G. Volpato (Verona, 1988), pp. 329–42.

[68] M. Azzi Visentini, 'Un esemplare giardino umanistico: Villa Brenzone a Punta San Vigilio', in Mosser and Teyssot (eds.), *L'architettura*, pp. 102–4.

Fig. 4.16 Aerial view of the Villa Brenzone at Punta San Vigilio (Verona)

small lakeside harbour to the *rotonda degli antichi* on the summit of the small promontory, a feature which may have suggested the idea of the Temple of British Worthies at Stowe to William Kent.[69] The famous garden at Villa Borromeo, on the other hand, occupies the whole of Isola Bella, which has been completely transformed into an artificial, symmetrical and none the less extraordinary complex which evokes the architectural form of a ship.

Although other aspects could be analysed, the above will be sufficient to illustrate how the architecture of the villa and its adjoining buildings and garden layout in the Veneto are always dictated by a careful survey of the peculiar features of the site. This appreciation of the site's natural qualities was intended to lead to the creation of a harmonious dialogue between the site and any human intervention: in the conception of the Veneto villa the garden was virtually regarded as a surrogate of a beautiful natural landscape. In fact, when the natural setting spontaneously presented a variety of attractive views from a hilltop position, the villa, whose porticoes and loggias ran along the building's central axes, thus allowing the surrounding environment to filter through the building, was encompassed by narrow open spaces, little more than panoramic terraces. When, on the other hand, the building stood in the midst of a

---

[69] As John Dixon Hunt suggested in his *William Kent. Landscape Garden Designer* (London, 1987), p. 54.

monotonous expanse of arable land, as in the case of the villas sited on the plain, art was called upon to create spacious gardens with a dual function: to serve as an area for 'recreation' and to furnish the 'beautiful vistas' which nature alone had failed to provide.

In conclusion, it is worth emphasising that during the construction of the Veneto villas over three centuries an attempt was always made to respect, with due discretion, the environmental setting in which the architectural project was located. And this context, which was and still is inseparable from the villa, should be safeguarded in the same way as the individual buildings. It is regrettable to note, therefore, that so-called industrial civilisation has drastically altered the layout of particularly important areas in several zones, ranging from the banks of the Brenta to the Terraglio and the Euganean Hills, which have been savagely eaten away by quarries, and on the outskirts of urban centres where historical residences, suffocated by a milieu which no longer respects them and often deprived of their gardens, appear as the gaunt survivors of a past age. It is to be sincerely hoped that similar destruction can be avoided in the future.

CHAPTER 5

THE GARDENS OF THE MILANESE 'VILLEGGIATURA' IN THE MID-SIXTEENTH CENTURY

IRIS LAUTERBACH

In memory of Jörg Gamer (1931-1993)

From the days of the Visconti and the Sforza onwards, many important villas, with gardens, appeared in the duchy of Milan. It is evident that their garden design borrowed from developments in other artistic centres in Italy, and also that European models and stimuli had a considerable influence. One reason for this was doubtless the fact that the Spanish Habsburgs, who ruled the city after 1535, and their Austrian cousins, who ruled it from 1706, facilitated and encouraged contacts with the outside world. French influence is also clear from the late Seicento onwards. Because of its geographical situation, Milan had long been open to countries on the other side of the Alps; and since the duchy of Milan was a neighbour of Savoy, which had dynastic links with France, it was the traditional first stop for French travellers to Italy. When the ideas and culture of the French Enlightenment, and later the Romantic movement, first reached the Italian peninsula, they found their most fertile ground not in Venice or Florence, nor yet in Rome or Naples, but among the aristocracy and in the intellectual atmosphere of Milan. It is therefore not surprising to find that one of the first Italian authors to write a treatise on landscape gardening, in the tradition of Hirschfeld, was a Milanese – Ercole Silva, a scion of an old noble family, with his *Dell'arte dei giardini inglesi* (1801).

In the course of the eighteenth century, in Rome and other places, the ideal of regularly patterned gardens, as seen in the Cinquecento and Seicento, began gradually to give way to the landscape model, more by natural evolution than by conscious alteration. But in Milan it was otherwise: landscapists looked to theory and started afresh with new gardens – as in Ercole Silva's own villa at Cinisello Balsamo, or the Villa Reale in Monza – and modelled them on examples beyond the Alps. Thus, from the middle of the Cinquecento to the beginning of the Ottocento, gardens appeared in the Milanese *villeggiatura* which were stylistically among the most advanced of their time. As the landscape around Milan is extremely varied, the gardens there often show an original and distinctive handling of the terrain. In none of the other Italian regions whose landscape

127

was artistically shaped by the culture of the villa – Piedmont and the Veneto, Florence, Rome and Naples – is such a varied garden topography to be seen in such a small space as in this countryside, along the *navigli* (canals) of Milan, in the Po valley, the hills of the Brianza and the lakes which lie among the lower slopes of the Alps.

Nevertheless, and in spite of the useful and important studies which have been published in the last few decades,[1] a glance at the historiography of Milan's villas and gardens will reveal numerous gaps. Although authors such as Arrigoni, Bascapè and Langè have produced masterly overall surveys of the theme, we still lack detailed research on many sites. Doubtless this is mainly because, in all probability, much source material is still gathering dust in the archives of the noble families of Milan, still largely unexplored by historians. Moreover, the villas of Milan are far less well represented in *vedute* and descriptions than are (for example) those of Piedmont, Florence or Rome. The ducal house of Savoy took care to advertise its artistic and political identity through innumerable panegyrics. In Rome, the seat of many noble families who competed among themselves in artistic achievement – as in other things – and the goal of in-numerable pilgrims, artists and travellers, there was a kind of compulsion towards pictorial representation, most profitable to art historians. There was nothing compar-able in Milan, where the desire for self-representation may have been muted by foreign rule, by the plagues of 1575-7 and 1630, and by political and economic decline through the Seicento. Unlike Rome or Florence, where every traveller would visit, and often describe, the famous villas in and around the city, Milan had comparatively few gar-dens: only at the end of the eighteenth century did Piermarini's Giardino Pubblico do something to remedy this. As for the many villa gardens outside the city, they seem to have been so far off the usual tourist routes that they often receive only a brief mention in guide books, and therefore in travellers' descriptions.[2] This is not true of the Isole

---

[1] See especially the relevant volumes in the series *Ville italiane*: Pier Fausto Bagatti Valsecchi, Anna Maria Cito Filomarino and Francesco Süss, *Ville della Brianza*, vol. I (Milan, 1978); Santino Langè, *Ville della provincia di Milano* (Milan, 1972) and *Ville delle province di Como, Sondrio e Varese* (Milan, 1968); Carlo Perogalli and Paolo Favole, *Ville dei navigli lombardi* (Milan, 1967). See also Paolo Arrigoni, *Mostra delle ville milanesi del Sei-Settecento* (Milan, 1928); Pier Fausto Bagatti Valsecchi, 'Le ville storiche nell'ambiente lombardo', in *Lombardia, il territorio, l'ambiente, il paesaggio* (Milan, 1982), vol. III, pp. 125–32; Giacomo Bascapè, *Mostra storica dei giardini di Lombardia*, Exhibition catalogue (Milan, 1959) and *Arte e storia dei giardini di Lombardia* (Milan, 1978); Giacomo Bascapè and Carlo Perogalli, *Ville milanesi* (Milan, 1965); Maria Teresa Boriosi Cruciani, 'Il giardino lombardo', *Antichità viva* 5 (5) (1966), pp. 27–42; Aldo Castellano, 'Il paesaggio come spettacolo: la villa', in *La Lombardia spagnola* (Milan, 1984), pp. 77–86; *Il giardino a Milano, per pochi e per tutti. 1288-1945*, Exhibition catalogue (Milan, 1986); *Mostra del giardino italiano*, Exhibition catalogue (Florence, 1931); Francesco Süss, *Le ville del territorio milanese. Aspetti storici e architettonici*, 2 vols. (Milan, 1988-9).

[2] Paolo Morigi, *La nobiltà di Milano . . . Aggiuntovi il supplemento . . . del Sig. Girolamo Borsieri* (Milan, 1619), p. 551: 'nel ricco, e populoso contado di Milano si veggono gran numero di bellissime, e superbissime fabriche, con appartamenti, e loggiamenti signorili da Prencipi, tutti delitiosi, con fonte, peschiere, boschetti, lamberinti, pergolati, e prospettive, che per essere eglino un grandissimo numero li trapasserò di raccontare'. ('In the rich and populous county of Milan you may see a great number of most beautiful and distinguished buildings, with apartments and noble lodgings for Princes, all delightful, with fountains, fish-ponds, groves, labyrinths, arbours and vistas, which are so numerous that I shall not attempt to describe them.') Galeazzo Gualdo Priorato, *Relatione della città, e Stato di Milano . . .* (Milan, 1666), pp. 149ff, on 'Borghi, Terre, e Ville con loro feudi più riguardevoli del Ducato di Milano', p. 163: 'Tutto all'intorno poi di Milano vi sono casamenti, cassine, e casali de'Cittadini, con horti, giardini, & altre delitie insigni per la qualità del paese fertile, & abbondante, e diverse

Borromee in Lake Maggiore, which lay on the standard route for tourists from the north and north-west to Milan, and were often the subject of enthusiastic comments. For travellers who continued their journey via Pavia and along the Po valley, the Villa Belgioioso was also conveniently accessible.[3]

If we look at the work of only two artists, quite apart from the surviving villas themselves, we can see that these 'lacunae' in the guide books result in a wholly inadequate picture of the villa culture of Milan. Both of the following are therefore of the greatest importance. In 1559, the jurist and *litterateur* Bartolomeo Taegio published his (unfortunately scantily illustrated) treatise *La villa. Un dialogo*, in which he gives a convincing account of the villa culture flourishing in Milan in his time. Nearly 200 years later, in 1726, the engraver Marc Antonio Dal Re published his seminal work *Le ville di delizia*, which no historian can afford to ignore, although it documents only a rather late stage in the villa culture (a second, enlarged edition appeared in 1743).[4] In a chapter of this length it would be impossible to give more than a brief survey of Milanese horticulture from Taegio to Dal Re, particularly as the sources are, as I have said, often inadequately researched. What I shall attempt, therefore, is to describe the culture of villa and garden in Milan in the middle of the Cinquecento, paying attention to Taegio's treatise and examining two important sites by way of example.

At an early stage, the Visconti and Sforza had created several hunting parks in and around Milan. Although our knowledge of these is scanty, owing to the lack of detailed evidence,[5] we do know that there was a very extensive wooded area, stretching from the Castello Visconteo in Pavia to near Certosa: a *barco* rich in game. Memories of this game park, which must have suffered greatly from the ravages of the battle of Pavia which took place in the area in 1525, persisted for a long time.[6] Another hunting park,

---

picciole Ville.' ('All round Milan there are houses, dwellings, and citizens' residences, with orchards, gardens, and other delights, notable for the quality of the fertile and abundant landscape, and diverse little villas.') Johann Georg Keyszler, *Neueste Reisen durch Deutschland . . . Italien* (Hanover, 1751), vol. I, pp. 259ff, on gardens around Milan; Abbé Jérôme Richard, *Description historique et critique de l'Italie* (Paris, 1766), vol. I, p. 267, on the Milanese *villeggiatura*: 'Dans le printemps & l'automne il y a une multitude de châteaux & de belles maisons peu éloignées de la ville où la plupart de ces gentilshommes vont passer les beaux jours.' ('In the spring and autumn there is a multitude of châteaux and fine houses, not far from the city, where most of these gentlemen go in fine weather.') Maria Cristina Gozzoli, 'Artisti e viaggiatori fra città e campagne lombarde all'epoca del "Grand Tour"', in *Lombardia, il territorio*, pp. 201–85.

[3] The Villa Belgioioso is described in detail in e.g. Richard, *Description historique*, p. 193.

[4] Marc Antonio Dal Re, *Le ville di delizia o siano palagi camparecci nello Stato di Milano*; many of the engravings are included in the selection edited and introduced by Pier Fausto Bagatti Valsecchi and Giansiro Ferrata (Milan, 1963). However, by no means all of Dal Re's engravings are easily accessible today, because, except for the editions of 1726 and 1743, they survive only as scattered, very rare single sheets. A large number can be found in the Raccolta Bertarelli in Milan (Castello Sforzesco). See also the 1987 reprint of Dal Re's engravings of the Castello Belgioioso (Milan, 1987). The next sizeable publication in the Dal Re tradition on villas in the Milan region, illustrated with lithographs, was Federico and Carolina Lose, *Viaggio nei monti di Brianza* (Milan, 1823; reprint Milan, 1959).

[5] Authoritative studies of fifteenth-century villas are Luisa Giordano, '"Ditissima Tellus". Ville quattrocentesche tra Po e Ticino', *Bollettino della Società Pavese di Storia Patria*, 40 (1988), pp. 145–295; Carlo Magenta, *I Visconti e gli Sforza nel castello di Pavia* (Milan, 1883); F. Prato, 'Il parco vecchio o il campo di battaglia di Pavia', in *Memorie e documenti per la storia di Pavia* (Pavia, 1897).

[6] See, e.g, Franz Schott, *Il nuovo itinerario d'Italia* (Rome, 1649), p. 121, where he writes on the buildings which were still visible.

near the Castello in Milan, was steadily expanded under Galeazzo Maria Sforza and his successors.[7] The earliest villa of any size, the so-called Sforzesca, completed in 1486, was built near Vigevano for Lodovico il Moro.[8] An inscription on the building says that Lodovico had dedicated himself to the peaceful pursuit of agriculture and ensured that the earth of his villa became fruitful: 'VILIS GLEBA FUI MODO SUM DITISSIMA TELLUS'.[9] Mulberry trees, planted at the time, remind us that the luxury fabrics of Milan were eagerly sought after in fourteenth- and fifteenth-century Europe. Lodovico had a *barco* to hunt in, and the labyrinth of trees he planted indicates an artistically planned garden. Here we already see the characteristic combination of usefulness and pleasure which was to mark the villa culture of Lombardy in later centuries. The architects employed at the Sforza court around 1500 evinced a renewed interest in garden design. Not only Leonardo, but also Filarete often mention gardens, and Filarete's numerous designs for 'labyrinths' may be explained by the Sforzas' predilection for mazes.[10]

The claims of the French royal house and the Spanish Habsburgs on the dukedom of Milan led to war in the 1520s and 1530s.[11] The victory of Charles V's armies in the battle of Pavia in 1525 brought the dukedom under Habsburg sway; it again fell to the Habsburgs after the death of the last Sforza in 1535. The political situation of Milan, unstable for decades, was consolidated by the Habsburg takeover, which was codified in a new constitution imposed in 1541. Until 1706, when the dukedom was conquered by Prince Eugene and passed to the Austrian Habsburgs, Milan remained under the domination of Spain, represented by a governor.

Between about 1530 and 1580, when the after-effects of the first great plague of 1575-7 made themselves felt, the newly stabilized political situation brought to both town and country an economic prosperity which found expression in increased building activity. Most of the land in the dukedom belonged, by long custom, to the leading Milanese patrician families, who occupied the highest offices of state, dominated the senate, and decided policy in both city and state. The nobility, here as in the rest of Italy, defined themselves through this possession of land, and while the political theorist Nicolò Machiavelli severely criticised their feudal rule, he also bore witness to their power:

[7] Luca Beltrami, *Il castello di Milano sotto il dominio dei Visconti e degli Sforza* (Milan, 1894) and works mentioned in note 1.

[8] Giordano, '"Ditissima Tellus"', pp. 251ff; Ludwig Heydenreich, 'La villa: genesi e sviluppi fino al Palladio', *Bollettino CISA*, 11 (1969), pp. 11–22, esp. pp. 14–16; Richard Schofield, 'Lodovico il Moro and Vigevano', *Arte lombarda*, 62 (1982), pp. 93–140, p. 132: without 'suitable gardens . . . no Sforza settlement was complete'.

[9] Giordano, '"Ditissima Tellus"', p. 268.

[10] On Leonardo's plans for villas and gardens see Carlo Pedretti, *Leonardo architetto* (Milan, 1978); Aldo Castellano, 'La "villa" milanese nella prima metà del Cinquecento. Un prototipo inedito: la "Gualtiera-Simonetta", in *La Lombardia spagnola*, pp. 87–128, especially pp. 122ff; Filarete, *Trattato di architettura*, ed. Anna Maria Finoli and Liliana Grassi (Milan, 1972): see e.g. vol. II, plates 14, 19, 88; there were intricate mazes at the Sforzesca and at the Milan Castello. See also Schofield, 'Lodovico il Moro'.

[11] See Ada Annoni, 'Milano, lo stato conteso, nella politica internazionale dei secoli XVI-XVII', in *La Lombardia spagnola*, pp. 9–38; Roberto Mainardi, 'I territori lombardi nel XVI secolo', in *Lombardia. Il territorio*, vol. II, pp. 7–22; *Storia di Milano*, IX: *L'epoca di Carlo V (1535-1559)* (Milan, 1961).

gentiluomini sono chiamati quelli, che oziosi vivono dei proventi delle loro possessioni abbondantemente, senza avere alcuna cura o di coltivare, o di alcun' altra necessaria fatica a vivere. Questi tali sono perniciosi in ogni repubblica ed in ogni provincia, ma più perniciosi sono quelli, che oltre alle predette fortune comandano a castella, ed hanno sudditi che ubbidiscono a loro. Di queste due sorte d'uomini ne sono pieni il regno di Napoli, terra di Roma, la Romagna e la Lombardia.

('the term "gentry" is used of those who live in idleness on the abundant revenue derived from their estates, without having anything to do either with their cultivation or with other forms of labour essential to life. Such men are a pest in any republic and in any province; but still more pernicious are those who, in addition to the aforesaid revenues, have castles under their command and subjects under their obedience. Of these two types of men there are plenty in the kingdom of Naples, the Papal States, the Romagna and Lombardy.')[12]

However, a fief (*feudo*) could also be acquired by purchase. Ownership of land carried the title of Marchese or Conte, according to the number of vassal families which went along with it. It is true that for many years such a newly acquired title of nobility gave no rights to high office – for which a suitable genealogy and several generations of aristocratic lifestyle (*more nobilium*)[13] were essential – but it did offer exemption from certain taxes. Such a position, therefore, not only allowed its holder to rise socially in the Milanese patriciate, but also brought him concrete economic advantages. The Spaniards, and later the Austrians, often showed their gratitude to their faithful Milanese supporters – mostly government officials and tax-gatherers – by gifts of land and an accompanying title of nobility.

The enthusiasm of merchants and officials for the possession of land was a feature of the second half of the Cinquecento, and not only in Milan. This is shown, for example, in the comments made by Anton Francesco Doni, a Florentine by birth who later settled in the Veneto, but who was also familiar with the state of affairs in Lombardy.[14] In his treatise *Le ville* (first edition Bologna, 1566) he divides villas into five categories according to social rank. Merchants (*mercatanti*) are assigned to the third category, the relatively modest *possessione di ricriatione*; but he complains that thanks to their extensive means they often rise to a 'higher' rank: 'bene spesso con un prezzo da cittadino, comprano una villa da Re' ('very often for the price of a citizen, they buy a villa fit for a king').[15]

---

[12] Niccolò Machiavelli, *Discorsi sopra le deche di Tito Livio*, in *Opere*, vol. III (Florence, 1813): book I, 55; *The Discourses*, ed. Bernard Crick (Harmondsworth, 1970, repr. 1983), pp. 245–6.

[13] Mainardi, 'I territori', p. 10.

[14] See note 22 for source of Doni's comments on Giovio's villa.

[15] Anton Francesco Doni, *Le ville* (1st ed. Bologna, 1566), reprint ed. Hugo Bellocchi, *Deputazione di storia patria per le antiche provincie modenesi*, n.s., 12 (Modena, 1969), p. 57. In a manuscript of *Le ville* which remained unpublished in his lifetime, Doni added a verse composition which is a harsh invective addressed to newly rich social climbers and villa owners. It culminates in the lines, 'Credete che le vesti, sì supreme / L'aplauso, i servitor, palagi e forza / Faccin che la Virtù paventi e treme?' (p. 108). ('Do you think that clothes, however fine, applause, servants, palaces and power, make Virtue fear and tremble?')

The stunningly rapid development of Milanese villa culture in the middle of the Cinquecento is more easily explained against this social background. Ownership of land was essentially confined to the patriciate and the high nobility, but the newly rich classes were muscling in. The most impressive evidence for the highly developed villa culture in Milan is given by Bartolomeo Taegio, who lists well over 200 villas. Taegio's treatise clearly describes the pattern of ownership of these villas and their customary use, and his descriptions hold true into the Settecento. The 'villa' included a tract of land which was mostly under cultivation; the greater part of it was rented out. The owner, who spent most of the year pursuing his own affairs in the city, did not just repair to the country for rest and recreation: it was particularly in spring and autumn that he was to be found at the villa, to supervise the agricultural labours of his tenants. In many cases the villa, with its farm buildings and gardens, was structurally very similar to the villages around.

I shall now examine two important gardens from the middle of the Cinquecento, which are conceptually closely related: Paolo Giovio's *museum* on Lake Como and the Milanese villa of the governor, Ferrante Gonzaga, who was advised by Giovio, and in the process I shall look more closely at Bartolomeo Taegio's treatise.

The villa which the clerical humanist and polymath, Paolo Giovio, had built beside Lake Como to house his collection of portraits of famous men has been well documented and researched.[16] Attention has been focused especially on the concept of the *musaeum*, which was the first modern use of this classical notion to denote a particular building.[17] The series of portraits of *uomini famosi* was a model for many later collections.[18] Also of importance, especially in the context of Lombard villa architecture, is Giovio's conscious and express determination to imitate the villas of antiquity. His humanist *villeggiatura* is quite unlike the concept outlined above, with its frequent overtones of agricultural utility.

Paolo Giovio (1483–1552) was a native of Como who lived for many years in Rome; he began collecting portraits some time before 1519. In 1531 comes the first indication that he was planning to build a villa on the banks of Lake Como, some 15 km from the town, to receive his growing collection (fig. 5.1). We do not know whether the architect Domenico Giunti ('Giuntalodi', 1505–60) was responsible for the work from the outset, but Giovio himself mentions that Giunti was at work on the villa, and, in a

[16] See Matteo Gianoncelli, *L'antico Museo di P. Giovio in Borgovico* (Como, 1977); Paolo Giovio, *Opere*, vol. VIII: *Gli elogi degli uomini illustri*, ed. R. Meregazzi (Rome, 1972), esp. pp. 1–21; Eugène Müntz, 'Le Musée de portraits de Paul Jove . . .', *Mémoires de l'Académie des Inscriptions et Belles-Lettres* 36(2) (1900); Paul Ortwin Rave, 'Das Museo Giovio zu Como', in *Miscellanea Bibliothecae Hertzianae* (Munich, 1961), pp. 275–84.

[17] Thus Rave, 'Museo'. The building is first termed a museum in a letter of 1539 (ibid., p. 277).

[18] See, e.g., Heidy Böcker-Dursch, 'Zyklen berühmter Männer in der bildenden Kunst Italiens – Neuf Preux und "uomini illustri" – eine ikonologische Studie', dissertation, Munich, 1973; Maria Monica Donato, 'Gli eroi romani tra storia ed "exemplum". I primi cicli umanistici di Uomini Famosi', in *Memoria dell'antico nell'arte italiana*, ed. Salvatore Settis (Turin, 1985), vol. II, pp. 97–152, with exhaustive bibliography; Wolfram Prinz, 'Vasaris Sammlung von Künstlerbildnissen', *Mitteilungen des Kunsthistorischen Institutes in Florenz*, 12, Beiheft (Florence, 1966); Paul Ortwin Rave, 'Paolo Giovio und die Bildnisvitenbücher des Humanismus', *Jahrbuch der Berliner Museen* 1 (1959), pp. 119–54.

Fig. 5.1 Paolo Giovio. Map of Lake Como, *Descriptio larii locus* (Como, 1559)

letter of 1547 to Ferrante Gonzaga, refers to him as 'my' architect ('el mio maestro Domenico da Prato').[19] Building began in 1536 under the supervision of Benedetto, representing his brother Paolo, who still lingered in Rome; it must have been almost finished by the summer of 1539. Giovio spoke enthusiastically about the planned 'iovalissimo edificio sopra il laco proprio dedicato al Genio e alle Muse' ('most jovial/Giovial building on the lake, entirely dedicated to the Genius and the Muses').[20] However, Giovio, still in Rome, was so absorbed in work on the publication of the *Elogia*, the *vitae* of the persons represented in his collection (the first edition appeared in 1546),[21] that he at first paid only sporadic visits to his *museum*, and lived there for long periods only in his old age. Nevertheless, at an early stage he had his ever-increasing

---

[19] Paolo Giovio, *Lettere*, ed. Giuseppe Guido Ferrero, vol. II: *1544-52* (Rome, 1958), no. 187, 15 December 1547. On the architect, see the section on the Villa Gonzaga.

[20] Cited from a letter of Giovio to Cardinal Gian Maria del Monte: *Opere*, ed. Meregazzi, p. 8.

[21] Giovio, *Opere*, ed. Meregazzi, pp. 1–21.

collection transferred to the villa, where it was visited by innumerable scholars and exalted personages. This golden age for the villa and museum did not last long: a few decades after Paolo's death the villa was sold off, and the collection, still in the possession of his descendants, was dispersed. The buildings, directly over the lake, had been damaged by floods, so that the new owner, Marco Gallio, had a new villa built further inland, probably using material from the earlier site.

Several documents provide information about the appearance of the villa and the intentions of the man who commissioned it: there is a letter from Benedetto to his brother in Rome, dating from 1542; in 1543 Anton Francesco Doni visited the site, and reported on it in two letters to Jacopo Tintoretto and Agostino Landi; and of special importance, naturally, are Giovio's own descriptions, particularly the masterpiece of rhetoric entitled 'Musaei Ioviani descriptio', which he put as a preface to the *Elogia* of 1546. In it he gives an ideal portrait of the *villeggiatura* of a humanist who wishes to enjoy his leisure, far from the cares of the city, in a place dedicated to the arts and sciences, to Apollo and the Muses. A painting dated to 1619, now in the Museo Comunale at Como, gives us some idea of what the building looked like (fig. 5.2).[22]

The very first sentence of Giovio's description (after some introductory remarks) alludes to the exceptional site of the villa, which is on a kind of peninsula jutting into the lake. Even this choice of site is a conscious reference to antiquity: not only were the remains of one of Pliny's villas to be seen nearby, under the lake, but the site was supposed to be the place where an 'opacissima Plinii platanus' had formerly stood.[23] That this *platanus* (plane tree) really had stood near a villa belonging to Pliny the Elder is now thought to be improbable; but what is important is simply that Giovio thought so, and uses the idea to make an explicit link with the legendary villa of that famous resident of Como.[24] On the outside walls of the building nearest the water were paintings of warriors, together with a portrait of the Spanish governor, Alfonso Davalo Marchese del Vasto, who was a connection of Giovio's. An inscription marked it as the actual museum. Further buildings and courts followed. In the colonnades and rooms were frescoes with allegorical and mythological subjects, provided with numerous mottoes which developed and commented on the iconographic schema. Many of them related to legends of Apollo, and so alluded to the villa's designation as a home of the Muses. Towards the mountains stretched a walled garden divided into rectangular compartments; according to descriptions, it contained gardeners' work (*opera topiaria*), vine pergolas and an avenue which Giovio called a 'hippodrome', of which nothing is

[22] Letter of Benedetto to Paolo, quoted in Gio. Battista Giovio, 'Elogio di Monsignor Paolo Giovio il Seniore Vescovo di Nocera', in *Elogj italiani*, ed. Andrea Rubbi (Venice, 1782), vol. VIII, pp. 91–3; Anton Francesco Doni, *Tre libri di lettere de Doni . . .* (Venice, 1552), pp. 75–86; Paolo Giovio, *Elogia veris clarorum virorum imaginibus apposita* (Venice, 1546), also in *Opere*, ed. Meregazzi, pp. 35–8; *Collezioni civiche di Como: proposte, scoperte, restauri*, Exhibition catalogue (Como, 1981), no. 10; Gianoncelli, *L'antico Museo*, has as far as possible adapted the descriptions to outlines and site plans.

[23] Giovio, *Descriptio Larii Lacus* (Como, 1559), p. xv.

[24] Gianoncelli, *L'antico Museo*, p. 6. A similar reference to Pliny may be found at the Villa Giulia in Rome (begun in 1551), where originally four plane trees shadowed the courtyard of the nymphaeum.

Fig. 5.2 Giovio's villa on Lake Como, 1619

to be seen in the later painting. Special mention is made of a particularly unusual fountain in the so-called 'Doric colonnade', which was next to the lavishly decorated main court. Hidden conduits led to a statue of the goddess Natura, from whose breasts pure spring water flowed into a marble basin.[25] In deference to antiquity, Giovio's description tells how the fountain was made by the nymph of the spring, who deigned to leave her quiet and distant woods and dwell at the villa, and so among men. There is another instance in which Giovio rejoices in the presence of a nymph.[26] Not far from the villa, near the lakeside, there was a little island, surrounded by a wall and planted with tall fruit trees. On the side nearest the villa was the hidden nymph known as the 'Doric Echo',[27] who would again and again repeat and return the visitor's greeting. As we shall see, this 'surprise echo' feature of villa and garden architecture, typical of the mannerist concept of the *maraviglia*, recurs in the villa of Ferrante Gonzaga, which had been developed in close cooperation with his friend Giovio.

Giovio was familiar not only with more modern reflections on villa life (he mentions Petrarch and his sojourn in the Vaucluse),[28] but also, and above all, with ancient sources.

---

[25] This statue may have resembled (e.g.) the later Ceres on Ammanati's Juno Fountain for the Palazzo Vecchio in Florence (now in Florence, Museo Nazionale del Bargello); see Detlef Heikamp, 'Bartolomeo Ammanati's marble fountain for the Sala Grande of the Palazzo Vecchio in Florence', in *Fons Sapientiae. Renaissance Garden Fountains*, Dumbarton Oaks Colloquium on the History of Landscape Architecture 5 (Washington, D.C., 1978), pp. 115–73.

[26] Giovio, *Opere*, ed. Meregazzi, p. 36: 'Ab ipso quoque insulae adverso latere illa immortalis virgo abdita intus, quae Dorica vocatur Echo excitantibus, quum laeto clamore salutatur, celeri liberalique obsequio semper respondet, nam duplicatas reddit voces ac hisdem accentibus recantat.'

[27] 'Doric' here probably refers to the musical mode.   [28] Quoted in Giovio, *Opere*, ed. Meregazzi, p. 2.

Earlier, when still a young man in 1504, he had written a letter[29] describing the Villa Lissago, a family property, and referring to similar descriptions in Cicero's letters.[30] As mentioned earlier, Giovio often engages with traditions concerning ancient Como's most famous son, Pliny the Elder. Pliny had built two villas on Lake Como, one called 'Comoedia' directly on the lake shore, and the other with a panoramic view over the lake, called 'Tragoedia'; the former presumably had a more cheerful, rural character, while the latter was more serious and sublime. The character of Giovio's own villa was evidenced in an inscription over the entrance, which ended with the words MUSAEUM CUM PERENNI FONTE AMOENISQUE PORTICIBUS AD LARIUM PUBLICAE HILARITATI DEDICAVIT. This dedication of the villa to public pleasure and good cheer may be a reference to Pliny's 'Comoedia'. However that may be, in other places the humanist refers quite clearly to the villas of his fellow-countryman from classical times.[31]

It was not enough for Giovio to site his villa near the remains of one of the elder Pliny's. The building, and various other elements of the plan, also hark back to Pliny the Younger's description of his Laurentian and Tuscan villas in the two famous letters (II, 7 and V, 6), which have been many times reinterpreted. Rave has pointed out[32] that the siting of the *musaeum*, open to water on all sides, probably derives from Pliny's seaside villa at Laurentium: one of its rooms looked over the sea on three sides, and Giovio in his *Descriptio*, like Pliny before him, is very insistent on the beauty of the view over his surroundings and the effects of the sun's light on it. *Opera topiaria* and a racing track or hippodrome are attested for both the Tuscan villa and the later site on Lake Como.[33]

The garden of Giovio's villa, as far as it is known from the only surviving picture, retains the division into regular rectangular compartments which remained the norm well into the Cinquecento. Significant for our purposes are both the concept of the villa held by Giovio, who commissioned it, and the references to ancient models. That Giovio's ideas were not only influential in Lombardy, but also attracted attention in Rome (where he lived while the villa was being built) is shown by a comparison made in 1550 with the Villa Farnesina, built by Peruzzi in 1509-11, which noted that both were built near water.[34]

The villa of Don Ferrante Gonzaga, governor of Milan, known originally as the Villa Gualtiera, and generally called after subsequent owners the Villa Simonetta,[35] is fre-

---

[29] Letter to Giano Rusca, contents reproduced in Giovio, *Elogj*, p. 7.

[30] Cicero on his villa in Arpinum: *M. Tulli Ciceronis Epistolae ad Quintum Fratrem*, book III, 1. See Otto Eduard Schmidt, 'Ciceros Villen', in *Die römische Villa* ed. Fridolin Reutti (Darmstadt, 1990), pp. 13–40, esp. p. 26.

[31] For the citation from Pliny and allusion to Giovio's letter see *Opere*, p. 2, note 1; Pierre de La Ruffinière du Prey, *The Villas of Pliny from Antiquity to Posterity* (Chicago and London, 1994), *passim*.   [32] Rave, 'Museo', pp. 280–1.

[33] What Giovio's hippodrome looked like is unclear. He probably gave the name to the broad central avenue of the garden, which would have been lined with trees or pergolas: cf. later proposals for the Villa Gonzaga 'ad uso d'uno ippodromo'. It was surely not a hippodrome of the 'circus' type, as is often suggested in later reconstructions of Pliny's villa.

[34] In a letter to Giovio, Cardinal Farnese compared the site of the villa on Lake Como with the Villa Farnesina, which also lay near water, on the banks of the Tiber: quoted in Giovio, *Elogj*, pp. 51–2.

[35] According to Baroni, Alessandro Simonetta acquired the villa from Ferrante Gonzaga: Costantino Baroni, 'Domenico

quently held to be the most important early villa in the dukedom. In view of the powerful position of its owner, it must surely have been the most prestigious design of its kind in mid-sixteenth-century Milan. As early as 1574 the biographer Giuliano Gosellini wrote that with this building Don Ferrante had set his fellow Milanesi a goal and sought to encourage them to build villas for themselves[36] – although, as it turned out, the governor had scarcely any opportunity to enjoy his own, owing first to the cares of government and subsequently to his dismissal. If we bear in mind that the appointment of an Italian governor (faithful to Spanish interests) in Milan was greeted with the greatest optimism, and that Don Ferrante's entry into the city on 19 June 1546 was something of a triumph, this idea of him as a pioneer probably has some truth in it, even if we allow that the author, Gosellini, a former secretary to the governor, intended a panegyric.

Ferrante Gonzaga (1507-57), third son of Francesco Gonzaga and Isabella d'Este, who in 1539 founded the line of Guastalla and became prince of Molfetta, grew up in Mantua, and was sent in early youth (1523-6) to be educated at the court of the Emperor Charles V, in Spain.[37] There he won the trust of the emperor, who in later years encouraged the career of this general and diplomat with a series of appointments. From the 1530s onwards Ferrante's generalship ensured many a victory for the Habsburgs; from 1535 to 1546 he held the important position of viceroy of Sicily. In 1546 Charles V again showed his confidence in him by appointing him Spanish governor of Milan – where, as an Italian, he was expected by the Milanesi to use his influence to promote their interests more effectively. Don Ferrante's decline began when he was accused of various dubious dealings and summoned to defend himself before the imperial court in Brussels (1554). He was found not guilty, but the emperor none the less dismissed him from the governorship and granted him a far less important dignity in the kingdom of Naples. After Charles V's abdication, Ferrante never gained the complete trust of King Philip II; he died in 1557.

The *vitae* written in Ferrante's own lifetime, or shortly afterwards, make only marginal references to his artistic interests; he seems to have taken his military duties far

Giunti architetto di don Ferrante Gonzaga e le sue opere in Milano', *Archivio storico lombardo*, n.s., 3 (1938), pp. 326–57 (p. 351); Pompeo Litta, *Famiglie celebri italiane* (Milan, 1819-83), vol. VI, genealogy of the Simonetta family of Calabria, table II, on Alessandro Simonetta; Litta's assertion that Gonzaga bought the villa from Alessandro is based on a misunderstanding.

[36] Giuliano Gosellini, *Vita dell'Illustrissimo et Generosissimo Sig. D. Ferrando Gonzaga Principe di Molfetta* (2nd edn, Venice, 1579), p. 58: 'Et per invitar gli altri ad ornar di ville, et di giardini il contorno, fabricò fuori le mura il bel palagio, che da lui e dinominato il GONZAGA; ma per la sua partita si rimase imperfetto.' ('And to encourage others to beautify the environs with villas and gardens, he built outside the walls the fair palace that was called by him GONZAGA; but it remained unfinished at his departure.') By the mid-1550s Gosellini had assembled the biographical details about Don Ferrante which the latter intended to advance in defending the charges brought against him by Charles V; but the *Vita* itself was not published until 1574 (Litta, *Famiglie celebri*).

[37] Gosellini, *Vita*; Alfonso Ulloa, *Vita del valorosissimo e gran capitano D. Ferrante Gonzaga principe di Molfetta* (Venice, 1563); I was unable to consult Guido Gabrielli, *Laudatio Ferdinandi Gonzagae Molfictae principis et Ariani ducis* (Venice, 1561). On the relevant genealogical literature see especially Litta, *Famiglie celebri*, vol. III; Felice Ceretti, 'Don Ferrante Gonzaga alla corte di Spagna', *Atti e Memorie della Reale Deputazione di storia patria per le province modenesi*, Series V, vol. II (1903), pp. 135–48.

more seriously than the ensuing leisure.[38] At any rate, as far as his biographies can tell us, he paid much more attention, both in Sicily and in Milan, to fortresses than to palaces. This picture may be deceptive. It is certainly true, however, that Ferrante was not so much a humanist, familiar with the literature and art of ancient and modern times, as a pragmatist, who had his children taught German and Spanish rather than Latin.[39] But, apart from the fact that Ferrante must have absorbed culture in his cradle, he often frequented humanist circles and was acquainted with the poets Trissino and Aretino, and with Paolo Giovio, whose *museum* on Lake Como he visited.[40] Giovio, for his part, reciprocated the interest, asking insistently for a portrait of Don Ferrante for his collection, and acknowledging him in his *Elogia* (1551) as a notable general.[41]

Unlike later Spanish governors such as the duke of Alba, Ferrante's successor, who saw his position in Milan merely as a springboard for his later political career and never had any intention of settling there, Ferrante showed his attachment to the city by acquiring an existing villa not far from Milan, and by having it greatly enlarged and altered to suit his own purposes (figs. 5.3-6). What remains of this much-altered and severely war-damaged building is now in the heart of the town.[42] The garden had already vanished by the end of the eighteenth century.[43]

Surprisingly, the development of the building before Don Ferrante acquired it is better researched than the works he himself set in motion.[44] In 1502 Gualtiero Bascapè, a high civic official under Lodovico il Moro, acquired the land, where hitherto there had been nothing but a vineyard and some unimportant buildings. He commissioned the main buildings of the villa, constructed probably in 1502-5, including a five-arched colonnade which was incorporated into the later building, and which until the study by Castellano (1984) was attributed to the circle of Bramante. Since the so-called 'Villa Gualtiera' is always described in official documents as a *zardino*, it probably included a garden of some kind. Gualtiero only occasionally lived in the villa, whose buildings

---

[38] See note 36; Ulloa, *Vita*, fo. 180r: 'Dilettossi particolarmente di fabriche, e di fortificationi, e tal volta s'impiegava nell'agricoltura; & di questa sua inclinatione lasciò honorati testimonij come un Guardino a Palermo di molte diversità di piante e di arbori di soavissimi frutti adorno; una Gonzaga a Milano, e diversi altri edificij sul Mantovano de grande eccellenza.' ('He delighted particularly in architectural works and fortifications, and took some interest in agriculture; and of this inclination he left distinguished testimony such as a garden in Palermo adorned with a great diversity of plants and most sweet and fruitful trees; a 'Gonzaga' at Milan, and diverse other buildings of great excellence in the region of Mantua.')   [39] Thus Litta, *Famiglie celebri*.

[40] Paolo Giovio, *Lettere*, no. 268 and Appendix, p. 254; letter of Ferrante to Paolo Giovi, 26 July 1547.

[41] The portrait was executed by Domenico Giunti, architect to both Giovio and Ferrante. The *Elogio* of Ferrante appeared in Giovio's *Elogia virorum bellica virtute illustrium* (Florence, 1551), pp. 335-6.

[42] The villa is near the modern Cimitero Monumentale.

[43] Carlo Bianconi, *Nuova guida di Milano* (Milan, 1787), p. 361, on the Villa Simonetta: 'Palazzino suburbano . . . fu costrutto con fina eleganza . . . Dalla parte del non più esistente già ornato giardino. . .' ('A small palace near the town . . . it was built with refined elegance . . . on the side of the ornate garden, which no longer exists.')

[44] The standard works are Castellano, 'La "villa" milanese'; Aurora Scotti, 'Per un profilo dell' architettura milanese (1535-1565)', in *Omaggio a Tiziano. La cultura artistica milanese nell'età di Carlo V* (Milan, 1977), esp. pp. 101-2; Aldo Castellano, 'Un giardino distrutto: Il giardino della Simonetta a Milano', *Atti del sesto colloquio internazionale Sulla protezione e il restauro dei giardini storici* (Florence, 1987), pp. 143-7. Also on the villa: Ugo Tarchi, 'La villa detta "La Simonetta" nel suburbio di Milano', in *I monumenti italiani*, series II, fasc. II (Rome, 1953); Tarchi's account of the building of the villa has been partially revised by Castellano. I have not been able to consult the doctoral thesis by Nicola Soldini.

Fig. 5.3 Dal Re. General view of the Villa Gonzaga-Simonetta, 1726

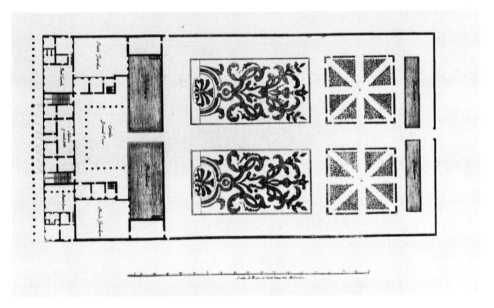

Fig. 5.4 Dal Re. Plan of the Villa Gonzaga-Simonetta, 1726

were reckoned to have seigneurial character, and left all farming matters to his tenant, from whom he received, in addition to the annual rent, a fixed quantity of agricultural produce. This fact is worthy of attention in so far as Cinquecento treatises on the villa, including the oft-mentioned work by Taegio (1559), always suggest (in deference to antiquity) that the ideal villa owner finds his foremost satisfaction in practical agriculture. This requirement seems to be really a fiction born of the study of antiquity and of Arcadian imagery, and can scarcely have corresponded to reality.

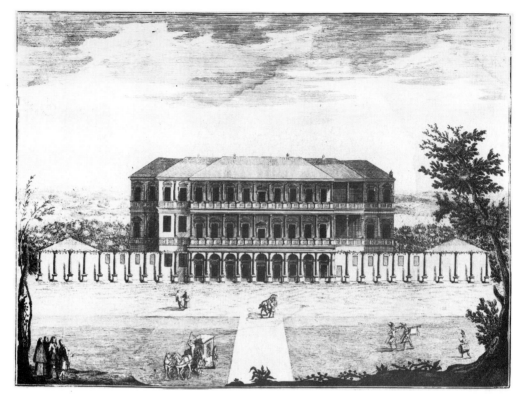

Fig. 5.5 Dal Re. Prospect from the entrance of the Villa Gonzaga-Simonetta, 1726

After Gualtiero's death in 1508 the complete sequence of ownership, down to Ferrante, is known to us. There is a bill of sale from late 1544 which gives information about the composition of the villa: the main building had been turned into a *palatio*; on one side – near the five-arched colonnade, and thus not on the later site – there was an enclosed garden. Castellano has reconstructed the striking use of loggias and porticoes to lead into the surrounding countryside, and derived them from Leonardo's studies for villas.

By a bill of sale, dated 27 April 1547, Giovanni Pietro Cicogna transfers what Castellano calls the 'prima villa-palazzo milanese' to Ferrante Gonzaga, including a '*pischeria*' and '*seu fontanile*', a vineyard and the meadows round about. In spring of the same year work was begun on what amounted to virtually a completely new building and new design. The architect was Domenico Giunti of Prato (1505-60), also known as Giuntalodi, whom we have already met in the service of Giovio.[45] He had been educated in Rome and had already worked for Ferrante some years previously. According to Vasari and Miniati, Giunti had followed Ferrante to Sicily in about 1540; there he had been

[45] See Baroni, 'Domenico Giunti'; Giuseppe Campori, *Gli artisti italiani e stranieri negli stati estensi* (Modena, 1855), pp. 246ff, on Giunti.

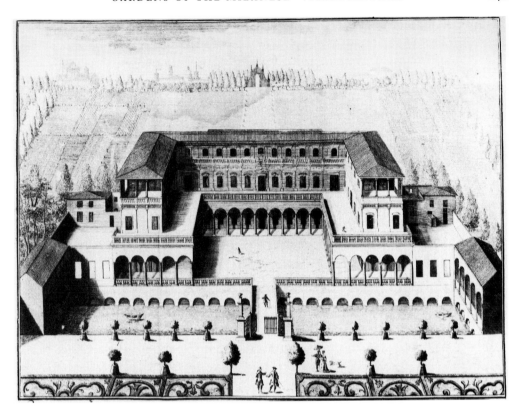

Fig. 5.6 Dal Re. Prospect of the Villa Gonzaga-Simonetta towards the garden, 1726

principally responsible for the fortification of Messina, though (according to Miniati in 1596) he had also built 'palagi, giardini, fontane, ed altre opere mirabili ed eccellenti' ('palaces, gardens, fountains and other wonderful and excellent works') for the viceroy and other clients.[46] Giunti pursued this twofold architectural specialisation – fortresses and villas[47] – in later days in Milan.

As Ferrante was often away, the architect, who was obviously working independently for much of the time, reported progress on the work in a series of letters.[48] Apart from two letters by Giovio giving his ideas on the character and appearance of the villa,[49] Giunti's correspondence is the only source at present available – certainly the

[46] Giorgio Vasari, *Le vite de' più eccellenti pittori, scultori ed architettori*, ed. Gaetano Milanesi (Florence, 1906), vol. VI, pp. 39–53; p. 40 quotes from Miniati, *Narrazione e disegno della terra di Prato* (Florence, 1596). The literature unfortunately does not make clear what sites in Palermo were involved. There is only a published letter from Giunti to Ferrante, dated 31 May 1542, in which he mentions an orchard and rabbit warren: Campori, *Artisti italiani*, p. 245; see also quotation from Ulloa in note 38.

[47] Don Ferrante also commissioned another villa in Milan, the so-called 'Senavra', about which we know virtually nothing: see Gian Battista Maderno, 'Milano – La Senavra', in *Studi e ricerche nel territorio della provincia di Milano*, ed. M. L. Gatti Perer (Milan, 1967), pp. 159–63. Giunti mentions it only once in his correspondence on the Villa Gonzaga-Simonetta: letter of 26 February 1550, which says that the work is going extremely well. Campori, *Artisti italiani*, p. 260.

[48] Ed. in Campori, *Artisti italiani*.

most important – for the history of the site. Giunti mentions several times that he is sending Ferrante drawings of the design,[50] but no research has so far brought them to light. The appearance of the garden can be deduced only from the engravings by Marc Antonio Dal Re, which are almost two hundred years later (figs. 5.3-6).[51] Unfortunately, the garden must have changed much more over the centuries than did the actual building.

Giunti's correspondence shows that from the beginning there was intensive work not only on the villa and its numerous outbuildings but also on the surrounding landscape. Purchases of neighbouring pieces of land continued even after 1547, evidently because reluctant neighbours sometimes had to be talked into selling. Vines were planted in the vineyard, which was cultivated by tenant farmers (Giunti even asked Ferrante if he preferred vines from the Brianza or from Gattinara!); a piece of ground was expressly designated as a *brolo* (orchard). The garden, probably rectangular, was surrounded by a wall, still to be seen in the Dal Re engraving. There is mention of a *prato* and also a *peschiera piccola* and a *peschiera grande*; from the context it appears that this refers to the larger fish-pond directly by the villa, which was divided into two halves by a bridge leading to the garden, and the two interconnected smaller ponds at the other end of the garden. A contract for the water supply was signed in April 1549; all commentators are enthusiastic about the abundance of water in the garden. In spring 1550 work began on the *fontanone*.[52] Espaliers were planned from the beginning. The main avenues of the garden were probably lined with pergolas or trees, hiding the surrounding wall from view.[53] Dal Re shows these transitory pergolas, which had gone out of fashion by the eighteenth century, as surviving only on the entrance side, where they visually prolong the arcades of the central *risalto* to either side and harmonise the appearance of the outbuildings behind them. Giunti often mentions that he is waiting impatiently for deliveries of marble for columns and balustrades, and probably also for fountains, which would confer due magnificence on the ensemble.

Some very interesting letters by the sculptor Leone Leoni refer to the decoration of the garden with statues, not mentioned at all by Giunti.[54] While staying in 1549 in the

---

[49] Giovio, *Lettere*, nos. 287 and 318.

[50] Baroni mentions these plans. See letters of 24 April 1547; 19 June 1549; 24 October 1549; 'il disegnio in pianta di tuta la Gonzaga come va finita' ('plan of the design of the whole Gonzaga as it is to be finished'); 2 May 1552: 'li disegni della Gonzaga e sono pezi n.o 3 cioè la pianta, la faciata di tramontana e quella di mezo giorno' ('the designs for the Gonzaga, three items viz. the plan, the northern façade and the southern one'); 5 August 1553: 'la pianta del disegnio della aggiunta al casotto' ('the plan of the design for the addition to the house'). All in Campori, *Artisti italiani*.

[51] Marc Antonio Dal Re, *Ville di delizia* (lst ed., 1726). Dal Re puts the Villa Simonetta at the very beginning, evidently because of its artistic importance.

[52] Whether this was the same fountain as the *fontanino belissimo* which was completed in summer 1553 (see letter of 5 August 1553) is unclear. *Fontanino* and *fontanone* seem to imply distinctly different dimensions. Since Giovio is most enthusiastic about the abundance of water on the site, we may assume that there were several fountains.

[53] Contemporary treatises, including Taegio's (see below), always recommend that the main avenues should be lined with pergolas or trees. Giovio's letter of 15 December 1547 also refers to pergolas; on 19 October 1549 he speaks of dense arbours of trees. Cf. also the frescoes in the villa.

Flemish dominions with Prince Philip, the son of Charles V, Leoni made a trip to Paris to acquire the moulds of the best ancient statues which Primaticcio had made in Rome in 1540 and 1545 by order of Francis I. Some of these moulds had already been used to cast bronze statues which were to decorate the gardens of Fontainebleau – turned thus into 'una nuova Roma'.[55] After Francis I's death, the moulds were of no further use, and in 1549 Leoni succeeded in getting them in his possession. Bronze statues from some of these moulds were to decorate the gallery of the palace of Binche, inhabited till its destruction in 1554 by Mary of Hungary, queen-governess of the Netherlands. Leoni, longing to return to Milan, wrote a letter to his Milanese protector, Ferrante Gonzaga, on 15 August 1549. In it he solicits him to use his influence to have the casting of the statues for Queen Mary made in Milan. In return for his help, the sculptor offers to cast another set of bronze statues from the Primaticcio moulds for Don Ferrante's villa: 'con poca spesa noi faressimo una Roma a la Gualtiera'.[56] Nothing else is known about this project which does not reappear in either Leoni's or in Ferrante's correspondence. Leoni seems to have taken the moulds back to Milan where the collection of statues modelled on them finally made a real 'Roman' statuary court in the sculptor's own Casa degli Omenoni. But Leoni's idea to create of Gonzaga's villa 'una nuova Roma' on the model of the famous Roman statuary gardens remained unrealised, probably for the same reasons which left the whole ensemble unfinished.

The increasing cares of government seem to have distracted Don Ferrante from the villa he had embarked on with such enthusiasm. In spring 1552 Giunti had to request payment for himself and the gardeners – though he realised that his patron had other problems on his mind. The announcement on 26 June 1552 that he would find the Gonzaga most beautiful ('troverà la Gonzaga bellissima') does not seem ever to have induced Don Ferrante to pay a visit, for even a year later (5 August 1553) he seems never to have set eyes on the site, where much of the work was nearing completion.

When Ferrante left Milan in 1554 to obey the summons to Brussels, his architect also departed, and our information on the villa dries up; according to Gosellini it remained unfinished.[57] Giunti certainly remained in the service of Ferrante's family even after the latter's death in 1557, but he concentrated more on extending and altering fortifications and buildings in the dukedom of Mantua and the *feudo* of Guastalla. Johann Georg Keyszler visited the villa on his Italian journey in 1729-30 and laments the poor state of the dilapidated building;[58] this implies that Dal Re's engravings, which had appeared a little earlier, had somewhat glossed over it.

[54] See Carlo Casati, *Leone Leoni d'Arezzo scultore* (Milan, 1884), pp. 21–3; Eugène Plon, *Leone Leoni sculpteur de Charles V et Pompeo Leoni sculpteur de Philippe II* (Paris, 1887), pp. 48–9; Bruce Boucher, 'Leone Leoni and Primaticcio's moulds of antique sculpture', *The Burlington Magazine* 123 (1) (1981), pp. 23–6; see also Sylvie Pressouyre, 'Les fontes de Primatice à Fontainebleau', *Bulletin monumental* 127 (1969), pp. 223–39.

[55] Giorgio Vasari, *Le vite*, vol. VII, p. 408.

[56] Amadio Ronchini, 'Leone Leoni d'Arezzo', *Atti e memorie per le provincie modenesi e parmensi* (1865), vol. III, pp. 2–41. The original letter here referred to is quoted on pp. 26–7.

[57] See Baroni, 'Domenico Giunti', note 93, quoted after Miniati; Gosellini, *Vita*, p. 58.

[58] Keyszler, *Neueste Reisen*, vol. I, p. 293.

It has often been said that Ferrante Gonzaga's villa was the first important three-winged design in Milanese villa architecture, which thereafter concentrated on a type of building open to the surrounding landscape and gardens. While the present chapter is concerned with the garden of the villa rather than its architecture, some remarks on the whole design may be in order. Dal Re's engravings show the layout of the buildings, although he embellishes, regularises and, in the interests of better representation, simplifies parts of the building.[59] In the bird's-eye view we can see the little colonnaded courtyard from the early Cinquecento, which links on the east with the south-facing entrance side of the main wing. Giunti's unusual reorientation of the building, which meant that the garden court was open to the north instead of the south as was customary, is probably due to his desire to link with the earlier villa. Around the small courtyards to the left and right of the main wing are the outbuildings and – on the east side – a chapel. Only on the diagonal did the two side wings meet with the main building.[60] There was no direct connection between them: the main façade of each of the side wings opened on to a little *giardino segreto*, at the end of which was a wall pierced with window openings through which the larger garden could be seen. As the different wings of the building were not closely related by architectural means, the architect harmonised the view from the garden by lining the courtyard with a portico, surmounted by a terrace, a sort of *ambulatio*, which ran round the garden frontage of the side wings and advanced as far as the pierced garden walls on all three sides, and to the arcades of the pavilions beside the *peschiera*. Such a theatrical piece of architecture can only have been intended for a representative function: probably for the parades, displays of horsemanship and water-games which were a necessary part of the aristocratic lifestyle and are so often attested in similar places.[61] The paved garden court and the *peschiera*, divided in two by its bridge, were a ready-made stage for theatrical displays of this sort. Furthermore, Giovio – and we shall return to this later – suggested in one of his letters that the central avenue of the garden could be 'ad uso d'uno ippodromo', used as a racetrack and surely also for tournaments, indicating just such a representative and theatrical function for the site.[62] Certainly the conception of a court opening onto the garden by means of porticoes and terraces is without direct precedent in Cinquecento architecture.

Our main interest lies with the garden, which, like the villa itself, has never hitherto

[59] See also the reconstructions by Tarchi, '"La Simonetta"', though some details are hypothetical, e.g. the architectural structure of the walls in the garden courtyard.

[60] Dal Re's view from the garden (fig. 5.6) is incorrect in the way it shows the roofs in this detail.

[61] See e.g. Claudia Lazzaro, *The Italian Renaissance Garden* (New Haven and London, 1990), plate 42: the Villa Medici in Castello as represented by Giusto Utens (fig. 2.1). See David R. Coffin, *Gardens and Gardening in Papal Rome* (Princeton 1991), chap. 13, 'Entertainment'. On the later Villa Garzoni see Bernhard Rupprecht, 'Die Villa Garzoni des Jacopo Sansovino', *Mitteilungen des Kunsthistorischen Instituts in Florenz* 11 (1) (1963), pp. 1–32.

[62] Cf. the description of garden festivities in e.g. Doni, *Le ville*, p. 51: besides boating, music and conversation the visitors amused themselves with 'honesti, et dilettevoli giochi: palla, pallone, pallamaglio, trucco, biliardo, caselle, rulli, morelle, zone, aliossi, lacchetta, mestola et pallottole' ('decent and delightful games: ball games, football, pall-mall, conjuring, billiards, skittles, stone-throwing, knucklebones, ducks and drakes, marbles . . .').

been subjected to a detailed typological analysis. This is particularly difficult, of course, because we have so little information about the original appearance of the garden. One thing is obvious, however: the access to the garden via a bridge over a large *peschiera*, close to the house and its courtyard, was inspired chiefly by Mantuan examples. The important Gonzaga villa in Marmirolo near Mantua, which was built in 1523–5 and whose appearance is, unfortunately, only imperfectly known, had a main building directly beside a water course which was spanned by a bridge, with a loggia opening on to it.[63] The Milanese arrangement of fish-pond, bridge and garden recurs at the Palazzo del Te in Mantua, which had been built by Giulio Romano for Ferrante's brother, Federico II, as an extension to an earlier building, beginning in late 1525.[64] Little is known of this Mantuan *giardino grande* situated in the well-watered countryside except that it was evidently a magnificent design.[65] We know that the exedra which borders the garden behind the Palazzo del Te was not built until the seventeenth century,[66] so that Ferrante's garden in Milan, like the Mantuan example at that time, was rectangular in outline, although it had no grotto. What is innovative about Giunti's villa design is that it does not belong any more to the traditional one-winged or four-winged type; rather it was a three-winged building open to garden and landscape, further distinguished by the surrounding portico.

The fact that we know so little about the appearance of the garden increases the importance of the above-mentioned letters by Giovio. At the least they reveal something of the design concept as it was suggested by the humanist to the military man. Essentially we are referring to two letters, one written from Rome on 15 December 1547 – some nine months after building work began – the other on 19 October 1549, from Como, when the building was substantially complete.[67]

After Don Ferrante had visited Giovio's *musaeum* in the summer of 1547 and expressed his liking for 'così rare abitazioni',[68] he may have written to his host, then resident in Rome, about his own plans for the building then in progress. In the earlier of the two letters, written before he had seen the site, Bishop Giovio invented a christening ceremony to bestow a name on Ferrante's villa, 'il bel luogo qual fa Vostra Eccellenza per diporto e recreamento delli quotidiani fastidii' ('the beautiful place which Your Excellency is creating for pleasure and recreation from your daily cares'). The 'godparents' were to be 'li signori Capilupi', probably the brothers Ippolito, Lelio and perhaps also Camillo Capilupi, members of the Mantuan aristocracy which had long been closely connected to the Gonzaga, and also of the circle of humanists around

---

[63] See *Giulio Romano*, Exhibition catalogue (Manuta, 1989), pp. 520–1, with further bibliography on Marmirolo.

[64] See Kurt W. Forster and Richard J. Tuttle, 'The Palazzo del Te', *Journal of the Society of Architectural Historians* 30 (4) (1971), pp. 267–93. Also cf. the fish-ponds in front of the Villa Medici in Castello, under construction from 1537 (Lazzaro, *Italian Renaissance Garden*). The ponds at Castello, unlike those of Ferrante's villa, were not in front of the garden façade of the casino.

[65] Forster and Tuttle, 'Palazzo del Te', pp. 280–1.   [66] Ibid.

[67] See note 49. Hitherto only odd words from these letters relating to the Villa Gonzaga-Simonetta have been quoted; no detailed attention has been made to the concept suggested by Giovio.   [68] Giovio, *Lettere*, Appendix, p. 254.

Giovio in Rome.[69] The name he suggested, disregarding its etymology, was 'Ninfeo', which in its masculine form was suited to the sex and character of the owner, and would also recall 'uno antico Romano' who had given the same name to his well-watered garden. By this he may have meant the Tuscan villa of the younger Pliny, which was famous for its water-works.[70] Here 'Ninfeo' means the whole place and not only an architectural structure or grotto. Giovio is probably also referring to literary topoi in the description of the *locus amoenus*, which since Theocritus' first Idyll had always been characterised as the abode of the nymphs. Last but not least, it recalls Giovio's description of his own villa on Lake Como, in which he often evokes the presence of wood and water nymphs. Concerning the siting and design of Ferrante's villa, Giovio advises:

> in questa Gualtiera è una mirabil copia d'acqua viva corrente, sorgente, ovi si puono fare elegantissimi compartimenti di peschiere, ucellere, conigliere e parchetti de varii animali, ad imitazione delli antichi, come insegnano Varrone e Columella. E sono certo ch'el mio mastro Domenico da Prato troverà milli vaghi disegni di fare una facetissima fabrica del edificio e de' compartimenti, de orti, giardini e pergolati.

('In this Gualtiera there is a wonderful abundance of fresh running and spring water, where one can make most excellent enclosures for fish-ponds, aviaries, rabbit warrens and enclosures for diverse animals, in imitation of antique examples, as shown in Varro and Columella. And I am sure that my master Domenico da Prato will find a thousand charming designs for making a most pleasing construction for the building and of enclosures, orchards, gardens and pergolas.')

Giovio refers even more clearly to examples from antiquity than he does in relation to the gardens of his own villa. The treatises on agriculture by the authors he names, Varro and Columella, were available at the time both in individual editions and in compendia, and were frequently cited as authorities in modern literature on villa culture.[71] The aviaries (*uccelliere*) which are so common everywhere in Italian garden design from the Cinquecento onwards are probably to be explained as a harking back to

---

[69] On the Capilupi brothers see *Dizionario biografico degli italiani*, vol. xviii (Rome, 1975). Ippolito regularly kept Ferrante informed on political intrigues and developments in Rome.

[70] Though as far as I know, Pliny did not call his Tuscan villa a 'Nymphaeum'. On the building style and concept of the nymphaeum see Frank Joseph Alvarez, 'The Renaissance nymphaeum. Its origins and its development in Rome and vicinity', dissertation, Ann Arbor, Michigan, 1982. On p. 70 the author quotes from Giovio's letter, but without any further indication on the location of Ferrante's villa; also Ulrika Kiby, 'Poggioreale – Das erste Nymphäum der Renaissance', *Die Gartenkunst* 7 (1) (1995), pp. 68–79. Bramante's nymphaea in the Belvedere court of the Vatican and in Genazzano certainly hark back to classical models, but as far as I know were not so called at the time. Since there are no architectural reasons to compare the Villa Gonzaga with earlier Roman examples, it must be assumed that by 'Ninfeo' Giovio was referring not to architecture, but to literature.

[71] See *Rei rusticae scriptores* (Venice, 1472), a compendium containing Cato, Varro, Columella and Palladius; the same authors were published in 1514 by Aldus Manutius, also in Venice, under the title *Libri de re rustica*. See Bernhard Rupprecht, 'Villa. Zur Geschichte eines Ideals', *Probleme der Kunstwissenschaft* (1966), vol. ii, pp. 210–50 (p. 222 and *passim*).

reconstructions of Varro's *aviarium*.[72] Giovio's advice to make enclosures for animals alludes to a garden amusement which had been common since antiquity.[73]

To give the entrance 'dignità e pomposa vista' ('dignity and an impressive appearance') and to follow 'l'ordine delli antichi mastri delle bell'opre' ('the practice of ancient masters of fine design'), Giovio suggests an inscription giving information about the architect and purpose of the place: FERNANDUS GONZAGA A CAROLO V IMP. AUG. MAX. CISALPINAE GALLIAE PRAEFECTUS QUUM EX BELLICIS ATQUE CIVILIBUS CURIS MERITAM NON IGNOBILIS OCII REQUIEM QUAERERET NYMPHAEUM SUBURBANI SECESSUS HONESTAE VOLUPTATI DEDICAVIT.

The villa, in other words, was intended to provide its owner with honourable relaxation from the cares of office. Whether this inscription was in fact used is uncertain. Other sources, such as Giunti's letters, mention that the entrance portal was decorated with sculptures and with pillars, topped with spheres, on either side of the gate, along with the arms of Ferrante, his wife and the emperor – but there is no mention of an inscription.

Giovio's second letter was written after he had visited the villa, so the remarks in it can claim a closer relation to actuality than the mainly conceptual expressions in the earlier letter. But we must again be careful to distinguish the metaphorically expressed praises, which are clearly intended to flatter the owner, from more concrete judgements. Thus Giovio sums up his impression of the 'estrema bellezza' conveyed by the unusually magnificent architecture ('architettura altiera a magnifica ... fuore de l'ordine de la prattica de' presenti tempi'), with its many loggias and porticoes, in the words, 'restai stupefatto perchè mi parve entrare ne la maravigliosa casa di Merlino celebrata da' poeti come cosa possibile e non trovata' ('I was amazed, because it seemed to me that I had entered the marvellous house of Merlin, celebrated by poets as a thing possible, but never found').[74] The *tertium comparationis* in this comparison between the castle of the legendary enchanter Merlin and Don Ferrante's villa is the image of an architecture so beautiful that it seems unreal. Evidently Giovio had had some conversation with the architect, whom he knew well, and had discussed some architectural details. Thus he suggests that it would show wise foresight to shape the balustrade (*ghirlanda*) over the portico in the court in a way that would allow, if necessary, the erection of a canopy over the terraces – because the rainy weather so frequent in Milan could easily ruin both the terraces and the vault underneath.

The garden, so far as we can reconstruct the site and its state of decoration at this time (autumn, 1549), prompted Giovio to make some comparisons much more definite than mere literary fiction: 'si potrebbe ben poi dire che le tre delizie di Spagna sareb-

---

[72] S. W. van Buren and R. Kennedy, 'Varro's aviary at Casinum', *Journal of Roman Studies*, 9 (1919), pp. 59–66; see also Pirro Ligorio's reconstruction.

[73] See note 46, on the *conigliera* which Giunti had earlier created for Ferrante in Palermo.

[74] Merlin the Enchanter is a figure from late medieval courtly romance who also appears in the literature of the Cinquecento, e.g. in Canto III of Ariosto's *Orlando Furioso*. Ariosto there describes Merlin's grave, which is scarcely germane to Giovio's purpose; but it is said to be made of exceptionally noble materials.

bero tre magre fantesche de la pomposa Gonzaga, dico l'Alzafaria de Saragozza, l'Alcazera de Siviglia e l'Alambra di Granata' ('thus it could well be said that the three delights of Spain were three meagre phantasms of the magnificent Gonzaga – I mean the Aljafaria of Saragossa, the Alcázar of Seville and the Alhambra of Granada'). Those three marvels of architecture included the famous 'Patio of the Lions' in the Alhambra with its fountains, which pales by comparison with the Villa Gonzaga, whose fountains Giovio sees in his mind's eye as if they were already complete: 'io vedo già la fontana vostra, così ampla, così chiara e così copiosa, che darà acqua de cristallo in ogni luogo, a complimento de la fecondissima pischera' ('Already I see your fountain, so ample, so clear and so abundant, that it will provide crystal water in every place, as well as the teeming fish-pond'). Moreover, Don Ferrante is advised to channel 'quella leggiadra corsa da la pischera al casino' ('that charming path from the fish-pond to the house'), probably the central avenue from the smaller fish-pond to the main building, 'ad uso d'uno ippodromo': 'sarà proprio un viale armato da le bande o d'arbori frondosi, o di cancelli con rosarii, che avanzerà d'amenità e prospetto ogni bella cosa' ('it will be a veritable avenue lined with hedges or leafy trees, or rose-covered pergolas, which will outdo every other beautiful thing in its pleasantness and its views'). Giovio mentions another such 'hippodrome' in connection with his own villa on Lake Como and, as we have seen, relates it back to a feature of the younger Pliny's Tuscan villa. This, and other details mentioned by Giovio, help make our image of the garden more vivid – although once again we do not know whether Giunti and his gardeners put any of Giovio's suggestions into effect. The *bande*, *arbori frondosi* and *cancelli con rosarii* give a picture of the garden which is quite different – more varied and 'greener' – than Dal Re's much later bird's-eye view, which shows, besides the flowerbeds, only a few neatly pruned trees here and there. Several rooms in the 'casino' had surviving frescoes showing landscapes and vine-pergolas, which must have existed in reality in the garden. Landscape and garden motifs were very prominent in the interior decoration of Gonzaga's villa, creating a pleasant area for leisurely relaxation between the real nature outside and the painted nature within the building.

Giovio concludes his letter by strongly advising Don Ferrante to retain the numerous outbuildings (dairy, kitchens, stable, barn), since their variety increased the dignity of the main building.[75] At the same time, by way of a mild warning to the ever-busy owner, Giovio advised him to take good care of his villa, because a 'mania for stonework' is one of the virtues of a prince: 'E quella tenga presente che 'l Principe non può essere galantuomo se non ha il mal de la pietra'.

If Giovio esteems the garden of an Italian in the service of Spain more highly than the most famous Spanish examples, this may be for reasons of panegyrics or patriotism. But the comparison in itself indicates that a Spanish governor, especially one who had visited Spain as Ferrante Gonzaga had, knew well the palaces and gardens there. More-

---

[75] 'perchè quella frequenzia di piccioli edificii augumenta la dignita del luogo mastro'.

over, Ferrante must have been viceroy of Sicily for long enough to know the refinements of Arab–Norman gardens and water-gardens, and perhaps to imitate them as far
as possible in the 'palagi, giardini, fontane' created for him there by Giunti.[76] Giovio
himself can have known Spanish examples only from descriptions: in particular, by the
numerous Venetian ambassadors who had written down their impressions after a visit
to Charles V's court in Granada. The report most interesting to art historians is by the
ambassador Andrea Navagero, who travelled through Spain in 1525-6 and, in a letter,
gave a long and enthusiastic description of the Generalife. This letter was not published
until a quarter of a century later,[77] but this or other information about Spanish gardens
must have reached Giovio, who knew Navagero well enough to include his *vita* in the
Elogia (1546).

Besides the Alhambra, Navagero also visited (*inter alia*) the Alcázar in Seville, but he
does not mention the Aljaferia in Saragossa.[78] The Moorish gardens, especially the
Alhambra, aroused admiration with their abundant water and their strikingly imaginative fountains, water-stairs and *scherzi d'acqua*. Navagero loudly laments that the Spaniards were letting the countryside – so flourishing under the Moors – and the Moorish
gardens fall to rack and ruin. It has often been suggested, by historians of (e.g.) the
Palazzina Farnese in Caprarola or the Villa Lante in Bagnaia, that the passion for water
in Italian Renaissance gardens is of Arab origin;[79] but there are few clearer indications
of it than Giovio's comments on Ferrante Gonzaga's villa. Giovio's *tertium comparationis*
includes the abundant water supplied to fountains and fish-ponds. It is all the more
regrettable that nothing has been preserved of the site and its ornamentation – which is

[76] Ferrante spent half a year at the imperial court at Granada in summer 1526. His two letters written from there do not
mention anything concerning architecture or gardens. See Raffaele Tamalio, *Ferrante Gonzaga alla corte spagnola di Carlo V*
(Mantua, 1991), pp. 278–80. Still indispensable for the Sicilian examples is Adolph Goldschmidt, 'Die normannischen
Königspaläste in Palermo', *Zeitschrift für Bauwesen*, 48 (1898), pp. 542–90; Giuseppe Caronia, *La Zisa di Palermo, Storia e
restauro* (Bari, 1982); Ursula Staacke, *Un palazzo normanno a Palermo. La Zisa* (Palermo, 1991). Hans-Rudolf Meier, 'Die
normannischen Königspaläste in Palermo. Studien zur hochmittelalterlichen Residenzbaukunst', dissertation, Basle,
(1992); idem, "... das ird 'sche Paradies, das sich den Blicken öffnet'. Die Gartenpaläste der Normannenkönige in
Palermo', *Die Gartenkunst* 6 (1) (1994), pp. 1–18. That the Norman palaces and gardens of Sicily were known outside their
own immediate area in the Cinquecento is shown by the descriptions in guidebooks: see Leandro Alberti, *Isole appartenenti
alla Italia* (Bologna, 1567); Tommaso Fazello, *Le due deche dell'historia di Sicilia* (Venice, 1573; Latin edn, Palermo, 1558),
Decade I, Book VIII, pp. 247–8. Sources such as these also show that the Norman gardens were in a poor state at the time,
and that (for example) the fountains of the Zisa were not working. For concrete and demonstrable examples of the impact
of Moorish and Norman garden design on Italian gardens see Gottfried Kerscher, 'Islamische Kultur für den Osten? Ein
verlorener islamischer Palast in Italien und seine Nachfolge', *Kritische Berichte* 20 (1) (1992), pp. 29–42; see also Kiby,
'Poggioreale'.

[77] *Lettere de diversi autori* (Venice, 1556), pp. 718–38: letter from Navagero to Gio. Battista Ramusio, dated 31 May 1526, with
a description of the waterworks of the Generalife; there is a later edition of Navagero's collected letters, *Il viaggio fatto in
Spagna et in Francia* (Venice, 1563), same letter, fols. 18v–25r. See Mario Cermenati, 'Un diplomatico naturalista del
Rinascimento: Andrea Navagero', *Nuovo Archivio Veneto*, 24 (1) (1912), pp. 164–205. Ferrante Gonzaga himself knew
Navagero well enough from his sojourn in Granada in spring and summer 1526. On Moorish and Spanish gardens in
European travel literature see Iris Lauterbach, 'Die Gärten spaniens in der europäischen Reiseliteratur', in *Im Blick des
Fremden - Die Kunst spaniens*, ed. Gisela Noehles (Frankfurt-am-Main, 1996).

[78] James Dickie, 'The Islamic garden in Spain', in *The Islamic Garden*, ed. E.B. MacDougall and R. Ettinghausen
(Washington, DC, 1976), pp. 87–105.

[79] Lazzaro, *Italian Renaissance Garden*, p. 299, n. 94 with further bibliography.

why students of such gardens have hitherto paid so little attention to Giovio's letters.

The Villa Gonzaga-Simonetta was famous well into the nineteenth century – but not for its garden: the attraction was an echo. Interest in this curiosity was so widespread that foreign travellers considered the Gonzaga to be the most important villa in the environs of Milan, absolutely not to be missed.[80] The echo could be experienced only from one window in the top floor of one wing. It was said that a pistol shot (for example) would echo up to thirty times. To this echo we owe a hitherto unnoticed picture of the villa from the middle of the seventeenth century (fig. 5.7): the Jesuit Athanasius Kircher devoted a lengthy chapter to the Villa Simonetta in his scientific treatise *Musurgia universalis* (1650).[81] In 1657 Gaspar Schott, another Jesuit, borrowed the engraving and the accompanying text for his *Magia universalis naturae et artis*; Kircher likewise reprinted both engraving and text in his later work *Phonurgia* (1673).[82] In Praelusio II to chapter IV, 'Magia Echotectonica sive De Acusticis Fabricis', entitled 'De mirifica Echo Villae Simonetta Mediolani', the author mentions it along with the most famous examples of acoustic effects from both antiquity and modern times. So as to determine the causes of this echo, Kircher, at that time employed in Rome, had asked Matthäus Storr,[83] a fellow-Jesuit from Milan, to procure for him a view of the villa and the exact dimensions of its courtyard. The result was the engraving (fig. 5.7) which shows the three-winged building and its courtyard, marking the famous window on the upper floor, as well as the bridge which led over the *peschiera* into the garden. The main reason for the astonishing echo was that the plane surfaces of the walls in both wings lay parallel to each other.

It is not known when the echo first appeared, or whether it was deliberately 'designed' or happened by chance. It is surprising that, although Kircher is the first to mention it in 1650, he dates it back to Ferrante Gonzaga's time. If earlier authors do not mention it, it may be for a wholly different reason. If, for example, the author of a guide book, such as Gualdo Priorato, has nothing to say about it even in 1666,[84] it may be because he had never been into the villa and so never got as far as the only window from which it was to be heard. It is not mentioned by Ferrante's biographers, Ulloa (1563) and Gosellini (1574), who can be reproached for their lack of interest in art; Borsieri, author of the supplement to Paolo Morigi's genealogical work *La nobiltà di Milano* (1619) is

[80] Keyszler, *Neueste Reisen*, I, pp. 292–3, with a detailed description of the physical causes of the echo; Bianconi, *Nuova guida di Milano*, p. 361; *Guide de l'étranger* (Milan, 1805); Aubin Louis Millin, *Voyage dans le Milanais* (Paris, 1817), pp. 275–6; Luigi Bossi, *Guida di Milano* (Milan, 1818), part II, p. 3; Cesare Cantù, 'Palazzo detto l'Eco della Simonetta', *Cosmorama pittorico* (1844), pp. 295–6.

[81] Athanasius Kircher, *Musurgia universalis sive Ars magna Consoni et Dissoni*, vol. II (Rome, 1650), pp. 289–91; see also Jörg Jochen Berns, 'Die Jagd auf die Nymphe Echo. Künstliche Echoeffekte in Poesie, Musik und Architektur der Frühen Neuzeit' in *Die Mechanik in den Künsten*, ed. H. Möbius and J.J. Berns (Harburg, 1990), pp. 67–82.

[82] Gaspar Schott, *Magia universalis naturae et artis*, 4 vols. (Würzburg, 1657–9), vol. II, pp. 122–5; Athanasius Kircher, *Phonurgia Nova* (Kempten, 1673), pp. 78–81.

[83] There is no mention of Storr in Augustin and Aloys De Backer, *Bibliothèque de la Compagnie de Jésus*, part I: *Bibliographie*, vol. VII (Brussels and Paris, 1896).

[84] Gualdo Priorato, *Relatione della città di Milano*, p. 163, on the Villa Simonetta.

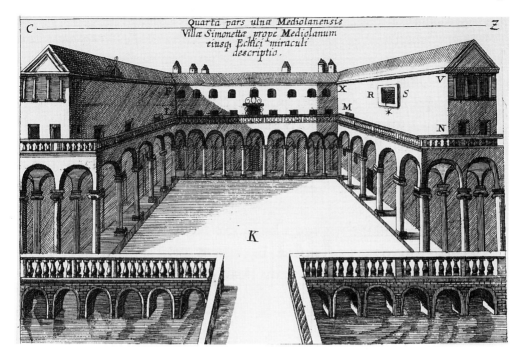

Fig. 5.7 View of the garden range of the Villa Gonzaga-Simonetta from Kircher, *Musurgia universalis* (1650)

obviously ill-informed about the Villa Gonzaga in any case.[85]

The weightiest argument is that the architect himself gives no indication that he intended to set up an echo in the inner courtyard – but can such an immaterial phenomenon as an echo *be* deliberately constructed? Since Giunti left the building unfinished in 1554, we can only conclude that the echo materialised, more or less by chance, a few years or even decades later, when the villa was finished under the auspices of the Simonetta family. Perhaps the effect was discovered later and a window opening then made. Also in favour of a later date is that the effect is typical of late Cinquecento architecture's aiming to astonish visitors. Kircher himself mentions, in the same connection, the whispering vault in the Palazzo Farnese in Caprarola, as well as an earlier example in the Palazzo del Te in Mantua. Vincenzo Scamozzi, in his great work *L'idea della architettura universale* (Venice, 1615), also deals with the echo phenomenon and adds a passage on the subject to his chapter XXIV, on 'Portici, Gallerie, Luoghi da Passeggi, Ventidoti, & altri luoghi per delitie . . .' Thus he expressly considers echoes as *delitie* and connects them with the concept of pleasure buildings. A similar effect, though it was 'landscape' rather than 'architectural', was possibly being sought in Ferrante's own time, and in a garden context: the echo at Giovio's villa on Lake Como.

---

[85] Borsieri, in Morigi, *Nobiltà di Milano*, pp. 59–60, names (e.g.) Ambrogio Alciato as Don Ferrante's architect but does not mention Domenico Giunti at all.

There, according to Giovio, the nymph Echo lurked on the little island near the villa, and would return the visitor's greeting. Obviously, such a phenomenon would have been excellently suited to Giovio's suggested 'Ninfeo' concept of the Villa Gonzaga.

When Taegio wrote his treatise, *La villa. Un dialogo*, in the late 1550s, Ferrante Gonzaga and his times were already gone and forgotten; Taegio never once mentions his name – despite the fact that he was so intimate with Ferrante's biographer, Gosellini, that the latter composed an introductory sonnet for Taegio's work.[86]

Thanks to Argelati and Morigi, we are well informed about the author (fig. 5.8).[87] Taegio, a native of Milan, is described as a highly cultured individual with a great interest in the arts, a jurist by profession who devoted much of his energy to literature.[88] Through his juridical activities he doubtless made the acquaintance of many villa owners, mostly high Milanese officials, whose administrative dignities he is always at pains to note.[89] Being himself in an assured social position,[90] he knew the social obligations of such men, one of which was 'vivere in villa'. Taegio has a notable literary vein: his treatise on the villa certainly has more poetic qualities than those of Gallo or Doni, for example.[91] This is the more understandable in that his treatise is not a disquisition on agriculture, but takes the form of a dialogue modelled on classical and humanistic literature in praise of country life. He comes across as an author with access to a good library, familiar with the protagonists of classical and contemporary villa culture. Whether he knew the great artistic models in the rest of Italy from personal observation or only from hearsay is an open question; he seldom makes comparisons or notes stylistic affinities. Taegio seems to intend his treatise as homage to a social class to which he belonged by right of intelligence rather than birth or wealth. In fact, his work – although it appeared only as a pocket book with few illustrations – was and remained the only one of its kind in the artistic literature of Milan. No other treatise of either the sixteenth or the seventeenth century gives such detailed information about Milanese villa culture; and in his importance to art history, if not in his intellectual pretensions, only the much later Dal Re can compare with him.

Taegio felt an especial affinity with the old noble family of Simonetta, for he dedicated his work to Giulio (later Cardinal) Simonetta and devoted particular attention to the gardens of various members of the family. In his preface, the author describes

---

[86] This detail is from Filippo Argelati, *Bibliotheca Scriptorum Mediolanensium*, 2 vols. (Milan, 1745), vol. II, p. 1472, since Gosellini did not put his name to the sonnet.

[87] Argelati, *Bibliotheca*, pp. 1472–3; Morigi, *Nobiltà di Milano*, p. 217, on Taegio: 'Historico e Poeta fecondissimo, e dottissimo' ('a historian, and a most prolific and learned poet').

[88] Argelati, *Bibliotheca*, gives a list of Taegio's publications, including no. XI, *La villa*.

[89] Taegio was the author of a *Tractatus varii ad Criminales causas pertinentes* (Milan, 1564). This *Tractatus is dedicated to Pietro Paolo Arrigoni, president of the senate of Milan, whose garden Taegio describes in La villa*, p. 101.

[90] The family was only ennobled by Charles V: Argelati, *Bibliotheca*, p. 1472.

[91] Doni, *Le ville*; Agostino Gallo, *Le dieci giornate della' vera agricoltura e piaceri della villa* (Brescia, 1st ed., 1550). Taegio's book is treated in James S. Ackerman, *The Villa. Form and Ideology of Country Houses* (London, 1990), chap. 5, 'The image of country life in sixteenth-century villa books'.

Fig 5.8 Portrait of Bartolomeo Tegio, from *Tractatus* (Milan 1564)

his intention to 'lodar la Villa & biasmar la città' ('to praise the villa and blame the city') as a herculean task, and already imagines that he sees it cast to the four winds by ill-wishers. With this *captatio benevolentiae* he not only announces himself as a new-comer to the field, but also displays his mastery of classical rhetoric. Then follows the actual dialogue between Partenio, the city-dweller, and Vitauro/Taegio, defending country life; it is not subdivided, either thematically or into chapters. The conversation, dated 30 May 1559, is set within the overall theme of the wickedness of this world, which is no more than 'una gabbia di pazzi maldicenti' ('a cage full of evil-tongued madmen' – thus the Preface). Vitauro terminates the conversation abruptly with a reaf-firmation of this theme, though not before he has almost convinced Partenio of the advantages of country life. Vitauro ends the treatise with an ironical hit at himself, for 'chi savio esser si crede è piu de gli altri pazzo' ('he who thinks himself wise is madder than the rest', p. 181). He has, of course, spent the previous 181 pages explaining that the only choice for the wise man must be a life in the country.

Taegio cites all the known authorities on the subject, both classical and contempor-ary, to bolster his argument that the hectic and busy city, with its crowds and cares, is greatly inferior to his concept of country life, 'vivere in villa'.[92] This formidably well-read author knows the agricultural treatises by the Romans Cato, Columella, Varro and Palladius[93] as well as the relevant passages from Virgil, Horace, Cicero and both Plinys. The literary fictions in the works of Poliziano, Ficino, Pico della Mirandola, Sannazaro and Bembo are as familiar to him as the remarks of Annibale Caro or Claudio Tolomei on the subject of villa life. The trenchant contrast between town and country has a long tradition in humanistic literature back to Petrarch. Though Taegio places himself in this tradition, his contribution to it, thanks to his

[92] In this context see Rupprecht, 'Villa. Zur Geschichte eines Ideals'; rather surprisingly, Rupprecht does not mention Taegio.   [93] See note 71.

individual prose style, is completely original. His prose is characterised most strikingly by paratactic structures, namely numerous fantastical descriptions and other elements. Thus, not devoid of humour, he uses vivid animal imagery to give the reader an overview of the vices of the city, turning on its head the argument that the city belongs to men and the villa to beasts:

> la crudeltà della Tigre, la impietà dell'Orso, la bestialità del Cinghiale, la ferocità del Leone, la superbia del Cavallo, la rapacità del Lupo, l'ostinatione del Bue, l'inganno della Volpe, la malitia del Cameleonte, la varietà del Pardo, la mordacità del Cane, la disperatione dell'Elefante, la vendetta del Camello, la petulantia del Becco, la brutezza del Porco, la pazzia dell'Asino, la buffoneria della Scimia, la ribalderia delle Sirene, la furia de Centauri, la ingordigia delle Harpie, la lussuria de Satiri, & quanta malvagità d'animali irragionevoli, & spaventosi mostri creò giamai la natura. (p. 7)

('The cruelty of the Tiger, the impiety of the Bear, the bestiality of the Boar, the ferocity of the Lion, the pride of the Horse, the rapacity of the Wolf, the obstinacy of the Ox, the cunning of the Fox, the artfulness of the Chameleon, the inconstancy of the Leopard, the mordacity of the Dog, the desperation of the Elephant, the vengefulness of the Camel, the impertinence of the Goat, the ugliness of the Pig, the folly of the Ass, the buffoonery of the Monkey, the treachery of the Sirens, the fury of the Centaurs, the greed of the Harpies, the lustfulness of the Satyrs, and all the wickedness of all the irrational animals and fearful monsters ever created by Nature.')

In the continual play of question and answer Vitauro demolishes every one of Partenio's arguments in favour of city life. Townsmen are in fetters of servitude, whereas in the country man and the human spirit are free. Vitauro would rather have trees around him than servants, leaves than cloth of gold, open countryside than palaces, frugal rather than refined fare. Only in the villa is the _vita contemplativa_ of a philosopher and thinker really possible, such a life really contributing more to the well-being of a state than the _vita activa_ of a general or politician; for virtue and the human mind's striving after truth promote the good of the republic and the worthiness of the state. A sojourn in the 'amena, et solitaria Villa' ('pleasant and solitary villa') serves the three aims of human activity ('i tre fini delle humane operatione'), that is to say 'la gloria, l'utile, & il diletto' ('fame, usefulness and pleasure'), all three being closely interconnected. Pleasure is evoked by the contemplation of gardens and the natural world. Fame and usefulness are increased both by study of natural science and by the 'divine, & humane speculationi' (p. 4) which can be indulged 'in villa' and which help to perfect the mind. Agriculture, too, serves these aims. In the greatest detail and with an abundance of citations from classical Latin literature, as for example the well-known story of Cyrus and Lysander, Taegio argues that _agricoltura_ is a noble, useful and delightful occupation, which was engaged in by many rulers of the ancient world, to the edification of modern princes. Hunting, fishing and birding are part of this occupation, and mingle pleasure with utility.

The relationship of art to nature is also discussed. When Partenio complains that art falsifies nature, and that (for example) pergolas are 'mostruose fabriche di piante, strani innesti, & methamorfosi d'alberi' ('monstrous fabrications of plants, foreign engraftings and metamorphosis of trees', p. 54), while fish-ponds and caves imprison nature's creatures, Vitauro emphasises that the work of the gardener is to achieve an interplay of *arte* and *natura*, the so-called *terza natura*: 'l'industria d'un accorto giardiniero, che incorporando l'arte con la natura fa, che d'amendue ne riesce una terza natura' ('the industry of a wise gardener, who by incorporating art with nature brings forth from both a third nature', p. 66).[94]

Life in the civilized villa, with its fine gardens, gains in *gioia* and *felicità* by often standing out against the background of a threatening, wild, natural landscape:

> minacciosi monti, tanne da serpi, oscure caverne, horride balze, strani greppi, dirupati bricchi, rovinati sassi, alberghi d'heremiti, aspre roccie, alpestri diserti, & cose simili, le quali … senza horrore rare volte riguardar si possono. (p. 115)

('Menacing mountains, serpents' lairs, darksome caverns, fearful crags, strange banks, craggy precipices, fallendown stones, hermits' refuges, jagged rocks, wildernesses, and other such things, which … can seldom be contemplated without horror.') This repellent contrast is a pseudo-romantic panorama to be set in contrast to the villa.

Only in the last few pages (pp. 155ff) is there any discussion of practical gardening,[95] and even this is clothed in a literary fiction. A suitably costumed gardener appears before the assembled guests at a feast in the villa of Camillo Porro 'quasi in atto di comedia', and asks for advice on gardening. The advice he receives mostly belongs to the realms of superstition, but is evidently taken seriously.

The concluding passage (pp. 171ff) deals with the organisational structure of the villa and the choice of an ideal steward or *fattore di villa*. Vitauro explains in detail what qualities such a steward ought to possess, showing the importance of his position, which involved responsibility for the practical and agricultural side of the villa. The *padrone* ought to be his model in all things, but the 'master' of the house ought to concentrate on his own interest in, and use of, the villa rather than on practical tasks. The social hierarchy emerges clearly from Taegio's characterisation of the ideal steward. The master must supervise even his subordinate's marital relationship and friendships, so as to be sure of monopolising his loyalty and care.

When assigning Taegio's work to its true place in contemporary villa literature,[96] one thinks first of the treatise by Giuseppe Falcone, *La nuova vaga et dilettevole villa*, which was published in Brescia in the same year (1559); and of Agostino Gallo's *Le dieci*

---

[94] This is almost the only passage from Taegio which has hitherto attracted any attention from historians of the garden: see Lazzaro, *Italian Renaissance Garden, passim*, and Elisabeth MacDougall, 'Ars hortulorum. Sixteenth-century garden iconography and literary theory in Italy', in *The Italian Garden* (Washington, D.C., 1972), p. 51. Coffin, *Gardens and Gardening*, p. 104, refers '*terza natura*' back to Jacopo Bonfadio.

[95] Coffin, *Gardens and Gardening*, fig. 173, shows Taegio's illustration of the gardeners with a water level.

[96] See note 91.

giornate dell' agricoltura, published some years earlier (1550), again in Brescia. For both Falcone and Gallo, however, the pleasure of villa life springs from direct involvement in agriculture, and in this both works, and also Herrera's *Agricoltura* (1577), differ from Taegio's.[97] But the primarily literary outlook of the learned humanist is found also in Alberto Lollio, who in 1563 brought out a *Lettera in laude della villa* in Ferrara.[98] All these works have the common aim of publicising and reinforcing the villa culture in the environs of their author's own city, be it Brescia, Ferrara or Milan.

This inclination to praise his own city emerges with particular clarity when Taegio, describing a villa culture which by 1559 was highly developed, adds an enumeration of more than 200 villas and their owners. This is what gives the work its high documentary value, which, astonishingly, has not yet been appreciated by historians of the villa or the garden.[99] There is no room here for a full appreciation, but I shall analyse a few descriptions of particularly interesting gardens.

In most cases Taegio gives only a general opinion of the beauty of the garden, if he does not merely list the name and place; he could not, in any case, have known them all. However, a significant number of gardens is described in more detail. It is noticeable that the author says no word about architecture: his descriptions of villas are concerned exclusively with gardens, and he distinguishes between pleasure gardens and orchards.

As Taegio had connections with the Simonetta family, it is not surprising that he should mention gardens belonging to three members of that family. Besides Giulio Simonetta's in 'Toresella' (p. 70, meaning Torrigella near Parma),[100] there is the botanical garden of Scipione Simonetta in Milan itself (pp. 102–3), which was open to the interested visitor, contained a wide variety of rare plants from all over the world and could challenge comparison with the greatest examples in Padua and Pisa. The most detailed description of the whole book refers to the garden of Cesare Simonetta near his Villa Castellazzo at Rho (pp. 67ff).[101] Unfortunately, this Cesare, a provost and brother to Giulio and Scipione, is the least documented personality in a large family highly productive of churchmen and high state officials,[102] so that the character of the man who commissioned what Vitauro calls the 'piu bello & delicato giardino, ch'io mi vedessi mai' ('most beautiful and refined garden I ever saw') remains quite unknown.

Taegio, making use of individual details to convey topography, gives us a colourfully poetic and convincing picture of the garden which draws on all the traditional topoi for describing the *locus amoenus*.[103] The garden, which is divided into four by straight

---

[97] G.A. D'Herrera (Francesco Sansovino), *L'agricoltura tratta da diversi antichi e moderni scrittori* (Venice, 1st ed., 1557).

[98] Alberto Lollio, *Delle orationi . . . aggiuntavi una lettera del médesimo in laude della villa* (Ferrara, 1563).

[99] *Il giardino a Milano*, p. 48, does stress the significance of Taegio's treatise, which is also discussed by Ackerman, *The Villa*. chap. 5.

[100] Litta, *Famiglie celebri*: since 1530 the *feudo* of Torrigella had been in the hands of the branch of the Simonetta family to which Cesare, Giulio, Scipione and Alessandro belonged.

[101] See Langè, *Ville della provincia di Milano*, p. 510: the first villa, which was later altered, was built by the Simonetta family in the middle of the sixteenth century.   [102] Litta, *Famiglie celebri*, merely mentions Cesare's office.

[103] See Rupprecht, 'Villa. Zur Geschichte eines Ideals'; Lise Bek, 'Ut ars natura, ut natura ars. Le ville di Plinio e il concetto del giardino nel Rinascimento', *Analecta Romana Instituti Danici*, 7 (1974), pp. 109–56.

avenues, is enclosed by a hedge which affords shelter to many birds. Low hedges of sweet-smelling herbs line the avenues and square flowerbeds. The crossroads in the middle is marked by a pergola overgrown with roses, jasmine and vines, whose 'cunning grafts' (*ingeniosi innesti*) demonstrate the *terza natura* of the garden. In the bottom right-hand quarter the wind wafts gently over a sward of grass and flowers, surrounded by citrus trees which offer blossom and fruit simultaneously to the view. There are strange, fragrant plants from distant lands 'd'alle parti d'India'. Tall deciduous trees and pines form a shady grove alive with birds and animals; only scattered rays of sunshine reach its grassy floor. From a grotto on the left side of the garden springs a clear, murmuring brook of which one branch runs round the garden while another pours into a *peschiera* surrounded by a marble parapet decorated with inlay and statuary. Antique statues ('infinite bellissime antichaie') are reflected in the water, seeming to rejoice in their own beauty. Vitauro/Taegio says that the most overwhelming impression is given at sunrise and sunset, when the statues and their reflections unite in unearthly visions of *amore* and *gioia*, seeming to transport the observer to Venus' kingdom on the isle of Cyprus. Vitauro then draws back from this poetic vision and returns to the realm of fact, referring to the many ingenious messages and mottos to be found in the flowerbeds.

The gardens of Cardinal Giovanni Angelo de' Medici in Frascarolo and of the Spanish chancellor Francesco Taverna at his Villa Canonica, near Monza, are considered comparable to the most famous sites of antiquity, but here the descriptions do not go beyond a conventional presentation of their appearance. The villa of Paolo Giovio on Lake Como is mentioned, but not Ferrante Gonzaga's, perhaps because neither villa nor garden was complete by the end of the 1550s. The attractions of other gardens are described in more detail.[104] At Monsignor Landriano's Villa di Vidigolfo there is an island in the *peschiera* which is inhabited by animals and serves as a menagerie (p. 81). Pietro Novato, at his Villa in Voghera, has a labyrinth of nut-trees (p. 104) in whose bark are cut the letters of a richly allusive inscription. In the middle of the labyrinth there was a marble statue of a laurel-crowned Apollo in mourning for Daphne, sitting, as if on Parnassus, on a 'rozzo et humido sasso' ('rough, wet stone') from which gushed a clear spring.[105] If a visitor came near the statue he was sprinkled with fine sprays of water; clearly the intended effect of these water-jets is to make fun of a respectfully admiring passer-by. Bernardo Brebbia has at his villa 'una fontana fabricata per mano di Bramante, & fregiata da una giocondissima selva di aranci, limoni, & cedri' ('a fountain made by the hand of Bramante, and embellished with a delightful grove of orange, lemon and cedar trees', p. 105).

In the garden of the Caimo family villa there was an 'artificiosa et notabile fontana'

[104] E.g.: 'l'alta, et incomparabile fabrica del meraviglioso theatro dell'eccellentissimo Giulio Camillo' at the villa of Pomponio Cotta (pp. 71–2). Taegio must have known *L'idea del teatro dell' eccellentissimo M. Giulio Camillo* (Florence, 1550); see Frances A. Yates, *The Art of Memory* (London, 1966), pp. 129–59.

[105] Compare e.g. Ammanati's 'Appenine' at the Villa Medici in Castello.

('cunningly made and notable fountain', pp. 92–5; see fig. 5.9), which had been designed by the mathematician Alessandro Caimo, called the 'modern Archimedes' (p. 162). This fountain, which 'per forza d'aria, o sia di vento getta acqua quasi di continuo' ('by the force of air, or perhaps the wind, throws water almost continually'), is a complicated structure that calculated the movements of air and water. Taegio, following Caimo, calls it the 'machina di Herone', alluding to works on pneumatics by the ancient Greek mathematician Hero of Alexandria that were often consulted and interpreted in the Renaissance.[106] Vitauro/Taegio, who had discussed with Caimo himself the 'causa di si lodevole effetto' ('cause of such a laudable effect') as the ever-playing fountain, describes the mechanism in detail with the help of a diagram. It may have some connection with Leonardo's studies of hydraulic apparatus: since the beginning of his artistic career Leonardo had been interested in 'Hero fountains', which he also designs as table-fountains. Obviously he was harking back to the table-fountains in the 'Heronic' mode which Leon Battista Alberti had described exhaustively in his *Ludi Rerum Mathematicarum* (c. 1450).[107] Caimo, as a scientist, must have been familiar with these precedents; but the fountain described by Taegio is, as far as I know, one of the earliest known examples of Hero fountains from the Renaissance and had been erected perhaps even earlier than the Fountain of the Birds at Tivoli. The works of the classical scientist had been translated into Italian at least as early as 1501, but the translation by Giovanni Battista Aleotti, which gave Hero's knowledge wide currency so that it could be applied on a larger scale to fountain-building, appeared only in 1589.[108]

Taegio's treatise shows the extent of his literary and scientific learning as he combines interest in technical innovations such as the 'Hero machine' with a genuine poetic talent for describing scenes and situations. Most convincing, from a literary point of view, are the passages in which he describes his impressions of nature and his emotional responses to aspects of nature and landscape. Taegio sums up his long lists of Milanese villa owners (intended to show the popularity of *vivere in villa*) and his garden descriptions with the sweeping question, who would not rejoice in nature, which speaks to all the senses: in a clear spring, in flower-decked meadows and dewy blossoms, shady groves, budding trees and verdant branches, waterfalls and murmuring brooks, playful animals and singing birds and the endless, clear sky over all? Finally, as

---

[106] Hero of Alexandria, *De Expetendis et Fugiendis Rebus*, ed. Valla (Venice, 1501); *De gli automi overo Machine se moventi . . .*, trans. by Bernardino Baldi (Venice, 1589); Marie Boas Hall, *'Hero's pneumatica: A study of its transmission and influence'*, in *Philosophers and Machines*, ed. O. Mayr (New York, 1972), pp. 90–100; Alexander Gustav Keller, 'Wasserkünste und Hydromechanik der Renaissance', *Endeavour*, 25 (1966), pp. 141–5, and 'Pneumatics, automata and the vacuum in the work of Giambattista Aleotti', *The British Journal for the History of Science*, 3 (1967), pp. 338–47; *Fons Sapientiae: Renaissance Garden Fountains*, ed. E. MacDougall (Washington, D.C., 1978).

[107] Leon Battista Alberti, *Ludi Rerum Mathematicarum*, in *Opere volgari* (Bari, 1973), vol. III, pp. 146–8, with a description and diagram of the table-fountain on which Caimo's version described by Taegio may have been based. However, the first printed edition of the *Ludi* did not appear until 1568 (in *Opuscoli morali di Leon Battista Alberti*, ed. Cosimo Bartoli (Venice, 1568), pp. 225–55), so Caimo must have known a copy stemming from Alberti. On Leonardo's designs for fountains see Pedretti, *Leonardo architetto*, pp. 96, 310–16.

[108] Giovanni Battista Aleotti, *Gli artifiziosi et curiosi moti spiritali di Herrone tradotti da M. Gio. Batt. Aleotti d'Argenta. . .* (Ferrara, 1589); see also Agostino Ramelli, *Le diverse et artificiose machine* (Paris, 1588).

Fig 5.9 Fountain (*machina di Herone*) in the garden of the Caimo family, from Taegio, *La villa*
(Milan, 1559)

Taegio speaks of the singing of shepherds and villagers as they deck their rustic altars,
the vision of an Arcadian Golden Age is complete. In this, the author is following
literary tradition, just as he did with his apotheosis of the *vita contemplativa* (pp. 9–11),
which seems to anticipate the romantic world of Giacomo Leopardi.

CHAPTER 6

HARD TIMES IN BAROQUE FLORENCE: THE BOBOLI GARDEN AND THE GRAND DUCAL PUBLIC WORKS ADMINISTRATION

MALCOLM CAMPBELL

I

During the fourth decade of the seventeenth century a constellation of interconnected events, political, social and economic, occurred which profoundly changed the Boboli Garden (fig. 6.1.). The purpose of this chapter is to document and review these events and to examine their transforming effects on the garden, the adjacent palace, the Palazzo Pitti, and the city of Florence. Although a number of initiatives affecting the Boboli were undertaken in this period, I will focus on one of the most important, the creation of a new aqueduct system for garden, palace and city.

There is nothing unusual about the fact that scholarly consideration of gardens should involve several frames of reference. In the past thirty years, historical studies of the garden have moved from principally descriptive considerations to levels of interpretation that include the study of primary literary and archival sources, iconographic analysis, and horticultural and archaeological exploration, to name some of the more salient of these diverse lines of inquiry related to understanding the form and function of the historic garden.[1] What makes the circumstances of the Boboli Garden unusual in the 1630s is the degree to which developments affecting garden and palace were integrated with the city of Florence and the multiplicity of levels at which this integration took place. Unusual, too, I believe (although future researches elsewhere may refute the claim) is the degree to which this integration reflected a programmatic agenda that addressed the separate but related issues of the plague,

[1] These multiple frames of reference for the Italian Renaissance garden in central Italy have been well summarised in Claudia Lazzaro's *The Italian Renaissance Garden. From the Conventions of Planting, Design, and Ornament to the Grand Gardens of Sixteenth-Century Central Italy* (New Haven and London, 1990). In addition to scholarly debts listed in the footnotes that follow, I would like to acknowledge special appreciation for the advice and assistance of Marco Chiarini, Sabine Eiche, Claudia Lazzaro, Cristina Acidini Luchinat, Claudio Pizzorusso and Katharine Watson. Gino Corti is warmly thanked for his assistance in reviewing my archival transcriptions. Eric Carey assisted with Latin transcriptions. I would also like to recall here the lectures of David Coffin that introduced me – like so many students – to a very special place, the Italian garden, and that it was James Holderbaum, who on a sunny summer day nearly four decades ago, literally opened my eyes to the wonders of the Boboli.

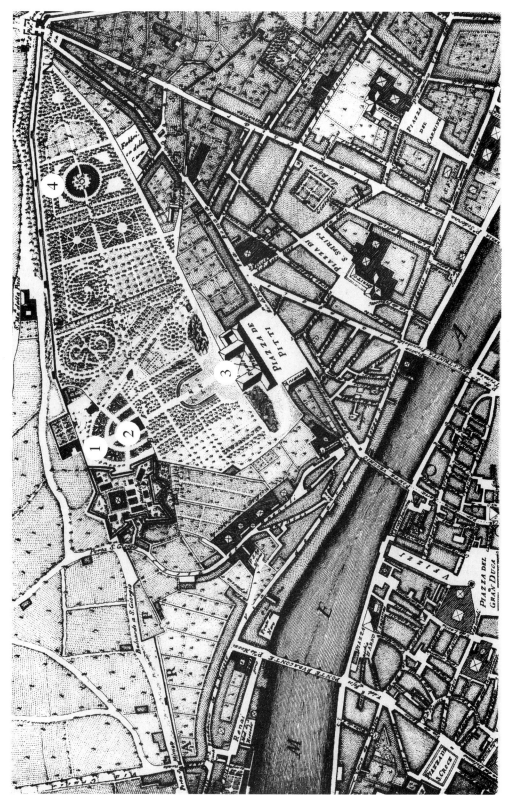

Fig. 6.1 Plan of the Boboli Garden from a map by Ruggeri, 1731, showing (1) *Dovizia*, (2) the Neptune Fountain and Vivaio Grande, (3) Fontana del Carciofo and the Moses Grotto, and (4) Isolotto

economic depression (especially in the textile industry and the building trades), a critical shortage of potable water in the city and, as an overarching consideration, the enhancement of the *Magnificenza* of the grand ducal Medici and their court.

The importance of the last element in this 1630s agenda should not be under-estimated. Although the alleviation of economic depression and human suffering was central to Medician response to conditions in the city, documents associated with the response to these multiple catastrophes indicate that these circumstances were per-ceived to offer reduced construction costs and an abundant labour supply. Also, as we shall see, the works of art introduced into this project and their inscriptions celebrate the success of grand ducal intervention by evoking mythological and biblical heroes and thus rendering the overcoming of those catastrophes as evidence of the heroic character, moral rightness and divine ordination of Medici rule.

Finally, there was an additional page in the Medici agenda: the Palazzo Pitti–Boboli Garden complex needed to be in an appropriately regal state to welcome and to celebrate the long-planned marriage of the young Grand Duke Ferdinand II to Vittoria della Rovere, only direct heir to the magnificent art collection of her grandfather and putative heiress to the duchy of Urbino, held in fief from the papacy. The official nuptials with attendant celebrations, which were to include an opera held in the main courtyard of the palace and an equestrian spectacle in the newly constructed amphitheatre (part of the 1630s work project), were scheduled for July 1637. Thus 1637 must have been a target date for the completion of many parts of the work project and a spur for the final over-all effort. The justification and celebration of Medici rule as expressed in the Boboli Garden, the Palazzo Pitti and in the city of Florence in the 1630s significantly expanded the representation of Medici rulership in the capital city of the grand duchy. The role of the Palazzo Pitti and the Boboli in these unfolding events was conclusive evidence of the shift in the centre of Medici governance, which had actually occurred in the reign of Grand Duke Ferdinand I (1587-1609), when the grand ducal household was transferred from the Palazzo Granducale (the former Palazzo della Signoria) to the Palazzo Pitti.[2] Only in this later period do the Palazzo Pitti and the Boboli become the primary locus for the representation of the grand duke as the divinely authorised dispenser of justice and mercy, as ruler and protector of the state, and as assurer of the prosperity and peace – *quietus* as the Medici traditionally termed it – of the Tuscan state and its people.[3] To date this emergence of the Palazzo Pitti and Boboli as an integral construct, a *reggia* consisting of both residence and garden, has received scant attention.

---

[2] For the role of the Palazzo Pitti complex during the reign of Ferdinand I, see L. Satkowski, 'The Palazzo Pitti: planning and use in the grand-ducal era,' *Journal of the Society of Architectural Historians*, 42 (4) (Dec. 1983), pp. 336–49. Further to the early history of the palace: F. Bottai, 'Bartolomeo Ammannati: una reggia per il Granducato di Toscana," *Antichità viva*, 18 (5-6) (1979), pp. 32–47; and M. Mosco, 'Una "Descrizione dell'apparato delle stanze del Palazzo de' Pitti in Fiorenza" edita a Venezia nel 1577,' *Antichità viva*, 19 (2) (1980), pp. 5–20.

[3] See, for example, the application of *quietus* as noted by Giorgio Vasari in his 1534 portrait of Duke Alessandro (M. Campbell, 'Il Ritratto del Duca Alessandro de' Medici di Giorgio Vasari: contesto e significato,' in *Giorgio Vasari. Tra decorazione ambientale e storiografia artistica*, ed. G. C. Garfagnini (Florence, 1985), p. 352.

In 1960, in an exhibition sponsored by the Florentine State Archives, a limited attempt was made to research the Boboli Garden and Pitti Palace as an entity.[4] Fifteen years later the exhibition and catalogue *Il luogo teatrale a Firenze* opened a new phase in Boboli–Pitti studies.[5] In an introductory essay to the catalogue, Ludovico Zorzi tellingly linked the ducal theatre and spectacle loci in the city, the Salone of the Palazzo Granducale, the Uffizi theatre, and the events held in the Piazza Santa Croce to theatre-related developments at the Palazzo Pitti and in the Boboli.[6] In 1977 in the context of the fresco cycles added to the Palazzo Pitti by Pietro da Cortona and others, I briefly discussed the Palazzo Pitti and the Boboli Garden, linking them to Roman imperial traditions of the palace-cum-garden as found, for example, on the Palatine Hill in Rome and to such later examples as the Villa Giulia and the Cortile Belvedere of the Vatican Palace.[7]

The full scope of the projects of the 1630s was vast, embracing the continuation of the ambitious initiatives of Cosimo II, Ferdinand II's father, begun c. 1618 and interrupted by his death in 1621. It was Cosimo II who had commenced the expansion of the Palazzo Pitti from seven bays to twenty-three bays on the design of Giulio Parigi (figs. 6.2 and 6.3), removed Giambologna's Ocean Fountain from the Prato Grande, the grassy amphitheatre immediately behind the palace, and installed a temporary set of bleachers in this location, thus adumbrating the permanent amphitheatre that his son would commission Giulio Parigi to design and which would be carried to completion by Alfonso Parigi the Younger. It was also Cosimo II who breached the western wall of the original Boboli, extending the formal gardens with an extraordinary prolongation that greatly increased their size and created a visually powerful cross axis to the original central allée that extended from the main courtyard of the palace southward to the city walls. Comparison of the 1731 Ferdinando Ruggieri plan of the garden (see fig. 6.1) and the well-known and frequently published 1599 depiction of the garden in the lunette painting by Giusto Utens (fig. 6.2) dramatically records the scope of this expansion. The projects of the 1630s represent Ferdinand II's continuation – and modification – of his father's initiatives, enriched by an ambitious programme of mural and ceiling decorations in the enlarged palace and, most important for our consideration, by the development of a new aqueduct system and an attendant programme of fountains that are the focus of this chapter.

---

[4] F. Morandini, *Mostra documentaria e iconografica di Palazzo Pitti e Giardino Boboli*, Archivio di Stato di Firenze, Exhibition catalogue 4 (Florence, 1960). A study particularly useful for its compendium of seventeenth- and eighteenth-century plans of the Pitti Palace and Boboli Gardens, documentation, and reconstruction of the history of the Boboli amphitheatre is G. Capecchi, *Il giardino di Boboli: un amfiteatro per la gioia dei granduchi* (Florence, 1993). Unfortunately, this publication came to my attention too late to be incorporated in the argument.

[5] *Il luogo teatrale a Firenze: Brunelleschi, Vasari, Buontalenti, Parigi*, ed. M. Fabbri, E. G. Zorzi and A. M. Petrioli Tofani (Florence, 1975).

[6] *Il teatrale*, especially pp. 47–9.

[7] M. Campbell, *Pietro da Cortona at the Pitti Palace. A Study of the Planetary Rooms and Related Projects* (Princeton, 1977), pp. 157–64.

Fig. 6.2 Giusto Utens. *Palazzo Pitti and Boboli Garden*, 1599

Fig. 6.3 Buoninsegna Cicciaporci. Drawing of the Palazzo Pitti, c. 1670

II

In 1628, just prior to the celebration of his majority, Ferdinand II completed a grand tour of central European capitals and a sojourn in Rome in the company of his brother Cardinal Giovanni Carlo, who reported on their stay in the city: 'Mentre siamo stati in Roma, habbiamo havute tante e tali occupazioni e per vedere le anticaglie, e le cose moderne, oltre alle infinite visite . . .'[8] It is likely that the 'antiquities' and 'the modern things' would have included many of the ruins of ancient Rome, including the palaces on the Palatine Hill and such modern Roman palaces as the Vatican, Casino and Palazzo Borghese, the Palazzo Barberini, then under construction, the Villa Giulia, the Villa Madama and, of course, the Villa Medici. The fountains in the city, especially those commissioned by Popes Sixtus V and Paul V, would have been unavoidably evident, and the 'infinite visits' would have made available the recent developments in painting and sculpture. In retrospect the visit to Rome in 1628 seems timely and auspicious.

Much less auspicious, however, were conditions in Florence at the time the new grand duke assumed power. The city had suffered economic depression during the reign of his father, and now in the 1630s the problems occasioned by a faltering economy were compounded by the return of the plague, which had infested Florence and the Tuscan state c. 1620-2. Florentine economic problems were a reflection of a pan-European economic depression that in the 1620s and 1630s affected most of the great trading and early modern industrial centres of the continent. In Florence the wool and silk workers were particularly hard hit, but the impact was felt throughout the

---

[8] G. Pieraccini, *La stirpe de' Medici di Caffaggiolo* (Florence, 1986), vol. II, p. 556.

economy, particularly by the construction trades.[9] With the benefit of hindsight the long economic depression that weakened the state of Tuscany can be seen as part of broader developments occasioned by the shift of trade routes to the Atlantic Ocean and the emergence of new nation states that decisively moved the centres of European power away from the Mediterranean basin. So, too, the plague that engulfed Florence — and much of Italy — in the period 1630-3 (it struck Florence in the winter and spring of 1630-1 and returned during the spring and summer of 1633) was part of a larger pandemic cycle of recurrent typhus epidemics that devastated the European subcontinent between 1613 and 1666. The terrible effects of this succession of epidemics was greatly intensified by the fact that during much of this period, roughly from 1618 to 1648, Europe was engulfed in the Thirty Years War. Considerable attention has been given to issues of public policy with regard to questions of health in Tuscany during this pandemic, especially during the 1630-3 epidemic.[10] However, except for the publication of grand ducal archival citations in the form of raw data in the 1975 catalogue, *Il luogo teatrale a Firenze*, the remarkably modern public works project initiated by Ferdinand II in response to these devastating events has received little attention.[11]

Faced with the multiple catastrophes of economic depression and plague, Ferdinand II and his administrators embarked on an ambitious governmental programme that encompassed the sponsorship of public sanitation, public welfare, and public works. The sanitation measures, among the most enlightened in Europe in the period, were largely in the hands of board of health magistrates, who were given extraordinary powers and who were remarkably successful in combating the plague, considering the inadequacies of their epidemiological concepts. The organisation and activities of the health magistrates need not detain us save for the observation that, although their decrees did not give it more than nominal attention, it is evident that these administrators were apprised of the need for an adequate supply of potable water for sanitation and for human consumption.

In contrast, the welfare programme and the public works project are of concern to us, for they were, in their application to the plight of the wool and silk workers and the building trades, especially sculptors, masons and stone cutters, inextricably bound to interconnected projects in the city, at the Palazzo Pitti, and in the Boboli. The volume of material in the State Archives, Florence, related to these interlocking projects is extensive. Most of this documentation consists of laconic payment records that

---

[9] For a lively account and bibliography see E. Cochrane, *Florence in the Forgotten Centuries 1527-1800* (Chicago and London, 1973), pp. 195-207.

[10] C. M. Cipolla, *Cristofano and the Plague. A Study in the History of Public Health in the Age of Galileo* (Berkeley and Los Angeles, 1973), C. M. Cipolla, *Public Health and the Medical Profession* (Cambridge, Mass., 1976), and C. M. Cipolla, *Faith, Reason and the Plague in Seventeenth Century Tuscany*, trans. by M. Kitter (Ithaca, 1977).

[11] See especially *Il luogo teatrale*, 49 and Cat. No. 11.1. This catalogue entry, prepared by Anna Biancalani, contains an enormous corpus of archival citations, generally untranscribed, often uninterpreted and with no indication of previous publication. The idea of a public works programme *per se* is not articulated. I hereby acknowledge this entry; it should be consulted, but I will not attempt to cite it for individual documents.

contribute little to our understanding of the policies that directed this enormous administrative undertaking. I will cite only a small portion of this documentation and limit this discussion to material that best illuminates the scope and intent of these projects as they relate to the Boboli Garden.

In comparison to policies of other European governments, grand ducal response to the combined catastrophes of plague and economic depression in Florence was remarkably progressive. Elsewhere the medieval tradition of alms giving and other eleemosynary practices were used to alleviate starvation and economic deprivation, but I have not found evidence of government-sponsored welfare programmes that targeted specific, depressed industries and provided alternative work for the unemployed. In fact, historians have assumed the conventional situation obtained in Florence. Eric Cochrane has summarised this position: basing his observations on earlier published research and his own study of a populous sector of the city, he concludes that 'The only alternative to mass starvation was the mass distribution of public charity. Ferdinand distributed some 150,000 *scudi* of it in 1631 alone, not counting his subsidies of monasteries bereft of their usual alms and the special outlays voted by the city magistrates.'[12] I would not contest the fact that the grand duke allotted substantial sums for charity; I would, however, argue that significant funds were distributed in the form of a structured dole, that at least in the city of Florence it was administered by public officials, not the clergy, and that it was integrated with a public works programme. Finally, I would contend that the programme was initiated in 1630, before the 1631-3 period studied by Cochrane.

The earliest document connected with this programme that I have located is a copy of an entry made on 13 February 1630, recording the fact that 200 silk workers have been put to work on the bastions of the Fortessa da Basso 'because His Highness wishes to offer some help to the weavers of the Arte della Seta who are suffering in such penurious times'.[13] This work programme appears to have started at the bastions of the Fortezza da Basso; however, it soon shifted to the Palazzo Pitti, the Boboli, and to an enormous project, the building of a new aqueduct for the city.

The directive initiating this work was followed by a second, dated 22 February 1630, that added fifty more workers to the rolls and also spelled out the terms and qualifications for work.[14] All men physically able to shoulder the *corbello* loaded with earth, a wicker basket still used by farm labourers in Tuscany, were to be paid one *lira*

---

[12] Cochrane, *Florence*, p. 198.

[13] Archivio di Stato di Firenze (hereafter ASF), Fabbriche Medicee, F. 126 (Memorie e Ricordanze, 1625-33), c. 118v: 13 February 1629 (1630 stile comune): 'Copia di un ordine di fare lavorare 200 tessitori di seta a' bastioni del Castello [San Giovanni Battista, a.k.a. Fortezza da Basso]. Volendo S.A. in tempi tanto penuriosi porgere qualche aiuto alli tessitori del' Arte della Seta che si stanno otiosi . . .'

[14] For this and the following: ASF, Fabbriche Medicee, F. 126 (Memorie e Ricordanze, 1625-33), c. 118v: '22 Febb. 1630 (stile comune): S.A. aprova che si acreschino al numero di dugento (tessitori di seta), altri cinquanta per al corbello, a lire una il giorno, e si vadino ritirando le polizze delle elemosine alle donne, massimo quelle che possono esser da fatica et si mettino al corbello a sette crazie il giorno per ciascuna, e in luogo separato dalli huomini con buono ordine, per ovviare ogni sorte di scandolo . . .'

per diem; women who met the same qualification were to receive 7 *crazie* for a day's labour and to work in a separate location in 'good order' so as 'to avoid every sort of scandal'.[15] The number of women working was significant: among the wool workers 163 women were reported shouldering the *corbello* by January 1631.[16] Under these provisions women not physically able to enter the grand ducal work force were denied alms, but they remained eligible for the dole of wine and food discussed below.

By May 1630 the work force was enlarged to include 100 wool workers, men and women, hired on the same basis as the silk workers.[17] The work at the Pitti commenced with a grand ducal letter of authorisation dated 22 October 1630. This letter transferred 15,000 *scudi* from the Depositeria Generale to the account of the Fabbriche 'for the expenses of new construction at the Palazzo Pitti in order to give employment to the artisans in this penurious year' and established a 100,000 *scudi* account at the Monte di Pietà, to be drawn against at the rate of 500 *scudi* a week to carry forward these activities.[18]

In November 1630 a directive gave more details of the work programme.[19] For families in which no adult could meet the work requirements, a nascent child labour code was enacted: male children, fourteen years of age or older, were to be accepted into the work crews if they were physically able to shoulder the *corbello*. Also, special provision was now made, probably because of the onset of winter, for days when rain prevented work. On inclement days—except for feast days—five *crazie* were to be distributed to all workers. Because this outlay was considered *elemosina*, it was not charged to the account of the Fabbriche. Except for these eleemosynary outlays, the wage distributed through the work project and the dole, that is, the distribution of bread and wine, was in the hands of the Fabbriche, whose records contain census books listing, *quartiere* by *quartiere*, the guild members and their status in this public work project.[20] Through the offices of the Fabbriche those unable to work received measured amounts of bread and wine which were distributed by a grand ducal representative standing at the portal of the guild hall. By January 1631, the work force drawn from the silk and wool guilds at work on the extension of the Palazzo Pitti, in the Boboli, and on a new aqueduct numbered 600.[21] In March the Fabbriche reported

---

[15] The monetary relationship of *crazie* and *lire* is somewhat complicated; there are 5 *quattrini* in 1 *crazia*, 3 *quattrini* in 1 *soldo* and 20 *soldi* in 1 *lira*. Hence the women were paid 35 *quattrini* per diem or 11 and two-thirds *soldi* or approximately 58.33 per cent of a man's wage. This rate of remuneration means that women were paid slightly less than 60 per cent of men's wages. In judging this disparity, we must bear in mind the backbreaking nature of the work; the men may have been harnessed to a more demanding schedule of production. Also, the rates of remuneration do in fact somewhat generously replicate those traditionally found in the building trades, where women's wages were half those of men (R. A. Goldthwaite, *The Building of Renaissance Florence. An Economic and Social History* (Baltimore and London, 1980), p. 322).

[16] ASF, Fabbriche Medicee, F. 140, fasc. 1630, unnumbered entry.

[17] ASF, Fabbriche Medicee, F. 126 (Memorie e Ricordanze, 1625-33), c. 127v.

[18] ASF, Depositeria Generale, F. 1020, No. 518.

[19] ASF, Fabbriche Medicee, F. 140, fasc. 1630, ins. 9.

[20] Ibid., f. 140, unnumbered fasc. cover these accounts and those discussed below. The surviving documentation is far from complete.

[21] Ibid., F. 140, fasc. 1630, ins. 9.

feeding an additional 400 guild members who were unable to shoulder the *corbello* between December 1630 and 19 January 1631.[22]

Given the criteria for their employment, it is obvious that the silk and wool workers constituted the pool of unskilled labour used in the construction and earth-moving required by these grand ducal projects. To their number were added many of the unemployed in the construction industry. These workers, skilled stone cutters and masons, together with the clerks who measured and inventoried cut stone, mouldings and curbing, proved more contentious than the weavers. Concerned that their allotted work was being transferred to less qualified, lower paid workers, six master stone cutters submitted a petition to the grand duke in April 1631, on behalf of forty other *maestri* and *compagni* (masters and journeymen), reminding him that when they, unemployed stone cutters from Fiesole and Settignano, had been hired, it had been agreed that the price of their piece work would be maintained and that work would be divided evenly between the Fiesolani and the Settignesi.[23] These skilled workers humbly requested that their prices be maintained and that their work not be allocated to others, especially those who had not been advanced to *maestro*. The petition was vetted on behalf of the grand duke by Francesco de' Servi, who explained that he had made the original agreement with the master masons which, he claims, specifically applied to ornamental stone work. At issue, he states, is the work of thirty *poveretti scarpellini* who are cutting lengths of *pietre forte* (a hard sandstone) for the new theatre and for the *stradone*, the broad pathway that serves as a spine for the western extension of the garden (see fig. 6.1, between nos. 2 and 4). He adds in his brief on the case that the grand duke can rest assured that where the *poveretti* are working a cost saving of 2/3 per *braccia* is realised on the stone cut! The petition appears to have been denied. Another petition was more successful.[24] Four clerks (*scrivamani*) working out of doors and hence at the mercy of the weather asked that their salaries be raised to 9 *scudi* per month. The rescript on the petition indicates grand ducal approval but for a total increase of 32 *scudi* per month for the foursome.

Obviously, depending on their particular skills, different classes of workers had a variety of negotiating options with the grand ducal administration; however, as near as I can determine, in no case did participants in the works project have the prerogative of setting their rates of remuneration or of 'bidding' for contracts. Thus, for example, when four sculptors, some of whom were members of the Accademia del Disegno, sought work at the palace, the architect-in-charge, Giulio Parigi, wrote on their behalf directly to the grand duke explaining that 'a handful of sculptors' were making supplication for work in, as usual, this time of penury.[25] Parigi proposed they be put to work on twelve statues 3 *braccia* high of sandstone and four lions' heads of hard stone

[22] Ibid., F. 140, fasc. 1631, ins. 14.
[23] Ibid., F. 140, fasc. 1631, no. 13 (April, 1631).   [24] Ibid., F. 140, fasc. 1631 (March 1632).
[25] This document has been transcribed and published in C. Pizzorusso, *A Boboli e altrove, Sculture e scultori fiorentini del Seicento* (Florence, 1989). p. 80.

(*pietre forte*) to be placed beneath the ground floor windows of the new addition to the palace.[26] In this case the rescript on the petition indicates that only the lions' heads were approved for completion. No mention of remuneration appears. Presumably this issue already had been determined by prior estimate and, as was customary in transactions involving members of the Accademia, final payment would have been adjudicated by a panel of fellow *maestri*. The massive public welfare and works project initiated by Ferdinand II in the 1630s summarised here is an important chapter in the history of such programmes and deserves further consideration in terms of its social and economic significance.

III

From an art historical perspective what is of especial importance in the initiatives undertaken by Ferdinand II in the 1630s is the fact that they combined public welfare and a work project that embraced the ducal residence, its garden, *and the city*. What unified this programme in the socio-economic sphere was of course the work project for battalions of unemployed labourers, construction workers, sculptors, artisans and functionaries who, at various levels, staffed this enterprise. At the hygienic and artistic levels we have a coalescence of concerns centered on the availability of a relatively abundant flow of potable water. The need for such a water supply was exacerbated by the plague. In the 1620s and also in the 1630s, the evidence gathered by the Uffiziali della Sanità indicates that sanitary conditions in Florence and elsewhere in the grand duchy were appalling, particularly, of course, among the poor in whose dwellings the cisterns and canteens were found overflowing with foul and fetid water, where the wells with drinking water (*pozzi da bere*) had their water commingled with the liquids of the cesspools (*pozzi neri*).[27] As early as 1621 the Uffizio della Sanità angrily reported to the grand duke that the city of Florence 'has totally lost that neatness and cleanliness that was the special quality that made it so worthy among the cities of Italy'.[28]

These conditions are in fact particularly shocking because we know that in the fifteenth and sixteenth centuries Florence enjoyed an abundance of potable well water and an efficient street drainage system that emptied surface and wash water into the Arno river. Typically, residences were fitted with interior latrines and cesspools. It was perfectly common for residences – and certainly for palazzi – to have private wells and plentiful fresh water. Both Goro Dati and Benedetto Varchi, chroniclers respectively of the fifteenth and sixteenth centuries, enthusiastically record these healthful conditions as enhancing the condition of urban life in Florence.[29] What caused the shocking

---

[26] Two of these lions' heads survive; two others once located beneath windows on the end of the palace facing eastward were destroyed or removed when the nineteenth-century stairwell was added to this end of the palace. See Pizzorusso, *Boboli*, p. 80, for further comment.

[27] C. M. Cipolla, *I Pedocchi e il Granducato* (Bologna, 1979), esp. pp. 12–27.   [28] Ibid., pp. 13–14.

[29] For a summary and further bibliography, see Goldthwaite, *Building of Renaissance Florence*, esp. pp. 16–26.

change of conditions by the 1620s? Flooding may have been a factor, but Florentines had been coping with periodic floods for centuries. It is also possible that fluctuations in the water table may have created new and severely deleterious conditions.

In addition to the precipitous decline in the availability of potable water from wells within the city, the conduits bringing water to the Boboli Garden from springs near the church of San Leonardo on the Costa San Giorgio were in a severely debilitated condition. The evidence is in the form of a report Giulio Parigi submitted to the grand duke on 25 September 1629, in which he explained that water from these springs was no longer reaching the Vivaio Grande (that is, the reservoir fish-pond at the top of the central allée: fig. 6.1, no. 2).[30] Parigi reported that in many places the water, unable to move forward in the pipes and conduits, was backflowing and furthermore that in functioning conduits as much as two-thirds of the supply was lost in transit. It is highly likely that the conduit connecting this water source and the one that linked the older spring near S. Miniato al Monte to urban Florence, for which the monumental Neptune Fountain (fig. 6.16) in the Piazza Granducale served as the principal monument, were in similar states of disrepair.

At a date not as yet precisely known but certainly within a year of Parigi's report, work was underway to create a new aqueduct for the city and the Boboli. In his guidebook to the Boboli published in 1789, Francesco Maria Soldini claimed that Grand Duke Cosimo I had planned to build this new aqueduct which had as its source an abundant aquifer located on a hillside on the slopes of Montereggi north-west of Fiesole near the Mugnone river and at a short distance from the church of the Crocifisso di Fontelucente in the locality called Burrone al Calderaio.[31] According to Soldini, Cosimo was able to construct a large-scale fish hatchery at this location and to start work on a conduit which he planned to bring into the city with the intention of 'enriching many public places in Florence and his garden which he was in the process of creating'. Soldini wrongly assumed that the projected aqueduct was instigated by Ferdinand I, who assumed rulership when his brother, Cosimo's eldest son Francesco, died in 1587. Soldini's account is of interest, for it verifies the fact that Grand Duke Cosimo played a visionary role in the development of an aqueduct system for the city of Florence and the Tuscan state and that this effort was probably carried forward by Ferdinand I. The presumption, however, that inscriptions at the Palazzo Pitti and in the Boboli celebrate the completion of the new aqueduct, the Acqua Ferdinanda, as a major accomplishment of Ferdinand I is incorrect. This enterprise was a central feature of the work project of the 1630s and thus an accomplishment of his grandson and putative namesake, Ferdinand II. This new aqueduct was, in point of fact, a singularly

---

[30] ASF, Fabbriche Medicee, F. 1928, no. 59. In this document the *vivaio* in question is referred to as the 'Vivaio di Boboli'. Following C. Acidini Luchinat ('La Fontana del Nettuno, viaggi e metamorfosi', *Boboli '90: Atti del Convegno Internazionale* (Florence, 1991), vol. I *passim*), I have consistently referred to this *vivaio* as the Vivaio Grande, although it is often called Vivaio Quadro in later documents, especially in connection with the *vivaio* at the Isolotto, which is sometimes referenced as the Vivaio Grande. See ASF, Fabbriche Medicee, F. 140, fasc. 1636, ins. 34.

[31] F. M. Soldini, *Il reale giardino di Boboli* (Florence, 1789), p. 15.

expensive element in the all-embracing plan to ameliorate living conditions and to enhance aesthetically the urban environment.[32] Typically (and consistent with the hundreds of weekly entries for the project which fill the ledgers of the Fabbriche and the Depositeria Generale), the aqueduct is referred to simply as the *condotto* associated with Montereggi, the mountainside source of its waters, rather than by its official nomination as the Acqua Ferdinanda, which pretentiously identified it in the manner of the aqueducts of Imperial Rome.

IV

To date no seventeenth-century plan of the aqueduct has been located; however, an eighteenth-century one probably prepared by Giuseppe Ruggeri in the 1740s and now in the collection of the city museum, Museo di Firenze Com'era, retains the major aspects of the original system of conduits and fountains.[33] In addition, an eighteenth-century cache of documents dating from 1768 to 1788 includes plans and reports on the aqueducts of Florence that shed further light on the original Acqua Ferdinanda.[34] The aqueduct consisted of conduits made principally of terracotta but also of lead. Water was piped downhill from its sources on Montereggi and carried in conduits in the river bed of the Mugnone.[35] Provision was made for the supply to be tapped by certain villas along the river. Water pressure was provided by gravity and, to assure consistency in flow and pressure, a water tower was built out of a bastion on the northern periphery of the city wall near the Porta San Gallo, where the aqueduct entered the city walls. The water tower, known as the Torre (or Torrino) del Maglio, survived into the late nineteenth century.[36] The name derived from the odd shape of the tower, its massive base suggesting the head of a hammer and its tall shaft housing the water column resembling a handle. The passage of the aqueduct into the city was rendered visible and accessible to the populace by a series of public fountains through which, for the first time, water was broadly distributed throughout the city and into the

---

[32] When in July 1640 this vast project was reaching completion, Andrea Arrighetti, Soprintendente of the Fabbriche, gave an interim summation of expenses to the grand duke on the project as 94,842 *scudi*, 2 *lire*, 10 *soldi* and 2 *denari* (ASF, Depositaria Generale, F. 1044, no. 1 and also ASF, Fabbriche Medicee, F. 140, fasc. 1640, ins. 106).

[33] This plan, entitled 'l'Acqua all'Imperial Palazzo de Pitti, e ad altre varie Fontane Pubbliche della Città di Firenze, Giardini e fatta l'anno 1754', is wall-mounted in the museum. Measuring several metres in length, it resists illustration through normal photographic publication.

[34] ASF, Segreteria di Finanze, F. 201, under 'Affari diversi'. The condition of the aqueducts of Florence is reviewed in detail. The quantity and quality of sources and the flow of water at the fountains of the city is recorded. This file of documents was brought to my attention by Sabine Eiche.

[35] This at least was the intended routing. In a report prepared in 1782, it is stated in a memorandum (see note 34 above) that the conduit does not actually reach the springs; rather, the water from the springs is received at a terminus in the river bed after flowing freely downhill and powering small water mills en route to the collecting point.

[36] There is a painting of the water tower in the Museo di Firenze Com'era by E. Marko dated 1837 (see P. Magi, *Firenze di una volta* (Florence, 1973), p. 83 for an illustration). The tower was located at a point in the city wall that marked the initiation of the Via Lamarmora, which was in fact formerly called the Via del Maglio. The oddly shaped tower is visible near the Porta San Gallo in the panoramic view of the city in G. Zocchi's *Scelta di XXIV vedute . . . della Città di Firenze* (Florence, 1754), plate 1.

farthest confines of the Boboli Garden situated on the southern perimeter of the city.

The entry of the aqueduct at the Porta San Gallo meant that the physical arrival of the new water supply from the north of the city was diametrically opposite the desired symbolic emergence of its waters in the Boboli and their implied distribution *from the Boboli to the city*. The *concetto* that the symbolic headwater of the aqueduct within the city should be situated in the Boboli was a fundamental premise of the visual representation of the aqueduct and was intended to underscore the flow of water to the populace as a manifestation of grand ducal munificence. Following the precedent of the extant conduit system in which the entry of water into the Boboli was marked, as we have seen, by the Vivaio Grande, the reservoir and fish-pond located close to the southern terminus of the central allée (fig. 6.1, no. 2), this site was to serve as the *inferred* entry point of the new aqueduct into Florence. In fact the new water supply arrived in the garden – after traversing the city – in closer proximity and elevation to the Prato Grande, the grassy plateau immediately behind the palace (see fig. 6.1, 'Teatro').[37]

The thematic recasting of the central allée of the Boboli to celebrate the young grand duke's role as a preserver of peace, restorer of prosperity, provider of water, and munificent benefactor of the Florentine people was given an annunciatory figure by the installation of a colossal marble statue representing Dovizia (Abundance) at the uppermost point in the allée (fig. 6.1, no. 1; fig. 6.4). With this statue we encounter the first of the extensive series of sculptures that were recycled, redistributed, and modified to ornament and to provide visual testimony to the accomplishments and aspirations of the new Medici regime. The *Dovizia* was originally commissioned by Grand Duke Ferdinand I as a figure honouring Johanna of Austria, consort of his deceased brother Francesco I and the mother of Maria de' Medici, who at the time of the commission (1600) was the promised spouse of Henry IV of France.[38] Originally commissioned from Giambologna, the figure was actually carried out by Pietro Tacca, who, aided by his pupil Bartolomeo Salvini, modified the figure for its new hilltop location in the Boboli between 1635 and 1637.[39] In keeping with the conventional presentation of Abundance, a gilded sheaf of wheat was placed in Dovizia's upraised left hand, an appropriate accompaniment to the cornucopia overflowing with fruit and flowers crooked in her right hand.[40] The inscription on the base declares that while all Europe

---

[37] The original conduits leading from the *vivaio* down the allée to fountains on the Prato Grande and atop the terrace of the palace courtyard certainly remained functional, but this source was significantly superseded in quantity by the supply of the new aqueduct.

[38] For a full account see D. Heikamp, 'Die Säulenmonumente Cosimo I', *Boboli '90* (Florence, 1991), vol. I, pp. 3–17, esp. pp. 12–13. See also K. Watson, *Pietro Tacca Successor to Giovanni Bologna* (New York and London, 1983), pp. 128–59.

[39] An extensive discussion of the *Dovizia* and documentation of its transport and installation is provided by Watson, *Pietro Tacca*, pp. 141–9. See also documents in F. Guerrieri and J. Chatfield, *Boboli Gardens* (Florence, 1972), pp. 76–7. Additional, mainly confirmatory documents are to be found in ASF, Aquisti e Doni, F. 74 and Fabbriche Medicee, F. 75 bis and Fabbriche Granducal, F. 1929 (B), fasc. 181.

[40] The spray of gilded stalks of grain was definitely a modification made in 1635 (ASF, Fabbriche Granducali, F. 1929 (B), insert no. 181).

Fig. 6.4 Giambologna, Pietro Tacca and Bartolomeo Salvini, *Dovizia*, marble.
Florence, Boboli Garden

was plunged in terrible warfare and Italy suffered from famine, Tuscany enjoyed the
benevolent reign of Ferdinand II, most perfect prince of a felicitous people: PARIO E
MARMORE SIGNVM COPIA / HIC POSITA SVM A.D. MDCXXXVI. / MEMORIA / AETERNVM VT
VIGEAT QVOD / OMNIS FERE EVROPA DVM FVNESTISSIMO / ARDERET BELLO ET ITALIA
CARITATE / ANNONAE LABORARET ETRVRIA SVB / FERDINANDO II. NVMINIS
BENEVOLENTIA / PACE RERVM OPTIMA ATQVE VBERTATE FRVEBATVR / VIATOR ABI /
OPTIMVM PRINCIPEM SOSPITEM EXPOSTVLA / TVSCIAE FELICITATEM GRATVLARE ('A figure
in Parian marble, I was placed here as an Abundance in AD 1636. May the memory last
forever that while almost all of Europe was consumed with most grievous wars and Italy
was struggling from a lack of grain, Etruria under Ferdinand II, because of the kindness
of his will, was enjoying peace, the best of affairs, and prosperity. O passer-by, go your
way, urgently request that your most excellent ruler be safe, and wish joy for Tuscany.')
Today the statue presides from within a niche composed of bay and ilex; lacking these

Fig. 6.5 View of the Cortile Grande with the entrance to the Moses Grotto, Fontana del Carciofo, the Prato Grande amphitheatre, the Neptune Fountain at Vivaio Grande (barely visible) and *Dovizia* (in the distance). Florence, Palazzo Pitti/Boboli garden

plantings in 1636, the grand duke ordered the city wall behind the statue to be painted green.[41] This effort to accentuate the visibility of *Dovizia* underscores a fundamental problem that vexed this attempt to construct a readable programme in visual terms of the young grand duke's accomplishment at the Boboli. The length of the tiered central allée obviates the intended effect of this colossal figure; the distance reduces her to a mere incident in the perspective even when the spectator's viewpoint is the floor above the *piano nobile* of the palace (see fig. 6.5). Her inscripted message, we should note, is accessible only to those who undertake the ascent of the allée. The limited and intermittent appearance of such readers is appropriately captioned in the phrase VIATOR ABI. The suggestion that the statue is made of Parian marble is apparently purely rhetorical; Katharine Watson's researches indicate that the marble came from the quarries of Carrara.[42]

The Vivaio Grande (fig. 6.1, no. 2) is located immediately in front of and below *Dovizia*. Concomitant with the installation of *Dovizia*, Stoldo Lorenzi's bronze

[41] Watson, *Pietro Tacca*, p. 142 and n. 46.   [42] Ibid., p. 136.

Neptune, originally commissioned by Cosimo II in 1566 for this location and removed after 1584,[43] was returned to this site but under radically different terms than its initial debut (fig. 6.6). Originally posed atop a cylix fountain located at a short distance from the Vivaio Grande, Neptune appeared in his threatening aspect that Giovanni Paolo Lomazzo described as *turbato*.[44] In this installation the water in the bowl of the fountain beneath his poised trident would have spilled over the lip of the bowl, pouring around the cringing tritons and nereids who were crouched beneath the cylix bowl.[45] In its original position I believe that in addition to interpreting this figure as *Nettuno turbato* we can perceive him as initiating the deluge commanded by his brother Jupiter in Ovid's *Metamorphoses*.[46] The deluge as an initial thematic entry point for water in a hillside garden was probably a *concetto* employed in earlier gardens, even if the theme was less tellingly explicated. In later gardens the theme is indeed explicit: the two most famous examples are the sixteenth-century Grotto of the Deluge at the Villa Lante, Bagnaia, and, in the early seventeenth century, Gianlorenzo Bernini's Neptune and Triton Fountain, originally located above and adjacent to a large *vivaio* at the Villa Peretti, Rome, where the same *concetto* was re-enacted. Lorenzi's Neptune Fountain can be seen in its original configuration above a cylix fountain, but after its initial transfer from the Vivaio Grande, in the Utens lunette (fig. 6.2), where he appears as the centrepiece in the strictly compartmented garden to the left of the palace.

Neptune returned to the Vivaio Grande in 1634 but without his cylix fountain.[47] Upon his return, he was installed on a steep, rocky promontory that rises abruptly at the centre of the Vivaio Grande. The nereids and their triton companions, who originally crouched beneath the bowl of the cylix fountain, have been transposed so that one pair acknowledge one another, almost seeming to genuflect, while they regard the fall of water upon a large scalloped shell that has been introduced between them. The shell, open and bowl-like, is like the marble fish, an addition to the original fountain and

---

[43] Acidini Luchinat, 'La Fontana del Nettuno', p. 42.

[44] G. P. Lomazzo, *Trattato dell'arte de la pittura* (Milan, 1584), book VII, chap. 25, p. 584: 'Nettuno Dio del Mare, fu formato in diversi modi, hora tranquillo, quieto e pacifico, e hora tutto turbato come si legge appresso Homero, or Vergilio, imperoche tale anco si vede il mare in diversi tempi.' It is to the indispensable research of B. Wiles (*The Fountains of Florentine Sculptors and their Followers from Donatello to Bernini* (Cambridge, Mass., 1933)) that we owe the topological distinctions of cylix and candelabrum fountain types (pp. 22–31, 59–67). The importance of the writings of the sixteenth-century theorist Giovanni Paolo Lomazzo for the multiple contemporary interpretations of Neptune statues was first noted by Wiles (pp. 22, n. 1; 53, n. 1; 60, n. 2). After the completion of this chapter, the informative discussion of the aspects of Neptune in I. Lavin's essay, 'Giambologna's *Neptune* at the Crossroads' (*Past-Present. Essays in Art from Donatello to Picasso* (Berkeley, Los Angeles and Oxford, 1992), pp. 63–83) came to my attention.

[45] Acidini Luchinat, 'La Fontana del Nettuno', pp. 31–45, provides a detailed discussion and definitive reconstruction of the fountain.   [46] Ovid, *Metamorphoses*, I. 275–92.

[47] As noted by Acidini Luchinat, the Neptune was certainly returned to the Vivaio Grande by 1635 because a final accounting and recording of the last phase of restoration was recorded on 10 June 1636 (p. 43 and n. 44); however, there are entries for work on the Vivaio and the Neptune between August and December 1633 (ASF, Aquisti e Doni, F. 74). These include payment to the bronze caster Bartolomeo Cennini for 'restaurazione della statua di metallo e per mettere nel vivaio' (13 August 1633) and, in the midst of numerous weekly payments for the Vivaio Grande, also called the Vivaio Quadrato, we have a payment on 19 August 1634 for 'spese del vivaio e per dette a Francesco Betti Scarpelino . . . per rassettare la statue di bronzo per la fonte'.

Fig. 6.6 Stoldo Lorenzi, The Neptune Fountain in the Vivaio Grande, bronze, marble and
artificial rock. Florence, Boboli Garden

offers a clue to the reinterpretation occasioned by this new installation. Tour guides in the Boboli tell their credulous listeners that Neptune is fishing which, needless to say, is scarcely the case. More thoughtful observers have noted the transfer of the bronze Neptune from his more formal sixteenth-century sculpted cylix to a rocky islet as a manifestation of the nascent naturalism of the Seicento, while others have lamented the destruction of the logic of the original design.[48] But what if the transformation of Neptune's setting was occasioned by an altogether new intention in terms of subject? The raised trident from which water spews forth onto the rocks and into the scalloped shell is an event given special emphasis by the interacting nereid and triton who create a parenthetical group, framing the shell. If we can interpret Neptune's action as *bringing forth water* – and I think that we can do so – then this new setting for Neptune revises the intention of his action and introduces a new text: we witness Neptune-Poseidon striking the earth, rather than roiling Ovidian flood waters, to offer his gift of gushing water from the earth, in competition with that of Athena-Minerva, to the Athenian polis.

The setting for Neptune has been modified to make reference to the competition that occasioned the naming of Athens and, by inference, the bringing of water to Florence. The goddess won the original competition with the gift of the olive tree, succeeding against Poseidon, whose trident pierced the earth and brought forth his gift of water. The immediate source for the introduction of the theme into the Boboli is probably Ovid's *Metamorphoses*, where the contest between the gods is described as presented by Minerva-Athena in her tapestry-weaving contest with Arachne: 'Minerva showed the hill of Mars in Athens / And that old conflict over name of the land. /.../ And there stood Neptune, smiting with his trident / The cliff of rock, and the gush of sea-water / Proving his title to the rule of the city.'[49]

Here on the lofty heights of the Boboli beneath the presiding statue of *Dovizia*, Neptune, in the revised version of Stoldo Lorenzi's fountain, makes a second strike, this time for Florence, thematically linking the city with Athens. This subject was certainly well known at the Medici court.[50] The return of Lorenzi's *Neptune* to the upper reaches of the central allée and its adaptation to the service-oriented civic theme of water-provider, was, as we shall see, to occasion significant changes along the central axis of the garden. These changes will be taken up in detail below, but it will be useful

---

[48] Cf. Acidini Luchinat, 'La Fontana del Nettuno', p. 44: 'La fontana del Nettuno ci è stata tramandata nel suo inalterato allestimento 'naturalistico' del Seicento'; and C. Avery, 'The "Garden called Bubley": Foreign impressions of Florentine gardens and a new discovery relating to Pratolino', *Boboli '90* (Florence, 1991), vol. I. p. 149: 'It [the Neptune Fountain] had lost its tazza in this move, while the original logic of its design was also destroyed.'

[49] Ovid, *Metamorphoses* VI. 65–6; 70–2, trans. R. Humphries (Bloomington, 1964), p. 131.

[50] The reference to the Athens-based contest with its suggestive overtures of association of Florence with Athens is a subject closely related to other contemporaneous or near-contemporaneous representations in the palace. The Florence–Athens *paragone* was certainly implied in Giovanni da San Giovanni's fresco cycle then in progress in the main Salone of the grand ducal apartments on the ground floor of the palace (M. Campbell, 'The original program of the Salone di Giovanni da San Giovanni', *Antichità viva* 15 (4) (1976), pp. 3–25), and the subject was expressly represented in a lunette in the Sala di Giove in which the bestowal of Minerva's gift, the olive tree, was depicted by Pietro da Cortona c. 1642-4 (Campbell, *Pietro da Cortona*, p. 133 and fig. 111).

Fig. 6.7 Giambologna, The Ocean Fountain, marble. Florence, Boboli Garden, Isolotto

to review them here. With the threat of a hillside deluge eliminated, the role of Neptune on top of Giambologna's Ocean Fountain (fig. 6.7) as a calmer of waters was no longer required, and this fountain could be removed from the Prato Grande (fig. 6.2), leaving an unimpeded space appropriate to its new use as an amphitheatre (fig. 6.5). The Fontana del Carciofo (fig. 6.8), located atop the palace terrace, where Ammanati's Juno Fountain had stood in 1599 (fig. 6.2), served as a festive celebration of the arrival of water from Neptune's generosity (even though most of the water that vivifies this fountain arrived by conduit from the new aqueduct and not from the spring near San Leonardo that flowed out of the trident held by Lorenzi's *Neptune*). In the grotto below the terrace, accessible from the palace courtyard, a third and final new set of fountain installations was contemporaneously created (figs. 6.9-10). Here the antique classical water theme is transformed; the new aqueduct is celebrated in religious

Fig. 6.8 Giovan Francesco Susini et al. Fontana del Carciofo, marble and bronze. Florence,
Palazzo Pitti/Boboli Garden

terms, and the grand duke's magnanimity is seen as adumbrated in Moses bringing forth
water from the rock for the Israelites (fig. 6.11).

   Of these new installations, the first we will consider is the Fontana del Carciofo,
placed on the terrace above the courtyard of the palace. Recently, thanks to the
researches of Claudio Pizzorusso, the complex history of this fountain, the last
monumental example of the candelabrum type, has been largely unravelled.[51]
Following the removal of Ammanati's Juno Fountain in the period 1635-6, it appears
that the terrace area where it had stood remained vacant until the period 1639-42, when
work was carried out on the new fountain under the direction of Giovan Francesco
Susini.[52] These dates seem quite correct; however, one important element in the
documentation, Filippo Baldinucci's entry on Susini, needs to be reviewed because it

---

[51] Pizzorusso *Boboli*, pp. 35–54 and C. Pizzorusso, 'Indizi per una Fontana di Venere', *Boboli '90* (Florence, 1991), vol. I, pp.
    83–8. The earlier literature is found in Pizzorusso's publications.
[52] Ammanati's Juno Fountain appears on the terrace in the Utens lunette (fig. 6.2). For its history, see D. Heikamp,
    'Bartolomeo Ammanati's marble fountain for the Sala Grande of the Palazzo Vecchio in Florence', *Fons Sapientiae:
    Renaissance Garden Fountains*, ed. E. MacDougall (Washington, D.C., 1978), pp. 115–73. The dates for the Fontana del
    Carciofo are confirmed by the researches of Giovanni Lombardi ('Giovan Francesco Susini', *Annali della Scuola Normale
    Superiore di Pisa, classe di Lettere e Filosofia*, vol. III, 9, 2 (1979), pp. 770–1. See also Pizzorusso, 'Fontana di Venere', p. 83.

Fig. 6.9 The Moses Grotto. Interior view: Raffaello Curradi and Cosimo Salvestrini, *Moses*, porphyry (centre); Antonio Novelli, *Laws*, marble (left); Domenico and Gioven Battista Pieratti, *Imperium*, marble (right). Florence, Palazzo Pitti

has been interpreted selectively.[53] I believe that too much attention has been given to the date of 1639 offered by Baldinucci for 'completion of the great model' of the fountain, and, conversely, too little note has been made of what his comment on the fountain yields in its entirety. Consulting a memorandum book 'written in Susini's own hand', Baldinucci states that 'in 1639 [Susini] finished the great model of the fountain that was to be placed above ... [the Moses Grotto], and that the dedicatory plaque [*cartella*] for the side of the basin [*sponda del vivaio*], the snails, the outer angles of the fountain and the small stairs; all of these were underway in June 1641, and then in 1646 were added two wild animals of bronze'.[54]

In terms of the commission and design of the fountain, the date of 1639, when the great model – which I take to be a full-scale mock-up – was finished, is a belated

[53] F. Baldinucci, *Notizie dei professori del disegno da Cimabue in qua*, ed. Ranalli (Florence 1846), vol. IV, pp. 119–20.

[54] Baldinucci, *Notizie*, vol. IV, pp. 119–20: 'Come egli del 1639 avea data fine al modello grande della fontana, che dovea andare sopra essa grotta, e a quello della cartella per la sponda del vivaio, delle chiocciole, degli angoli di essa fonte, e delle scalinate, le quali cose incomincio a mettere in opera nel mese di giugno 1641, e poi del 1646 vi accommodò due animali salvatici di bronzo.'

Fig. 6.10 Bronze and marble wall fountain. Florence, Palazzo Pitti, Moses Grotto

terminus post quem. Plans for this fountain, consisting of detailed drawings and probably small *modelli*, must have been worked up several years earlier. Previously uncited documents record the payment for the transport of a large fountain bowl, identified as a *contratazza* brought from the port at Pisa to Florence in the autumn of 1636, that is, immediately after the removal of the Juno Fountain.[55] Another archival source sheds further light on this enterprise.[56] The *contratazza*, like the great bowl of the Ocean

[55] The entries for this operation begin on 8 November 1636, shortly after the fountain of Ammanati, previously located on the terrace, was removed (25 October 1636). The transport operation was a complicated one requiring not only portages but the enlargement – and subsequent repair – of the city gates at the Porta San Frediano and also at the gate to the Boboli near S. Pier Gattolino. The transport of the *contratazza* even resulted in damage to the streets. Payments for this work continue until 24 December 1636 (for all these entries see ASF, Fabbriche Medicee, F. 75 bis).

[56] ASF, Fabbriche Medicee, F. 35 (Debitori e creditori della Nuova Fabbrica de' Pitti di S.A.S. 1636-1639), *c.* 62 *sinistra*: 'Spese della tazza venuta di portoferraio ch'è . . . sul terrazzo dello Am[m]annato di dare addì 6 di dicembre [1636] . . . '; then follows an itemised expense list with, on *c.* 62 *destra*, payment in full at *scudi* 5313.4.2.

Fig. 6.11 Raffaello Curradi and Cosimo Salvestrini, *Moses*, porphyry. Florence, Palazzo Pitti, Moses Grotto

Fountain, came from Portoferraio on the island of Elba, and its destination was the terrace formerly occupied by Ammanati's Juno Fountain (fig. 6.1, no. 3). This bowl, like its predecessor from Elba, is of granite and of such size and weight that part of the expense of transport entailed enlarging and then repairing the city gates at the Porta San Frediano and at the entry to the Boboli. Clearly, we are dealing with a fountain bowl of exceptional size.[57] It is highly unlikely that the expensive quarrying and transport of the

[57] I once confused entries for the 1636 *contratazza* with the installation of a ground-level basin under the Ocean Fountain at the Isolotto, to which this bowl can have no relation (Campbell, *Pietro da Cortona*, p. 16, n. 56). Apparently baffled by the material used in the great bowl of the Fontana del Carciofo, Cinelli (F. Bocchi, *Le bellezze della città di Firenze*, ed. G. Cinelli (Florence, 1677), p. 134) states that it is made of *pozzolana*. While its grey coloration suggests cement, this would have been technically impossible, given the diameter of the bowl and its minimal central support, before the era of reinforced concrete.

large bowl was carried out prior to the execution of the fountain design. The upper bowl of the Fontana del Carciofo does not appear in the recorded portages, but this is not surprising, for it was almost certainly an extant bowl recycled into this commission. In all likelihood, this upper bowl is in fact the one which formerly served the cylix fountain that originally supported Stoldo Lorenzi's *Neptune*.

Essentially completed in 1642, the Fontana del Carciofo consists of a central double-tiered candelabrum topped by a stylised *giglio* which bears a presumably unintended resemblance to an artichoke; whence came the nickname of the fountain (fig. 6.8). The stem of the candelabrum is enlivened with harpies, conventional ones beneath the upper bowl and below the lower bowl, male figures equipped with 'harpesque' wings and serpentine legs. The basin in the fountain is an elongated hexagonal in plan. The short sides of the basin facing east and west are enriched by enormous marble scalloped shells flanked by curving steps. Several marble snails – so dutifully noted by Baldinucci – are dispersed around the fountain. The long side of the basin facing the palace is fronted by a curvilinear cascade on which two satyrs, male and female, are perched.[58] On the garden side the long wall of the basin carries an elaborately ornamented cartouche sculpted by Susini with a lengthy exhortatory inscription: AVLICI NARCISSI MEMORES FONTEM NE INSPICITE VOBIS FORTVNAM STRVERE HINC HAVRITE EGO PROCVL INTER SPAELEA FERARVM GENITA QVIA OPTIMA HVC MAGNO IMPENDIO DEDVCTA GLORIOSO FERDINANDI COGNOMINE CLARA INCEDO ET LICET ORTA IN SVMMIS MONTIVM CONCAVA VALLIVM TVBIS INCLVSA PERCVRRERE NON DEDIGNATA REGIAE PVLCHERRIMVM LOCVM TENEO ITA NEMO IN AVLA EMERGET AVT FIRMO STABIT VESTIGIO NISI MODERATIONI ET INTEGRITATI INNIXVS ('Courtiers mindful of Narcissus, do not look upon the fountain so as to contrive an [evil] fate for yourselves, but drink up from here, since I, magnificent, born far away from here among the caverns of wild animals, and brought here at great expense, enter here renowned because of the exalted name of Ferdinand, and although born on the peaks of mountains, did not disdain to travel enclosed in conduits through the hollows of valleys. I hold the most beautiful place in the royal residence such that no one will appear in the court or will stand on [this] firm spot unless endowed with moderation and integrity.') The inscription is positioned on the southern side of the fountain basin, presumably so that it could be read by spectators in the theatre; however, legibility is actually limited to occupants of the terrace.[59]

It is evident that the bronze wild animals that Baldinucci said Susini added to the fountain in 1646 – and which are no longer on the site of the fountain complex – were part of the original scheme; they were the 'wild animals' mentioned in the inscription who had strayed from their 'caverns' to admire the courtly fountain. Their presence

---

[58] These two figures (visible in figs. 6.5 and 6.8) are made of an indeterminate, badly weathered material. One wonders if they were part of the original full-scale model that was never translated into marble. Perhaps their cement-like medium gave rise to Cinelli's misconception that the great bowl, the *contratazza* of the fountain, was made of *pozzolana* (see note 57 above).   [59] For an illustration of this cartouche and its inscription, see Guerrieri and Chatfield, *Boboli Gardens*, fig. 62.

would have heightened the spectator's consciousness of the other bronze elements on the fountain – the garlands of fruit and aquatic life on the candelabra – and thus strengthened thematic connections with Lorenzi's bronze *Neptune* and the sheaf of wheat and cornucopia held by Dovizia. The giant marble sea snails (also mentioned by Baldinucci) would have further underscored the theme of abundance and strengthened the references to sea life implicit in the action of Lorenzi's *Neptune*, installed on his islet in the act of bringing forth sea water from his rocky base.

Ironically, the most striking aspect of the Fontana del Carciofo and the source of its status as Giovan Francesco Susini's masterpiece owes little to his talents. The dozen little marble amorini who discharge their bows while cavorting and riding turtles on the angles of the basin, astride swans in its waters and perched on shells at the eastern and western ends of the fountain base are not only in large part the work of other artists but were executed twenty years earlier for the original project at the Isolotto commissioned by Ferdinand's father Grand Duke Cosimo II (fig. 6.1, no. 4). These little charmers were part of the original 'Cythera' complex created there, together with the marble statues of more adolescent cupids, still *in situ*, who cheerfully abuse dissected hearts with hammers, open them with keys, and indiscriminately fire arrows. From the researches of Claudio Pizzorusso we now know that these figures – amorini and cupids – were the work of an équipe of artists including, in addition to Susini, Giovan Simone Cioli, Andrea Ferrucci, Antonio Novelli, Bastiano Pettirossi, Giovan Battista and Domenico Pieratti, Bartolomeo Rossi, Cosimo Salvestrini and Agostino Ulbaldini.[60] This is, indeed, a group quite distinct from the sculptors documented at work with Susini on the Fontana del Carciofo in 1639-42: Andrea Bigazzi, Michelangelo Bozzolini and Francesco Generini.[61] Repositioned on the Fontana del Carciofo, the playful amorini add an overtly libidinous quality to the general theme of abundance and fertility represented in *Dovizia*, the Vivaio Grande teeming with fish, and the fruits of the land and sea that decorate the Fontana del Carciofo. When the fountain was completed, the amorini would have both commemorated the wedding festivities of July 1637, when Grand Duke Ferdinand II married Vittoria della Rovere and anticipated the birth of an heir, which occurred when Grand Prince Cosimo was born in 1642.

The Fontana del Carciofo is a nodal point in the actual water flow in the aqueduct system and in the rhetoric of its representation. Normally the display of water at this fountain would have followed the pattern of the traditional candelabrum fountain in which water emitted from the top of an extended central stem splashes forth into an upper bowl, falls evenly into a larger bowl below – the *contratazza* – and then overflows, again evenly, into a large ground-level basin. The splash and steady spill of this water play would have been appropriate to the small-scale character of the figural elements that enliven the austere linearity of the steps and basin of the Fontana del Carciofo. However, the hydraulics of this fountain were designed to play, on occasion,

---

[60] Pizzorusso, 'Fontana di Venere', p. 84. Pizzorusso has attempted – convincingly – to attribute specific figures to the hands of individual artists.   [61] Lombardi, 'Susini', pp. 770-1.

a highly dramatic role, one more in keeping with the ostentatious character of its inscription. This special effect is not documented until the late eighteenth century, when the status of the Florentine aqueduct system was reviewed in detail. From a report made in 1766, we learn that when the valves on the other fountains connected to the aqueduct were closed, the Fontana del Carciofo discharged a geyser measuring 14½ *braccia* (or approximately 28 feet) in height when measured from the rim of the fountain basin to its crest.[62] This water jet would have been of sufficient magnitude to capture the observer's attention and, in the case of a spectator positioned on one of the palace loggias and thus able to distinguish the distant figure of Lorenzi's *Neptune*, to permit the desired fictitious connection between Neptune's implied action and the geyser triumphantly emitted from the stem of the *carciofo*.

From the Fontana del Carciofo the aqueduct water flowed westward, enriching the supply of water at the Isolotto, but also passed to the grotto beneath the terrace of the palace courtyard (fig. 6.1, nos. 3 and 4). The original Isolotto sculpture programme was, as we have noted, disassembled to provide sculpture for the Fontana del Carciofo. Shorn of its most charming amorini marksmen who had been installed on Susini's fountain, it retained part of its Cytherean iconography in the cupids who abuse hearts. The decision to locate Giambologna's Ocean Fountain (fig. 6.7) on the island at the centre of this vast *vivaio* was effected in 1637.[63] Commissioned in 1567, this fountain had stood on the *prato* of the natural amphitheatre behind the palace – where it can be seen immediately behind Ammanati's Juno Fountain in the Utens lunette (fig. 6.2) – until 1618, when it was removed and apparently reconstituted in the compartmentalised garden to the east of the palace.[64] In contrast to the recycled state of *Dovizia*, the revised Neptune Fountain, the Fontana del Carciofo, and the Moses Grotto beneath the courtyard terrace, the Isolotto and its island-based Ocean Fountain are not part of the highly charged, symbolic vista provided by the central allée of the original garden in which the alignment with the palace plays a central role (fig. 6.5).[65] This fountain and its *vivaio* do, however, connect with the garden complex via the long avenue, the Viottolone, that forms a central spine for the western expansion of the garden and connects with the principal allée of the original garden at a point just below, that is, to the north of, the Vivaio Grande (fig. 6.1, note the avenue connecting nos. 2 and 4). The Viottolone provides a physical link between Lorenzi's *Neptune* at the Vivaio Grande and Giambologna's Ocean Fountain at the Isolotto, a relationship that

---

[62] ASF, Segreteria di Finanze (Anteriore al 1788), F. 201, Affari diversi, fasc. XI, no. 5, Oservazione sul alzata dell'acqua allo zampillo della Fontana del Carciofo dei Pitti. This and other documents in this section of the filza are reports on extant conditions; there is every reason to believe that this system of manipulating the valves in the aqueduct for special effects was part of the original aqueduct as constructed in the 1630s. This document was brought to my attention by Sabine Eiche.

[63] For details and documentation, see M. Campbell, 'Giambologna's Oceanus Fountain: identifications and interpretations', *Boboli '90* (Florence, 1991), vol. I, pp. 89–106, at p. 105. See also C. Avery, *Giambologna. The Complete Sculpture* (Oxford, 1987), pp. 215–18, 254.

[64] Campbell, 'Oceanus Fountain', p. 102.

[65] Claudio Pizzorusso has also noted the importance of the conjunction of monuments along the central allée (*Boboli,*, pp. 51–4).

partially re-establishes the more immediate visual association they enjoyed in the late sixteenth century when both were located on the central allée behind the palace. The linkage is conceptual rather than immediately visual, but if the visitor to the Vivaio Grande traverses the Viottolone to the point where it breaches the old western wall of the original garden, the reward is a spectacular view down the Viottolone to the Isolotto, where the Ocean Fountain serves as a major terminus to the vista. Viewed in relation to Lorenzi's *Neptune*, the Neptune that surmounts the Ocean Fountain, a self-assured presence who clasps a conch shell to thigh with his left hand and wields a baton, a *bastone del comando*, in his right, represents a polar opposite of *Nettuno turbato*. He is Neptune in his pacifying mode, the Neptune of tranquillity and *quieta* as Lomazzo described him, thus exemplifying those aspects of the sea god that the Medici claimed as characteristic of their regime.[66]

Placed at the centre of the Isolotto atop the Ocean Fountain with a trio of river gods perched beneath him, Neptune can be understood as bringing these controlling qualities not only to the waters of the encircling *vivaio* but even to the mischievous cupids, the grotesque fountains that ornament the vivaio's borders, and the rustic sculptures that inhabit the adjacent woodlands – and beyond. Indeed, we should note that Neptune faces to the west and north and thus extends his pacifying gaze toward the Arno river, its flood plain, and, far out of sight, the maritime ports of Tuscany on the Tyrrhenian Sea. We know from a grand ducal directive that the decision to place the Ocean Fountain on the Isolotto was made late in the aqueduct project and that its selection for this location was reached only after the fountain originally proposed for this site, a Fontana d'Ottone (literally the Fountain of Brass), was rejected as too small.[67] The latter fountain was placed instead in the Cortiletto, the small courtyard to the east of the main palace courtyard, where, an archival source informs us, a base of jasper was to be prepared for it 'like the one that is under its companion piece in the grotto.' We do not know anything more about this pair of fountains, but if one had been placed on the Isolotto, the perceptive seventeenth-century spectator would have recognised it as a pendant to one in the grotto of the palace courtyard. In the event, this connection was replaced by the pairing of Neptunes at the Vivaio Grande and the Isolotto, and a visually much more powerful conclusion was achieved at the principal terminus of the western extension of the garden.

For a visitor arriving at the courtyard of the Palazzo Pitti for the first time, the water display of the Fontana del Carciofo – even in its quotidian mode – would have been impressive. Directly below the terrace fountain within an archway was the Moses Grotto flanked by two extensively restored Roman antique sculpture groups (fig. 6.5). Then as now in the niche to the left of the grotto was a *Hercules and Antaeus*, and to the right was a group then referred to as *Alessandro Magno* but which is actually *Menelaus*

---

[66] G. Lomazzo, *Trattato dell'arte de la pittura* (Milan, 1584), p. 584. This is the Neptune of Virgil (*Aeneid* I. 125–43), who calms the sea and by analogy pacifies men.

[67] Campbell, 'Oceanus Fountain', 105 and n. 52.

Carrying the Body of Patroclus.[68] The archway between the sculptures opened onto the courtyard grotto (fig. 6.9). The oval floor of the grotto is largely taken up by a *vivaio* of such dimension that the spectator cannot easily advance more than a pace or two into the space. In terms of labour and materials, the grotto decorations and its sculpture ensemble constitute one of the most lavishly developed celebrational points in the aqueduct project. These decorations include extensive mosaic work consisting of grotesque work on the walls, and on the saucer vault a central oval mosaic depicting a winged *Fame* with tablet and trumpet.[69] Around *Fame* the vault is divided into ribbed segments defined by *spugna*, calcified sponge, which also covers much of the sculpture niches below. The segments of the vault are frescoed with flora and fauna, as if to suggest that the *spugna* ribs are an open-air trellis. The two wall fountains at the long ends of the oval space are bizarre constructions; their basins are ancient sarcophagi from which erupt elaborately shaped shell-like bowls of richly veined marble, *mischio da Serravezza*, upon which are poised bronze grotesque caryatid creatures who support crossed bronze boughs of laurel and oak and clusters of 'golden apples', representing the union of the Medici and Della Rovere (see fig. 6.10). Overhead, seen against conch-shell half domes, once gilded grand ducal crowns are held aloft by pairs of air-borne putti. Of the five statues in the remaining niches, the dominant one, and clearly the pivotal element in the entire grotto, is the figure of Moses (fig. 6.11), who is positioned directly opposite the courtyard archway and hence the spectator.

Fashioned by Raffaello Curradi and Cosimo Salvestrini from a fragmentary porphyry statue of a Roman emperor, Moses is posed as if in the act of bringing forth water from the rock. The staff once grasped in his extended right hand is now missing. The relevance of Moses' act in the context of the grotto decorations is enunciated by the inscription on a marble cartouche that appears to be held aloft by the Marzzocco, the heraldic lion of Florence. The inscription represents the keynote statement in celebration of the Acqua Ferdinanda; it reads: EN ISRAELIS DVX E CAVTE / FERDINANDAM AQVAM EDVCENS. / INTVERE HOSPES, / HINC LEGES CAELESTIA DONA / ET VINDEX IVSTITIAE STVDIVM / HINC PRINCIPATVS / OCVLATO SCEPTRO INSIGNIS / ET CHARITATE MATERNA / SVBIECTORVM IMBECILLITATI / PARCENS TOLERANTIA / HEROEM COMITANTVR VNDE DISCAS, VT AVRIBVS / QVI PARET, OCVLIS VTI / DEBERE QVI IMPERAT / ET REGNAM SINE LEGIBVS / LEGES SINE VLTIONE / AC SAEPIVS CLEMENTIA / NON CONSISTERE. ('Behold the leader of the Israelites as he is drawing out the Ferdinandian water from the rock. Visitor, look upon this. From here you will gather the Divine

---

[68] For descriptions of these statues, see Bocchi, *Le bellezze*, p. 133. See also F. Haskell and N. Penny, *Taste and the Antique* (New Haven and London, 1982), pp. 232–4, fig. 119 and pp. 292–6, fig. 155. The *Menelaus Carrying the Body of Patroclus* group was later moved to the Cortiletto that housed one of the fountains identified as a Fontana d'Ottone in our documents.

[69] The mosaic work was carried out by Giovanni delle Dame and a team of assistants. Mosaic tesserae used in the grotto were secured from Venice, the Pisa cathedral depository and from Rome. The ones from Rome were presumably antique spolia. There are innumerable entries for this work in ASF, Fabbriche Medicee, F. 75 bis. For Boschi's contribution see L. Lucchesi, *Il Seicento Fiorentino*, vol. III (biographical volume) (Florence, 1986), p. 40. For extensive illustrations of the Moses Grotto, see Guerrieri and Chatfield, *Boboli Gardens*, figs. 49–58.

Laws. Both Zeal, the avenger of Justice, and from here Imperium, remarkable with its starred sceptre, and with maternal Charity, Endurance that is sparing of his subjects' weakness, accompany the hero, whence you may learn that one who rules or is preparing to do so ought to make use of his ears and eyes and that a kingdom without laws or laws without vengeance, but more often with clemency, does not remain firm.') The representation of Moses striking the rock to bring forth water for his people in conjunction with the opening of a new aqueduct is most closely associated with the wall fountain of the same theme in Rome designed by Domenico Fontana for Pope Sixtus V. Also, Moses is a traditional Medici trope, as is demonstrated by the seminal presentation of the motif in the Cappella di Eleonora in the Palazzo Vecchio.[70] As the 'Medicean' Moses, his role here is not only to connect the bringing forth of water with the grand ducal family, but to sanctify and render miraculous an action that was initiated in the uppermost reaches of the garden, as we have seen, by the Graeco-Roman god of the seas and waters of the earth.

Moses is ringed by an unusual quadrumvirate of allegorical figures based on a programme devised by Francesco Rondinelli, grand ducal librarian, and denoted by the inscription on the cartouche beneath Moses.[71] The viewer is exhorted to view the grotto's personae as representative of a divinely ordained rule, and as such the statues accompanying *Moses* constitute an idiosyncratic version of good government, the *buon governo* theme, long a popular image in Italian communes of the early modern period. Moses is clearly the pivotal figure. Leader and benefactor of his people, he occupies pride of place and is also set apart by the specialness of the extremely hard, purple-red stone of which he is carved. *Zeal*, the work of Giovan Battista and Domenico Pieratti, is presented in ancient shepherd's attire (fig. 6.12). Flames burst forth from his head and for an attribute, a miniature structure, apparently a mortuary chapel or a baptistery, appears at his feet. *Laws*, by Antonio Novelli, wears antique dress and holds a tablet with Hebrew script signifying the Ten Commandments (fig. 6.9). Her extended right hand may once have held an attribute. Paired to the left of *Moses*, these two allegories suggest *buon governo* infused with religiosity. To the right of *Moses*, *Imperium*, also by the two Pieratti, is represented by a figure armed *all'antica* (fig. 6.9). His left foot rests on a miniature crenelated fortress, and, according to the inscription, he once held a starred sceptre in his upraised right hand. Recent research has revealed that both *Zeal* and *Imperium* were part of a different but unidentified project underway at least as early as 1629.[72] So too, *Charity* by Agostino Ubaldini; this allegory was part of an earlier project in which this statue, carved before the death of the artist in 1623, was a distressed *Latona* clutching her offspring (fig. 6.13).[73] The statue has been converted to *Charity*

---

[70] For Moses as a Medici model, see J. Cox-Rearick, *Bronzino's Chapel of Eleonora in the Palazzo Vecchio* (Berkeley, Los Angeles and Oxford, 1993), pp. 294–319.

[71] For the role of Rondinelli and the attributions of the statues, see Pizzorusso, *Boboli*, pp. 25–6.

[72] Pizzorusso (*Boboli*, pp. 25–6) cites M. C. Cornaggia, 'Domenico e Giovan Battista Pieratti'. Degree thesis, Florence, Università di Studi, Facoltà di Magistero, 1973–4, for extensive documentation.

[73] Pizzorusso, *Boboli*, pp. 63–4.

Fig. 6.12 Domenico and Giovan Battista Pieratti. *Zeal*, marble. Florence, Palazzo Pitti,
Moses Grotto

Fig. 6.13 Agostino Ubaldini. *Charity*, marble. Florence, Palazzo Pitti, Moses Grotto

with virtually no adjustments. True to their original roles, her offspring seem more fearful than famished. This ensemble of statues was installed in the Moses Grotto between 1635 and 1642.[74]

Endurance, as noted in the inscription, incorporates these attributes which we are to understand as collected in the person of Moses, enduring and stern leader who is proclaimed the moral embodiment of the strict code of rulership here celebrated. The rule of law propounded redounds with the harshness of the Old Testament. Of the four Cardinal Virtues, not one survives in conventional form, although the phrasing implies that Justice is subsumed under Law. Only one traditional Theological Virtue is included, and she is designated as 'maternal' rather than 'Christian' Charity *per se*. Interpreted in light of the inscription, these virtues collectively emphasise the ruler-as-avenger, the idea of Justice-Law as epitomised by the Mosaic decalogues, the preference given to Zeal over the communal themes of Hope or Faith, the substitution of Imperium for Fortitude, and the absence of Prudence and Temperance impart a harshly Counter Reformation tone to the assemblage that is certainly not assuaged by the recurrent reference to vengeance as the agency of enforcement.

The severity of the inscriptions very nearly distracts the viewer from the central action and the *incipit* of the inscription whereby Moses provided water for the Israelites; so, too, the waters of the Acqua Ferdinanda symbolically pass from the Moses Grotto to the citizenry of Florence.[75] Tracing the main conduit of the aqueduct into the city, we arrive at the Ponte Vecchio, where a version of the figure group referred to in seventeenth-century payment records as the *Alessandro Magno* was located.[76] As pointed out by Haskell and Penny, this sculpture group, which actually depicted *Menelaus Carrying the Body of Patroclus*, may have been in place and therefore its incorporation in the aqueduct may have been primarily one of modification for plumbing and the addition of duly recorded *mascheroni*, the face-like masks that served as water spouts, and the attendant basins. Presumably it was thought that the subject matter of this fountain, which repeats that of so-called *Alessandro Magno* adjacent to the Moses Grotto, would serve to connect it with the Acqua Ferdinanda.

Also on the Oltrarno side of the river, a marble fountain was installed in the narrow wall fronting on the Via Maggio that marked the juncture of the Via dello Sprone and the Borgo San Jacapo. Generally identified as the Fontana della Nicchia (Shell Fountain), this was executed between 1638 and 1639 by the sculptor Francesco Generini (fig. 6.14).[77] Its elaborate, shell-like bowl is very close in form to the bowls of

---

[74] Ibid., p. 125 and n. 47.

[75] In the weekly payment records (ASF, Fabbriche Medicee, F. 75 bis and Aquisti e Doni, F. 74), work on the 'fountains of Florence' occurs on 24 April 1638; thereafter there are continuous entries to the end of the account book (28 June 1641).

[76] Specific payments to Matteo Stagi, Francesco Generini and Andrea Bigazzi for work on the installation of the *Alessandro Magno* as a fountain at the Ponte Vecchio occur between 24 April and 17 July, 1638 (ASF Fabbriche Medicee, F. 75 bis). For illustration and discussion, see Haskell and Penny, *Taste and the Antique*, pp. 292, 295 and fig. 154. The group was subsequently removed to the Loggia dei Lanzi.

[77] Payments to Generini are recorded in ASF, Fabbriche Medicee, F. 35 (Debitori e creditori della Nuova Fabbrica de' Pitti de S.A.S., 1636–9), cc. 165 *sinistra* and *destra*. Work was carried out between 17 April 1638, and 21 May 1639. The initial

Fig. 6.14 Francesco Generini, Fontana della Nicchia, marble. Florence

the wall fountains in the Moses Grotto, and its *mascherone* water spout bears a striking likeness to the faces of the harpies on the fountains on the balustrade of the Isolotto. These tenuous associations with the aqueduct project are reinforced by the presence of a small grand ducal coat of arms affixed to the wall above the fountain.

The main line of the aqueduct conduit proceeded across the Ponte Vecchio, a branch of which carried water to the Mercato Nuovo (now popularly known as the Straw Market), where its waters emerged from the dripping mouth of the *Porcellino*, as Pietro Tacca's great bronze boar cast from an antique work in the grand ducal collection has been known for centuries (fig. 6.15). Tacca was commissioned to execute the cast by Ferdinand II's father, but it was probably not put into effect until shortly before 1634, just in time to serve as a fountain.[78] The choice of a boar was

entry clearly states that the work is for the 'fountain at the S. Trinità bridge', i.e. the Fontana della Nicchia. The later credit entries imply the work was at the Ponte Vecchio; however, these entries are in a second, successive hand in the accounts which suggests that confusion occurred when the second hand took over the accounts.

[78] For further details, see Haskell and Penny, *Taste and the Antique*, p. 163. Payments for installation in the Mercato Nuovo began on 2 July 1639 (ASF, Fabbriche Medicee, F. 75 bis). Pietro Tacca was involved in the installation, as was Cosimo Salvestrini who carved the original base, now replaced by a bronze replica. For discussion and documents, see P. Torriti, *Pietro Tacca da Carrara* (Carrara, 1975), p. 39 and n. 37.

Fig. 6.15 Pietro Tacca. Fountain of the Porcellino, bronze (nineteenth century installation). Florence, Mercato Nuovo

appropriate to the market place where it was installed; it also reflected – albeit at a distance – the inscription on the Fontana del Carciofo with its references to the head waters of the aqueduct near the lairs of wild creatures. One wonders if this work had some connection with the bronze wild animals Baldinucci claimed were added – or projected to be added – to the Fontana del Carciofo in 1646.

The main conduit of the Acqua Ferdinanda leads into the former republican core of the city, the Piazza Granducale, the site of the Palazzo della Signoria, which the grand duke's great-grandfather Cosimo I had converted into his residence and which, although still potent as a symbol of Medici power, was now superseded by the Palazzo Pitti and colloquially known, then as now, as the Palazzo Vecchio. Adjacent to the palace is Bartolomeo Ammanati's Neptune Fountain (fig. 6.16).[79] The largest urban fountain in Florence, it was created between 1560 and 1575 to mark the arrival of water from the first Florentine aqueduct commissioned by Cosimo I to bring water from

[79] For a more detailed discussion, see M. Campbell, 'Observations on Ammannati's *Neptune Fountain*: 1565-1567', in *Renaissance Studies in Honor of Craig Hugh Smyth*, ed. A. Morrogh, F. Superbi Gioffredi, P. Morselli and E. Borsook (Florence, 1985), vol. II, pp. 113-29.

Fig. 6.16 Bartolomeo Ammannati. The Neptune Fountain, marble and bronze. Florence,
Piazza della Signoria

springs near the church of San Miniato into the city centre and, significantly, to the
Boboli Garden, which his wife, Duchess Eleonora, had then recently acquired.
Ammanati's marble *Neptune* is a truly colossal figure. Borne by a marble chariot driven
by hippocamps and clasping a *bastone del comando* instead of the conventional trident, he
renders a stolid performance of the sea god's *Quos Ego!*, as recounted by Virgil, when he
calms the sea for Aeneas and, metaphorically, pacifies unruly citizenry.[80] It is clear, too,
that Giambologna critiqued Ammanati's *Neptune* with his later, baton-wielding
Neptune in the Boboli (fig. 6.7). In context of the Acqua Ferdinanda, however, these
two *Neptunes* collaborate to iterate the theme of Neptune as bringer of peace and
Quietus and celebrate the new aqueduct, the one from the Isolotto at the farthest
westward extension of the Boboli, the other here at the urban core of the city.

Ammanati's Neptune Fountain, like the Fontana del Carciofo, enjoyed a privileged
role as a nodal point in the new aqueduct system, serving on occasion for special
hydraulic display. In the eighteenth-century aqueduct reports noted above, it is

[80] Virgil, *Aeneid* 1.125–43. See notes 44 and 66 for the aspects of Neptune.

stated – and illustrated with a drawing – that when the other valves of the system were closed and this fountain offered its solo performance for the populace or visitors, the result was a geyser, known as the *vela* (sail) that rose $37\frac{1}{4}$ *braccia* (c. $71\frac{1}{2}$ ft) in the air from the pavement level.[81] In its mix of marble Neptune, bronze sea creatures and satyrs, richly veined, porphyry-like marble, known as *marmo mischio*, the materials of this fountain recall Lorenzi's *Neptune*, the marble and bronze of the Fontana del Carciofo and the *marmo mischio* and bronze of the wall fountains in the Moses Grotto. The theme of abundance initiated at *Dovizia*, repeated at the Fontana del Carciofo with its garlands of sea bounty, are echoed here in the cornucopias of sea life and great fish in the hands of the bronze tritons and nereids that sprawl on the lip of the fountain basin. Furthermore, to the visitor familiar with the crouching sea creatures at the rocky base of Lorenzi's *Neptune* and the pair of forest creatures who clutch fish adjacent to the little cascade on the Fontana del Carciofo, these bronze figures astride the basin of Ammanati's fountain or crouched along its sides would appear to iterate the themes of their kin on the Boboli fountains.

The aqueduct programme included a utilitarian candelabra fountain situated at the western end of the Piazza Santa Croce (fig. 6.17).[82] Provisioned from the older and limited water source near S. Miniato al Monte, the Santa Croce fountain provides a modest water display from spouts on its central stem. The most striking visual element in this fountain, however, is the ornamentation that caps the central candelabrum stem (fig. 6.18). Here, carved in marble, is a richly foliated acanthus. Its coiled leaves form in silhouette the time-honoured Florentine republican symbol, the tripartite *giglio*. The upper acanthus leaves are held within the circular band of the Medici grand ducal crown, and the lower leaves support or clasp Medici *palle*, thus creating, as an ensemble, a three-dimensional, multi-faceted grand ducal coat of arms in which the essential political reciprocity and hierarchy of the Tuscan state are visually summarised. Major payments for this fountain are combined with those for the Porcellino Fountain in the Mercato Nuova, leaving little doubt that it was considered part of the new water system.[83]

The main aqueduct conduit extended northward from Ammanati's Neptune Fountain to the Piazza della Santissima Annunziata, where its waters were rendered visible by the twin grotesque Marine Fountains located before the façade of the church from which the piazza takes its name (fig. 6.19). These two fountains, executed in 1626-9, were originally intended as embellishments for the piazza Granducale in Livorno.[84] The twin fountains were never installed and instead were commandeered for the Acqua Ferdinanda programme and placed in the Piazza SS Annunziata, where

---

[81] See note 62 above. The extraordinary effect of the *vela* is presented in an anonymous drawing in this report.

[82] Work on this fountain is first recorded on 21 July 1638 (ASF, Fabbriche Medicee, F. 75 bis). The fountain appears in its original position – in the middle of the street – at the western end of the piazza in the view published in Zocchi, *Scelta di XXIV vedute*, plate XXIV.

[83] ASF, Depositeria Generale, F. 140, no. 73 (27 June 1639).   [84] Torriti, *Pietro Tacca*, pp. 34–5.

Fig. 6.17 Fountain in the Piazza Santa Croce, marble. Florence

they form an ensemble with the great equestrian statue of Grand Duke Ferdinand I conceived by Giambologna and executed with the assistance of Pietro Tacca (1601-8). Ferdinand II had Tacca add dedicatory plaques on this equestrian group concomitantly with the installation of the fountains, a fact which suggests that he wanted to underscore the association of the recycled fountains with a statue of his grandfather and family namesake without, however, placing the fountains in such close proximity to his grandfather's statue as to make a unitary composition.[85]

Tacca's Marine Fountains are wondrous compounds of vividly naturalistically rendered sea life and totally fantastic sea creatures. The latter dominate the fountains in the form of two opposed imaginary sea monsters who spit water into equally bizarre ones who serve as bowls. Whereas these creatures suggest weirdly inspired imaginings provoked by the sea lions, manatees and other marine animals found in the distant seas

[85] The plaques were added in December 1640, and the following June the fountains were officially unveiled (C. Guasti, *Le carte strozziane . . .* (Florence, 1884), p. 60).

Fig. 6.18 Detail of fig. 6.17

of the New World, the garlands of sea life that decorate the fountain bases seem cast from life, specimens from the sea's bounty that could serve as naturalists' study pieces. The twin fountains brilliantly illustrate two extremes of Florentine Seicento *invenzione*, the acutely descriptive observation of nature that is central to the scientific inquiry of the period and, on the other hand, the unbridled fantasy manifest in contemporaneous Florentine decorative arts, polarities that resonate throughout the fountains of the Acqua Ferdinanda. Situated in their intended location adjacent to the harbour of Livorno, the twin fountains would have evoked obvious connections with the marine world. Here, far from the sea, the appropriateness of these monuments is certainly less immediately intelligible. And yet, when we recall other fountains of the aqueduct, Giambologna's *Neptune* centred in the Isolotto and facing toward coastal Tuscany, Lorenzi's *Neptune* on high ground in the Boboli bringing forth water, and the *Neptune* of the Piazza Granducale with its geysering water *vela*, the Santissima Annunziata

Fig. 6.19 Pietro Tacca. Marine Fountain, bronze. Florence, Piazza Santissima Annunziata

fountains read more plausibly as marine trophies thematically linked to the gestures of this triad of Neptune's and to their accompanying minions and sea life.

v

One of the features of the Acqua Ferdinanda fountain system which is most striking and which documents the intentionality of its underlying programme is the concern evinced in the distribution of motifs within the Boboli to create a fountain system which, with the most dedicated sort of contrariness, makes the water of the new aqueduct appear to emanate from the Vivaio Grande in the Boboli (when in fact I find no evidence that at the time of construction the waters from Montereggi even reached that location), but which, as we have noted, entered the city at the opposite compass point. This extraordinary fiction is, to the best of my knowledge, without precedent. Effecting this message at the Boboli was fundamental to the aqueduct project, and thus there is a concentration of inscriptions and sculptural representations that support this aspect of the project within the precincts of the Boboli, most notably on the central allée: the *Dovizia, Neptune,* the Fontana del Carciofo, the Moses Grotto and the enlarged grand ducal residence from where these representations could be collectively witnessed and through which, thematically if not physically, the waters of the new aqueduct were distributed to the city. The essential agenda was to establish this relationship: the Boboli as source and the grand duke, represented by sculpture and grand ducal palace-residence, as munificent provider.

It should therefore come as no surprise that the initial outlay of funding for sculpture installations and fountains occurred in the garden precinct rather than in the city. Financial constraints limited this effort and led to extensive reuse of sculptural elements both within the Boboli and, later, in the city. Time factors, both those of the project and others extraneous to it, played a role as well. Enrichment of the supply of potable water in Florence was, after all, a matter of pressing urgency, and the fountains in the city played a practical as well as a symbolic role in its distribution. The grand ducal marriage, with public festivities projected for July 1637, served to establish, if not a date for the completion of all of the constituent projects – palace enlargement, construction of the garden theatre, and the aqueduct and its fountains – then at least a point in time at which it would be eminently appropriate for these projects to be sufficiently visible to provide auspicious evidence of the well-being of the Medici regime and the prosperity and *buon governo* of the Tuscan state. Only on these state occasions, however, when the amphitheatre of the Boboli was the scene of equestrian events, when operatic performances were held in the courtyard, when crowds invaded the garden, and the Fontana del Carciofo received the full pressure of the Acqua Ferdinanda, would the effect be one of public spectacle. Except for these special events, the Boboli Garden fountains and indeed the entire constellation of fountains linked by the Acqua Ferdinanda would seem to confirm Richard Goldthwaite's assertion that the Medici court – like that of other Italian principalities – was, in spite of its splendour, in many ways markedly private and familial in character and scale.[86]

It would be an error, however, to view the Medici court as domestic in character and the grand duke, together with his administrative and courtly entourage, as merely an engrandised version of a traditional Florentine merchant-prince's household. Rather than merging the ruling Medici with the economically and politically rising mercantile bourgeoisie of the city state, the visible expression of Medici power coalescing in the 1630s in the Palazzo Pitti and its attendant garden, the Boboli, by the sheer scale of this undertaking, set them apart from other citizenry. When the enlarged palace, the new amphitheatre, and the new fountain and sculpture installations are perceived as a unified whole, it is apparent that this visible representation of Medici authority was concentrated in this palace-garden complex to an unprecedented degree and that the new city fountains mediate between the city and its ruler rather than impose grand ducal authority in the urban sphere. By the end of the 1630s the most official representations of Medici power were concentrated in the enlarged palace, in its frescoed rooms, in the new amphitheatre, and in the garden. Henceforth, a preponderance of the significant spectacles associated with the regime will take place in this setting rather than in the streets and piazzas. Seen in this perspective, Ferdinand II's transformation of the Palazzo Pitti and the Boboli Garden marks an important stage in a development that reaches its apogee at Versailles.[87]

[86] R. A. Goldthwaite, *Wealth and the Demand for Art in Italy 1300-1600* (Baltimore and London, 1993), pp. 170–5.

[87] See the summary provided by Jurgen Habermas, *The Structural Transformation of the Public Sphere*, trans. by T. Burger (Cambridge, Mass., 1989), pp. 9–10.

CHAPTER 7

FRUIT AND FLOWER GARDENS FROM THE NEOCLASSICAL AND ROMANTIC PERIODS IN TUSCANY

ALESSANDRO TOSI[*]

It is not difficult to imagine the surprise and amazement of the guests attending the spectacular evening reception held by Lord John Tylney, 2nd earl of Castlemaine, in his Florentine garden in the late summer of 1780: a cleverly lit series of *vues d'optique* of Vesuvius, which clearly revealed the host's keen interest in vulcanology, created an evocative and spectacular setting amidst the pineapple conservatories, the vases of citrus fruits, the rose garden, the fruit trees and an aviary containing garishly plumed Chinese and Brazilian pheasants.[1]

Owing to Lord Tylney's expert directions, this strange theatrical set succeeded in recreating the atmosphere of those explorations which aroused the enthusiasm of contemporary dilettanti, travellers and painters, and appeared to reflect a new awareness of the problems concerning the relationship between nature and artifice, science and art. The opportune association between the views of Vesuvius, taken from paintings by Joseph Wright of Derby or Pierre-Jacques Volaire, and the garden, itself embellished since 1760 with numerous species of flowers and fruits by Lady Walpole, wife of Lord Robert Walpole and sister-in-law of the famous Sir Horace,[2] in fact represents an important tribute not only to the growing interest in newly emerging scientific disciplines, but also to the trends of contemporary taste which were ready to give an enthusiastic reception to the theoretical principles of the 'picturesque'. Deprived of all its ephemeral connotations, the garden was suddenly transformed into a sort of romantic *cabinet de physique*, which was both didactic and experimental.

In Enlightenment Florence at the end of the century, engaged in laying the foundations for a more modern organisation of scientific knowledge (the 'public'

[*]Translated by Lucinda Byatt.

[1] F. Borroni Salvadori, 'Personaggi inglesi inseriti nella vita fiorentina del '700: Lady Walpole e il suo ambiente', *Mitteilungen des Kunsthistorischen Instituts in Florenz*, 27 (1983), pp. 83–124, p. 109.

[2] Kunsthistorischen Instituts in Florenz, Ms. Ka 48t, 'Relazione fatta nel giardino di S. E. Madama Miledi', cf. also Borroni Salvadori, 'Personaggi inglesi', pp. 95, 117; and A. Vezzosi, 'Pittura di macchia e di sfinge, isole romantiche e simulacri, vaghezze in giardini d'Esperidi', in *Il giardino romantico* (Florence, 1986), pp. 92–116, p. 93.

Natural History Museum had been founded in 1775, whereas in 1783 the 'economic and agrarian' Accademia dei Georgofili incorporated the suppressed Botanical Society), a theatrical setting of this nature was bound to meet with the unconditional support of intellectuals and dilettanti. Moreover, the spreading enthusiasm for the gifts of 'Flora' and 'Pomona', one of the major cultural phenomena of the time, also called for careful thought concerning the significance and appearance of the modern garden. Against this background of dreams of Arcadia, severe neoclassical themes and the first romantic transports, 'pleasurable botany' reflected the vivacity of scientific and literary circles, academic settings and even the fashionable society salons in Florence and other Tuscan cities in the same way that experiments in physics and chemistry had electrified the powdered ladies and inspired the pens and brushes of the most enlightened authors.

While such high-flown romantic scenes mingled with the sweet scent of flowers and fruits in Lord Tylney's garden, there were numerous connoisseurs in the capital of the grand duchy who took pleasure in growing particularly rare and sought after species. For example, in 1794 Count Leopoldo Galli became the first person in Tuscany to plant a camelia in his garden. During the same period Count Piero Bardi ordered a '*Magnolia grandiflora*' to be brought from London and a '*rosa gallica holoserica*' from France, which was referred to with legitimate pride as the 'Rosa nera de' Bardi'. What was more, in his garden at Palazzo Guicciardini he succeeded in cultivating the famous 'Arabian jasmine', the plant from which Magalotti had drawn poetic inspiration a century earlier but which had then disappeared after being affected by a mysterious disease when Pietro Leopoldo revoked Cosimo III's 'monopoly'.[3] The gardens belonging to Marchesa Luisa Feroni in Via dei Serragli were renowned for their abundance of plants which were 'rare at that time'. This was also true of Marchese Giuseppe Pucci's garden in Via dei Cresci: fuchsias – at once keenly sought after 'by gardening connoisseurs for their collections' – were introduced in 1805 and were followed in 1812 by new varieties of yellow-flowered chrysanthemums, also known as West Indian chrysanthemums, which Gaetano Savi had already introduced to Pisa's Botanical Gardens. Yet another famous garden was that belonging to the Elena Mastiani Brunacci – the noblewoman to whom Savi dedicated his *Materia Medica Vegetabile Toscana* in 1805 – 'in which the most beautiful plants were arrayed in a constantly changing spectacle'.[4] This enthusiasm for fruit and flower gardening was not confined to Florence alone. The numbers of keen gardeners rose steadily in cosmopolitan Leghorn, Siena, Cortona and Pistoia, not to mention Lucca. In Pisa, where Carlo Goldoni had been impressed by the refined hospitality reserved for members of the Arcadian Academy in the garden of

---

[3] A. Targioni Tozzetti, *Cenni storici sulla introduzione di varie piante nell'agricoltura ed orticoltura Toscana* (Florence, 1853), pp. 250, 267, 272, 295.

[4] Ibid., pp. 301, 303, 307; A. Tosi, 'Arte e scienza tra neoclassicismo e romanticismo: il Giardino in età moderna', in *Giardino dei semplici. L'orto botanico di Pisa dal XVI al XX secolo*, ed. F. Garbari, L. Tongiorgi Tomasi and A. Tosi (Pisa, 1991), pp. 213–74, 231–3.

Palazzo Corsini-Scotto, the tree known as 'Julibrissin' was brought from Constantinople to the Frugoni garden by the Florentine Filippo degli Albrizzi towards the end of the century.[5]

Underlying this enthusiasm for fruit and flowers, which were often sought after and collected not only for pleasure, lay an illustrious tradition of naturalist studies implemented and updated by botanical gardens and scientific academies during the course of the century. One need only recall the expansion of the ancient 'Giardini dei semplici' in Pisa and Florence which served as a model for smaller but none the less interesting gardens, such as that in Cortona; or the history of the Florentine Botanical Society and, more importantly, that of the Accademia dei Georgofili, an institution of international standing.[6] For example, the attempt made by the Florentine printer, Giuseppe Allegrini, to publish a *Pomona Toscana* in 1777 with copperplate engravings and a commentary by Marco Lastri and Attilio Zuccagni, is evidence of the full support for the latest trends in European scientific literature. Along the lines of the national *Pomonas* by Duhamel du Monceau, Mayer, Hooker and Knoop, this volume contained the first census of the region's 'fruit-bearing trees', not only as a means of demonstrating the new classification methods but also of emphasising 'the pleasing ornamentation they bring to Gardens and to the countryside as a whole'.[7]

The close relationship between the garden and the countryside, a fundamental principle of the poetics of the picturesque, is clearly expressed in the works of the most enlightened naturalists of the period as well as in the inspired verses by the 'Arcadian shepherds'. Starting with the erudite travels of the Florentine Giovanni Targioni Tozzetti, in whose *Relazioni d'alcuni viaggi fatti in diverse parti della Toscana* (Florence, 1768-77) the combination of science and antiquarian studies results in the adoption of a surprisingly modern approach to the study of the territory, up to *Viaggi per la Toscana* (Pisa, 1795-1806), written by the director of Pisa's Botanical Garden, Giorgio Santi, and one of the most convincing works of late eighteenth-century Italian scientific literature, an awareness of landscape in all its forms, whether natural or artificial, assumed precise theoretical shapes. During the same period readers could also dream about the mythical pastoral scenes eulogised by Salomon Gessner, whose *Idylles* had been translated into Italian and published in Leghorn in 1787:

---

[5] Targioni Tozzetti, *Cenni storici*, p. 241. On the Pisan gardens see also R. P. Ciardi, 'Vivere a Pisa. Abitanti e forestieri', in *Settecento pisano. Pittura e scultura a Pisa nel secolo XVIII*, ed. R. P. Ciardi (Pisa, 1990), p. 21, and A. M. Giusti, *Giardini pisani tra Arcadia e Pittoresco* (Siena, 1991), p. 13.

[6] On the Botanical Society of Cortona and on the garden see A. Tosi, 'Il giardino e l'Accademia: spunti figurativi nelle società Botaniche di Cortona e di Firenze', *Annuario dell'Accademia Etrusca di Cortona*, 21 (1984), pp. 219–39; L. Tongiorgi Tomasi and A. Tosi, '"Ars naturam fingens". L'Accademia etrusca di Cortona tra interessi scientifici, reperti da collezione, illustrazioni naturalistiche e giardini', *L'Accademia etrusca* (Milan, 1985), pp. 190–9. On the Accademia dei Georgofili and the Florentine Botanical Society see M. Tabarrini, *Degli studi e delle vicende della Reale Accademia dei Georgofili nel primo secolo della sua esistenza* (Florence, 1856); P. Baccarini, 'Notizie intorno ad alcuni documenti della Società Botanica fiorentina del 1716-1783 ed alle sue vicende', *Annali di Botanica*, 1 (1904), pp. 225–54.

[7] A. Tosi, 'Tra Flora e Pomona: arte, natura e scienza in Toscana nella prima metà dell'800', in *'Flora e Pomona'. L'orticoltura nei disegni e nelle incisioni dei secoli XVI-XIX*, ed. L. Tongiorgi Tomasi and A. Tosi (Florence, 1990), pp. 31–54, see pp. 34–5.

Fig. 7.1 G. Zocchi and G. Wagner. View of Pratolino, from *Veduta delle ville e d'altri luoghi della Toscana*

> I am sometimes driven to leave the city and seek refuge in the solitary fields whose spectacular natural beauty drives from my soul all disgust and all the unpleasant impressions to which it has been subjected. Transported by the sight of such a marvellous spectacle and overcome by a myriad delightful sentiments, I am as happy as a shepherd in the Golden Age and far richer than a king.[8]

Antonio Cerati, 'Filandro Cretense' in Arcadia, praised 'Nature's majestically beautiful negligence' in *Le ville lucchesi*, printed by Bodoni in 1783, drawing inspiration from Pietro Verri's inventions and anticipating the themes which would ensure the success of Jacques Delille's didactic poem *Les jardins ou l'art d'embellir les paysages*, published towards the end of the century in both Florence and Lucca.[9]

These scientific and literary evocations were endorsed by the development of a visual culture able to appropriate the profound linguistic innovations taking place in Europe during the Enlightenment. Giuseppe Zocchi's *Vedute delle ville e d'altri luoghi della Toscana*, published in Florence in 1744 and well known to Horace Mann and his friend Walpole, had built on the precedents of the genre of Venetian *veduta* painting to create a new taste in landscape painting (fig. 7.1).[10] Zocchi's drawings, in which the

[8] S. Gessner, *Idilli* (Leghorn, 1787), Preface.

[9] Filandro Cretense, *Le ville lucchesi* (Parma, 1783; repr. Lucca, 1981). On the translation of Delille's work see I. Belli Barsali, 'I giardini lucchesi tra Sette e Ottocento', in *Il giardino romantico*, pp. 61–9.

[10] See G. Zocchi, *Vedute delle ville e d'altri luoghi della Toscana*, ed. H. Acton and A. Tagliolini (Milan, 1981). The lively interest aroused by the views painted by the Florentine artist is borne out by the correspondence between Sir Horace Mann and Horace Walpole: W. S. Lewis, W. Hunting Smith and G. L. Lam (eds.), *Horace Walpole's Correspondence with Sir Horace*

seventeenth-century Florentine graphic tradition was updated following the example
of Van Wittel, Canaletto and Vernet, depicted the splendid Italianate gardens of the
most famous villas around Florence, together with a few evocative vistas of the Tuscan
countryside showing enraptured travellers ready to absorb the lyrical scenarios. The
calculated, formal instructions underlying the poetics of the picturesque style can be
glimpsed in the wide and airy perspectives achieved using the *camera ottica* and the
alluring climatic effects suggested by the use of pale expanses of watercolour.[11] These
account for the extraordinary success of Zocchi's graphic style, sanctioned by such
scrupulous connoisseurs as Horace Mann, Horace Walpole and Pierre Jean Mariette,
which was destined to exert a radical influence on Florentine figurative culture in the
second half of the century. Moreover, the original views of Paestum drawn by the artist
in around 1760 for that intrepid traveller, James Bruce of Kinnaird, and modelled on
the example of Antonio Joli and Hubert Robert, marked the start of an exciting period
in which antiquarian meditations and architectural virtuosity were used to convey a
new sensitivity towards nature.[12]

It is therefore easy to understand how the theories of landscape gardening which were
spreading throughout Europe were destined to meet with singular success in Florence
and other Tuscan cities.[13] In the early nineteenth century, when the neoclassical
experience had already taken on a romantic tinge, the vogue for the landscape garden
classified by Christian Cay Lorenz Hirschfeld in his 5-volume *Theorie der Gartenkunst*
(Leipzig, 1779-85), which had already spread through erudite circles owing to the
various editions of the *Encyclopédie* published in Lucca (1758-76) and Leghorn (1770-9),
infected architects and gardeners, nobles and dilettanti alike. Marchese Tommaso Corsi
was the first to construct an 'English' garden in Florence, entrusting its design to
Giuseppe Manetti's genius. Dense groves, winding paths and limpid lakes, dotted with
architectural features whose design was based on a vocabulary imbued with complex
philosophical speculations and erudite figurative and literary quotations, were also used
to embellish the Serristori, Corsini, Giucciardini, Mozzi Bardini and Gherardesca

Mann (New Haven, 1954-71), vol. I, pp. 57-8; vol. II, p. 181. Horace Mann himself owned an album of drawings by
Zocchi which was sold in 1979 (*Catalogue of Drawings of Views of Rome, Florence and elsewhere by Giuseppe Zocchi* (London,
Sotheby's 1989)).

[11] See G. Romano, *Studi sul paesaggio* (Turin, 1978), p. 127. John Dixon Hunt's studies are also fundamental on these aspects:
'Ut pictura poesis, ut pictura hortus, and the picturesque', *Word & Image. A Journal of Verbal/Visual Enquiry*, 1 (1) (1985),
pp. 87-107; Hunt, '"Ut pictura poesis": il giardino e il pittoresco in Inghilterra (1710-1750)', in *L'architettura dei giardini
d'occidente dal Rinascimento al Novecento*, ed. M. Mosser and G. Teyssot (Milan, 1990), pp. 227-37.

[12] Zocchi's views of Paestum, which he was commissioned by Bruce to draw in Florence in 1763 (see P. Hulton, F. N.
Hepper and L. Friis, *Luigi Balugani's Drawings of African Plants. From the Collection made by James Bruce of Kinnaird on his
Travels to Discover the Source of the Nile 1767-1773* (New Haven, 1991), p. 7) are kept at the Yale Center for British Art, New
Haven, Conn. On the relations between neoclassical culture and gardens, see A. A. Tait, 'The landscape garden and
neoclassicism', *Journal of Garden History*, 3 (1983), 4, pp. 317-32.

[13] On the success of the landscape garden in Italy see G. Venturi, 'Ercole Silva e l'arte dei giardini inglesi in Italia', in *Dell'arte
de' giardini inglesi*, ed. E. Silva (Milan, 1976), pp. 7-31, and also G. Venturi, *Le scene dell'Eden. Teatro, arte, giardini nella
letteratura italiana* (Ferrara, 1979), pp. 73-97; A. Tagliolini, *Storia del giardino italiano* (Florence, 1988), pp. 315ff; G. Venturi,
'I "lumi" del giardino: teoria e pratica del giardino all'inglese in Lombardia tra Sette e Ottocento', in *Il giardino italiano
dell'Ottocento*, ed. A. Tagliolini (Milan, 1990), pp. 19-35.

gardens. Under the careful directions of Luigi de Cambray Digny, they were also used to decorate Marchese Pietro Torrigiani's garden and the Orti Oricellari belonging to Giuseppe Stiozzi Ridolfi.[14] The garden at Marchese Amerigo Corsi's villa in Sesto was transformed *all'inglese* in 1815 following the recommendation and design of Hackert's erudite pupil, Francesco Inghirami,[15] whereas neomedieval evocations and the glorification of *exempla virtutis* – themes which, as in painting, would transform the garden into an ideal scenario for staging complex iconographic programmes – were the hallmarks of Alessandro Gherardesca's projects in Pisa and the designs elaborated by the latter and Cambray Digny for the Puccini garden at Scornio near Pistoia, one of the most outstanding examples of the period.

Moreover, the first two decades of the century saw the completion of radical re-structuring work on the gardens belonging to the grand duke at Poggio a Caiano, Poggio Imperiale, Petraia, Castello, Pratolino and Boboli involving such skilful architect-gardeners as Manetti, Cambray Digny, Joseph Frietsch, Giuseppe Cacialli and Giuseppe Del Rosso,[16] although not without criticism by the most strenuous defenders of the ancient charm of the Italian garden. Even in the Lucca of Elisa Baciocchi, where neoclassicism had penetrated to a deeper level, the large 'natural' park at the villa in Marlia, created at the wish of Napoleon's wilful sister during the early years of the nineteenth century, was an example viewed by many noblemen with obsequious interest: important testimonials of this are the elegant portraits of Olympia and Zoé Cenami painted between 1809 and 1811 by Pietro Nocchi (figs. 7.2 and 7.3); inspired by the works of François Gérard, the artist set his subjects against the background of 'a village meadow in the guise of a landscape garden as is now the vogue' in the evocative surroundings of the villa at Saltocchio.[17]

[14] On the Florentine gardens between the eighteenth and nineteenth centuries, see F. Von Waldburg, 'Die florentiner Gartenlagen, des ausgehenden 18. und frühen 19. Jahrhunderts', dissertation, Dr.-Ing. Techn. Hochschule, Stuttgart 1978; Von Waldburg, 'Appunti sui giardini fiorentini del tardo '700 e del primo '800,' in *Il giardino storico italiano. Problemi di indagine. Fonti letterarie e storiche*, ed. G. Ragionieri (Florence, 1981), pp. 235–42; V. Cazzato and M. De Vico Fallani, *Guida ai giardini urbani di Firenze* (Florence, 1981); F. Chiostri, *Parchi della Toscana* (Genoa, 1982); M. Dezzi Bardeschi, 'Le macchine desideranti', in *Il giardino romantico*, pp. 29–45; Vezzosi, *Pittura di macchia e di sfinge* (Florence, 1986); M. G. Vaccari, 'Il giardino delle Gherardesca e gli Orti Oricellari a Firenze', *Quaderni di Palazzo Te*, 5 (1986), pp. 67–74; M. Pozzana, 'L'influenza della introduzione di specie vegetali esotiche sulla formazione del giardino ottocentesco toscano', in *Il giardino italiano dell'Ottocento*, ed. A. Tagliolini (Milan, 1990), pp. 253–65; L. M. Bartoli and G. Contorni, *Gli Orti Oricellari a Firenze. Un Giardino, una città* (Florence, 1991).

[15] G. Guicciardini Corsi Salviati, *La villa Corsi a Sesto* (Florence, 1937), pp. 38–9; M. Pozzana, *Materia e cultura dei giardini storici* (Florence, 1989).

[16] Waldburg, 'Die florentiner Gartenlagen'; Waldburg, 'Appunti sui giardini fiorentini'; L. Zangheri, 'Joseph Frietsch un "giardiniere" boemo a Firenze', *Antichità viva*, 3 (1984), pp. 28–32; *Boboli '90, Atti del Convegno Internazionale* (Florence, 1991); C. Acidini Luchinat and G. Galletti, *Le ville e i giardini di Castello e Petraia a Firenze* (Pisa, 1992), p. 187. On Gherardesc's work in Pisa (in the Venerosi Pesciolini garden and at Villa Roncioni in Pugnano) see M. A. Giusti, 'Natura e cultura nei giardini di Alessandro Gherardesca', in *Il giardino italiano dell'Ottocento*, pp. 225–40; Giusti, *Giardini pisani*.

[17] A. Tosi, 'Aspetti della pittura lucchese durante il principato', in *Il Principato Napoleonico dei Baciocchi (1805-1814) riforma dello stato e società* (Lucca, 1984), pp. 302–23, at p. 315; A. Tosi, 'Pietro Nocchi', in *'Recensir col tratto'. Disegni di Bernardino e Pietro Nocchi*, ed. R.P. Ciardi and A. Tosi (Lucca, 1989), pp. 73–105. On the park in Marlia see M. A. Giusti, 'Le residenze dei Principi a Marlia', in *Il Principato Napoleonico dei Baciocchi*, pp. 465–90, and P. E. Tomei, *Il giardino della villa di Marlia e l'Orto Botanico*, in *ibid.*, pp. 504–7.

Fig. 7.2 P. Nocchi. Portrait of Olympia Cenami, 1809–11

The 'pleasant, delightful, vast wooded theatres' and the 'foreign plants' which made the 'erudite luxury' and 'rural simplicity' of the landscape garden a pleasure to be savoured[18] also called for careful reflection on questions closely linked to the development of botanical and horticultural studies. Fruit and flowers were presented and illustrated in brand new linguistic and figurative terms as precious collectors' items forming part of sophisticated natural collections, almost the *rariora* of modern vegetable 'Wunderkammern'. The plates of Gaetano Savi's *Materia medica vegetabile toscana*, printed in Florence in 1805, had already marked the start of a type of naturalistic illustration consistent with neoclassical stylistic elements. In 1817 young Antonio Piccioli, the son of the 'botanical gardener' who worked in the garden of the Museum of Physics and Natural History, presented to the Accademia dei Georgofili the first

---

[18] I. Pindemonte, *Il giardino inglese descritto da Ippolito Pindemonte nel poemetto de' Sepolcri . . .* (Verona, 1817).

Fig. 7.3 P. Nocchi. Portrait of Zoé Cenami, 1809–11

volume of *Plantarum pulcherrimarum Horti Botanici Musei Imperialis et Regalis Florentini Icones*, a collection of watercolours portraying the most beautiful specimens growing in the museum's garden (fig. 7.4).[19] The same year also saw the publication of the first volume of Giorgio Gallesio's *Pomona italiana*, the first of the major editorial undertakings destined to bring Tuscany to the forefront of the national scene, thus making up for Italy's backwardness compared to the rest of Europe, above all England and France (fig. 7.5).

Published in Pisa between 1817 and 1839 by the printing house belonging to the famous *letterato* and art historian Giovanni Rosini, *Pomona italiana ossia trattato degli alberi fruttiferi* marked the start of the study and classification of the different varieties of Italian fruit-bearing trees in a splendid iconographic format executed by an experienced team

[19] Preserved in the Biblioteca Nazionale Centrale of Florence: see Tongiorgi Tomasi and Tosi, '*Flora e Pomona*', pp. 107–8.

Fig. 7.4 A. Piccioli. *Peurretia speciosa*, from *Plantarum . . . Icones*

of draughtsmen and engravers. The specimens, drawn 'from real life' in the gardens of Florence, Pisa and Lucca, not to mention Genoa, Turin and Bologna, were reproduced using avant-garde copperplate printing techniques which were able to imitate the extraordinarily natural chromatic effects observed by Gallesio during his careful study of Jacopo Ligozzi's antique tempera paintings conserved in the Uffizi.[20] The success of *Pomona italiana* prompted Rosini to print another richly illustrated work, *Flora italiana ossia raccolta delle piante più belle che si coltivano nei giardini d'Italia* (Pisa, 1818-24), by the director of Pisa's Botanical Garden, Gaetano Savi. Conceived along the lines of the

[20] Tosi, 'Tra Flora e Pomona', pp. 31–44; M. Pozzana, *Il giardino dei frutti* (Florence, 1990), pp. 79–112; Tosi, 'Arte e scienza tra neoclassicismo e romanticismo', pp. 235–9.

Fig. 7.5 *Susino damaschino*, from G. Gallesio, *Pomona italiana*

most important Anglo-Saxon contributions to botanical literature – *The Botanist's Repository* by Henry Andrews and *The Botanical Magazine* by William Curtis – *Flora italiana* presented a 'collection' of plants selected 'from the most beautiful specimens cultivated in the gardens of Italy' in the form of Antonio Serantoni's elegant illustrations (fig. 7.6).[21] Addressed to the dilettanti in whose gardens it was possible to admire 'collections' of particular interest for their beauty or rarity, Savi aimed to convey a 'taste for Botany', a 'pleasant' and 'useful' science, using an approach which was not far removed from that adopted by Curtis who had first conceived his *Botanical Magazine* as 'a work in which Botany and Gardening . . . or the labour of Linnaeus and

[21] G. Savi, *Flora italiana* (Pisa, 1818-24), I. See also Tosi, 'Tra Flora e Pomona', pp. 44–5; Tosi, 'Arte e scienza tra neo-classicismo e romanticismo' pp. 239–40.

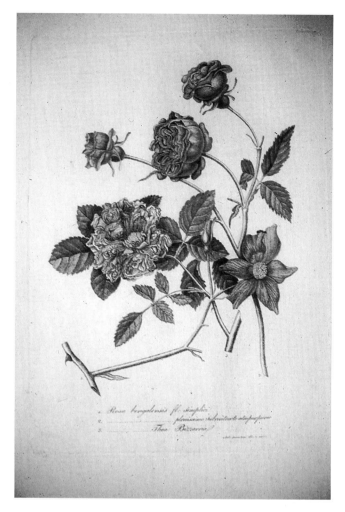

Fig. 7.6 A. Serantoni. *Rosa bengalensis*, from G. Savi, *Flora italiana*

Miller, might happily be combined'.[22] Thus, whereas Antonio Targioni Tozzetti's *Raccolta di fiori, frutti ed agrumi*—first published in Florence in 1822—was intended 'to respond to the needs of many gardening enthusiasts' and was dedicated to 'the most worthy plants destined for the ornamentation of Flora and Pomona' (fig. 7.7),[23] it was the *Almanacco per i dilettanti di giardinaggio*, the handbook edited by Savi himself from 1822 onwards, which put into concrete form the didactic intentions so keenly felt during the romantic period:

[22] W. Curtis, *The Botanical Magazine*, 1 (London, 1793), Preface.
[23] A. Targioni Tozzetti, *Raccolta di fiori, frutti ed agrumi piu ricercati per l'adornamento dei giardini disegnati al naturale da vari artisti* (Florence, 1825), Preface. In 1830 Antonio Targioni Tozzetti became director of the Florentine Botanical Garden: see Tosi, 'Tra Flora e Pomona', pp. 47–9.

Fig. 7.7 *Rosa Centifolia*, from A. Targioni Tozzetti, *Raccolta di fiori*

The taste for Gardening, which continues to spread during our Times, in addition to being an innocent, pleasant occupation, suited to both sexes and every age, and at the same time unending given that it concerns a vast number of extremely interesting items, is also a highly effective means of preparing the mind for the study of Botany . . .[24]

The Pisan scientist combined practical 'instructions' on the way to grow various plants with an essay by Luigi Mabil entitled 'Sopra l'indole dei giardini moderni,' 'humorous poems' by Angelo Maria Ricci and Ippolito Pindemonte's 'Prose campestri', which

[24] G. Savi, *Almanacco per i dilettanti di giardinaggio* (Pisa, 1822–34), vol. I, p. 1; see also C. Ridolfi, 'Elogio del Prof. Gaetano Savi', *Memorie della Società Italiana delle Scienze*, 23 (1845), pp. 1–24.

were justly singled out as the 'manifesto of the new awareness of the countryside seen as a garden'.[25] The close relation between garden and literature, between botany and poetry – a genuine topos of the Romantic movement – was thereby openly declared. From this point of view the collaboration between an illustrious botanist such as Savi and a well-known man of letters such as Rosini was destined to produce extremely significant results. During the same period, Rosini, who was then working on the first draft of the *Monaca di Monza*, translated into Italian the *Poesie* by the Sicilian Giovanni Meli (Pisa, 1821–3), the inspired author of 'Il Gelsomino', 'La Ruta', or 'Il sistema sessuale de' fiori di Linneo'. *La Georgica de' fiori* by Angelo Maria Ricci from Rieti was also published in Pisa in 1825 and was the first 'didactic poem' to be dedicated to the garden.

Ricci was well known for a number of minor scientific poems much appreciated by Vincenzo Monti, Pietro Giordani, Leopoldo Cicognara and Pindemonte; in his *Idilli* (Pisa, 1822) he had already expressed his debt to Pope, Dryden, Tasso, Guarino, Marino and above all to Salomon Gessner. In *Georgica de' fiori*, suggested by earlier literary works ranging from Delille's *Les jardins* to Darwin's *The Loves of the Plants*, Ricci emphasised the value of the didactic genre, crediting it with the merit of 'giving a certain degree of pictorial clearness to doctrines which are abstract by definition'. In an attempt to imitate 'those painters who paint flowers in their natural colours' – and therefore adhering to an Arcadian style of classicism in which the motto 'ut pictura poesis' was revised in the light of romantic experience and direct relations with Canova's and above all Bertel Thorvaldsen's sculpture, Ricci appealed for aid to science – namely botany – to 'instruct' the reader on the 'general rules for constructing any sort of garden'.[26] The 'solitary, shady cloister', the 'moss-covered sacred chair at the entrance', the 'singular green lake', the 'humbly sloping lawn' strewn with flowers carefully arranged in imitation of 'Pallas' or Arachne's ancient mantle' once again became the linguistic elements of the garden according to the landscape model:

> Vero è che l'Anglo, di cui l'orme adora
> L'età novella, in bel disordin tenta
> La Natura atteggiar libera ancora . . .[27]

To the *topoi* of the romantic garden Ricci added poetic instructions on how to make the divisions between different parts of the garden, how to ward off insects and destroy

[25] Venturi, 'I "lumi" del giardino', p. 27.

[26] A. M. Ricci, *La Georgica de' fiori* (Pisa, 1825), pp. XIX–XXII. On Ricci, known for the following works: *De gemmis* (1796), *Gli amori delle piante* (1802), *Le conchiglie* (1830) and the unpublished poem on 'Orti botanici', see A. Sacchetti Sassetti, *La vita e le opere di Angelo Maria Ricci* (Rieti, 1898); on his relations and collaboration with Bertel Thorvaldsen, see *Bertel Thorvaldsen 1770-1844, scultore danese a Roma*, ed. E. di Majio, B. Jøarnes and S. Susinno (Rome, 1989), p. 202; on his contacts with the literary figures of the time, see F. Fedi, *L'idealogia del bello. Leopoldo Cicognara e il classicismo tra Settecento e Ottocento* (Milan, 1990), pp. 52–4, 277–8, 290–3. On the success of the 'poesia didascalica georgica' in Italy in the late eighteenth century, see also F. Re, *Della poesia didascalica georgica degli italiana dopo il ristoramento delle scienze sino al presente* (Bologna, 1809).

[27] Ricci, *La Georgica de' fiori*, p. 48. Ricci was inspired by the garden of the villa belonging to the duke of Cassano near Portici, whose attractions had already been praised in *Poesie* (Pisa, 1824), pp. 121–44.

ants, how to choose vases or position the stoves. The project for the cottage intended for the 'Gardener' or 'Florist' is a particularly elaborate and curious pastiche, between an ancient *studiolo* and a modern scientific laboratory, where valuable glass showcases could be used to collect the most beautiful and rare flowers:

> Sì come soglion gli orafi, che in teca
> D'oro, o d'argento al passeggier fan mostra
> Ne' scrigni lor di quanto India a noi reca[28]

He also imagined a botanical laboratory full of butterfly specimens, instruments for experiments on fertilisation and grafts, 'simple lenses, microscopic lenses for magnifying, a solar microscope which would cast immense images of minute items onto the wall, garden shears, ferrules, probes, shells, crystal jars for acids, alkali and other chemical reagents', the walls of which were covered with botanical plates:

> E i fior d'altra contrada, e d'altro sito
> Delineati in candido papiro
> Col titolo patrio dell'ameno lito[29]

This was followed by a richly endowed library and a dried herb collection:

> E ne' vari scaffali accolti in giro
> Gli aurei volumi di color che tutti
> I misteri di Flora a noi scopriro,
>
> O sotto grave lapide ridutti
> D'erto papiro tra i bibuli fogli,
> E in odorati scheletri rasciutti.
>
> D'altri fior, d'altre piante i bei germogli,
> Cemeterio di Flora, in cui di molti
> Suoi vaghi parti le reliquie accogli ...[30]

And lastly the observatory where all the observations necessary for the correct management of the garden could be performed. In other words, an abode

> ... ove sarai
> Pittor, Vate di Flora, e Geometra.[31]

The hymns to nature which had delighted an entire generation of poets enraptured by the myth of Arcadia gave way to precise, formal indications and methods behind which it was not difficult to glimpse Pisa's lively scientific milieu. Whereas the botanical garden became the privileged source of inspiration for eulogies on the ideal garden – it is worth noting that Ricci mentions the herbarium precisely at the time when the Pisan collection was being considerably enlarged – the advice given by its

---

[28] Ricci, *La Georgica de' fiori*, p. 93.   [29] Ibid., pp. 98, 105–6.   [30] Ibid., pp. 98–9.   [31] Ibid., p. 88.

director, Savi, resulted in the outstanding international success of 'Orologio di flora', namely 'the calendar of flowering plants and the tasks appropriate to each month' with which Ricci concluded his short poem. The latter was reprinted in Pisa in 1827 and immediately translated into several languages, including Greek distichs and Latin verse, set to music, reproduced on canvas and embroidery, and even affixed to watches made in Germany.[32]

Ricci's poetic description of the garden in *Georgica de' fiori* anticipated the figurative portrayal of some of the most renowned Florentine and Tuscan gardens. For example, in 1832 Emilio Burci published a series of views of the Orti Oricellari (fig. 7.8), which had been designed from 1813 onwards by Luigi Cambray Digny for Giuseppe Stiozzi Ridolfi. The rules laid down by Silva and put into verse by Ricci appear to have been perfectly translated in the images of the gothic abbey of Sant'Anna, the small temple of Venus, the ruins of the ancient temple and the circus, Polyphemus' colossus and the grotto, the 'flower garden' in which vases containing lemon trees were flanked by white statues, the fort and the Pantheon destined to commemorate illustrious *exempla virtutis* – in this instance the members of the Accademia Platonica.[33] Ricci also deliberately included the 'small tower' used as an observatory which was modelled on the prototype designed by Gaetano Baccani for the Torrigiani garden.[34]

Described or imagined, painted or praised in verse, the garden was therefore the faithful mirror of an epoch of profound cultural renewal. Even the determined opposition to the landscape garden by architects and gardeners in the name of an entirely Italian form of classicism disguised the need to re-establish an identity and linguistic autonomy *vis-à-vis* the foreign models which were dramatically gaining ground. The 'Considerazioni sulla convenianza dei giardini italiani rapporto a quelli di altre nazioni', written by Giuseppe Del Rosso in 1819 after Cambray Digny's project for the Orti Oricellari and published in the 1831 edition of *L'osservatore fiorentino*, formed part of that *querelle* which, as in painting and literature, was destined to connote a romanticism characterised by manifold and complex nuances. Aiming to demonstrate how both Cambray Digny and his client had 'falsely tried to imitate English gardens, and how the emblems of sadness dotted here and there throughout the garden were poorly suited to a place in which everything should emanate pleasantness, and where every object should serve to inspire gaiety and good humour', Del Rosso vindicated ancient and not solely formal values.[35] In *Antotrofia, ossia la coltivazione de' fiori*, published in Florence in 1834, Antonio Piccioli also extolled the 'pleasantness',

---

[32] See Sacchetti Sassetti, *La vita e le opere*, pp. 159–60, and F. Marzotto Caotorta, 'Tendenze culturale nel giardino romantico in Italia', in *Il Giardino italiano dell'Ottocento*, pp. 169–76. Savi also included 'L'Orologio di Flora' in his *Almanacco di giardinaggio* in 1835.

[33] E. Burci and T. Salucci, *Vedute del giardino del marchese Stiozzi Ridolfi già Orti Oricellari* (Florence, 1832). See also L. Passerini, *Degli Orti Oricellarii. Memorie storiche* (Florence, 1875), pp. 44–51, and L. Scott, *The Orti Oricellari* (Florence, 1893); Bartoli and Contorni, *Gli Orti Oricellari*, pp. 57ff.

[34] Waldburg, 'Die florentiner Gartenlagen', pp. 87–95; M.P. Maresca, 'Da Osiride al Torrino (Il Giardino Torrigiani)', in *Il giardino romantico*, pp. 56–60. See also *Guida al Giardino Torrigiani* (Florence, 1824).

[35] Passerini, *Degli Orti Oricellarii*, pp. 44–5; see also Bartoli and Contorni, *Gli Orti Oricellari*, pp. 72–3.

Fig. 7.8 E. Burci. The *Giardino dei fiori* at the Orti Oricellari

'gentleness' and 'grace' of 'cultured, classic Italy' and inveighed against 'so much indecency in the arts and letters' occasioned by the 'horrors of romanticism' imported 'from the Scandinavian mists'. In addition to numerous practical hints on gardening, the Florentine gardener also presented a series of flower etchings and engravings (see fig. 7.9). These were associated with 'emblems' conceived by Marco Malagoli Vecchi from Modena, the translator of Thomson's 'Seasons' and the poem by Delille, as well as with excerpts from Teresa Bandettini, Darwin, Delille, Dubos, Domenico Gazzadi, Gianni, Montani and Salomon Gessner. The debt owed to the authors of handbooks for flower painters, a genre which was extremely widespread in England, did not prevent Piccioli from reinstating the Arcadian myths, emphasising their symbolic importance and even their humanitarian concessions: 'Flowers are such beautiful things! . . . It is not possible to do without them at feasts; the poor use them to cheer up and decorate their humble abodes. On a par with nature and all its sentiments, flowers are better than social conventions.'[36]

This vision was not far from that, laden with romantic aspirations, which during the same period led Niccolò Puccini to exhalt the educational and didactic function of the

[36] A Piccioli, *Antotrofia, ossia la coltivazione de' fiori* (Florence, 1834), pp. 9–11. See also A. Tosi, 'Tra Flora e Pomona', pp. 50–3.

Fig. 7.9 A. Piccioli. *Rosa gallica*, from *Antotrofia, ossia la coltivazione de' fiori*

garden. The splendid English-style park at the villa in Scornio, near Pistoia, which the scholar had commissioned from Luigi Cambray Digny, except for the monumental elements which had been assigned to Alessandro Gherardesca, was perhaps the most complete and evocative expression of the romantic garden in Tuscany (fig. 7.10). The emblematic features, characteristic of an architectural language capable of translating in refined and convincing tones the literary and figurative raptures of contemporary culture, were combined with the client's philanthropical and humanitarian leanings. The Pantheon (fig. 7.11), the 'Torre di Catilina', the retreat, the castle, the marble sculptural group of *Gli orfani sulla rupe* by Luigi Pampaloni, the monuments to

Fig. 7.10 Frontispiece, *Monumenti del giardino Puccini*

Fig. 7.11 View of the Pantheon, from *Monumenti del giardino Puccini*

illustrious Italians – ranging from Dante to Machiavelli, Tasso, Vico, Michelangelo, Raffaello and Canova – but also 'Galileo's hemicycle' and the statue to Linnaeus ('Prince of botany'), all transformed the garden from *locus amoenus* into a privileged receptacle of noble didactic messages. The amused description which Diego Martelli wrote of the Puccini garden conveys the redundant and artificial scenography which welcomed the visitor:

> Having visited the villa we passed into the park, designed in the English manner, of which the principal marvels may be summarised as follows: the Pantheon of illustrious men. A dilapidated gothic temple. A terracotta statue of Diana . . . busts, cippi, statues to great Italian figures, to Ferruccio, Michelangelo and Machiavelli, all embellished by epigraphs prophesying the Italian recovery which made one pardon the inadequacy of the materials and the paltriness of their execution. Among the marvels was also Catiline's Tower standing on the site of her last battle and Pythagorus' temple on the island in the lake, embellished by two enormous weeping willows sufficient to move even the frogs. After the island [we visited] a gothic podesterate on the mainland, a hermitage in an even more pronounced gothic style flanked by a small house with smooth, well plastered walls painted to resemble wood, which appeared impossible; a medieval castle – this is an arch-gothic style – and numerous other busts, columns, statues, the majority in terracotta, to commemorate either leading citizens or men of virtue; and lastly, Napoleon's bridge.[37]

The romantic triumphs of the Puccini garden appeared to mark the end of an epoch. The 'First Meeting of Italian Scientists', held in Pisa in 1839, was a sign of the radical change awaiting not only the scientific sphere but Italian culture in general. Moreover, innovative experiments had already been successfully performed by Marchese Cosimo Ridolfi in his 'extraordinarily well-stocked' garden at Bibbiani, a felicitous combination of agrarian and botanical studies which had conceded little or nothing to architectural whims and literary evocations.[38] The loyal subjects of Flora and Pomona were replaced by seasoned collectors of camelias, orchids, petunias or cacti – such as Conte di Bouturlin, Conte della Gherardesca, Marchese Bardo Corsi Salviati, Prince Anatolio Demidoff, Marchese Pietro Torrigiani, Marchese Ferdinando Panciatichi and Emilio Santarelli.[39] In order to 'encourage the promotion of fruit and flower gardens' and 'regretting the complete absence in our country of institutions which already flourish north of the Alps', the Accademia dei Georgofili laid the foundations for the

---

[37] D. Martelli, 'Romanticismo e realismo nelle arti rappresentative' (1895), in *Scritti d'arte*, ed. A. Boschetto (Florence, 1952), pp. 198–212. See also *Monumenti del Giardino Puccini* (Pistoia, 1845); P. Luciani, 'La committenza di Niccolò Puccini', in *Cultura dell'Ottocento a Pistoia. La collezione Puccini*, Exhibition catalogue (Florence, 1977), pp. 23–8; M. Di Giovine and D. Negri, *Il Giardino Puccini di Pistoia. Studi e proposte per il recupero* (Pistoia, 1984). Between 1840 and 1841 Puccini commissioned a fresco cycle from Sabatelli, Bezzuoli, Cianganelli and Martinelli for the ground floor stables of the villa. The frescoes illustrated episodes in the lives of Raffaello, Michelangelo, Benvenuto Cellini and Andrea del Sarto (see C. Mazzi and C. Sisi, 'La collezione di Niccolò Puccini', in *Cultura dell'Ottocento a Pistoia* (1977), pp. 13–20).

[38] See C. Ridolfi, *Catalogo delle piante coltivate a Bibbiani e cenni su qualcosa delle medesime* (Florence, 1843); G. Moggi and L. Falciani, *Guida botanica al Parco di Bibbiani* (Florence, 1991).

[39] Targioni Tozzetti, *Cenni storici*, pp. 192, 202, 211, 215, 220, 256–7; Guicciardini, *La villa Corsi a Sesto*, pp. 39–40, 82.

Società Toscana di Orticultura, which was officially founded in 1854.[40] Once the society had begun to organise plant and flower exhibitions, under the expert guidance of the gardener Attilio Pucci, Florentine gardens appeared to discard their complex symbolisms and, even for a short period, returned to being those baroque 'theatres of greenery' which had delighted princes in earlier centuries. The floral triumphs with their dazzling combinations of colours and scents, the naturalistic *tromp-l'oeil*, the ingenious fruit and flower arrangements in plaster, wax or marble which were the delight of ardent horticulturists and their increasingly large following of dilettanti, represented the ephemeral nature of modern industrial society overflowing with positivist enthusiasm. The spectacle offered by the Gherardesca garden when it was used as the venue for the fourth exhibition of the Tuscan Horticultural Society in 1857 was the most obvious sign of the final decline of that sense of nature which had characterised the many-faceted development of neoclassicism and romanticism:

> all those who visited the Gherardesca garden during the hottest hours early yesterday afternoon and watched the numerous couples of ladies and gentlemen strolling up and down the pleasant boulevards, or sitting in the shade of the cool, green trees listening to the marvellous music of two musical ensembles hidden amidst the bushes and woods, must, if they succeeded in forgetting our merciless sun, have imagined themselves momentarily transported into Armida's enchanted gardens.[41]

[40] M. Dezzi Bardeschi, *Gli orti di Parnaso. Il giardino dell'Orticoltura a Firenze: storia e progetto* (Florence, 1989), pp. 29ff.
[41] Ibid., p. 32.

CHAPTER 8

GARDENS AND PARKS IN LIGURIA IN THE SECOND HALF OF THE NINETEENTH CENTURY

ANNALISA MANIGLIO CALCAGNO★

During the nineteenth century the landscape of the city of Genoa and some parts of Liguria – especially the strip of land next to the coast and the more manageable terrain on the flat valley bottoms – underwent important large-scale transformations in both urban and rural areas. The main causes of these changes are to be sought in the advent of industrialisation in Liguria, the development of transport and the marked increase in population. The effect of these factors was felt on both urban and rural landscapes: they brought about profound changes in the appearance of Liguria's coastal landscapes and valleys, which up to that time had remained largely natural or had retained an archaic rural character.

The urban scene underwent considerable change following expansion in construction in the part of Genoa that lies outside the city walls, along the coast and on the lower slopes of the hills. Genoa's great natural amphitheatre, which slopes down towards the sea, was given a new urban shape and a new road network was superimposed on top of the old one.

The poorest areas of the agrarian countryside began to be neglected as people moved away from the country and towards the city and the new industrial zones to the west of Genoa. The expansion of the port, the construction of the first railway lines and the improvement of roads which at the beginning of the nineteenth century were still behind the times, facilitated mobility in Liguria in many areas where travel was difficult owing to the harsh and inaccessible nature of the landscape. Numerous seaside villages expanded as the Ligurian rivieras[1] began to feel the impact of a first wave of high-class

---

★Translated by Ian Harvey.

[1] Salmon's famous eighteenth-century guide book explains the division of Liguria into the western and eastern riviera as follows: 'The Riviera is the area between the Apennines and the sea, which stretches along the territory of Genoa. The regional capital divides this area into two parts, the one to the east (Levante), the other to the west (Ponente)': ('ciò che in Genova dicesi la Riviera di Levante e di Ponente non è una riviera o un fiume che porti un tal nome, ma significa quello

tourism, which brought in its wake luxury hotels, tree-lined promenades, public parks and private villas with gardens full of rich exotic vegetation.

Other areas further inland, but still close to the city or within easy reach by the new means of transport, became holiday resorts for the middle classes who now dominated the newly industrialised scene. These places transmuted and miniaturised, as it were, the aristocratic villa life of previous centuries. The idea of the holiday generated a new interest in nature and was linked to a concern with health and hygiene which had its origin in the eighteenth century, to the spread of naturalistic studies and to an interest in the introduction of new plants.

In this chapter I will look at the principles and models which shaped the relations between landowners and the natural environment during the latter half of the nineteenth century; I will also examine the ideas and events which influenced the naturalistic aspirations of the nineteenth-century bourgeoisie in its impact on the Ligurian environment; and I will look at the figurative and spatial models which expressed the century's idea of nature, its opposition to urban sprawl and the value it placed on new natural and artificial landscapes.

The change in the landscape of Genoa was largely connected with the spread of new types of buildings which reflected the urban and social lifestyle of a nineteenth-century bourgeoisie that chose to live in the hilly part of the city, in multi-family houses which imitated the prestigious single-family residences of the old declining aristocracy. The Ligurian coastal landscape, on the other hand, was transformed by the numerous villas-with-parks of the bourgeoisie and the holiday residences of a rich international clientele who began to frequent picturesque seaside resorts with mild climates and splendid panoramas.

Villas of different sizes surrounded by parks were constructed in great numbers in some hilly places in inland Liguria, in localities which became ideal for spending holidays on account of their natural picturesque character and because they offered the healthy lifestyle held in such high esteem by Enlightenment thinking.

The bourgeoisie of the latter half of the nineteenth century sought its identity in these villas. The bourgeois villa was smaller than the eighteenth-century or Renaissance villa; its type was very often that of the *villino* (small villa), whose eclectic forms were intended to embody the decorum and new rules of social life. At the end of the nineteenth century the formal prestige of the feudal northern European castle or of the Anglo-Swiss cottage better expressed the aspirations of new clients who were trying to enhance their status by building dwelling places according to models and types taken from a past laden with significant images.

spazio ch'è tra l'Appennino e il mare, lungo il territorio di Genova. La capitale divide questo spazio in due parti, l'una delle quali le rimane a Levante, l'altra a Ponente: è questo il significato di Riviera de Levante e di Riviera di Ponente. Più propriamente direbbesi la Spiaggia o la Costiera'). Salmon, *Lo stato presente di tutti i paesi e popoli del mondo, naturale, politico e morale, con nuove osservazioni e correzionidegli antichi e moderni viaggiatori*, XVIII: *Dell'Italia cioè della Savoja, del Piemonte, del Monferrato e del Genovesato*, trans. by G. Albizzi (Venice, 1740-51), p. 211. T. G. Smollett uses the same expression in his travel diary: *Travels through France and Italy* (1st ed., 1766; Oxford, 1979), p. 203.

Around the numerous houses and large and small villas constructed for an affluent class space was set aside for a garden. Sometimes these gardens were only modest in size but they ensured the house a green setting – both a symbol of wealth in this end-of-the century city and an image of continuity with nature. Confined to ever narrower spaces, the art of the garden took on new forms and adopted a language more appropriate to radical social change and the ideals imposed by the industrialisation of the city. At times the nearness of the villas to each other – in a kind of specially set aside 'garden city' – made the residential quarters on the edge of the city into a kind of private domestic scale green belt.

The desire – or rather the attempts – to reconstruct a landscape which would fulfil the ideals expressed by the landscape designers of the end of the eighteenth century re-emerged during the nineteenth century in the wake of urban growth. Potential property owners, now largely urbanised, began once again the need to blend with a beneficial although tamed nature, concentrated in the few private or public green spaces of the city.

These attempts assumed various forms and styles during the course of the nineteenth century: some were expressions of the idea of the 'garden-city' envisioned and put into practice in the British Isles, first by social utopians and later by Ebenezer Howard, who wanted to join the city to the countryside, society to nature. The 'rediscovery' of nature was part of a heated philosophical–cultural debate about the restoration of a landscape in which people could enjoy the benefits of nature at the same time as maintaining their essential social links. However, the sections of garden city that were created – such as at Pegli[2] and later in other areas on the outskirts of the city – fell far short of fulfilling the utopian ambitions of their inventors. The desire to reunite with nature was enshrined more completely and explicitly in the numerous holiday residences beyond and far away from the narrow spaces of the city, in contact with that countryside which best expresses the beauty and variety of nature.

The middle of the nineteenth century saw the last great landscape estates with villa-parks built by the aristocracy on noble landed property situated near the city. While this pattern, of particular importance for the environment and the landscape, was drawing to a close, on the outskirts of the city of Genoa numerous new bourgeois residences were beginning to spring up, and large and small villas for the Italian and foreign bourgeoisie started to spread in some areas along the Ligurian rivieras and inland.

Tourism, the speed of rail transport[3] and ease of movement led the new social classes interested in acquiring residences in natural settings towards places on the coast chosen for holidays because of their mild climate and attractive landscapes. The Ligurian

---

[2] Pegli used to be a small fishing village to the west of Genoa; as part of the great expansion of the metropolitan area it has now been incorporated into the city.

[3] The railway – dubbed the 'magic road' in the nineteenth century – reached Italy, along the western riviera, from France in 1870. A. Maniglio Calcagno, *Giardini, parchi e paesaggi nella Genova dell'800* (Genoa, 1984), pp. 116–19. Very interesting on this subject are the *Views on the Railway between Turin and Genoa*, Lithographed at the establishment of Day and Son, Lithographers to the queen. From drawing by Carlo Bossoli (London, 1853), plates 14, 15 and 16.

rivieras became the destination of foreign tourists, particularly from Great Britain. But the intensive development of private gardens belonging to villas and hotels, of parks and public walks which accompanied the phenomenon of the seaside holiday was not matched by a corresponding creativity in landscape design.

The end of the century was dominated by various nineteenth-century theories about the role of garden designers. On the one hand there was the landscape-gardener whose role was to recreate nature by imitating its environmental balances, and on the other, the architect-gardener whose task it was, through a search for new harmonies, to impose on nature either those historical forms which belonged to gardening tradition or his own innovative solutions.

In the gardens of Liguria one can find both these concepts, but with a prevalence of the latter in the landscape creations on the coast where the mild climate, the privileged exposure of the slopes, the protection from the cold tramontana winds, encouraged owners to experiment with the acclimatisation of exotic and often rare plants. In the last great aristocratic parks, on the other hand, the designs still show evidence of a search for interesting compositional forms and a meticulous application of the landscape canons of the continuously evolving English type of garden. By this time the English garden had become widely known through numerous writings by attentive observers and theorists. The French theoretician Edouard André[4] recommended that the artists who composed these gardens – the practitioners were Canzio, Rovelli and Roda – should have the ability to conceive a unified composition. He also saw them as possessing creative gifts which belonged properly to the poet, the painter and the architect, at the same time as having a sound knowledge of botanical problems. Specific tasks – in the technical spheres of hydraulic engineering, horticulture and moulding the terrain – were assigned to people with the relevant professional skills. The precise definition of these skills had begun to emerge in the post-Enlightenment period with the gradual specialisation of scientific disciplines involving the natural environment. Even Ercole Silva, the theorist of the art of English gardens, had taken part in this discussion about the skills and knowledge necessary for the artist-gardener. He maintained that this professional should have 'the qualities of a painter and man of taste . . . an eye and a spirit capable of judging beauty'; he was to work in a different way from that of the architect, 'who is hampered by rigid proportion, confined by the invariable rules of austere geometrical exactitude'; and he was supposed to have a knowledge of botany as well as the ability to observe nature carefully.[5]

THE LAST VILLAS OF THE NOBILITY

The last important villas with large parks were constructed in the middle of the nineteenth century around the city of Genoa for the prominent families of the local

---

[4] E. André', *Traité général de la composition des parques et des jardins* (Paris, 1879), pp. 113–19.

[5] E. Silva, *Dell'arte dei giardini inglesi* (Milan, 1801; augmented and illustrated, 1813), pp. 30–1. New ed. by Gianni Venturi (Milan, 1976).

aristocracy. These parks, departures from the classical style that had been employed continuously throughout the previous three centuries, drew inspiration for their design from the theories and artistic ideas of the northern European romantic-picturesque school, modified to fit the steep slopes of the Ligurian landscape. This accomplished appendix brought to an end the long and important chapter of large-scale suburban villas with gardens and parks built by the most wealthy aristocratic families with the dual function of summer residence and farm. Many visitors were inspired to write enthusiastic descriptions by this remarkable landscape phenomenon—a succession of beautiful villas spreading continuously along the coastline adjacent to the city.

The large park of the villa of the marquis of Pallavicini at Pegli (fig. 8.1) is an emblematic example of a romantic idiom that reflects contemporary landscape theories. Completed in the middle of the nineteenth century, this interesting construction resulted from a happy relationship between client and designer: the marquis of Pallavicini, a man of sophisticated and cosmopolitan culture on the one hand, and Michele Canzio, a skilled architect and expert scenographer on the other.

It was precisely this latter ability that permitted Canzio to construct[6] on the steep slopes of the hill a succession of suggestive and picturesque views, and to introduce a variety of backdrops to the numerous vistas offered by the park: now the sea, now the cultivated countryside. The irregular-shaped lake, the grotto, the cascade, the variously styled pavilions, the ruins, the greenhouses—these were the representative elements of a majestic and eclectic composition. The views which opened up from specific observation points as the visitor walked along set itineraries, now climbing steeply, now going downhill, possessed that similarity with works of painting which (paradoxically) constituted an undeniable value in 'naturalistic' gardens. These views were constructed using architectural features drawn from various places and styles—classical, gothic, Chinese, Turkish—with playful decorations made in wrought and cast iron using the modern technologies of the time; with bridges across the lake and waterways; with rare and beautiful trees, each different from the other in colour and shape; with sudden panoramas which came into view at the end of winding paths.

The sequence of views afforded the visitor descending the hillside towards the sea was thus skilfully contrived, as were the clumps of vegetation, and the timely effects of light and contrasts of shade that were all made to appear natural. The sum effect was designed to stimulate in the visitor a mingling of memories and allegories of ancient imaginary events, evoked as a way of celebrating the fame of the owner. The stroller was meant to experience a variety of feelings and emotions aroused by the unexpected fountains and innumerable devices which appeared at intervals along the path. The whole idea was to produce in the visitor ever-changing thoughts, emotions and pleasures.

---

[6] The construction of the Villa Pallavicini park went on for about nine years, from 1837 to 1846. A little guide book was sold at the entrance: A. Gassarini, *Souvenir du Jardin Pallavicini de Pegli et itinéraire de Gênes à Voltri* (Gênes, 1857). See S. Ghigino, F. Calvi, *Il Parco Durazzo Pallavicini a Pegli.* (Genoa, 1987).

Fig. 8.1 The lake at Villa Pallavicini, Pegli, a small seaside resort to the west of Genoa

The most spectacular effect was without doubt the descent towards the lake from the top of a hill covered with dense vegetation and crowned with a medieval castle. The visitor reached the lake, often glimpsed along the rocky path, after a short trip in a boat through a broad grotto skilfully reconstructed with stalactites and stalagmites. The abrupt transition from the darkness of the cavern to the luminosity of the lake generated precisely the kind of emotions that were dear to the hearts of the romantics. The particular orographical position of the park allowed the beholder to take in the broader and more luminous view of the horizon of the sea which projected the enclosed views of the park towards the infinity of the ocean.

The romantic park at Pegli was open – with special permission – to local inhabitants and to the ever-increasing numbers of visitors to the Ligurian riviera. Perhaps for this reason it was decided to combine in the park the typically nineteenth-century interest in a variety of images and a rich wealth of vegetation with a search for the new and the surprising. Besides the pine woods, the thickets of camellias, the numerous botanical rarities, there were various lively scenes designed to evoke distant places: roundabouts and cast-iron swings were introduced, fountains, boat rides, and all kinds of surprises and discoveries. In this way this outstanding park was able to contribute to the tourist exploitation of the old fishing village of Pegli at a time when it was becoming a fashionable resort for high-class tourists. The division of the territory into a number of large private farming estates made possible the construction of a small railway station, large hotels, meeting places, bathing establishments, public promenades and an interesting succession of small holiday villas, in a wide variety of styles, surrounded by small gardens with exotic vegetation.

Another villa with a park built only a few years after the Villa Pallavicini is the Villa Duchessa di Galliera, situated at the extreme west of Genoa on a woody hill sloping down towards the sea. For a long time, because members of the family were prominent in the political and social life in Genoa, it was a prestigious gathering place for prominent personalities from both the local and the European cultural and aristocratic world. Earlier, in the seventeenth century, the building had been a summer residence, owing to the particularly mild and airy local climate. The park that surrounded it had been modified and expanded several times over the course of the years to meet the varying needs of the family.

At first the garden had consisted simply of regular flat terraces surrounding the building. However, the space it occupied extended visually in an ordered arrangement of terraces on the slopes of the vast surrounding property set aside for the cultivation of olive trees, fruit trees, vines and vegetables.

In the eighteenth century the agricultural land was expanded to include areas of chestnut-tree copses and was divided up into holdings in line with new agronomic techniques designed to increase production. In the nineteenth century the duchess of Galliera, the owner of the villa, decided to transform the vast agricultural estate into a landscape garden. In keeping with nineteenth-century ideas, the costly and complex task of transforming the land – which extended over an area of 33 hectares with a difference in height of 150m from the main ridge to the sea – was entrusted in 1865 to Giuseppe Rovelli, a landscape gardener from a Lombardy family of gardeners and nurserymen.

Rovelli's achievement was a kind of summary and amalgam of the eclectic tendencies which were the hallmark of the nineteenth century. His response to his client's demands was to combine the romantic desire for contact with nature with a taste for agricultural land in the form of a park. He maintained unaltered the rigorous classicism of the terraced garden in front of the monumental building (fig. 8.2). The large geometrical lawns, the central basin, the pincer-like double stairway which joined the different levels of the garden, all served to accentuate the outstanding position in the landscape of the great neoclassical villa and to guarantee an uncluttered view of the sea.

But in designing this country park Rovelli was giving his own interpretation to Enlightenment concepts which sought to unite in the open spaces of nature utility, pleasure and beauty, cultivated countryside and garden. Thus he incorporated into the park large agricultural areas, places for experimental cultivation and orchards, skilfully inserted into wooded areas and between long serpentine paths which wound over the hillside for 18 kilometres.

For sheer pleasure the designer used numerous types of architectural and decorative

Fig. 8.2 Villa Duchessa di Galliera, Voltri, showing the large geometrical terrace

elements from the large repertoire of the nineteenth century, adapting them, by placing them amid native and exotic plants, to a rocky and poorly irrigated landscape. The triumphal arch with its two sides – classical and rustic – the chalet, the neo-gothic dairy, the grottoes, the tombs, marble stelae standing in the chiaroscuro created by various species of trees, were designed to provoke in the visitor, fascinated by the loveliness and spontaneity of nature, a pleasurable sense of amazement and surprise.

The remains of the ancient walls of the village of Voltri also formed part of the design of the park, adding the fascination of real ruins; the paths were widened at certain points to allow the visitor to stop and view the sweeping panoramas extending towards the sea and the countryside; grottoes, steep cascades, rocky flights of steps, narrow pathways, were constructed in large numbers along the ascending paths, in a succession of light and shade.

The third large villa park in Genoa, which is the final great landscape achievement of the Genoese aristocracy, is Villa Pinelli-Serra. Constructed by the architect Cusani for the Marquis Serra in the second half of the nineteenth century, it differs considerably from the preceding two both in terms of its compositional concept and its geographical position.

Situated in a valley on the side of a small river, it provides an interesting example of a villa park designed completely in accordance with English garden tastes. The neo-gothic forms of the building itself[7] are openly inspired by models disseminated by nineteenth-century manuals on garden design and it forms the perspective and compositional focal point of the 8-hectare park. The clearly English character of the park is the result of the skilful grouping of exotic trees foreign to the climate and local vegetation; these trees isolate the park from the surrounding farm land by creating a kind of screen of vegetation which over the course of time has become extremely dense. The nineteenth-century interest in botanical collections was responsible for the introduction of palms, cedars, sequoias, taxodium disticum, alternating with oaks and lindens, creating interesting contrasts in form, texture and colour.

The availability of water in the area made it possible to create an artificial lake, basins and waterways. Despite the decay of the park as a whole the long serpentine paths still offer a remarkable profusion and variety of backdrops and views: the lake, the garden pavilions, the neo-gothic tower, the villa itself, the numerous elements of the traditional repertoire of the garden – such as grottoes, small temples and greenhouses. Today most of these are in a derelict condition, while some have even disappeared altogether after the long period of neglect which the park has suffered.

With these three parks – Pallavicini, Galliera and Pinelli – which stand out for their fame and size in the cultural panorama of the time, and with other contemporary parks – such as those at Arenzano, Sestri Levante and Santa Margherita – which are less interesting and less attractive, the chapter of great noble landscape creations comes to an end.

In these parks one is always aware of an interest in the natural environment, but it is expressed in varying forms and ways: through the penetration of the garden into the landscape, in the Pallavicini and Galliera villas; through a multiplicity of views – the sea, the surrounding hills, the cultivated countryside; through the visual isolation of the surrounding environmental context and the attention directed towards interior space in Villa Pinelli. In all three examples, albeit with varying emphases, the rarity and beauty of plants from other climates becomes one of the defining elements in the landscape composition.

The planning activity of the landscape gardener was clearly guided by the observations of the Italian theoreticians, Silva and Mabil. The latter, in his nineteenth-century treatise (based largely on Hirschfeld's *Theorie der Gartenkunst*), recommended

> uniting [in the garden] that which is vague and interesting in nature, using its very own manner and its very own means; gathering together in a given site the beauty which is otherwise spread throughout the countryside; producing a whole which lacks neither unity nor harmony; creating by combining and arranging the various objects, without however straying too far from nature, and reinforcing the character of the positions, and

---

[7] The neo-gothic villa created by the architect Cusani was modelled on the garden cottages illustrated in J. C. Loudon, *Encyclopedia of Cottage, Farm and Villa Architecture* (London, 1833); J. C. Loudon, *The Suburban Garden and Villa Companion* (London, 1838); *The Architectural Magazine*, 1 (April, 1835). See L. Patetta, *L'architettura dell'Eclettismo: fonti, teorie e modelli, 1780-1900* (Milan, 1975), pp. 17–39.

Fig. 8.3 Villa Pallavicini, Arenzano, on the western Ligurian riviera

multiplying the effects by setting up contrasts; highlighting the attractive aspects of nature by coupling them with those of art.[8]

So the basic idea is not spontaneous nature, but an ideal nature which encloses within it an interesting variety of themes in the fundamental unity of the whole. Later, Tommaseo[9] (in a way which was anticipated by Rousseau in the previous century) was to criticise some nineteenth-century gardeners for failing to establish the right balance between art and naturalness, and also for an excess of imagination which produced the 'piling up in a small space of all kinds of different natural beauty...'

BOURGEOIS TOWN VILLAS AT THE END OF THE NINETEENTH CENTURY

As part of its attempt to acquire a symbolic countenance of its own, the late nineteenth-century bourgeoisie left the old town and went to live in the new residential districts of the city. The rich clients who commissioned the construction of villas and who lavished money on extraordinary buildings were typically bankers, ship builders or shop owners.

[8] L. Mabil, *Teoria dell'arte dei giardini* (Bassano, 1801), p. 41.
[9] Nicolò Tommaseo, 'L'Arte de' giardini inglesi', in *Bellezza e Civiltà* (Florence, 1857), pp. 140–3.

In Liguria in general, but especially in Genoa, they often chose to reside in gothic-style castles placed in panoramic hillside positions standing out over the city, or on promontories directly overlooking the sea, in an attempt to gain visual dominion over the surrounding territory. In this way they were trying to represent the economic prestige they enjoyed on the industrial scene. Medieval architectonic forms were accompanied by the 'naturalistic' integration of the building into the terrain, the use of symbols and historical references taken from the middle ages, and stone materials which properly belonged to the castle.

The gardens also contained turrets, ramparts, drawbridges, ramps, grottoes and step-like terraces which seemed to merge with the rocky slopes of the coastline and the mountains of Genoa. The structure of these gardens imitated the natural Ligurian landscape, and likewise the trees and shrubs were often those of the Mediterranean vegetation. Precipitous cliffs overlooking the sea formed the site for the garden, and into these were set stairs and bridges linking the various levels or symbolic defensive structures. But the previous visual domination over the seascape, typical of most of the prestigious long-standing Renaissance and baroque villas, became transformed in these new late nineteenth-century 'villa-castles' into 'visual prominence' over the city.[10]

In most cases the gardens created for these villas during this period failed to match up to those of the preceding three great centuries, with which middle-class entrepreneurs seemed to have lost all connection; nor did they seem to feel any more a need for a harmonious relationship with nature. Often large houses were built with small gardens that were no more than adjuncts, an ornamental setting for the house, a way of enhancing the overall outside view.

The first such villa-castle to be built in Genoa was Castello D'Albertis in 1886 (fig. 8.5), followed in the early years of the twentieth century by numerous similar constructions. This building, constructed in brick and stone on the earthworks of the sixteenth-century city walls, still remains – despite the urbanisation of Genoa – one of the characteristic elements of the turn-of-the-century cityscape. The outline of its crenellated towers makes it stand out, commanding and austere amidst the green mass of the park that unfolds around it and in keeping with the design of the ramparts and the shape of the steep rocky slope.

At the point where the slightly sloping shady path widens there is a pointed open arch which pierces the massive ramparts and leads the visitor through a dark tunnel into the garden itself. The garden, within the enclosing walls, is laid out with planted sections lined by walks that follow the irregular shape of the sloping hillside between tall trees, palms and shrubs. The visitor comes across statues, towers and rocks which suddenly appear in the midst of trees, along serpentine paths and at the frequent points where the paths widen. The steep gradient towards the valley gives the garden the appearance of a wood, with dense evergreen and deciduous vegetation. While limited

[10] Interesting examples of villa-castles continued to be built in and around Genoa into the early years of the twentieth century by the architect Gino Coppedè.

Fig. 8.4 Bruzzo castle, Genoa. An example of a neo-gothic castle placed in a panoramic
position overlooking the city

in size this landscape composition is precise in its placing of different forms of
vegetation and in its structuring of space. It creates a highly suggestive setting around
the castle and serves to accentuate the effect of eminence and isolation which the
designer sought to achieve: it evokes symbolic images from a medieval past, when
townships were protected by defensive structures built in isolated and inaccessible
spots. Here the forms of the castle, which in the romantic park had been decoration,
become the central elements in the composition.

In holiday residences along the Ligurian coast the interest in garden design coincided
with a widespread interest in nature, with the diffusion of naturalistic studies and with
the desire to acclimatise in the open air those plants, trees, shrubs and flowers which
were arriving in large numbers from overseas.

In holiday houses in the hinterland, on the other hand, the desire to possess a garden

Fig. 8.5 Castello D'Albertis, Genoa. The first villa-castle built in Genoa at the end of the
nineteenth century

coincided with the search for a natural secluded spot where one could isolate oneself.
At the end of the nineteenth century spending holidays in a villa with a park became a
widespread custom among the bourgeoisie. The construction of such spaces did not
reflect a desire to comply with new aesthetic canons or traditional compositional
modes; it was rather the response to the strong appeal of the plant world and – by taking
plants from various geographical regions of the world – it exploited the plant world's
potential for recreating surroundings closer to the state of nature.

   The large numbers of splendid trees which adorned these microcosms were different
from those which characterised the surrounding countryside. Often the large trees
became denser at the edges of the park, forming a kind of protective screen which
isolated the inside from the outside.

   The perspective axes that traversed the geometric spaces of the garden and
connected the villa with the cultivated countryside beyond disappeared. The hallmarks
of this Ligurian gardening art were: the variety of paths that defined space; the artifice of
rocky places such as grottoes, stairways, waterfalls, narrow passages cut out of
apparently natural rocks; the use of a large number of plants foreign to the local climate,
in particular all types of palms.

   At the end of the nineteenth and the beginning of the twentieth century the villa
with a park became an important landscape phenomenon as large numbers of

constructions invaded the holiday areas. Indeed, bourgeois families owning villas far outnumbered the villa-owning aristocracy of the past. This was a phenomenon which in a very short space of time introduced important transformations into a landscape characterised by ancient rural forms and long-established landscape images.

THE GARDENS OF THE WESTERN LIGURIAN RIVIERA

From the middle of the nineteenth century, with the coming of the railways and the improvement of the coast road several towns on the Ligurian riviera experienced a veritable tourist invasion on the part of a rich international public in search of 'eternal spring' and winter sun in the mild Mediterranean climate. This phenomenon evolved in close parallel with similar developments along the neighbouring Côte d'Azur.

The Ligurian coastal landscape was still marked by the presence of ancient rural villages perched on high ground, by cultivated land alternating with wild land of great naturalistic charm, and offered the many foreigners on the now classic 'Italian journey' attractions which corresponded to the ideology of the 'picturesque'. To naturalists and nature-lovers Liguria provided a large-scale laboratory for the study of geology, spontaneous vegetation, cultivated land and climate. In their diaries they reported on the flora of the Ligurian mountains, the productivity of the land, the mild climate, the rich coastal vegetation.[11] They painted or described in admiring tones the features of utilitarian gardens enclosed between walls, the terracing of slopes where citrus fruits, vines and olives were grown, where plantations extended to the slopes of hills strewn with villages, castles, churches and villas.[12] They talked of the 'affreuses beautés' of a landscape in which palm trees, lemon and orange trees dotted the countryside and the coast.

Members of the rich travel-loving international bourgeoisie were fascinated by this 'lande superbe cultivée comme un jardin'. They were struck by the 'oriental' appearance of the Ligurian riviera, dominated as it was by palm trees, citrus trees and olives. They desired to spend long periods on this coast where the climate, the sun and the sea were beneficial to health; where – as Henry Alford wrote[13] – the warm January days could be compared to the cool hours of a June day in England; where it was possible to acclimatise in gardens an infinite variety of flowers in the open air instead of inside greenhouses as in the cold Europe of the north.

In the space of only a few years the 'villes d'hiver' of Ventimiglia, San Remo[14] and Bordighera experienced a rapid increase in the number of big hotels and 'winter

---

[11] Liguria occupies an important position in the development of natural sciences and botany. Numerous local scholars and foreign travellers have described the botanical peculiarities of Liguria, in particular those along the region's coastline.

[12] E.g. T. G. Smollett, *Travels*, Letter xxv.

[13] For many years Henry Alford, dean of Canterbury, spent long resting periods on the riviera, and he described the western Ligurian coast in *The Riviera: Pen and Pencil Sketches from Cannes to Genoa* (London, 1870).

[14] In the period between 1874 and 1906, in the town of San Remo alone 25 new hotels and 190 villas were built to the east and to the west of the historical nucleus of the town and on the hillsides sloping down to the sea.

Fig. 8.6 A tourist poster of Bordighera, at the beginning of the twentieth century

residences' where people could stay for long periods between November and March. On the edges of old coastal towns palm-lined avenues, promenades and gardens were laid out; on terraces sloping down to the coastal strip, on fertile slopes exposed to the sun and with a panoramic view over the sea, hotels with large parks and many private villas with gardens rich in exotic plants were built.

Tree-lined promenades formed the natural extension of the private greenery of the villas. Embellished with the same plants used for the gardens, they contributed to the creation of those landscape images which are so characteristic of the riviera and which came to be identified with seaside holidays.

The first gardens on the Côte d'Azur and the Ligurian riviera were created by the English,[15] and applied the theories and compositional ideas of the landscape park and its

[15] Some years later Alice Martineau (*Gardening in Sunny Lands: The Riviera, California, Australia* (London, 1924), pp. 23–4), sought to explain this mainly English invasion of the riviera: 'In all countries, in all parts of the world, there is an

nineteenth-century developments. However, the use of exotic plants which were substantially different in shape and foliage from the vegetation to be found in English gardens, the light and colours of the coast, the numerous blooms introduced into the flowerbeds – these all produced a completely different landscape image.

Later, gardens no longer drew on precise stylistic canons and began to embrace other principles. They became places for collecting and, so as to enable the introduction of wonderful novelties, their creators began to seek environmental compatibility between plants and site. Illustrated catalogues displayed the wide range of exotic plants available for European gardens and in his or her layout of the garden the artist-gardener explored the possibilities offered by planting the numerous splendid and unusual botanical species coming from various regions of the world in different parts of the park.

Appropriate use was made of the characteristics of the terrain, and even the rockiest and least sunlit areas were turned to account by introducing plants capable of resisting heat and drought. The terrain was moulded and form and colour given to new 'picturesque' landscapes by exploiting the innumerable scenic possibilities of the exotic vegetation, and also by highlighting visual openings that revealed the sky and the Ligurian Sea.

The lessons of landscape gardening theorists were still valid, and the suggestions Ercole Silva gave to gardeners in his treatise were well known:

> When a gardener is given the task of executing and planting a garden, he will begin by studying the nature of the terrain he has to embellish. He will observe the contours of the site and the surrounding countryside which can provide him with lovely viewpoints . . . he will walk through it often in all directions and at all hours of the day so as to grasp the nature of the site . . .[16]

The best gardeners of the time were not only experts in cultivation techniques but were also artists; with their profound knowledge of horticultural practice they sought, like the German Ludwig Winter,[17] the creator of numerous public and private gardens in San Remo and Bordighera, to embody in the space of the garden what one could define as the age's 'new feeling for nature'.

The passion for botanical collections cleverly transformed holiday resort gardens into reproductions of landscape paintings of precisely those hot and sunny regions that had provided the trees, shrubs and flowers. The appreciation of nature found

---

ever-increasing migration from town to country on the part of the educated classes . . . For years the country cottage has been the refuge of many a weary brain-worker who, taking up gardening for relaxation, has found health in the pursuit. The discovery, and the delight of garden making, has so seized the human imagination that these gardeners must now go farther afield, where a more grateful climate will reward their efforts; and one of the outcomes of this migration has been a great invasion of the Riviera, both French and Italian, an invasion in which English-speaking people pre-dominate . . . Everyone wants to make a garden, but few know how to create one . . . Many amateur gardeners have bought their experience at a heavy price; others have profited by the mistakes of their friends.'

[16] Silva, *Giardini inglese*, p. 103.

[17] The German Ludwig Winter (1845-1912) played an extremely important role in the Ligurian riviera, both in the field of garden design and in introducing numerous tree species, in particular tall palms. His nurseries gained wide renown. His name is especially linked to the completion of Thomas Hanbury's grandiose botanical garden at Mortola: see below.

expression in an owner's scientific capacity to reproduce perfectly the variety and unity of nature present in the various regions of the world.

The owner and creator of the garden was the mediator in a technical and cultural operation whereby the characteristics of the vegetation contributed to the reproduction of idealised images of specific and bounded portions of the earth's surface. The reconstruction of 'orientalised' landscapes to be found in the most interesting and 'complete' gardens on the Ligurian coast was thus the result not only of the scientific idea of acclimatising plants but also of the creative mediation of history and nature.

These landscape compositions incorporated Australian eucalypti, large Virginian magnolias and every type of palm, all of which had a profound impact on the character of the gardens and the landscape of the Ligurian riviera. Complex structural work on the terrain and costly earth-moving operations modified the one-time terraced slopes, as the land was adapted to the great freedom of garden design forms and appropriate space was given to the extensive botanical collections.

Talking about the 'jardin du Midi', the theorist Edouard André emphasised that 'en presence de cette nature à profils heurtés, il a fallu adopter résolument le système en escalier, superposer les terrasses et imprimer aux jardins un aspect de construction. Tantôt les terrasses sont assez larges pour être traitées en parterres réguliers...'[18] As an example of a terraced garden he referred to the one being built at Bordighera by Charles Garnier, the architect of the Paris Opera House, at the time he was writing his treatise. This garden, called the 'palm palace' because of its numerous palms, both tall and short, and an extraordinary spontaneous palm forest which closes it off at the back, unfolds over a gradient with a difference of height of more than 80 metres and displays within it interesting architectural features and botanical rarities. Ramps, flights of stairs and terraces lend structure to the rocky slope. The tower-shaped villa stands out on the far side of the garden, thus keeping for itself the overall view of the garden, the sea and the Maritime Alps.

The exceptionally 'constructed' character of the whole is typical of many creations by the French architect on the Ligurian coast. It is not, however, a feature shared by other gardens where the slopes are shaped less radically, while still retaining some characteristic features of the morphology of the coast, such as grottoes, cliffs and scattered rocks. In San Remo the gardens of the Zirio, Ormond, Nobel and Emily private villas were laid out on gentle slopes enclosed between serpentine paths. The villa was always constructed on the highest part of the property to give it the best vista. The ground floor was raised to a panoramic terrace, supported by arches or grottoes. This classically inspired regular, geometric, sunny space stands in deliberate contrast to the gentle shaping of the slope of the rest of the park. Here, between paths and undulating fields, the garden design is very free, making it easy for the visitor to walk around and to get a better view of the numerous plants collected in the park. In contrast

[18] André, *La composition des parques*, p. 801.

Fig. 8.7 Villa Margherita di Savoia, Bordighera

Fig. 8.8 Villa Zirio, San Remo: a view of the garden with a huge ficus and numerous
luxuriant palms

to the regularly laid out garden and its axial branches, where the outstanding features
are architectural elements borrowed from the classical tradition: basins, statues and long
pergolas which define spaces where one can stop and behold the landscape, it is caverns,
rocky surfaces, basins of *rocailles* that make up the romantic–naturalistic parts of the park.

The main attraction of such gardens lies in their profusion of palm trees, placed in
areas of different shapes and sizes in order to show up the special quality and beauty of
the groupings of trees, lined up in majestic avenues which direct the gaze towards the
best vistas. Contemporary photographic documentation also shows the highly varied
tropical vegetation of these gardens, alternating with vast Victorian-style flowered
parterres of complex ornamental design. Deciduous trees which point their bare
branches skywards during winter were few in number in such coastal gardens. The
choice fell on trees that were interesting for their shape, their fruit or their blossoms.
The numerous outstanding gardens on the riviera were made possible by the

widespread interest in nature taken by numerous prominent English and German personalities and by the presence at Bordighera and San Remo of landscape gardeners such as Winter. He was not only the creator of the main public and private gardens on the coast but he also originated the trade in exotic plants that was later to become so important. The appearance of the coastline fully satisfied the foreign guests' desire for exoticism: diary entries frequently talk about arriving at San Remo or Bordighera and gaining the impression of having reached the coastline of Africa.

The landscape design of the parks shifted the cultivation of olives and citrus fruits farther up the hillsides. The rural buildings of the small villages found themselves next to an eclectic variety of villas and hotels that were often criticised by contemporaries for being out of keeping with the traditional surroundings. In 1887 Guy de Maupassant compared this type of architecture to 'oeufs blancs pondus dans le sable, pondus sur les rocs, pondus dans les forêts de pins par des oiseaux monstreux venus pendant la nuit des pays de neige'.[19]

Sites for villas were chosen according to the owners' appraisal of the panorama or were dictated by their search for a location suitable for the acclimatisation of plants coming from various climates. Sometimes, as in the Hanbury Gardens, the fortunate position of the terrain was able to fulfil both requirements. The botanical garden of the rich English collector, Thomas Hanbury,[20] is in many ways the archetype of 'acclimatisation' and holiday gardens[21] on the Ligurian riviera. While the garden's main focus was on collecting and acclimatising exotic plants, it also combined the themes and ideals of the exotic and the picturesque, the useful and the aesthetic. In addition to the extraordinary collection of about 6,000 cultivated plants in the open air, this garden also embodies the landscape ideals of nature as recreated by man in imitation of natural landscape, where the dominant theme is the diversity of different forms of trees and the colour contrasts afforded by the vegetation. But in this important garden the exclusively aesthetic idea of imitation is enhanced by a sense of the careful attention paid to the ecological principles of reconstructing numerous natural environments, an attention which anticipates modern movements in landscape ecology.

In the vast Hanbury estate, situated on Cape Mortola, the garden becomes a fantastic microcosm where spatial and temporal limits are obliterated, where an attempt is made to express the principles of unity in variety which govern the harmony and beauty of the universe, principles propounded by the great naturalistic geographers of the nineteenth century. Distant regions of the earth are present in the variety of their vegetation and architectural styles. The fascination with history takes on concrete form in archaeological finds, in inscriptions and statues which become part of the decoration of the garden. Local traditions and customs too are reflected in the long pergolas, in the

---

[19] Famous descriptions of the 'Côte d'Azur' and 'Riviera ligure' are in Guy de Maupassant, *Tutte le novelle*, edited by M. Picchi. I: *Sull'acqua*; II: *Appunti di un viaggiatore* (Rome, 1956).

[20] The Hanbury Gardens were purchased by the Italian State in 1960.

[21] This expression is the literal translation of the French term, *jardin d'acclimatation*.

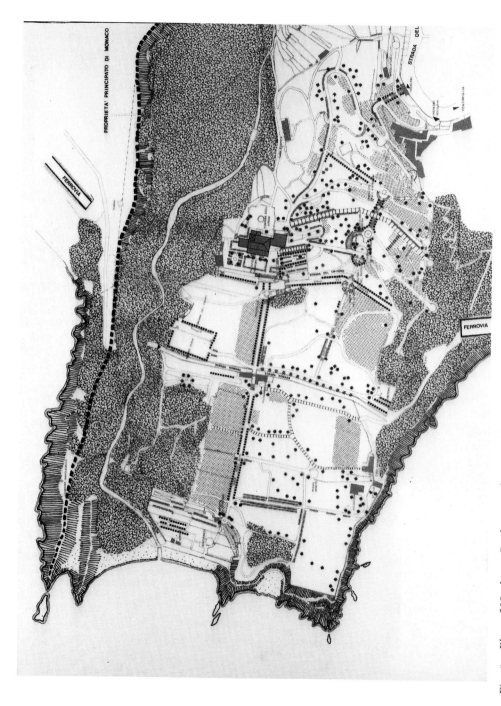

Fig. 8.9 Plan of Hanbury Gardens on the steep slope of Cape Mortola. The structure of the huge estate is shown clearly, with its Mediterranean vegetation, the straight avenues of cypresses, the long pergolas, the serpentine paths and the ancient Roman road (site survey and analysis by Francesca Mazzino)

paving of the paths, in the cultivation of citrus fruits, in olive groves and vineyards. Walking along the irregular serpentine paths, laid out on the steep slope, the visitor is presented with numerous and various views, which open up at the end of imposing straight avenues of cypresses or long vine-covered pergolas, or at the various stopping points.

These views reveal the landscape both inside and outside the garden. They present the architecture and decoration as symbols of the special relations that exist between man and nature; they offer literary quotations inscribed in stone as occasions for meditation on the evolution of the relationship between man and his natural environment; they invoke the concepts of 'paradise' which gardens have always expressed. 'Audiverunt vocem Domini Dei deambulantis in horto' is one of the inscriptions one finds as one walks along the garden paths.

Oriental civilisation, for example, has a place in the gardens: the owner's knowledge of the Orient, acquired during long stays there, is reflected in the Japanese bell, in the two lions next to the entrance, in the dragon and in the Moorish pavilion. These are symbols of civilisations which the owner – prompted by his memory – saw as expressing, better than any others, a love of nature and the interpenetration of garden and landscape.

Roman civilisation is also present in the form of numerous authentic archaeological finds that Hanbury had collected on his travels and which are proudly displayed along the Roman road – the ancient Via Julia Augusta – that runs through the vast estate. This road, unearthed during the construction of the site, came to form part of the compositional design of the gardens, together with their terraces, tall trees, pergolas, fountains and broad serpentine paths which mark off the areas set aside for various plants, according to display needs.

The collaboration between Thomas Hanbury and Ludwig Winter resulted in the creation of numerous areas in the botanical garden which succeeded in reproducing the beauty of particular aspects of tropical and subtropical regions. It led to two interesting fusions: one between the plants and flowers to be acclimatised and the traditional elements of the landscape garden, and the other between the sections which consisted of natural environment and those made up of agricultural land.

The old olive grove was preserved and the vineyard in the part near the sea was restored with great care. There was a flattened area where an extraordinary collection of citrus trees was introduced. In a section at the bottom of the valley Mediterranean *maquis* vegetation was preserved and reintegrated, creating a kind of 'natural reservation' with *Pinus halepensis* and appropriately transplanted trees (*Quercus ilex, Rhamnus alaternus, Cistus* ...) and shrubs (myrtle, rosemary, laurel, euphorbia, thyme ...). Small paths criss-crossed this area too, allowing the visitor to enjoy a corner of Mediterranean countryside in its wild state overlooking the sea – precisely the landscape whose luminosity, ruggedness, fragrances and colours had attracted so many foreign visitors to the Ligurian coast.

THE GARDENS OF THE EASTERN LIGURIAN RIVIERA

Towards the end of the nineteenth century and in the early decades of the present century also the eastern riviera, in particular the stretch from Nervi to Rapallo, saw the spread of holiday villas with large gardens. However, these holiday residences were different in character and they began to spread a few years later than in the west. The main difference was due to the morphology of the sites: the steeply sloping coast, the dense vegetation, the picturesque rocks and the small rocky inlets. Often the villa and its garden occupied a position facing and leading down directly to the sea: the steep rocks themselves became a garden, forming part of the park landscape, together with the sea and the hills at the back.

Here the gardens blend more into the natural landscape than in the west, and likewise the villa-garden is more isolated from its surroundings owing to the harshness of the slopes. For this reason even today the villas at Bogliasco, Portofino, San Michele di Pagana, Santa Margherita and Rapallo tend to be invisible from the road, isolated in the extraordinary landscape of the eastern Ligurian coast, enclosed within the recreated natural paradise of their gardens.

Again we have bourgeois residential estates, built with considerable means, according to the customs and fashions of the end of the century. Here too villa architecture made use of a repertoire that was foreign to local means of construction and building types. Eclectic forms were chosen that were similar to the cottage or the small castle. The gardens which replaced the cultivated terraces and the Mediterranean vegetation covered the hillsides until their upper limits reached the already existing woodland. New plants were also introduced in these gardens, but the emphasis was less on botanical collections and more on the relationship with the landscape.

In most cases, however, it is inappropriate to speak of the art of gardening, but of gardens which provide a splendid setting for the house. Gardening had become a tasteful and dilettante pastime that managed to achieve fascinating effects thanks to natural surroundings that were particularly generous in their spontaneous expression and scenic riches, and thanks to the skilful care of the artist-gardener. Despite the artificial nature of some effects, the garden 'harmonised' with the environment and, with time, gradually blended into it. In spite of changes in vegetation, on the whole respect was shown for the morphology of the terrain and there was a natural adherence to the lines that structured the landscape.

These gardens invoke the same elements and the same landscape compositions as in the western villas. There is similarity in the way buildings stand out against the garden, which is laid out with broad paths along the slope, with large areas set aside for exotic plants made available by a thriving nursery trade. Frequently one finds *rocailles*, grottoes with paths made deliberately difficult and picturesque by the presence of skilful artificial rock constructions and by a rich covering of vegetation. These shady spots contrast interestingly with the lightness of broad serpentine paths exposed to the luminosity of

Fig. 8.10 Villa Serra, Nervi, east of Genoa. The garden has replaced cultivated terraces, and merges with the existing woodland

the sky and the sea, belvederes and unexpected glimpses of the natural cliffs of the coast. Repeatedly we find the blending together of the exotic vegetation of palms, magnolias and cypresses on the one hand, and all those plants that fit happily into the rocky coastal landscape on the other – such as the tall umbrella pines typical of the Ligurian coast, holm-oaks, carouba, *Arbutus unedo* and the giant Pittosporum. As in the west, here too the fortunate exposure and climate have allowed the vegetation to grow in such a way as to provide quite different views today from those afforded by the original layout of the garden.[22]

INLAND HOLIDAY RESORTS

During the last years of the century in the hills of the Ligurian hinterland, within easy reach of the city, the phenomenon of the bourgeois summer holiday residences began to spread. It reached its peak at the beginning of the twentieth century and mostly involved Ligurians in search of a villa in the hills where they could enjoy the cool summer climate. The rediscovery of the natural landscapes of the countryside and the

[22] Villas with parks were also widespread in numerous other localities in eastern Liguria such as Chiavari, Sestri Levante and Lerici.

Fig. 8.11 Garden at Santa Margherita, on the eastern Ligurian riviera

love of gardens were certainly encouraged by the works of the Impressionists and also of the Macchiaioli,[23] whose paintings depicted scenes of bourgeois life set amidst a simple countryside, and were characterised by the search for contact with nature and the fusion of the everyday spaces of the garden with the large natural canvas of the landscape.

Here again we have gardens – this time in the countryside – recreating an image of nature that differs completely from the surrounding natural environment. It was the owner who decided on the type and characteristics of the building in which the family intended to spend the hot summer days. It was also the owner who decided on how to transform the surrounding space into a garden where they could live in contact with nature; and very often in this pursuit of naturalness he turned to other – as a rule Alpine – places for models.

Chestnut trees were replaced by fir trees, Lebanon cedars and cypresses which created dark patches on the landscape. Again large masses of rocks created shady paths, and formed grottoes, nymphaea and resting places overlooking the countryside; again

[23] The 'Macchiaioli' school of painting was an important Italian artistic movement which came into being in Florence between 1850 and 1860 as a revolt against the Academy and Purism.

Fig. 8.12 The belvedere of Villa Lo Faro, near Portofino

paths wound their way up slopes, imitating an often imaginary version of nature on a familiar scale, such as could be found in the paintings of Lega, Zandomenghi and Fattori.

Fig. 8.13 Nymphaeum at Villa Borzino, Busalla, in the hills of the Ligurian hinterlands

APPENDIX

The following works contain descriptions of Genoese and Ligurian gardens from the sixteenth century onwards.

Early publications

A. Giustiniani, *Castigatissimi Annali con la loro copiosa tavola della Eccelsa ed Illustrissima Repubblica di Genova . . .* (Genoa, 1537); J.C. Volkamer, *Nürnbergische Hesperides* (Nürnburg, 1708); M. P. Gautier, *Les plus beaux édifices de la ville de Gênes* (Paris, 1818-32), 2 vols.; D. Bertolotti, *Viaggio nella Liguria Marittima* (Turin, 1834), 3 vols.; F. Alizeri, *Guida artistica per la città di Genova* (Genoa, 1846-7), 2 vols.; F. Alizeri, *Guida illustrativa del cittadino e del forestiero per la città di Genova e le sue adiacenze* (Genoa, 1875); J. H. Bennet, *Winter and Spring on the Shores of the Mediterranean* (London, 1875); R. Reinhardt, *Palastarchitektur von Oberitalien und Toscana* (Berlin, 1886).

Recent publications

G. Masson, *Italian Gardens* (London, 1961, 1966), pp. 247–53; *Parchi e Giardini Comunali a cura della Direzione Giardini e Foreste e dell'Ufficio Stampa del Comune di Genova* (Genoa, 1964); *Catalogo delle ville genovesi*, Borgo S. Dalmazzo (1967, 1981); G. Masson, *Le ville del genovesato*, Istituto di Rappresentazione Architettonica della facoltà di Architettura di Genova (Genoa, 1983), 3 vols.; L. Magnani, *Tra magia, scienza e 'meraviglia': le grotte artificiali dei giardini genovesi nei secoli XVI e XVII*, Exhibition catalogue (Genoa, 1984); A. Maniglio Calcagno, *Giardini, parchi e paesaggio nella Genova dell'800* (Genoa, 1984); G. L. Gorse, 'An unpublished description of the Villa Doria in Genoa during Charles V's entry, 1533', *The Art Bulletin, 68* June, 1985; S. Ghigino and F. Calvi, *Il Parco Durazzo Pallavicini a Pegli* (Genoa, 1987); L. Magnani, *Il Tempio di Venere: Giardino e villa nella cultura genovese* (Genoa, 1987); A. Maniglio Calcagno, 'Giardini genovesi: la villa del Principe', *Spazio e Società. Rivista Internazionale di Architettura*, 41 (Jan.–Mar., 1988); A. Maniglio Calcagno, 'Ville e giardini genovesi', *Spazio e Società. Rivista internazionale di Architettura*, 43 (July–Sept., 1988); A. Maniglio Calcagno, 'La villa genovese del XV e XVI secolo', *Il Giardino Fiorito*, 6 (June 1988); E. Wharton, *Ville italiane e loro giardini* (Florence, 1991); G. L. Simonini, *Giardini italiani. Dal Piemonte all'Emilia-Romagna,*i: *Cremona* (1991), pp. 216–44; F. Mazzino, *Un paradiso terrestre. I giardini Hanbury alla Mortola* (Genoa, 1994); AA.VV., *I Giardini Botanici Hanbury* (Turin, 1995); R. Ghelfi, *Villa Marigola e il suo giardino* (Genoa, 1995); A. Maniglio Calcagno, *Il giardino di villa nella cultura genovese*, in *Attraverso i giardini: lezioni di storia, arte e botanica*, ed. G. Baldan Zenoni (Milan, 1995).

CHAPTER 9

SICILIAN GARDENS

GIANNI PIRRONE★

A GARDEN CALLED 'MYTH'

For those who continue to look for models in antique gardens, Marie Luise Gothein's categorical affirmation is still very much to the point: 'In the best period, when the other arts in Greece were rapidly advancing to their highest point of development, we hear nothing about garden culture'.[1] In order to dispel all doubt, Gothein 'scales down' the garden of Alcinous itself, tracing it back to the more reliable literary context of Homeric and Hesiodic mirages of fertility and 'eternal spring'.[2]

Sicily is part of these Hesperidian mirages: the solar *Trinachíe* of the pastures of Helios and fecund *Hortygía* (Odyssey XV, 404). But, if we set the myth aside to focus on history, Pierre Grimal rightly affirms 'that, as is natural, the first large ornamental gardens of the Greek world are to be found in Magna Grecia and Sicily'; he even goes so far as to classify them as 'models'.[3]

In 485 BC Deinomenid Gelon became ruler of Syracuse. A native of Gela and commander of the cavalry, his family were hereditary priests to the 'gods of the underworld' at Gela (namely Demeter and Kore, with a few Orphic appendages). At Olympia in 488 he was *hippónikos*, after becoming pindaric 'winner of the chariot race'. Ipponio, which lay almost within throwing distance of the walls around Syracuse, in the *contrada* of Targia,[4] was the place which, according to Athenaeus, Gelon later called the Horn of Amalthea, a magnificent grove embellished with swift flowing streams (fig. 9.1). Of this Gothein writes:

★Translated by Lucinda Byatt.
[1] M. L. Gothein, *A History of Garden Art* (New York, 1979), vol. I, p. 53.
[2] Ibid.
[3] P. Grimal, *Les jardins romains* (Paris, 1984; Milan, 1990), p.82.
[4] V. Amico, *Dizionario topografico della Sicilia*, 2 vols. (Palermo, 1757-1855), vol. II, p. 568. The location of the Horn of Amalthea at Hipponia (Vibo Valenzia), which has recently been suggested again, is not reliable. Gothein accepts this location, but Pierre Grimal does not.

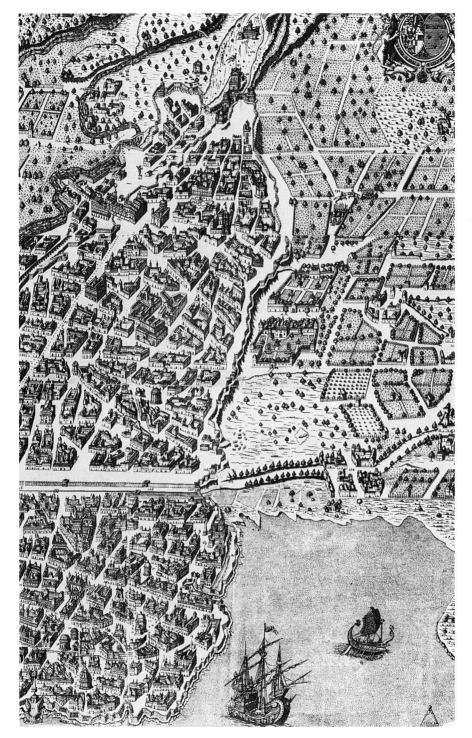

Fig. 9.1 V. Mirabella, *Pianta delle antiche Siracuse*, 1613 (detail) with 'Labdalo Fortezza posta nel principio di Tica' (top), 'Ipponio luogo di sollazzo' and 'Giardino Mittone, opera del re Gerone' (centre), 'Trogili' or 'Tragia' (bottom)

We can only take this to be a nymphaeum such as Homer described, one of those sanctuaries that included well-arranged trees, artfully enclosed water, and perhaps a grotto as well. What kind of water system was in Gelon's park we can only conjecture, but possibly the name *Horn of Amalthea* points to a fine waterfall, or possibly it only refers to the unusual fecundity of the place.[5]

Four centuries later, Pomponius Atticus took up Gelon's 'model' in Epirus. 'Why did the choice fall on Amalthea?' is the question Pierre Grimal asks himself.[6] The story of the broken horn which became *cornucopia*, and thus the symbol of abundance and fertility, is taken for granted. Pierre Grimal chooses to underline the Dionysian symbolism of this nymph, a marginal figure in the Greek Olympus. The goat, an initiatory wet-nurse, was in fact linked in chthonic and Bacchic terms to the Eleusinian mysteries of Demeter, who, it is worth remembering, was the central deity, the Great Mother of the Sicilian pantheon. But the horn also symbolised the flash of lightning. Amalthea in fact later became a leading star in the Auriga or Charioteer constellation. The key to this choice lies, I believe, precisely in the constellation of which this nymph forms part. The astronomical Auriga was depicted by the Greeks as a man holding a bridle in his right hand and a goat (or two kids) in his left: the *Capella*, the bringer of devastating storms or beneficial rain. The Charioteer knew how to master the passion and instinctive swerve of horses, thus symbolising inner equilibrium in the form of tension between opposing forces. His hand holding the reins is a perfect image of the 'knot' which unites spiritual and material forces: in Egypt the 'knot' was considered a symbol of life and Isis' 'knot' was therefore a symbol of immortality. Lastly, the Milky Way, which crosses the Auriga constellation, marks 'a frontier between the world of movement and immobile eternity',[7] thus enhancing the symbolic consequence of the whole. The bronze statue of the Charioteer at Delphi fully expresses this concept in his sidereal, almost hallucinated solemnity (fig. 9.2). It is this same statue that formed part of the dedication made by Gelon and Polyzelus at Delphi (c. 474 BC).[8] Emilio Paribeni has adopted a strange approch to the 'knot', almost as if to prise out its mystery: 'nothing can detract from the tremendous concentration, the secret reserve of the Charioteer, miraculously realised with edges as polished as crystal. Under such restraint, the vitality of the statue boils within like red-hot lava. . .'[9]

We know little more about Gelon of Syracuse: he was said to have been a good and generous man, which is already quite something for a tyrant; it is said that his rule represented a 'Golden Age' for Sicily. However, if his Hamáltheîon was a model, it certainly went further than being the superficial symbol of a conspicuous affirmation of power, or, on the other hand, the *hippónikos*' self-identification with the Charioteer. This is confirmed by Pomponius Atticus himself, whose gift of great equilibrium

[5] Gothein, *A History*, p. 61.   [6] Grimal, *Les jardins*, pp. 301–2.
[7] See J. Chevalier and A. Gheerbrant, *Dictionnaire des symboles* (Paris, 1982), pp. 86, 668–71.
[8] See B. Pace, *Arte e civiltà della Sicilia antica* (Rome, 1945), vol. III, pp. 723–31.
[9] See E. Paribeni, 'Centri greco settentrionali e greco pontici', *Enciclopedia Universale dell'Arte* (Florence, 1958), p. 877.

Fig. 9.2 Polyzelos, The Charioteer at Delphi, bronze, c. 474 BC. The inscription reads:
'Polizelos mi ha dedicato'

would be the envy of Cornelius Nepos: 'perpetua naturalis bonitas, quae nullis casibus agitur neque minuitur...elegans, non magnificus, splendidus, non sumptuosus'.[10] It was Atticus himself who, not having been *hippónikos*, confirmed, albeit four centuries later, that a garden could be created so that it became the faithful mirror of one's own personality and existence, the daily (and already humanistic) mentor of physical and spiritual well-being, 'secretly' linked to the cosmos and planets by which everything is governed.

Following the Deinomenids, Plutarch briefly mentions – as cited by Amico[11] – a Polyzéleios aulé which may perhaps have been built at the mouth of the Cassibile river near Leontinoi. The same Polyzelus, Hieron's 'much admired' brother who was involved in the Delphic dedication, was 'the founder or at least the owner of the villa'.

Equally intriguing is the garden belonging to Hieron I. The following entry appears in Amico's *Dizionario* under 'Fable':

> Garden of Hieron, King of Syracuse, created and planted at great expense before the walls of the said city; referred to by the Greeks as MYTHOS [the capitals appear in the text]; then as *Mitone* by Mirabella... It was here that the tyrant sat in judgement over the affairs of his people; wherefore Giacomo Avercampio affirms that the garden derived its name from *confabulation*.[12]

Myth, confabulation, fable; or again, speech, entertainment, dialogue . . . and lastly, orchard, garden.

A few years ago when Lionello Puppi came to talk on the subject of gardens in Palermo, he opened his paper by citing 'a very evocative passage' by Marcel Detienne. The latter 'insists on the ambiguity and ambivalence of mythical tales handed down by Greece and then attempts in turn to illustrate them with a story, which is in fact both parable and metaphor, involving the structure and image of the garden'.[13] Detienne significantly concludes his work *L'invention de la mythologie* with a description of Hieron's garden:

> On raconte qu'à Syracuse, dans les faubourgs de sa ville, Hièron ... avait aménagé un jardin magnifique, somptueux. Il amait s'y rendre pour traiter ses affaires. Le jardin d'Hieron s'appelait *Mythe*. Ironie à l'égard des audiences que le prince accordait à ses hôtes, ou, banalement, que c'était là son parloir, pour deviser entre les eaux vives, l'ombrage exquis de l'arbre à encens, et parmi les senteurs confondues de l'innocence et de la dépravation? La myopie seule nous empêche de voir que le *paradis* du roi de Syracuse faisait fleurir en toutes saisons l'espèce, hélas devenue introuvable, que de graves Observateurs de l'Homme, fâcheusement abusés par les écrits de certains botanistes, s'obstinent à confondre avec le chiendent ou je ne sais quelles herbes folles.[14]

[10] C. Nepote, *Le vite* (Milan, 1991) vol. XXV, pp. 9, 2–13, 4–5.
[11] Amico, *Dizionario*, vol. II, p. 377. [12] Amico, *Dizionario*, vol. I, p. 442.
[13] L. Puppi in *Il giardino come labirinto della storia* (Palermo, 1984), pp. 15–19.
[14] M. Detienne, *L'invention de la mythologie* (Paris, 1981), p. 242 and n. 42.

There is, next, the question of 'models': Xenophon had not yet been born at this time (Hieron died in 467 BC), and as a result his description of Cyrus' deeds in the *paradise* of Sardis was not available. Other sources and references must therefore have been used: Libyan, Egyptian, Phoenician-Punic . . . even if Sappho's song to her friend Arignota in faraway Sardis (98 Diehl) barely sketched the background ('. . . and the beautiful dew spread, / and the rosebuds opened and the suave chervil / and the florid yellow melilot . . .') given that we know that Sappho was in Sicily, in Syracuse between 604 and 595 BC.

Amico also tells us that at Epipolae, under the fortress of Labdalum, there was both a famous clock commissioned by Dionysius the Elder (405-367 BC) and the Royal Palace where plane trees, 'trees which had never been seen at that time', had been brought 'from the Island of Diomedes' for decoration.[15] Dionysius had planted other plane trees in his 'paradise' at Reggio, a palace surrounded by vast gardens (perhaps to exorcise the destruction and savage reprisals at the end of a long siege?).[16] This was 387 BC and Dionysius died twenty years later, viewed even by his detractors of antiquity as the 'saviour of Hellenism' in Sicily.

Hieron II (269-215 BC) completed the series with a gigantic ship-garden: the *Syracosía* ('Syracusan') was built in around 235 BC utilising Archìa's shipbuilding techniques and the genius of Archimedes. On the deck was a gymnasium and pathways in proportion to the size of the ship; flowerbeds of every sort, overflowing with the most beautiful and luxuriant plants, irrigated by hidden channels; pergolas of ivy and vines, planted in earth-filled barrels and irrigated in the same way as the flowerbeds, shaded the pathways. As for the *Haphrodisión*, it was large enough to accommodate three beds; its floor was paved in agate and other Sicilian stones and the walls were panelled in cypress. The 'doors were made of ivory and scented woods, and were beautifully painted. There was also a room . . . containing the library, and on the ceiling a sphere could be seen resembling that of the Sun, which is in Achradina'.[17] In Finley's opinion, 'the ship was useless for any purpose other than conspicuous display; Alexandria was the only harbour which could take it and so Hieron gave it to Ptolemy as a gift on the completion of its maiden voyage, and we hear no more of it'.[18]

But after the *Hamáltheîon*, why was a *Haphrodisión*, this prodigy of technology, then created? Was it perhaps in homage to the Egyptian Aphrodite in the sister land of the papyrus, or, in addition, the 'reinstatement' of an older Mediterranean Aphrodite? Without once mentioning Venus Erycina (which is after all only at the other end of the island), this question is answered by Biagio Pace. In brief, an unknown Sicel sculptor recarved Praxitele's chaste statue from Cnidus to create the immodest *'Landolina'* *Aphrodite* of Syracuse. Embroidering slightly maliciously on local gossip, it was

[15] Compared to Amico's assertion regarding the importation of the *Platanus orientalis* (at least from the Trèmiti), it is now accepted that an indigenous species existed in the south of Italy (Fenaroli, Giacomini, Pignatti).

[16] B. Caven, *Dionysius I. War-lord of Sicily* (New Haven and London, 1990; Rome, 1992), p. 194.

[17] T. Fazello, *L'Historia di Sicilia* (Venezia, 1574; Palermo, 1628), vol. IV, p. 87.

[18] M. I. Finley, *A History of Sicily. Ancient Sicily to the Arab Conquest* (London, 1968; Paris, 1986), p. 120.

considered a symbol of the sensual, curvaceous attributes of Syracusan girls. Pace himself therefore hypothesised the consequent presence in Syracuse of 'a sanctuary in which Aphrodite was worshipped together with Hermes'.[19]

Lastly, a handbook on agronomy is also attributed to Hieron II: this work is dated to a period shortly after the treatises by Theophrastus, a Greek, and Mago the Carthaginian.[20] This particular family passion (or luxurious pastime) appears to be brought to a fitting end by mixing cultures and aromas in gardens. Or, to borrow the words of Marie Luise Gothein again: 'Hieron II . . . probably links up with an unbroken tradition of princely gardens in Sicily'.[21]

'PALERMO, THE SO-CALLED PARADISE OF SICILY'

When Louis XVI was guillotined in Paris on 21 January, Domenico Scinà, abbot of Palermo, was just over a month short of his twenty-eighth birthday. Re-reading his biography we can relive the background to his works and plunge ourselves into full Siceliot hellenism with its emphatic interest in Empedocles of Agrigento, Archimedes of Syracuse, or bucolic verse (and Theocritus' *Jerone o le Grazie*): or even in *Hedypátheia*, 'the sweet taste', or manual of gastronomy, by the poet Archestratus, a native of Gela (fourth century BC).[22]

Among such wide-ranging predilections, Domenico Scinà, who was also physicist and geologist, found time to include a seminal work entitled *Topografia di Palermo*. In this he wrote of its 'accidental' fertility: 'The land around Palermo is a handful of fertile soil in the midst of piles of sand and tufa fragments, as might be expected of an ancient sea shore. And if it has a flourishing vegetation, with abundant trees and fruit, this miracle is entirely due to fertiliser, water, a large population and farming.'[23] But a deterministic ineluctability of 'site' prevailed over such physiocratic convictions, almost as if wishing to symbolise a causal relationship between the difficulties of husbandry and the ennobling (Arabian) contributions: the gardens and *solatii* at the two palaces at La Cuba, as well as at La Zisa, the Scibeni and Maredolce palaces and the park,[24] the Oreto, Cannizzaro and Eleuterio rivers, and fountains, springs and lakes like those at Favare, Gabriele, Uscibene, Danisinni, Averinga and Papireto (whose waters were said to derive miraculously from the Nile).[25]

[19] See Pace, *Arte e civiltà*, pp. 134–42.
[20] Finley, *Ancient Sicily*, p. 127; P. Lévêque, *Le monde hellénistique* (Paris, 1969), pp. 37–8. Amico also cites 'Gerone tiranno dell'agricoltura': *Dizionario*, vol. II, p. 517. On Mago and Carthaginian agriculture, see S. Lancel, *Carthage*, pp. 294–9.
[21] Gothein, *A History*, p. 77.
[22] On D. Scinà see G. Mira, *Bibliografia siciliana ovvero Gran Dizionario Bibliografico* (Palermo, 1881), vol. II, pp. 346–7; V. Di Giovanni, *La filosofia contemporanea in Sicilia* (Palermo, 1873; Bologna, 1985), vol. II, pp. 301–6.
[23] D. Scinà, *La topografia di Palermo e de' suoi contorni* (Palermo, 1818), p. 102.
[24] The extensive literature on the so-called 'Siculo-Norman park' focuses predominantly on architecture. An exhaustive bibliography is contained in G. Spatrisano, *La Zisa e lo Scibene di Palermo* (Palermo, 1982). See also G. Pirrone, 'Palermo, detto Paradiso di Sicilia', in *Ville e giardini XII-XX sec.*, with botanical and historical notes, ed. M. Buffa, E. Mauro and E. Sessa (Palermo, 1989).

Fig. 9.3 La Zisa castle, c. 1180. The hall (*iwan*) with fountain

As Leonardo Sciascia later wrote, this served to reveal, in a more realistic context, that the 'Sicily of water systems described by Idrisi, Ibn Hamdis and the other Arabian authors collected and translated by Michele Amari in his *Biblioteca arabo-sicula* . . . seems dreamlike to us' yet 'there are grounds for believing that the fable of the rivers of Sicily, Sicily's abundant water supplies, Sicily as the song and light of the waters, may have been started by Idrisi, the geographer'.[26]

As early as 972 (on the eve of the apogee of Fatimid rule), Ibn Hawqal, a travelling merchant from Baghdad, described the orchards and pleasure gardens along the banks of the Oreto river, then known as Wadi-al-Abbas (Abbas' river), and the doors of the *kasr* (castle) which were named after springs, health-giving fountains and gardens. Ibn Jubair, who visited *Balarmuh* in January 1185 (a few years before La Cuba and La Zisa were built) (fig. 9.3) described a 'marvellous city, built in the fashion of Cordoba' in which he 'walked from one garden and hippodrome to another'.[27] Henry Bresc would

---

[25] The third order of statues on the Fontana Pretoria in Palermo takes the form of four rivers, the Oreto, Maredolce, Papireto and Gabriele. See *Pantheon ambiguo. La Fontana Pretoria di Palermo* ed. G. La Monica (Palermo, 1987), pp. 156–74.

[26] See L. Sciascia, *Acque di Sicilia* (Bergamo, 1977).

[27] Ibn-Jubair, *Frammento del suo viaggio*, from M. Amari in *Journal asiatique* (1846).

later testify to the persistence of this 'atmosphere of an old Andalusian city',[28] leaving a wealth of information and studies on Palermo's gardens and orchards between 1290 and 1460 which virtually exhausted the available source material.[29]

Palermo, the elect, can therefore hardly avoid being identified with its Viridarium Genoard, or earthly paradise (which is the literal meaning of *genoard*): a garden which was the glory, symbol and emblem of royal power, but also a real image of a luxuriant – and orderly – nature which surrounded the city, and whose plants and waters penetrated the latter, finally reappearing and solemnly taking their place on the ceiling of Roger II's apartments in the mosaic iconology of the Royal Palace. 'In radiant gardens, accompanied by the garrulous cooing of doves, I have poured out / a well-matured wine, more exquisite than youth itself / Yes, I have made libations in a garden whose changing views and twittering birdsong charms the beholder /... Not to mention the splendour of those oranges suspended from branches like winecups borne by the cupbearer.'[30] The poet is anonymous, but was probably an emir in Palermo under the rule of the Kalbi family, together with numerous others, either exiles or Muslims, in an unredeemed Sicily: Ibn Hadmìs, or Abd-ar-Rahman as he was also known, from Trapani, could therefore write: 'Favara with its two lakes... Oh, splendid lake with two palms: oh, regal hostel surrounded by the lake!'[31]

However, this history of Palermo's gardens does not start, as might seem to be the case, in July 830 when the Arabs beseiged the city, nor does it end with the death of Federick II and his *viridaria*.[32] Once again, Fazello's words set the scene:

> This city stands on a plain running along the sea shore, which (as Herodotus confirms in Book VII) was known by the ancients as Litobello. Part of this city is washed by the Tyrrhenian sea, whereas the other three sides open onto a plain with large, flat fields which is completely enclosed by high, steep, harsh mountains, without a single tree... these form (you might say) a great Amphitheatre contrived by nature, and create a spectacular backdrop for those admiring them from the adjacent hills. These fields do not appear to be made of earth, but rather their wonderful forms look as if they have been beautifully painted, so that in whatever direction you look your eyes are wonderfully satisfied because the entire landscape is wide, beautiful, pleasant, varied, delightful and very fertile; and, above all, there is an abundance of oranges, lemons, pomegranates, and every other fruit. And there is also such a plentiful supply of corn, wine, oil and sugar cane that Ceres, Bacchus and every other planet responsible for preserving human generation vied against one another to make it fertile and beautiful,

---

[28] On the 'Andalusian' resemblance, in spite of the diversity and diachronous nature of the two 'reconquests', see H. Schreiber, *Halbmond über Granada* (Bergisch Gladbach, 1980; Milan, 1982).

[29] See H. Bresc, *Les Jardins de Palerme (1290-1460)* MEFRM, 84-1 (Paris, 1972) and 'Genèse du jardin méridional. Sicile et Italie du Sud. XIIe-XIIIe siècle', *Flaran* 9 (1987).

[30] U. Rizzitano, *Lezioni di storia e istituzioni musulmane* (Palermo, 1966-7) and *Storia e cultura nella Sicilia saracena* (Palermo, 1975), chap. 18.

[31] Rizzitano, *Storia e cultura*, pp. 267–89.

[32] On the *viridaria* of Federick II, see G. Agnello, *L'architettura sveva in Sicilia* (Rome, 1935) and *L'architettura civile e religiosa in Sicilia nell'età sveva* (Rome, 1961).

and to give it every possible advantage. This land is not only the most beautiful in Sicily, but in the whole of Italy. It is watered by wonderful fountains and sweet waters wherefore, owing to these perpetual springs and the lush greenness of its beautiful gardens, it gladdens the most melancholy and sorrowful spirit. Thus, in the 8th book of his History, as Athenaeus affirms in Book 12, Callias describes Palermo as consisting entirely of orchards owing to the abundance of fruit trees. It can therefore truly be said that it represents the delight and paradise of all Sicily.[33]

This is the lush image of a bowl-oasis, encircled by a harsh barrier of mountains, a bare wall which was formerly a desert and the watershed between the two Sicilies, namely the arid and the fertile areas: an 'enclosure' compared to the 'desert' of the sea and, beyond the mountain chain, the mythical *homphalós* of Pergusa, looking down towards the African sea, the arid kingdom of Ceres' granary. In this sense the 'flower-strewn meadow' in spring or the wild expanse of summer stubble or crops, and the worship of the divinities who rule them, are nothing but the 'arid', stereotypical counterpart of an (incredible) Sicily of the waters, which recently reappeared as the literary watershed between the 'damp' and the 'arid' (Quasimodo, Piccolo, Consolo, Frosini, Bufalino and Tomasi di Lampedusa, Sciascia).[34]

A closer examination of Fazello's description may be even more enlightening. The 'riviera', the 'Litobello', the city 'washed by the Tyrrhenian sea': this is a way of involving the 'desert' sea waters, which provide a permanent boundary to the plain, but at the same time broaden the landscape, almost as if allied with the 'high, harsh and steep mountains' in helping nature to 'conceive' the 'great Amphitheatre'. And the 'spectacular backdrop for those admiring them from the adjacent hills' is accompanied by pictorial observations which appear to anticipate 'Claudio' – in the same way that Goethe (and even Scinà himself) sometimes referred to Claude Lorrain.[35] The beauty of the landscape, which 'owing' to these perennial springs and the lush greenness of its wonderful gardens, 'gladdens the most melancholy and sorrowful spirit' is therefore considered as an aesthetic factor and the beauty and 'quality' of nature is seen as 'therapeutic'.

Piero Camporesi writes of a certain Scipione Mercuri, a doctor (who died in 1615), and the 'Belviso', or Belvedere which he created on the banks of Lake Garda. He also describes his diary, a work that 'is unequalled in the literature of the mid-16th century' and represents 'a rare and singular work' owing to its association of visual enjoyment with 'consoling therapy'.[36] If both these virtually contemporary observations, one by a

---

[33] T. Fazello, *L'Historia di Sicilia*, vol. VIII, p. 145.

[34] See V. Consolo, 'Il giardino di un poeta', Proceedings of the Congress, *Il giardino come labirinto della storia* (Palermo, 1984), p. 123.

[35] In his *Tagebücher* from Italy, Goethe mentions Claude Lorrain three times, including one occasion where he is referred to simply as Claudio (letter from Rome dated 19 February 1787). Scinà refers to the view of the Gulf of Palermo which His Royal Highness the duke of Calabria enjoys from his hunting lodge at the foot of Monte Caputo: 'From this height the eye sweeps over the landscape, the river, the city and running along the sea first encounters Bagheria, which delights as much as a beautiful landscape by *Claudio*' (the italics are in the text). See D. Scinà, *La topografia*, p. 21. On 'Le interpretazioni artistiche del paesaggio', see R. Assunto, *Il paesaggio e l'estetica* (Naples, 1973), vol. II, pp. 236ff.

[36] P. Camporesi, *Le belle contrade. Nascita del paesaggio italiano* (Milan, 1992), pp. 143–45.

Sicilian historian and the other by a Roman-Venetian doctor, are considered rare and singular, it is also worth underlining the equally rare coincidence of the common features which link the two extremities of Goethe's journey: Lake Garda and the Gulf of Palermo, both characterised by 'lemons' and landscape discoveries.[37]

Fazello's references to Callias and Athenaeus lead us back to Palermo, that strange Greek *képos* in a Punic setting, and, in all probability, to the many waterways and 'vast, well irrigated' gardens in Carthage seen by the Syracusan Agathocles and cultivated by Mago the Carthaginian. To the Greeks during the Hesiodic winters, this 'garden, orchard' or *képos* – as Athenaeus called the 'bowl' of Panormos – would represent a mythical Hesperidian garden. This was clearly not the utilitarian *pan-hórmos*, the 'all-port'. Its significance might differ if from the Greek *hormos* (derived from *eiro*, to 'wrap round') we were to adopt the meaning of 'necklace, jewel', already present in Homer, or 'garland' as in Pindar. Or if we were to follow Diodorus Siculus and his *liména kalliston* (XXII, 9) as he called Palermo's ports. Through the common root *slei*, *limén* or 'port' appears to be linked to water and gardens: from *límne*, 'lagoon, sea inlet, pond, swamp', to *leimón* 'a well watered, grassy field, pasture', or, by metaphor to 'extension, abundance, prosperity'; and, in general, 'that which delights the eye'.

GOETHE'S VILLA

Work on the construction of a public villa began in Palermo, along the sea front, in the spring of 1777 by the wish of the magistrate D. Antonino La Grua e Talamanca, marquis of Regalmici and, according to the project, by the architect Nicolò Palma.[38] The event was a source of inspiration to the Sicilian poet Giovanni Meli (1740-1815) and the closing lines of his 'anacreontic ditty' composed 'for the Magistrate Regalmici' have become proverbial.[39] Other sonnets were later dedicated to the villa itself: ' 'ntra ddi viali / d'arvuli e ciuri / jiri a tutt'uri / di ccà e di dda. / Lu friscu puru / di la marina, / ch'è assai vicina,/si godi ddà. . .'.[40]

The villa in Palermo, Italy's first public garden, was named 'Villa Giulia' or 'Villa del Popolo', but was also known more simply as 'La Flora' (fig. 9.4). Although the name 'Giulia' gradually became generally accepted over the years, this triad of names is still

---

[37] L. Puppi, *Verso Gerusalemme* (Rome, 1982) pp. 235-50 on 'Le Esperidi in Brenta'.

[38] See G. Pirrone, 'Palermo e il suo "verde"', in IEARM 'Quaderno 5/6/7' (Palermo, 1965), pp. 11–21, and 'Palermo: Villa Giulia, detta anche Flora o del Popolo', in *Il giardino storico all'italiana* (Milan, 1992), pp. 58–66; see Pirrone, '*Palermo, detto Paradiso*', pp. 240–255.

[39] 'L'abbundanza e scarsizza la fa Diu. / La pulizia l'à fattu Regalmici' ('God orders plenty and famine. "Cleanliness" [also in an aesthetic sense of order] was ordered by Regalmici'). See *G. Meli opere poetiche* (Palermo, 1982), p. 453. E. Caracciolo cites Meli and gives a historical and critical profile of the innovative work of Marquis Regalmici in R. La Duca, *Cartografia della città di Palermo dalle origini al 1860* (Palermo, 1962).

[40] 'among those avenues / of trees and flowers / you [could] wander at any time / to and fro / Even the breeze / from the sea / which is quite close / could be enjoyed from this spot.' These few verses expressed the enjoyment of free access to a public garden, immersed in nature and fanned by the sea breeze. Francesco De Sanctis later wrote of Meli: 'He had that divine faculty, granted to few – to Goethe and Manzoni – of spiritual equilibrium known as inner harmony.' See F. De Sanctis, 'Giovanni Meli' (conference held in Palermo on 8 March 1875) in *Saggi critici* (Bari, 1979), vol. III, pp. 187–218.

Fig. 9.4 N. Palma. Topographical map of the public Villa Giulia, engraving. Palermo, 1779

the subject of differing interpretations. The first name, linked to Giulia Avalos, wife of Viceroy Marcantonio Colonna, prince of Stigliano, to whom the villa was dedicated, was decidedly 'aristocratic'; the second was 'democratic' in opposition to the first, following the grumbling initially provoked by the obsequious dedication. 'However', as Villabianca remarked, 'having observed its warm reception by the populace and given that the villa had become one of the city's major attributes, it was again known as Villa Giulia'. Lastly, the name 'Flora' derived from its use as 'the place destined for the cultivation of flowers for pleasure, *Delightful orchard, garden, flower garden.* The public villa known as Villa Giulia in Palermo is called Flora or La Flora' – as Vincenzo Mortillaro affirmed in the *Nuovo dizionario italiano-siciliano* (Palermo, 1853).

There was a precedent for the homage paid to Giulia Avalos. Exactly two centuries earlier, on 25 April 1577, another Marco Antonio Colonna and his wife, Felice Orsini, made their triumphant entry into Palermo accompanied by great ceremony. On the beach, at the far end of the landing-stage, the couple were welcomed by an allegorical *mise en scène* representing the 'Golden Shell, the Epithet of Palermo, also known as the *Conca d'Oro*', in which stood 'the two statues of Palermo and *Felicitas*'. Four years after his arrival, Colonna ordered that the Cassero, the city's ancient main street, be prolonged as far as the sea. A new gateway was built which, as had been suggested by the allegorical programme, was named Felice after his wife.[41] In 1582 the same gateway was joined to that 'delightful road, to which he gave the name Colonna', running along the beach beside the walls. To Marco Antonio Colonna, the moral victor of Lepanto, it represented the ransom (at least in symbolic terms) from the Turkish and barbarian threat. But it also marked the 'birth' of the sea front, an (unconscious) anticipation of the discovery of the seaside promenade or, in short, the 'discovery' of the sea itself.

In 1754 the magistrate duke of Montalbo extended the promenade by demolishing a bastion, thereby creating a broader setting for the new promenade-villa system which was outstanding for the precocity of its town planning and scenic beauty (fig. 9.5). In many ways it represented the fitting conclusion, pushed right to the edge of the 'maritime theatre', of that operation of lacerating violence which had torn the ancient structure of the city. The straight cut made by Via Maqueda was the only one of its type in Europe and was intended to be a sign of the 're-establishment' of the new city plan whose 'cross-shaped' streets intersected in the main Piazza dell'Ottagono – also known as the Teatro del Sole. The symmetrical creation of four new street axes and as many new gateways onto the countryside or sea aimed to assign the role of panoptic measurer of the Conca d'Oro to the city's new four-square plan (and its internal cross).

Extra moenia, the square layout of the new public villa was therefore based on an idea of stabilising perfection which was all the more marked since its centre was represented by a circle and cross closely integrated with the square, in line with the ideal geometric homology of the city's intentionally square layout.

---

[41] On 'La rifondazione di Palermo nel Cinquecento', see M. Fagiolo and M. L. Madonna, *Il teatro del Sole* (Rome, 1981), pp. 126–35; G. La Monica, *Sicilia misterica* (Palermo, 1982).

Fig. 9.5 G. de Bernardis. Engraving of Palermo's sea front showing Porta Felice c.1815

The location of symbols within the villa, in particular along the east–west avenue, thus reflecting the line of the original Cassero, was equally homological and 're-establishing': a 'reproduction' of Porta Felice stood on the sea front; in the large central space, which corresponded to the seat of pretorial power in the city, stood a new Teatro del Sole, together with Palma's original design for a compass-card, and, later, the Putto-Atlas shouldering his dodecahedron, the axis of the world in the Hesperidean garden (fig. 9.6). To the west, against the backdrop of this new *kasr*, the fountain of the *genius loci* significantly replaced the Royal Palace, to seal and rule over this villa with its air of initiation. In 1778 the sculptor Ignazio Marabitti refashioned the mythical, archaic 'Genius of Palermo' (thought to be an ancient Afro-Egyptian Phoenician gnomon), using softer neoclassical lines (fig. 9.7).

Therefore, the homology was rooted even more profoundly in the chthonic myths of paganism, in the Pythagorean *tétraktys* and the most archaic and fabulous recreations of Hesperidean gardens in Sicily. While Eros snatched the golden apples before Heracles and the other Heroes who were with him, the Hesperides cried out loud and in their sorrow were transformed into trees: a black poplar, an elm, a willow. The list of the various arboreal species purchased for the villa in fact includes, as might be expected, 980 poplars and elms and 6,000 citrus fruit trees: bitter oranges being the only plants capable of actually displaying the mythical coexistence of flowers and fruits in the arbours, or *bersò* along the side paths, and a similar number of Hesperidean trees planted along the sides of the 'square'.

Fig. 9.6 Villa Giulia, central rotunda. Early twentieth-century photograph

It was from this 'paradise', this Garden of Eden, that Wolfgang Goethe looked 'uneasily' out over the gulf of Palermo and wrote 'the most unforgettable description of the Mediterranean landscape to be read in *Italienische Reise*'.[42] In a letter from Palermo dated 3 April 1787 he wrote:

> No words can begin to describe the vaporous clarity which hung around the coast on the wonderful afternoon of our arrival in Palermo: the purity of forms, the softness of the whole, the range of nuances, the harmony with which land, sea and sky were united. Whoever has seen this spectacle will treasure it in his heart for the rest of his life. Only now do I understand the paintings by Lorrain, and I hope one day, on my return north, to conjure up a pale image of this happy island in my spirit . . . I cannot begin to describe the way in which this Queen of Islands has received us – with mulberry trees in their freshest green, evergreen oleanders, hedges of lemon trees, etc. In a public garden I saw great beds of ranunculi and anemones. The air is mild, warm and fragrant, the wind gentle . . .'[43]

Sicily, the long coveted goal in the *crescendo* which accompanied his initiatory, tormented journey down the peninsula. This 'mania for Sicily' suddenly emerged at Naples: 'To me Sicily implies Asia and Africa, and it will mean more than a little to me

---

[42] See in J. W. Goethe, *Travels in Italy* (Milan, 1983), H. von Einem, p. 724; and again in Mira, *Bibliografia*, under the headings 'Paesaggio' (p. 821) and 'Antichità classica' (p. 827), the annotations by R. Fertoniani on the *Nausicaa* fragment. The English translations are taken from J. W. Goethe, *Italian Journey*, trans. by W. H. Auden and E. Mayer (London 1962).
[43] Goethe, *Italian Journey*, p. 228.

Fig. 9.7 I. Marabitti. Statue of the Genius of Palermo (1778). From '*L'Illustrazione Italiana*', 1908

to stand at that miraculous centre upon which so many radii of world history converge... in Sicily it will be even greener.'[44] In another letter from Palermo dated 7 April he wrote:

> I spent some happy, peaceful hours alone in the Public Gardens close to the harbour. It is the most wonderful spot on earth. Though laid out formally and not very old, it seems enchanted and transports one back into the antique world. Green borders surround exotic plants, espaliers of lemon trees form gracefully arched walks, high hedges of oleander, covered with thousands of red blossoms which resemble carnations, fascinate the eye. Strange trees, probably from warmer climes, for they are still without leaves, spread out their peculiar ramifications ...[45]

[44] Ibid., p. 221.   [45] Ibid., p. 235.

If the formality of its layout serves to limit fantastic mental adventures, what is the meaning and role of the *though*? In particular, in a villa whose late 'classical' style was already feeling the pressure of the vogue for the informal garden? But Goethe insists relentlessly: 'The enchanted garden, the inky waves on the northern horizon, breaking on the curved beaches of the bay, and the peculiar tang of the sea air, all conjured up images of the island of the blessed Phaeacians. I hurried off to buy myself a Homer so that I could read the canto in which he speaks of them.'[46]

On 17 April, the day before his departure, Goethe returned to 'his' public garden resolved to pursue his 'poetic dreams' (his Nausicaa). But the renewed sight of the plants 'growing freely in the open fresh air' (instead of being grown in pots or under glass) revived his 'old fancy' regarding the *Urpflanze*, 'the primal plant': 'Gone were my fine poetic resolutions – the garden of Alcinous had vanished and a garden of the natural world had appeared in its stead.'[47]

Oblivious of Alcinous – and oblivious of *The Odyssey* with which it had been identified,[48] and having revived interest in what he called 'my botanic philosophy', the public garden of Palermo was reproposed as a botanical garden, a reconstruction of the Earthly Paradise (a botanical garden was in fact laid out adjoining the villa in 1789).[49] But the long-lasting and veracious myth of eternal spring also applied to the Conca d'Oro, as was scientifically demonstrated a few years later by Domenico Scinà: 'and every month, except for July and August, the fields are dotted with new flowers'.[50]

Wolfgang Goethe left Palermo early in the morning of 17 April 1787. Among the papers on which he had composed the first draft of *Nausicaa* in the Villa Giulia (now in the Goethian archive in Weimar), he took with him the first two lines of the 'Anacreontic ditty' *Ucchiuzzi niuri* (*Little black eyes*) by the poet Giovanni Meli:[51] he would later include the same verses in his *Sicilianisches Lied*.

The 'elective affinities' were still far off. But not that far.

THE IMAGE OF FREEDOM

'The freedom of nature which is evident in the landscape, and likewise in its beauty, is cherished by the orderers of landscape gardens (whom Pindemonte believes to be Tasso's heirs) as a symbol of man's freedom . . . Nature free *from* man as the prospect of freedom *for* man, as *man's* freedom'; hence 'the garden seen as an image of freedom.'[52] While, in Rosario Assunto's works it may be licit to adapt this definition to 'freedom as

---

[46] Ibid., p. 236.

[47] Ibid., p. 258.

[48] On Goethe's identification with the figure of Ulysses, see H. Tuzet, *La Sicile au XVIIIe siècle vue par les voyageurs étrangers* (Palermo, 1988), p. 131.

[49] See Pirrone, 'Palermo e il suo "verde"', pp. 21–8; and also '*Palermo, detto Paradiso*', pp. 206–16.

[50] See Scinà, *La topografia*, p. 54 and note 191. On the subject of the 'imperishable flowering', see R. Assunto, *Il paesaggio e l'estetica* (Naples, 1973) vol. II, pp. 187–95.

[51] See *G. Meli opere*, pp. 385–7.   [52] R. Assunto, *Il paesaggio e l'estetica*, pp. 233–41.

an image of the garden', the appropriately named Viale della Libertà in Palermo (1848) and its Giardino all'inglese (1851) should be seen as an image of both the garden and of freedom. This use – or, rather, instrumental abuse – of the transitive property might prove to be not entirely arbitrary if aimed at inverting a thesis: the street is democratic given that it was created by a revolutionary act; a garden, on the other hand, is a symbol of reactionary restoration in that it was ordered by a Bourbon lieutenant, Carlo Filangeri, prince of Satriano.

Some forty years later, Pollaci Nuccio returned to the question:

> Although the memory of Satriano is not cherished by the Sicilians, it is nonetheless right to give him the praise he deserves. He was not a native Sicilian and represented a government which reverted the island to loathsome submission, but he nonetheless continued (the fact cannot be denied) a public work commenced by the revolution for the ornamentation of the city and oversaw it with commitment. Today Palermo can enjoy the results, and for this it is also indebted to the son of Gaetano Filangeri.[53]

But, after having created the first 'backdrop' in the form of the Giardino Inglese, Satriano had identified a second objective, which was already implicit in the change of names following the restoration from 'Strada della Libertà' to 'Strada della Favorita' (fig. 9.8).[54] In fact, this 'Royal Park' (1799) would give rise to new roads and leisure areas in Palermo; namely, the same pleasure of 'free time' to which fate would destine La Favorita – opened to the public after 1860 – and, at the turn of the century, the opening of the first bathing resort on the splendid bay of Valdesi-Mondello. We are here at the intriguing intersection of elite and popular, freedom (liberty) and absolute power, garden and city. To understand these congeries it is worthwhile returning to a passage in the resolution passed on 16 March 1848 to mark out the route of Via della Libertà: 'so as to reconcile the two ideas of giving work to the populace and adorning the city, it is hereby resolved to open the street *which has been proposed many times, at different epochs, but has never been implemented*' (author's italics). The accidental finding of a cutting from the newspaper *Il Gatto* dated 13 June 1848 gives details of both the times and the epochs of these proposals: in 1812 and 1821. 'The constitution of 1812', which, Rosario Romeo comments, 'represented the triumph of a conception inspired by modern liberty based on the world of *ancient freedoms...*' was followed by the 'repudiation' of 1816 and the Sicilian rebellions of 1820.[55]

Following the abortion of the Libertà project, Palermo saw the construction of the villa at Papireto for the marquis of S. Pasquale in 1831 and in 1834 the semicircular villa in Piazza Vittoria designed by the architects Puglia and Raineri: both were later

---

[53] F. Pollaci Nuccio, *L'Esposizione Nazionale e le sue adiacenze* (Palermo, 1892).

[54] On the park of La Favorita and on the Giardino inglese, see Pirrone, 'Palermo e il suo "verde"', pp. 28–30, 39–46; see also Pirrone, '*Palermo, detto Paradiso*', pp. 170–78, 187–97.

[55] R. Romeo, *Risorgimento in Sicilia* (Bari, 1973), pp. 152ff see also D. Mack Smith, *A History of Sicily* (Bari, 1970), pp. 435–583.

Fig. 9.8 Viale della Libertà, 1848. *La promenade*. From *Igiea: guide de Palerme*, 1909–10

destroyed during the 'war of factions' of 1848[56] (in the same way as the Botanical Gardens were destroyed in 1821).

Events in the island were more complex. To start with, in precisely the year 1821, Caltanisetta appears to have been the first in the series: a 'delightful, public villa' was constructed, on this occasion by the King of the Two Sicilies himself, Francesco I, in particular it would seem, to create work for the vast numbers of workers unemployed after the popular uprisings the previous year. Should the garden therefore be seen as an image of the restoration?

A 'promenade villa' (*villa da passeggio*) was built at Piazza Armerina around 1847, and another was laid out in 1845 at Termini Imerese with a belvedere overlooking the gulf of that name. Likewise, at Agrigento in 1850 a public villa was built whose 'surprising' position 'offers. . . an extremely attractive view to the south overlooking a calm blue sea' and 'a promenade of considerable length and breadth which showed the magnificent monuments of the ancient city. . .' The sea had again come to the fore. A 'pleasant promenade about half a mile long, adorned with trees and a large basin' was laid out in 1847 along the sea front at Mazzara. Other 'most pleasing' promenades were created by demolishing the fortifications at Milazzo in around 1853.

The same period saw the creation of a public promenade in Syracuse, 'adorned with

[56] See Pirrone, 'Palermo e il suo "verde"', p. 50.

Fig. 9.9 G. B. F. Basile. Panoramic view of the Villa Comunale, Caltagirone

orderly trees and flowers, running along the sea front . . . and during the summer evenings sweet music was played for the entertainment of the people'. In Catania, 'the square on the sea front was decorated and divided into a graceful pattern by trees which formed avenues embellished by granite columns, supporting lamps, and marble seats; the promenade was illuminated on summer evenings and musical bands played for the citizens' entertainment on Thursdays and on holidays'.[57]

Lastly, in perfect synchrony with Palermo, it was decided to construct a public villa in Caltagirone, even going so far as to draw upon the Botanical Garden in Palermo which had supplied the plants for the Giardino inglese and (at the suggestion of the director, Vincenzo Tineo) the same designer, the architect G. B. Filippo Basile, lecturer at the Botanical Garden (fig. 9.9).[58]

On 27 April 1853 the *Giornale Officiale di Sicilia* dedicated two columns to a description of spring which appears to have been particularly radiant that year: 'the

[57] See G. Di Marzo, notes to individual headings in Amico, *Dizionario*.
[58] S. Bruno, *Il giardino comunale di Caltagirone di G.B.F. Basile* (Palermo, 1990) (with archival documents).

"Giardino Inglese" which runs along the magnificent street of the "Real Favorita" is especially enchanting; it is always delightful, but particularly so this month when the winding paths are shrouded with roses, the rounded hills and gentle slopes are covered with that variegated vegetation which reveals the fertility of the soil in which plants from every region become acclimatised and grow strong and luxuriantly' (fig. 9.10). Maximilian of Habsburg, visiting Palermo in May 1852, went even further: 'A fairytale dream, a basket of flowers [*Blumenkorb*] overflowing with scents and fragrance in a large and wonderful shell: this is delightful Palermo.' He was fascinated by La Flora (Villa Giulia) and the Botanical Garden with its new *Bougainvillea spectabilis*, which he described as 'this garden's most precious jewel'. But he also observed:

> In the vicinity of Palermo is Olivuzza, another of Sicily's paradisiacal residential quarters. Whoever wishes to enjoy the perfection of all nature's beauties, the height of garden art, the quintessence of all floral grace, as only the luxuriant abundance of the most fortunate of countries can offer to man, should visit Villa Butera here in Olivuzza in the full splendour of May.[59]

This description was also borne out by Count Fedor de Karaczay in 1840: 'La jolie *Villa-Wilding*, dans le faubourg Olivuzza et son jardin anglais, très riche en plantes exotiques de toutes les parties du monde, meritent d'être visités. Cette plantation et la maison meublée avec beaucoup de goût et d'élegance, font les délices du prince Butera, botaniste passioné.'[60] Olivuzza, where 'you breathe the purest air in the whole region of Palermo', later housed the Russian Imperial Court in 1845-6, 'when Palermo was chosen as the most suitable place in Europe to cure the delicate health of Alexandra Feodorovna, August Empress of all the Russias . . .'[61]

The Giardino inglese (an offshoot of Palermo's Botanical Garden) appeared at that time to represent the emblematic *summa* of these remarkable 'amateur' precedents and, at the same time, the future popular model. The second half of the nineteenth century would in fact see the greatest changes in 'classical' gardens and the introduction of new fashionable layouts. Created as squares between 1860 and 1863, the Garibaldi Garden (also designed by G. B. Filippo Basile) was laid out in Piazza Marina,[62] together with another in front of Benjamin Ingham's house: these initiatives deserve a detailed examination, not only on account of their public/private distinction.

It is as if poles of attraction had suddenly been created on top of the previous pattern of seventeenth- and eighteenth-century villas. One of these was certainly the famous Olivuzza area (which perhaps found its strongest attraction in the nearby 'esoteric' La Zisa) with the Butera-Wilding, Serradifalco, Belmonte, Pignatelli Monteleone, Florio and Whitaker Malfitano villas. Another, like that along Corso Calatafimi, was centred

---

[59] Maximilian of Habsburg, *Aus meinem Leben* (Leipzig, 1867; Trieste, 1986), pp. 209–30.
[60] F. de Karaczay, *Manuel du voyageur en Sicile* (Paris, 1840), p. 99.
[61] Di Marzo, notes in Amico, *Dizionario*, p. 234.
[62] See Pirrone, 'Palermo e il suo "verde"', pp. 46–56.

Fig. 9.10 The Giardino inglese. Photograph of the avenue from the early twentieth century

on Villa d'Orleans and the 'romantic' gem of Villa Tasca (figs. 9.11-12). Likewise the hills could boast a superb sequence facing La Favorita in the form of villas such as Villa Mazzarino, Bordonaro, Castelnuovo; or Villa Sofia belonging to Renato Whitaker, which in the 1891-2 National Exposition of Palermo almost succeeded in routing the undisputed supremacy of the Botanical Gardens – which already in 1854 possessed 24,000 exotic plants. Lastly, overlooking the Giardino inglese, the park belonging to the princes of Trabia possessed an equally well-known orchid and palm collection.[63]

Albeit sketchily outlined, against this patchwork or 'leopard skin' background in which the citrus fruit orchards of the Conca provided the basic connective tissue, the Strada della Libertà succeeded in reaching and surpassing the objective set by Satriano, and preserved up until the 1930s the prerogative of being a garden 'among gardens', a 'prospect' as the image of Freedom.

As Onufrio had in fact already commented, 'Via della Libertà, *which everyone referred to as the 'Giardino Inglese'* [author's italics], should be visited in the evening. . .'[64] Without

<hr>

[63] For the places mentioned, see Pirrone, 'Palermo e il suo "verde"', pp. 28–30 and *'Palermo, detto Paradiso'*. On the gardens of the English colony in Palermo (and Sicily) see C. Quest-Ritson, *The English Garden Abroad* (London, 1992).

[64] E. Onufrio, *Giuda pratica di Palermo* (Palermo, 1882), pp. 26–27.

Fig. 9.11 Villa Camastra-Tasca, showing the villa and *parterre*. Oil painting of the first half of the nineteenth century

Fig. 9.12 Villa Tasca. *Il lago dei cigni*. From *L'Illustrazione Italiana*, 1908

needing to resort to Kevin Lynch and his 'environmental image',[65] this was confirmed by Fulco di Verdura: 'This *Giardino Inglese* is really neither a garden nor English. It was, and still is, a beautiful long avenue lined with plane-trees. Its real name is *Viale della Libertà*, but no one ever referred to it as such.'[66]

This avenue, the Giardino Inglese and La Favorita – for we are now talking about this century – were the setting for the Corsi dei fiori (flower processions) and the Sicilian Spring, a munificent tourist attraction devised by the Florio family; likewise, another esoteric floreal image of the Conca d'Oro as the garden of the Hesperides would be added to a vast pictorial cycle as part of the large paintings in the hall of Villa Igiea – also property of the Florio family.[67]

In 1927 the Royal Commissary of the Autonomous Institute for Tenement Housing declared that the new garden quarter at the end of Viale della Libertà was intended to meet 'the citizens' resolute desire that Palermo should also see the creation of a Garden City'.[68] This corollary was, however, almost too obvious owing to its location along a road that was also a garden: a repetition, in another epoch but along the same site, of G. B. Filippo Basile's design to build up around the Giardino inglese 'a modern quarter which would revive the memories of an exquisite art'.[69]

[65] K. Lynch, *The Image of the City* (Cambridge, Mass. 1960; Padua, 1964).

[66] Fulco di Verdura, *A Sicilian Childhood. The Happy Summer Days* (London, 1976; Milan, 1977), p. 164.

[67] See G. Pirrone, *Palermo, una capitale. Dal Settecento al Liberty* (Milan, 1989), pp. 116–29.

[68] See Pirrone, *Palermo, una capitale*, pp. 230–1.

[69] Ibid., p. 264; see also G. Pirrone, *L'Isola del sole. Architettura dei giardini di Sicilia* (Milan, 1994), pp. 146–71.

CHAPTER 10

JAPPELLI'S GARDENS: 'IN DREAMS BEGIN RESPONSIBILITIES'[1]

RAYMOND W. GASTIL

The English landscape gardens designed by Giuseppe Jappelli in early nineteenth-century Italy are so encrusted with the leavings of a long, hard century that it is difficult, at first, to see more than nostalgia amidst the yellow grass and the sham ruins made real by neglect. Jappelli's gardens, mostly in and around Padua, with an exceptional exercise in Rome, have lost a good deal of the props that energised their regenerative theatre, even as our late twentieth-century minds inevitably have lost the sensibility to comprehend much of the scenic intent. In the still private garden of Saonara, the celebrated grotto collapsed fifty years ago under Allied bombing. In the Parco di Treves, now a fully public park, many of the monuments remain, but the scattering of syringes around them, together with the angry graffiti of 'Fuori i tossico!' make Jappelli's delicate scenography appear rather lame alchemy. And at the Villa Torlonia in Rome, where Jappelli had laid out a literary *percorso iniziatico* for the prince and his guests, today's bureaucrats have established a *percorso attraversato*, a jogging and exercise track weaving among the hillocks, ruins and broken greenhouses that remain of Jappelli's intentions.

For all their crudeness of technique, the heroin and push-ups of this generation do illuminate the glades and grottoes of Jappelli's time. Drugs and exercise, in the garden and elsewhere, transform their adepts, take them out of the banal into a heightened sensibility, wherein it is possible to imagine a new, more powerful relationship with the world. And while Jappelli may have engaged in erudite reference along his garden paths, he, too, relied on surefire effects to generate that heightened sensibility – dark caves, frightening statues, startling views.

The difference, of course, lies both in the path – how you get high – and in the exit – how you come down. Jappelli and his peers intended more than a temporary

---

[1] The title is borrowed from the collection of short stories by Delmore Schwartz, *In Dreams Begin Responsibilities* (New York, 1938). This chapter was written with the support of Princeton University's Italian Studies Grant programme and the Dumbarton Oaks Summer Fellowship in Landscape Architecture Studies, with invaluable contributions from Dr John Dixon Hunt, Professors John Pinto, Allesandra Ponte and Georges Teyssot at Princeton University; and Drs Giuliana Mazzi and Franca Pellegrini in Padua.

intoxication: the sensate, intelligent visitor to the English landscape garden could follow an initiatory route meant to leave him with a permanently altered view of his relationship to nature and society. One entered the garden, envisioned the remaking of the world, and took the vision back to the everyday.

Jappelli's gardens *were* an escape from the world as it was. Not only did he invent new things, but he juxtaposed them in new relationships: a hill was next to a lake where once had been a plain, an exotic palm flourished next to a native pine, while a new, bric-a-brac mock-ancient tower rose next to a venerable ancient one. And if the unimproved landscape could serve as a level playing field for *things*, certainly it could offer the same occasion for *people* – princes, clients, friends, architects. Within the landscape garden, their relationships to history, place and one another could be reinvented.

The game was only fully played when visitors, as well as the proprietor, could successfully undertake the initiatory path, stop at the right places, feel the right things. The most critical element for the visitor's sensibility was the capacity to appreciate both the immediate and the associational, and to suspend disbelief – in the right way. One might recognise the physical artifact as fakery, and even admire the skill applied in manufacturing history or nature. But if one did not take the associated train of thought that interpreted the physical artifact as a valid metaphor of reconfigured social relationships, the garden was not working.

Jappelli's gardens offer a range of evidence of this way of thinking: as an ideology it is hardly unique to his designs, but his execution is especially adroit, and often refers to the most direct initiatory strategy of his time, that of the fraternal cults, especially the Freemasons, which will be discussed more fully in relation to the specific garden designs.

In addition, Jappelli's gardens stand out for the requirements they make on the client, guest and tourist. For all their showmanship, the garden and the cult offer an extraordinarily demanding vision: one could plant mature trees in new soil, one could imagine a new arrangement of place and history, one could construct a new self and a new fraternity, but then one had to live up to the reinvented role and take responsibility for the dream.

JAPPELLI'S INITIATION INTO THE ENGLISH GARDEN[2]

Jappelli's first biographer, Andrea Citadella Vigodarzere, a second-generation client and friend, described Jappelli's formative moment as a designer of gardens as an almost

---

[2] Several publications have been crucial for understanding Jappelli's garden designs and overall career through their texts, citations and illustrations. These include the seminal essay by Lionello Puppi, 'Jappelli: Invenzione e scienza, architetture e utopi tra rivoluzione e restaurazione', *Padova: case e palazzi*, ed. L. Puppi and F. Zuliani (Vicenza, 1977); Barbara Mazza, *Jappelli e Padova* (Padua, 1978); both volumes of *Giuseppe Jappelli e il suo tempo* (Padua, 1982), edited by Giuliana Mazzi; Paola Bussadori and Renato Roverato, *Il giardino romantico Jappelli* (Padua, 1983); M. Azzi Visentini, *Il giardino veneto tra Sette e Ottocento e le sue fonti* (Milan, 1988); idem, *Il giardino veneto dell'Ottocento, da Giuseppe Jappelli a Antonio Caregaro Negrin* (Milan, 1991).

mystical inspiration. In brief exile for his Napoleonic service, stationed at the Picenardi brothers' garden in Torri, near Cremona, Jappelli in his biographer's vision, suddenly saw his new mastery: 'si svegliasse in lui quella maestria nel comporre giardini, ignota prima'.[3]

Citadella Vigodarzere's version may be apocryphal, but Jappelli did visit the brothers' English landscape garden and he did begin designing landscape gardens soon after, usually with the same uninhibited taste for effect that the Picenardi twins had shown. The merchant brothers had turned their drab patch of ground into a wonderland of allegory and allusion, starting around 1780 with only one genuine twelfth-century ruin to go on, adding amphitheatres, Palladian arches, a pyramid, and a dozen other monuments of late eighteenth-century taste, with the literary flourish of inscriptions taken from Ariosto's epic, *Orlando Furioso* (c. 1502).

Jappelli must have been charmed by the effect, and may have contributed to it in turn. In doing so, he participated in a sensibility that valued the English landscape garden as a site for almost unlimited scenography. Dull ground became a fabulous garden, merchant brothers became cultured sophisticates, engineers became garden designers. Furthermore, for all its erudite references, the brothers' private garden was meant to be known and understood by the public. The owners promoted the garden again and again, just as Jappelli's later clients would promote their gardens through guides, letters and lithographs. In 1791, a guide to the antique inscriptions at Torri was published; in 1819, the letter of a 'cultivated young woman' was published as an introduction to the garden, and in 1820 the Picenardi themselves published a new guide.[4] The private refuge was a public forum, mystery existed to be demystified.

Jappelli was well prepared to find himself as a designer of English landscape gardens. His professional training as an engineer and architect, together with the political and intellectual setting of his time, suited him for the mix of technical knowledge, scenographic inspiration, and architectural facility required. Furthermore, with his youth spent at the hinge of the two centuries, rebirth and transformation were more than pungent metaphors to him: citizens of the Veneto saw their region reinvent its political identity a half-dozen times from the French Revolution to Napoleon's fall. Jappelli was in the thick of it, just as art and science, both in his grasp, were at the service of each new regenerative drama.

Born in Venice in 1783, Jappelli went to secondary school in Bologna, receiving his diploma in 1800 from the Accademia Clementina and returning to Venice where he

---

[3] Andrea Citadella Vigodarzere, 'Elogio di Giuseppe Jappelli', *Rivista dell'Accademia di Padova* (1854), cited in Paolo Carpeggiani, *Giardini cremonesi fra '700 e '800: Torre de' Picenardi – San Giovanni in Croce* (Cremona, 1990).

[4] The guide books and descriptions of the Torri garden include: I. Bianchi, *Marmi cremonese, ossi ragguaglio delle antiche iscrizione che si conservano nella villa delle Torri de' Picenardi* (Milan, 1791); G. Tiraboschi, *La Famiglia Picenardi, ossia notizie storiche intorno alla medisma* (Cremona, 1815); C. Fassati Biglioni, *Reminiscenze della Villa Picenardi. Lettera di una colta giovane dama che può servire a guida a chi bramasse vistarla* (Cremona, 1819); and Picenardi, *Nuova guida di Cremona* (Cremona, 1820). *Marmi cremonese* and *La Famiglia Picenardi* are reprinted in Paolo Carpeggiani, *Giardini cremonese fra '700 e '800: Torre de' Picenardi - San Giovanni in Croce* (Cremona, 1990).

frequented the studio of Giovanni Valle, and possibly that of the renowned neoclassicist Giantonio Selva, acquiring his professional accreditation in 1803. Two years later Napoleon reclaimed control over Venice, and at the same time Jappelli, according to his testimony to the Habsburg officials twenty years later, became a Freemason.

In his renunciation of Freemasonry in 1826, Jappelli explained his induction as a youthful indiscretion.[5] Yet his move appears less the act of an impressionable 22-year-old than the decision of a sensible professional. In the Italy of the time, Napoleon had created new lodges of Freemasons as one way of harnessing the goodwill that his ostensibly progressive programme engendered among professionals and other reformists. Jappelli's access to Napoleonic elite that controlled the public works projects could not but be improved by joining such a lodge.

In some accounts, when Jappelli was first documented as a professional in Padua in 1807 (as an engineer, second class) the city's coterie of Freemasons welcomed him as their own designer.[6] In any case, Jappelli, as he finished his professional formation in Venice, had become part of a culture which valued synthetic relationships, rather than those simply of family and history, and understood the array of tools available to create them, including the garden and the cult. Whether or not he kept any formal ties to Freemasonry, Jappelli had embarked on a way of thinking that lasted through the alchemic grottoes, monuments to friendship, and tournament fields of his landscapes over the next forty years.

Jappelli threw himself into the Napoleonic programme for Padua, ranging from the early planning of a new, hygienic slaughterhouse to decorating the *salle municipale* for a festival in celebration of the Corsican 'liberator'. (Six years later Jappelli would collaborate with the same team to celebrate the 'Feste' for Napoleon's Austrian replacement.) At the same time, Jappelli applied his more technical skills to the new order by enlisting in the army of Napoleon's viceroy, Eugène de Beauharnais, where he served as an engineer and captain through 1813. As an officer in Beauharnais' army, Jappelli may have seen a few landscape gardens in northern Italy in addition to Torri.

As an engineer and architect who discovered a new role for himself as an artist of garden design, Jappelli's evolution matches the best-known fictional narrative of the English landscape garden of his time: from a captain-engineer, capable of radically transforming the landscape for violent purposes – inventing new physical relationships at the scale of territories – to a garden designer moving earth for aesthetic ends – inventing new relationships for his clients and himself, parallels the career of the captain in Goethe's *Elective Affinities* (1809). Not that Jappelli would have read Goethe's

---

[5] The fullest discussion to date of Jappelli's relationship to Freemasonry is in Lionello Puppi, 'Giuseppe Jappelli e la Massoneria: una profezia inquietante', *Massoneria e Architettura*, ed. Carlo Cresti (Foggia, 1989), p. 175. Puppi cites two critical documents indicating Jappelli's membership in a Freemasonic Lodge: 'un rapporto databile sul finir del 1825 della polizia asburgica al Presidio di Governo del Lombardo Veneto', and 'una supplica di perdono alvicere' Ranieri ... sottoscritta da Jappelli nel gennaio 1826', p. 175.

[6] Puppi, 'Jappelli e la Massoneria,' p. 176.

novel, but he was part of a culture in which the game of constructing relationships, whether in war or at peace, was undertaken very seriously, and where an architect and engineer with a scenographic gift was among the best of players.

THE ENGLISH GARDEN IN JAPPELLI'S ITALY

However Jappelli came to his 'maestria', he would have to have been hard put to do it in a vacuum of knowledge of the talk and practice of the English landscape garden in Italy.[7] The English garden, more chauvinistically known as the *giardino irregolare*, had sparked a conversation that had already lasted in Europe for a century in 1814, and northern Italy, and Padua in particular, took a vigorous if ultimately regional role in the international discussion.

In 1813, one year before Jappelli's visit to Torri, the second edition of Ercole Silva's 1801 treatise on gardens, *Dell'arte de' giardini inglesi* was published, this time including illustrations of four English-style gardens in northern Italy.[8] As a well-educated architect in northern Italy, Jappelli might also have seen Luigi Mabil's 1801 abridged translation of Hirschfeld's monumental treatise on the English garden.[9] Finally, the topic was lively enough in 1817, only three years later (and the first year that Jappelli executed an English garden), for a Verona publisher to bring out a compendium volume of essays on the English garden, including both current writings and those from as early as 1783.[10]

If, in fact, Jappelli was versed in some or part of this material, he may have noted the conflicting attitudes toward the associational free-for-all of gardens such as the Picenardi brothers' retreat. On the one hand, the poet Pindemonte derided the value of artificially constructed nature in his 1792 essay (reprinted in the collection of 1817). He did not accept the value of invented physical-historical relationships: 'quando una bella scena artifiziale mi s'appresenta, certo io ricevo subito una senzasione assai dolce, ma la riflessione, lungi dall'accrescere il piacere, parmi anzi diminuirlo'.[11] The melancholic Veronese poet's taste for authenticity gave the artist no role in the garden, except for passing through. And as a matter of aesthetics, Pindemonte declared that garden design did not qualify as art, lacking the imitative remove of painting and sculpture.[12]

---

[7] Several texts have been crucial to understanding the cultural context of Jappelli's English landscape gardens. These include Gianni Venturi, 'The landscape garden in Lombardy', *Lotus International*, 30 (1981), pp. 39–45; Georges Teyssot, 'The eclectic garden and the imitation of nature', in *The Architecture of Western Gardens*, ed. M. Mosser and G. Teysott (Cambridge, Mass., 1991). Two additional texts have been essential to a more general understanding of the multiple levels of meaning in the English landscape garden: G. L. Hersey, 'Association and sensibility in eighteenth-century architecture,' *Eighteenth-Century Studies*, 4 (1) (1970), pp. 71–89; John Dixon Hunt, 'Ut pictura poesis, ut pictura hortus, and the picturesque', *Word & Image*, 1 (1) (1985), pp. 87–107.

[8] Ercole Silva, *Dell'arte de' giardini inglesi* (Milan, 1801; reprint Milan, 1985; 2nd ed. Milan, 1813, reprint Milan, 1976).

[9] P. L. Mabil, *Teoria dell'arte dei giardini* (Bassano, 1801). Trans. of C. C. L. Hirschfeld, *Theorie der Gartenkunst* (Leipzig, 1779–85).

[10] A. Torri et al., *Operette di varj autori ai giardini inglesi ossia moderna* (Verona, 1817).

[11] Ippolito Pindemonte, 'Dissertazione su i giardini inglesi e sul merito in cio dell'Italia', in Torri et al., *Operette di varj autori*, p. 32.

Jappelli, in reflecting on the Picenardi, might have taken the more commonsensical attitude of Silva (and Thomas Whately before him) that the artificial scene of a false ruin could give rise to virtually the same effect as a real one: 'possono fare quasi la stessa sensazione'.[13] Jappelli could also turn to Sir William Chambers to ratify an active artist-designer's role in creating landscapes. Chambers, long after the cycle of taste had spurned him in discourse if not practice in England, retained much of his reputation among the thinkers and makers of the English garden on the continent. Chambers' essays, in abridged or complete form, are issued as the definitive introduction to the topic in Mabil's translation of Hirschfeld (1801), in Silva's treatise (1801, 1813), and even as late as the compendium of Pindemonte, Mabil and Cesarotti (1817).[14]

The editorial comments accompanying these reprintings reveal a liberal attitude towards authenticity, whether of text or garden. For example, Chambers' assertion that the gardens he is describing are geographically Chinese is openly mocked as 'la fantasia di Chambers', but at the same time he is hailed as the greatest master of his art by Mabil. Thus, Chambers' deceptive texts, a half-century old, were appreciated for their effect, even when their deception was apparent. Just as Chambers defended the well-done artificial garden, so his admirers defend his false geography. It is as though they respect Chambers for his focus on the authenticity of feeling rather than origins, and admire him for his assertion of the artist's prerogative to invent not only new things, but also new relationships: Piranesi called for a complex architecture that surpassed the bareboned mimicry of Greek neoclassicism he saw in his contemporaries; Chambers campaigned for the plain idea of the more art the better, opposing it to what he saw as the ostentatious artlessness of Capability Brown and his admirers.

Finally, Jappelli could have turned to Mabil's essay from 1796 in the 1817 volume, which suggested that the best English landscape garden should neither simply *be* natural, nor simply *appear* natural, but rather, from the point of view of the observer, should *oscillate* between the real and the invented. The spectator could enjoy the pleasures of 'la disposizione, la fisionomia, l'attegiamento, ch'esso aver deve per generare un grato equivoco, una deliziosa dubitazione, se natura od arte abbia creata quala scena, preparata quella sorpresa, delineato quel quadro...'[15]

Mabil's is the attitude of a connoisseur, in which the premiated experience is that of

[12] Pindemonte, 'Dissertazione su i giardino inglesi', pp. 28–30.

[13] Silva, *Giardini inglesi*, p. 240. Whately wrote, 'Whatever building we see in decay, we naturally contrast its present to its former state, and delight to ruminate on the comparison. It is true that such effects belong to real ruins; but they are produced in a certain degree by those which are fictitious; the impressions are not so strong, but they are exactly similar.' Thomas Whately, *Observations on Modern Gardening: Illustrated by Descriptions* (London, 1770), p. 132.

[14] *Operette di vari autori intorno ai giardini inglesi ossia moderni* (Verona, 1817). William Chambers, *Designs of Chinese Buildings* (London, 1757); and *A Dissertation on Oriental Gardening* (London, 1772). The Italian volumes include the 1757 essay virtually complete, while a severely abridged version of the *Dissertation* is added by Silva. Hirschfeld had included an entire chapter against the Chinese origins of Chambers' garden descriptions: 'Grunde gegen die Wirklichkeit der chinesischen Garten, wie sie Chambers beschreibt,' *Theorie der Gartenkunst*, vol. I, pp. 84–103. Yet Hirschfeld, and Mabil after him, praise the falseness. Mabil writes that in calling his gardens 'Chinese', Chambers was exercising an 'ingegnoso strategemma, per discreditare l'antica maniera simmetrica...' *Teoria dell'arte de' giardini*, p. 28.

[15] Mabil, 'Sopra l'indole dei giardini moderni,' in Torri et al., *Operette di varj autori*, p. 98.

the observer defining himself through taste – a combination of education, snobbery and instinct – including a broad capacity to suspend disbelief. For the turn-of-the-century connoisseur, whether in gardens or interiors, the suspension of disbelief was accompanied by a ready knowledge and admiration of the techniques used to induce the various illusions at work. The designer and his peers – a fraternity of taste – exercised this connoisseurship in admiring the full range of the beaux-arts, from the dubiously ancient objects of art by the late Piranesi to the themed historicism of the rooms of Thomas Hope and William Beckford to even the garden ruins of John Soane.

Throughout his career, Jappelli exercised this especially English sensibility, which for him was always bound to a vision of how the world should work beyond the garden. He offered up this oscillating pleasure, repeatedly garnering praise for effective deceptions, as in the Treves garden, where his visitors imagined themselves in the far country, though they knew full well they were in Padua: 'che lo spettatore crede trovarsi lunge bene dalla città e fra i più selvosi siti de'colli'.[16]

THE GARDEN AS THEATRE

Jappelli's most provocative demonstration of his skill at this sophisticated equivocation came in his first commission as a landscape designer for the most prestigious client of his career. His first full English landscape garden was beneath a painted sky, a vivid scenography installed in the great hall of the Palazzo della Ragione in Padua.[17] An evanescent show, the garden lasted for one night, 20 December 1815 (a month after the police report on Jappelli's past activities was finished), to honour the city's new Habsburg ruler, Emperor Francesco I, now further titled king of Lombardy-Venetia, and his consort Maria Lodovico. The melodrama, a musical theatre piece, was a classical allegory of Padua's recent political past in which only the arrival of Caesar brought natural and political peace to the land.

Francesco, the putative Caesar (some, including Jappelli, may have considered the now rock-bound Napoleon the finer emperor), watched the play from his loggia. Like the rest of the audience, he must have taken pleasure in the mix of the real and artificial, from the allées planted with trees and flowers, to the scene of the Brenta's source, a spring on a rough hillside, adorned by a temple dedicated to Truth. At its foot, a river, a wet and real expanse, flowed to painted mountains beneath a rustic wooden bridge.

At the end of the show, the emperor took a stroll along the allée to the stage, where, having already admired the pleasing mix of real and painted scenery, he could admire the techniques that had produced them, such as the hydraulic system. Not that the mechanical revelation undid the seriousness of the theatre of the 'natural' that he had just watched.

---

[16] Pietro Selvatico, *Guida di Padova e della sua provincia* (Padua, 1842), p. 275.

[17] *Descrizione della festa drammatica offerta nella gran sala della Ragione* (Padua, 1816); cited at length in Puppi, 'Jappelli: Invenzione e scienza', p. 238.

The drama initiated Francesco, his court, and the citizens of Padua into the dominant sequential sensibility of the garden and the cult, in which one begins with disorientation – in this case the unexpected surprise of discovering, at the end of a very long stairway to a *piano nobile* in the urban core of Padua, a naturalistic garden ablaze with light. This surprise was followed by a ritual enactment of new relationships, observed in an atmosphere of suspended disbelief. Following the ritual, the sophisticated response was to take pleasure in the ruse without diminishing the earnestness of the performance. It is a pattern that courses through the designs and thinking of Jappelli and his era.

THE GARDEN INTERNALISED: THE CAFFÈ

After the one-night show at the Palazzo della Ragione, Jappelli had several opportunities to design actual gardens, on the ground. But, before turning to them, it is useful to begin by discussing the 'permanent theatre' of the Caffè Pedrocchi, which, for all its hard urban edges, perfectly demonstrates the basic experiential strategies that Jappelli would apply in his gardens. Only blocks away from the Palazzo della Ragione, the Pedrocchi was a long-running commission, begun in 1817. Jappelli would first complete the neoclassical front pavilions and main block of the Caffè, then finish the neo-gothic Pedrocchino in the early 1830s.

The vivid description of the Caffè in the 1842 *Guida di Padova*, one among several already published, was written by one of Jappelli's former students, Pietro Selvatico. The architect's written sketch of the building and its place in the city makes clear the contemporary sense of parallel relationships between reinvented building types and reinvented human types – a building type, like a person, could find a new role through its functions and associations (fig. 10.1). But this new role had to be validated by its grounding in natural and human history, which, as in Jappelli's English gardens, was presented as a mixture of real and invented relationships. The techniques and practice of the Caffè are almost a paradigm of those of the garden, where the architect changes the physical landscape with such fluidity and speed that the owner or visitor or passing citizen can imagine changing him or herself with equal facility. The reinvention of building type, nature and self is also construed in the context of an emerging community, whose members have the taste, knowledge and moral qualities to both suspend disbelief – see themselves in a new relationship to history and place – and to appreciate the process.

As in the theatrical production at the Palazzo della Ragione, the gardens of Picenardi, and the garden designs that followed, in the Caffè Pedrocchi virtually every relationship of thing and place and person is new or reinvented. First, the Caffè itself assumed an unprecedented role in the city as a new type of public edifice. It was the city's new centre, a *magnifico stabilimento* which was a caffè, a club and an exchange.[18]

---

[18] Selvatico, *Guida di Padova*, p. 262.

Fig. 10.1 G. B. Cecchini. Caffè Pedrocchi, from *Guida di Padova e della sua provincia*
(Padua, 1842), pl. 4

The contrast could not be greater between the urban role of the new Caffè, in the
commercial and institutional core, and that of the coffeehouses installed at the centre of
the still oval canal, ringed by statues of the famous at Padua's Prato della Valle
(1775-96), the last great public work of the old Venetian order.

Second, the Caffè's architectural character validates the building's monumental
place in the civic order not only by tying it to the pre-modern past through classical
scale and design, but also by incorporating literal classical elements – marble fragments
of Roman architecture dug up on the site during the excavations for the vast
ice-house. Part of the decoration of the hemicyclic room on the ground floor, these
remnants of the ancient, Roman forum, cheek-by-jowl with new design, are the spice
of real history and place mixing with new invention, the technique Jappelli used again
and again in his gardens.

Third, with the addition of the Pedrocchino, Jappelli connected his edifice with the
medieval history of the place, not only with the style, but with the direct visual
juxtaposition of a new, gothic artifact, against the skyline of authentic gothic towers
(fig. 10.2), a relationship evident in the published views of the time. Once again,
Jappelli put his design into the history of the city to deliberately provoke *dubitazione
deliziosa* as to its authenticity, as he would in his gardens. Finally, with regard to the real

Fig. 10.2 Caffè Pedrocchi, showing *Il Pedrocchino*

and invented history of things, the Caffè offered a free-ranging scenographic path inside, from Greek, to Moorish, to Egyptian, to Etruscan, to Pompei, to Quattrocento, to Baroque, all giving the Caffè multiple characters, unmoored to any stable historical reality, but rather asserting access to all.

But what did all the relationships of things mean for the relationships of humans? First, the Caffè's capacity to be reinvented as a new type matched the proprietor Pedrocchi's capacity to remake himself. Selvatico praises Pedrocchi in the *Guida* as a man *nato non ricco* who chose to give back his riches to the city by giving it the Caffè: 'consecrare le cumulate ricchezze ad aggiungere durevole vantaggio ed ornamento alla patria'.[19] The opportunities for self-invention were not simply the proprietor's, but also the customers'. Selvatico praises the opportunities of the Caffè by writing of 'la

[19] Ibid.

importanza morale dei nostri moderni caffè. Noi troviamo in questo stabilimento, quasi direi, la espressione della presente società tenera di conservare i vantaggi dell'indipendenza, senza perdere quelli della consociazioni.'[20]

Within the Caffè, the individual could define his relationship to society, yet at the same time be part of the humming, alchemic fraternity of caffeine. In a sense, it was as though he (or she, ultimately), had entered a desanctified Freemasonic lodge, in which the permanent theatre of Jappelli's set designs helped to shed the normal relationships of class and rank, allowing for both private contemplation and social reintegration. Thus, the Caffè Pedrocchi presents a haven of the sensibilities of the English landscape garden, in which the proprietor and his visitors establish authenticity through interpreting and acting in a field of real and invented historical artifacts. The desired effect was not casual, or temporary, but rather that of *importanza morale*. All that was required was a sensibility, one that could understand and interpret and invent, and, through contemplation, reimagine the order of the world.

THE FIRST GARDEN: PATERNITY AND THE CULT

Jappelli's first garden commission on the ground was identified in guide books as created first and foremost for the public good, giving it a moral weight of its own, although one rather different from that of the Caffè. Count Antonio Vigodarzere, who owned an estate in Saonara, a village a few miles east of Padua, was said to have initiated the garden as a public works project offering gainful employment for the Saonarans who had survived the famine of 1816.[21]

A drawing by Jappelli, most likely drafted at the beginning of the project in 1817, shows the 34.5 acre (14 hectare) garden much as it finally developed (fig. 10.3). The existing villa and its barchessa stayed in place, as did the late eighteenth-century *tempietto* by Angelo Sachetti at the entrance. At the south, where the drawing is fully rendered (it is mostly in black pencil, with a few shadings of green and brownish terracotta), Jappelli put meadows defined by sweeping arcs of regular plantings, shapes on the sheet that look like the rooms of a freed-up Baroque plan, one whose poché, however, is riddled with a vermicelli of tortuous 'Chinese' paths, demonstrating, as in much of his other work, his affinity for Chambers. Between these and the villa, there is a broad swath marked *tutto sabe*, identified in descriptions as the ancient bed of the Brenta. In the garden as in the Caffè, Jappelli exploited extant natural and historical artifacts to build up his narrative of invented relationships.

The light pencil work on the drawing shows the area north-east of the villa filled in with a lake, hillocks, and the basic plan of the Templars Chapel, possibly with a grotto nearby. The full complex of chapel, judgement room and grotto described in later

---

[20] Ibid., p. 266.   [21] Ibid., p. 54.

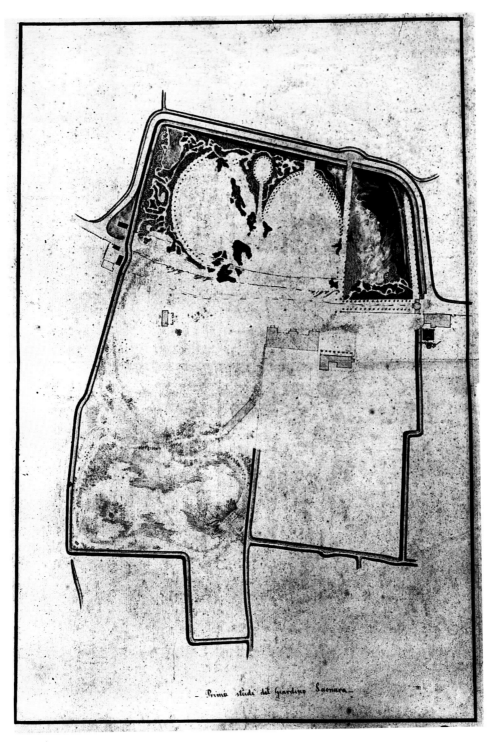

Prima studi del Giardino Saonara

Fig. 10.3 Giuseppe Jappelli. First studies for the Saonara Garden

accounts was not yet designed, but would be executed in a second round of building in the early 1830s.

The 'public' benefited from the Saonara garden not only in employment, but also by their access to the grounds, whether on foot or by reading through the several guides and descriptions published during and after Jappelli's lifetime. While hardly the public realm of the Caffè, the garden was no secret: the public was meant to know it, and, while perhaps not from as privileged a position as Emperor Francesco in the Palazzo della Ragione, intended to understand the technique – the hydraulics, the botanical expertise, the architectural sleight of hand – that went into it.

The Templars Chapel, today as in the nineteenth century, compels the most comment (fig. 10.4). The chapel survives, albeit with most of its ornament inside and out gone, while the later sequence of the room of judgement and grotto beyond has been largely destroyed. The chapel was completed before Japelli's voyage to England in 1836, most likely soon after the beginning of the project in 1817, definitely before 1834.[22] The provenance of its decorative materials, among other evidence, suggests an earlier completion date, as well as Jappelli's typical strategy of mixing genuine historical artifacts with invented ones. The gothic architectural fragments (some left, mostly gone), were taken from a desanctified church, S. Agostino, demolished in 1806 during Napoleon's rule. Jappelli could not have used them until 1817-18, when the church's ruins became legal building material. He did use some stone from the church for his slaughterhouse in 1820, and it is probable that he took the ornamental materials for the Templars Chapel at about the same time.[23]

Thus, deep in the count's garden, Jappelli put a 'Templars Chapel', which mixed real artifacts with new architecture, set amidst a new 'nature' of hills, trees, lakes and streams. Any visitor could experience the heart-stopping gloom of the place; the Chinese effects that Chambers had called for half a century before did not take any special knowledge; regardless of rank, the garden fabrics could 'excite a great variety of passions in the mind of the spectator'.[24] Yet if the English landscape garden privileged the immediate sensations which were at least potentially universal, some visitors might have had a higher perceptive resonance. Whately had argued that: 'nothing is unworthy of the attention of a gardener, which can tend to improve his compositions, whether by immediate effects, or by suggesting a train of pleasing ideas'.[25] Jappelli offered immediate effects, but connoisseurs, the knowledgeable fraternity, might understand the full range of references, while others might see nothing but the gloom.

---

[22] The most recent full discussion of the dating of the Templars Chapel is in M. Azzi Visentini, 'Il giardino Citadella Vigodarzere a Saonara', in *Il giardino italiano dall'Ottocento*, ed. A. Tagliolini (Milan, 1990). Azzi Visentini also provides extensive citations and interpretation of the fullest descriptions of the garden, including an 1833 description by Tullio Dandolo, partially restated in 1834: 'Saonara', in *I giardini d'Italia*, vol. I, pp. 96–102; and most importantly, Giovanni Citadella's booklet, 'Il giardino di Saonara desc ritto' (Venezia, 1838).
[23] Azzi Visentini, 'Il giardino Citadella Vigodarzere', pp. 185–6.
[24] Chambers, *A Dissertation on Oriental Gardening*, p. 35.   [25] Whately, *Observations on Modern Gardening*, p. 256.

Fig. 10.4 G. B. Cecchini. *Saonara*, from *Guida di Padova e della sua provincia* (Padua, 1842), pl. 20

Seeing the gothic vault, the trophies and tombs, some everymen would have understood that the 'Templars' stood for Freemasonry.

The Knights Templar were the legendary founders of Freemasonry, medieval warriors who had learned the secrets of masonry in order to rebuild the lost temple of Solomon. The legend played as a metaphor for the Freemasons' modern ambition of constructing a brotherhood bound by their initiation into secret knowledge, not for private gain, but ultimately for the reconstruction of the world – remade according to the plan of the Temple of Solomon.

But what was the point, for Jappelli, his patron, and the visiting connoisseur? While we can only speculate on the precise meanings Jappelli and his client intended to communicate, we do know that they could have been far more explicit. Elsewhere in Europe there had been direct Freemasonic narratives built into gardens and stage sets, whether far to the north in Scandinavia,[26] or on the stage in Vienna in Mozart's *The Magic Flute*.[27] Even in northern Italy there were English landscape gardens with very deliberate Freemasonic agendas, with initiatory paths built by clients and designed by architects who were members of active Freemasonic lodges. Contemporary examples included the Marchese Pietro Torrigiani's garden in Florence, with an iconographic array of tombs and towers designed by Luigi Cambray Digny (1809-17). Cambray Digny designed a similarly ideological garden for Niccolò Puccini in Pistoia (1821-8), which was sufficiently inflammatory for the police to insist on his removing its revolutionary inscriptions.[28]

The architectural manifestation of Freemasonry's initiatory path, at least as it was developed in late eighteenth-century France, had a fairly precise sequence, one which Vigodarzere's garden reflected at a more general level. The lodges documented in Paris followed a vertically ascending path of entrance, chamber of reflection, cleansing room, oath room, and final banqueting hall: a path which the adept began blindfolded and alone, then cleansed and led into a dark and noisy ritual of various trials, arriving for his questioning by the grand master in brilliant light, and finally joining the banquet as a brother.[29]

---

[26] Magnus Olausson, 'Freemasonry, occultism and the picturesque garden towards the end of the eighteenth century', *Art History*, 8 (4) (1985), pp. 413–33.

[27] See Geza Hajos, *Romantische Garten der Aufklarung: Englische Landschaftskultur des 18. Jahrhunderts in und um Wien* (Vienna and Cologne, 1989), p. 45.

[28] Paolo Maresca, 'Architetti e committenti Massoni nella Toscana del XIX secolo: i giardini come "iter" simbolico e iniziatico', *Massoneria e architettura*, pp. 171–3. In case the visitor did not quite understand enough of the iconography, there was a contemporary guide, at least to Torrigiani's sequence of tomb and tower, *Guida al'Giardino Torrigiani* (Florence, 1824).

[29] See Anthony Vidler, 'The architecture of the Lodges', *The Writing of the Walls* (Princeton, 1987), in which he writes: 'For a second and equally powerful vision of initiatory space had asserted itself in the late [seventeen] seventies as the corollary to the Egyptian temple, that of the *jardin-anglais*, the allegorical representation of the landscape of the Elysian Fields. Rousseau had proposed the natural landscape as the site of mankind's regeneration; now the increasingly popular forms of the English landscape were adopted as the environmental agents of an initiatory state of mind,' p. 99; see also Monique Mosser, 'Paradox in the garden: a brief account of Fabriques', in *The Architecture of Western Gardens*, ed. Mosser and Teyssot (Cambridge, Mass., 1991), pp. 263–80.

Jappelli and his client may not have had the budget or the belief for a strict Freemasonic sequence as in Paris, or the sculptural and architectural programme of Torrigiani's Egyptian sculpture and hulking tower. In addition, it may have behove them to be more discreet, if that was their intention, because dramatising a secret brotherhood was not a light or innocent gesture in 1817. Following the Spanish revolution in 1820, revolutionary sects, variously connected to Freemasonry, were intensely active in northern Italy: more so in Piedmont and Lombardy than the Veneto, but none the less recruiting among the same class of officers, aristocrats and professionals as Jappelli and his colleagues and clients. The multiple sects of the time, including the *adelfia, federati, carbonaria,* and *guelfia,* were united in a loose federation with the overall mastery of Filippo Buonarotti, an unreconstructed radical who pragmatically hid his views from the rank and file, a practice possible due to the sects' 'ritual symbolism, rigid hierarchical structure, and gradual revelation of aims'.[30]

Jappelli and his client may have had only an indirect connection to this revolutionary programme, or seen the garden as a place to retreat from revolution into metaphor. There is no evidence that the 'real' secret brotherhood of Freemasonry met or plotted in the Templars Chapel, yet such activity was real enough around them, with consequences beyond metaphor as the officers who instigated insurrections in northern Italy were discovered and prosecuted from 1821-4. The issue was also real enough for the Habsburg police to oblige Jappelli to renounce Freemasonry in 1817 and again in 1826.

The cult, and a building in a garden representing it, hardly offered the liberal programme of the Caffè, but even in the first phase of the Templars Chapel at Saonara it does dramatise how the paths towards initiation into the Freemasonic cult, and the path through an English garden, could parallel and overlap, whether literally or only metaphorically. An initiate into the rituals and aims of the Freemasons, like the connoisseur-initiate of the English garden, underwent a willing sequence of disorientation (in the garden, a grotto or a glen), followed by induction into special knowledge – weak as fact but strong as theatre, and probably recognised as such by the adept.[31] There is no reason to assume that most Freemasons fully believed in the mystical portion of their rite, any more than that the patron of an English landscape garden believed that his new ruin proved that he had medieval ancestors, but in the cult, and in the garden, the mythic and mystical were useful fictions in validating the adept's rebirth as an individual oriented to his brothers and the public good.

Jappelli's later design for the Saonara garden, like his designs for Dr Giacomini and Prince Torlonia, went much further than the first essay in recreating a sequential path

---

[30] Stuart Wolf, *A History of Italy 1700-1860: The Social Constraints of Political Change* (London, 1979), pp. 252–63.

[31] Vidler, 'The architecture of the Lodges', p. 101; see also Mary Anne Clawson, *Constructing Brotherhood* (Princeton, 1989); René Le Forestier, *La Franc-Maconnerie Templière et occultiste aux XVIII et XIX siècles* (Paris, 1970); and for a more general discussion of late eighteenth-century attitudes towards irrational effects, Robert Darnton, *Mesmerism and the Enlightenment in France* (Cambridge, Mass., 1968).

reminiscent of the initiatory route of Freemasonry. Antonio Vigodarzere, Jappelli's original patron at Saonara, died in 1835, and his nephew Citadella, whom Vigodarzere had adopted as his son, developed the initiatory sequence more fully. Andrea Citadella Vigodarzere put the garden and its artifacts at the service of a thesis of a reinvented self. In addition to modernising the villa itself, he expanded the Templars narrative from his father's time, adding a 'judgement room' and a grotto with a colossal statue of 'Baffamateo' to the Templars Chapel, creating a sequence that would be repeatedly described and illustrated in letters and guide books, and would inspire Jappelli's first and last Roman client, Torlonia.

The fullest description of Saonara as Citadella Vigodarzere completed the garden is in an account by Giovanni Citadella, who imagines visiting the garden on a summer evening with his friends Agostino Sagredo, Pietro Selvatico Estense and the owner. Their *percorso* begins along a path of cypresses to an Ionic temple holding the remains of the first proprietor, represented by a statue of the ageing father blessing his adopted son. The next stop is a hill dedicated to spring, where, amidst the flowers and marbles, one is in an asylum of meditation (itself a rough equivalent to the room of reflections in the Freemasonic route). After the brusque appearance of a sandy riverbed, the path divides, to a hillock with poplars, to a wood of magnolia and catalpa. The walkers take tiny twisting paths, offering multiple views and the illusion of covering vast territories, and then travel on to the woodland paths near the lake, finally arriving at the Templars Chapel.

Inside the chapel, full of tombs from the desanctified Paduan church, reissued as those of ancient Templars, the friends pass through to the hall of trials, circular in plan, with the marks of the test of fire and water, and they remark on the seven-pointed star, the stork of love, and, at last, within the stalagmite-filled grotto, the statue of Baffamateo, holding the chain of the centuries and other Freemasonic accoutrements. If the references are obscure, they are also largely explained, and even in Selvatico's *Guida* four years later, what might have remained inexplicable is adumbrated for public consumption. From the entrance through to the interior, Selvatico describes the Templar iconography (with its direct reference to Freemasonry, but not the word itself): 'le arme ed i trofei appesi alle sgrottate parete ricordano i prodezza templare', and beyond were the trials, 'Nel camminare questa grotta veggonsi i due battesimi ad acqua ed a fuoco usati dei Gnostici, a cui, secondo lo stesso Hammer, si acconciavano i degenerati cavalieri del Tempo.'[32]

In Citadella's account, the visitors (in this case all men) exit through to the summit, see glimpses of the lake, hear a rivulet, and arrive at the miller's house, which has a storeroom filled with marbles dug up in the construction. As at the Caffè Pedrocchi, the real past turned up during the construction of history. The tour ends with a view from the highest hills, to Venice, to Piove, the Euganean Hills, back to the public world.

---

[32] Selvatico, *Guida di Padova*, p. 52.

How had the dangerous notion of a secret brotherhood become, by the 1830s, innocuous enough to publicise, or was it simply that the practice of 'secrecy', like the practice of the English garden, oscillated between different levels of exposure? There is a parallel from half a century earlier in France, before the collapse of the old regime, when the secret fraternity of Freemasonry became increasingly bold, enough so that by the time the ageing Voltaire was initiated, it was reported in the newspapers. Freemasonry had become a public secret, meant to be known, just as the Parisian private, English landscape gardens of the same era were intended ultimately as public artifacts.[33]

In addition, if one looks for the binding theme of Saonara as reconfigured by the first client's adopted son, it is one of invented paternity, rather than constructed brotherhood. The statue of the hermaphroditic Baffamateo, a father figure for the Templar knights who elides the need for a mother in the order's myth, surely stands for Citadella's own invented filial relationship to the dead count. Grown men could become sons (or brothers), mature trees could be planted in new soil.

THE GARDEN AS URBAN ALCHEMY

For all the focus on secret brotherhoods and motherless sons, neither Saonara nor Jappelli's other narrative-rich garden designs were the reserve of men. Women, too, were shown at Saonara, approaching the chapel in G. B. Cecchini's drawing (published in the 1842 *Guida*) with their escort (fig. 10.4), and in a later engraving with the full domestic complement of children and dogs.[34] Cecchini also depicted a man and a woman at the heart of the grotto, already past the vicarious trials of fire and water, hard by Baffamateo. On the one hand, this could be read as signifying that even the deepest secrets of the Temple could be domesticated, on the other, it could be understood as showing how women, too, could participate in the transformative ideology, and were integral to any personal or cultural process of reinvention.

The 1842 guide book also includes an illustration of the Treves Garden, where while sacred friendship, chivalry, and other Freemasonic effects retain a special place in the programme, any 'secret brotherhood' represented seems more sedate than revolutionary. The lithograph shows two couples and a lone woman, gazing at a pair of swans (fig. 10.5). Italy had not, in fact, passed beyond the era of active secret political fraternities, but the metaphor in the garden had taken a far gentler mien. The 'initiation' was into connoisseurship of the intimate perceptions possible in a semi-public pleasure garden.

Completed between the first and second phases at Saonara, the Treves Garden was explicit in its analogies of natural and personal reinvention and relationships. First, there

---

[33] Monique Mosser, 'The picturesque in the city: private gardens in Paris in the 18th century', *Lotus International*, 30 (1981), pp. 29–37.

[34] 'La cappella dei Templari nei giardini di villa Citadella Vigodarzere a Saonara', lithograph by A. Gloria, *Il territorio padovano illustrato*, vol. II (Padua, 1862).

Fig. 10.5 G. B. Cecchini. *Giardino Treves*, from *Guida di Padova e della sua provincia*
(Padua, 1842), pl. 5

was the site, a piece of leftover land behind the aristocratic Treves brothers'
sixteenth-century palace, in a corner of the venerable city walls. As so often with
Jappelli's work, there was a genuine natural and historic context to start with, which he
resolutely stretched into a fantasy that oscillated between the natural and the new.
Jappelli dramatised the Alicorno canal into a natural body of water, and then, by
thinking through the distant sights and organising the hills and dales of the new site, set
up views to the real, exotic towers of Il Santo in the distance. For the chapel at Saonara,
Jappelli had used fragments of a demolished, desanctified church; at the Treves Garden,
as at the Pedrocchi Caffè, he employed views of the city's medieval monuments to add
authenticity to the stage set. In this English landscape garden, the distant eyecatchers
were the real, three-dimensional artifact; it was the foreground that held the new ruins.

Everywhere in the garden, Jappelli pushed through an iconography of invented
human relationships to complement the invented natural ones. There are numerous
false ruins, including among the most prominent a monument to friendship: caryatids
support a lintel framing the inscription: 'Concordiae Amicitae, AN MDCCCXXIX,
Sacer Locus' (fig. 10.6). Beyond this monument to amity and peace, there still stands on
the hillock a temple to love, once graced by sculptures of Amore and Psyche on top
(fig. 10.7).

Fig. 10.6 Treves park

The garden was the scene for alchemy, for constructed relationships, human and natural, and in case anyone missed the point, there was a grotto, now gone, which had inscriptions about 'Beppo dei Zardini', apparently inscribed as a sort of local Merlin, whose cavern was crammed with animal bones and cabalistic inscriptions. The more modern magic of botany was housed in a building that was gothic on one side – Jappelli's second neo-gothic façade, but without bric-a-brac, and neoclassical on the other. This was the sort of startling contrast championed by Richard Payne Knight, both on his own estate and in his writing: 'we perpetually see a mixture of Grecian and Gothic architecture employed with the happiest effect in the same building . . . far from interrupting the chain of ideas, they lead it on and extend it in the pleasantest manner, through different ages, and successive revolutions in tastes, arts, and sciences'.[35] (Payne Knight is one of the few English influences Jappelli ever directly credited.)[36] Inside Jappelli's two-faced structure, the chain of ideas ended in botany, storage for seeds and bulbs.

It is difficult to imagine the scenographic effect today, but Jappelli had a full narrative

[35] Richard Payne Knight, *An Analytical Inquiry into the Principles of Taste* (London, 3rd ed., 1805), p. 157.
[36] Jappelli, in his unpublished 'Memorie del giardiniere e dell'agricoltore' (1842) refers to English authors on gardening, mentioning 'Kent-Payne Knight-Uvedal Price-Repton-Henry Stewart', cited in Azzi Visentini, *Il giardino veneto tra Sette e Ottocento*, p. 245.

Fig. 10.7 Giuseppe Jappelli. *Pianta e prospetto de tempietto Treves*

team, including a sculptor and painter, which produced a setting calling for medieval knights battling in the exiguous tournament field (a feature which would be repeated with more effect for the Torlonia), a clearing filled with tombs of ancient sires, and, long since gone, a pagoda at the highest point, a homage to the English garden aside from the alchemic, chivalric theme.

Certainly the Treves, unlike the Pedrocchi, had no great need to reinvent themselves; they were nobles, they had a historic and contemporary role in the city. Yet they, too, were characterised as living up to an assumed role. Selvatico in the *Guida* may simply have been singing for his supper (one suspects he was doing so quite literally in praising the Caffè-owner Pedrocchi), but in any case he felt compelled to note how the Treves, through their garden as through their other patronage of 'the arts of the beautiful', were defining themselves. Selvatico footnotes the generous public role of the Treves, in art exhibitions in Venice as much as in their Paduan garden, almost at the same length as the description of the garden: 'Questi colti signori meritana di essere annoverati fra quei pochi ricchi che incoraggiano con intelletto d'amore le arti di bello.'[37] Perhaps they did not need to reinvent themselves, but their visitors did.

---

[37] Selvatico, *Guida di Padova*, p. 275.

PROFESSIONAL BROTHERHOOD AND THE GARDEN

In 1839, ten years after he began the Treves park, Jappelli initiated a project not for an aristocrat, but for a professional like himself. While lacking the gloom of the Saonara chapel-judgement room-grotto sequence, the house and garden offered probably his most earnest exposition on the garden as an initiatory space. The invented history was still neo-gothic, the metaphors of secret brotherhood and reinvention were not abandoned, but they were contained within a responsible, domestic realm.

The property, a house and garden on the Via del Santo, had a very public site – the main thoroughfare to Padua's most famous square and monument – but a very internalised programme. The public façade was a heavily rusticated, classical elevation, but the interior elevations and garden were an extraordinary neo-gothic exercise of 'pointed' window surrounds and castellated towers. Jappelli had carried out a similarly two-sided project a decade before, where the gothic-arched garden side of the gardener's house at Treves contrasted to the other side's orthogonal discipline, but here it had a clear programmatic rationale.

Only a score of yards away from the gothic court, but given greater distance through its setting on a small rise, stood the octagonal, Moorishly-detailed tower. Like the interior court's neo-gothic ornamentation, this was invisible from the street, but from within the garden it blends with the monuments of the city, a tower among the neighbouring towers, as at the Pedrocchino. At its base, there are (as at the Templars Chapel) a mix of real and invented fragments of Padua's earlier monuments.

For the client, this visual integration with the history of the city was also literally grounded in history, not only of a general kind, but of the most august annals of his public, professional 'brotherhood', the medical fraternity. G. A. Giacomini, as a prominent doctor, had bought a property where he could assert a direct physical connection to the greatest doctor Padua had known, G. B. Da Monte. While the sixteenth-century physician had established a medical clinic of which no one knew the exact whereabouts, Giacomini asserted that he had found the clinic itself, listing among his various evidence that in the excavations for the tower he had come across an array of human skulls and bones laid out as though for anatomical study.

Giacomini's colleagues did not all agree, but for the Paduan doctor this was a public issue. He decided to stake his claim of professional ancestry by publishing his letter to one of his doubters, G. Cervetto, a Veronese doctor, in 1844 in the *Giornale Eugeneo*. In the letter, Giacomini writes of how 'in piccolo estensione di scavo per costruire una toricella si rinvennero non meno di dieci carra di ossa umane, tra le quali parecchi crani segati come si usa nelle anotomiche dissertazione'.[38]

Thus his tower had an irresistibly alchemic base of human bones touched by a great doctor's hands, grounding it in the critical 'brotherhood' of the nineteenth century, the

---

[38] Letter dated 28 November 1843, published in *Giornale Eugeneo*, 15 April 1844; cited in Mazza, *Jappelli e Padova*, p. 106.

professional association. The tower had Freemasonic references, such as its three levels, rising from white to blue to yellow, from a dark base to an enlightened crown. Inside the tower, instead of the Templars' trophies of war, was a shelf of 'books' in plaster, relics of professional power. It was a curious transformation of the Freemasonic tower, whether it drew on the example of Torrigiani's Tuscan garden from the 1820s, or even earlier examples such as Louisenlund (1779–84) in Schleswig, Germany.[39]

Whatever the iconographic shifts, and absent evidence that any Freemasonic group other than the circumstantial one that the architect and his client and friend had visited the tower together, the doctor had none the less established an English landscape garden ideal for serious play-acting, where through suspending disbelief he could convince himself that he believed in the past presence of his historic predecessor, in order to affirm his constructed relationship to the ongoing narrative of society. Within his domestic retreat, Giacomini could cross the yard, clamber up the hillock, enter the dark tower, ascend the initiatory stairs, and arrive at the bright lookout. Through arabesques he could look out over the rooftops to the towers of Il Santo (fig. 10.8). The medieval frame was art, the medieval domes and minarets were history.

THE BAD CONNOISSEUR: TORLONIA'S ROMAN GARDEN

The prince of Torlonia, whose fortune came from his father's franchise of the mail system, had a vast budget and property compared to that of Giacomini, but in the end even he had only a suburban back yard for Jappelli's work, far tighter and more urban than Saonara. Torlonia had seen the garden in Saonara, with its winding paths, woods, waterways, and most impressively, its dark sequence of Templars Chapel, judgement chamber and grotto. Enchanted, the prince brought the Paduan architect to Rome in 1839 to do the same for his villa on the Via Nomentana, a scene already bristling with the artists and architects decorating the life of the prince (the better known Villa Torlonia, originally the Villa Albani, was purchased by the same Alessandro Torlonia decades later, in 1866).

Jappelli did his work, sketching out a *percorso iniziatico*, offering stock items from an English landscape garden's itinerary such as pagoda, grotto, dairy, lakes, isles (the drawing itself is a sketch coded to identifications of the various stops along the path: fig. 10.9). As built, Jappelli turned out a series of buildings and places enlivened by their apparent reference to Ariosto's *Orlando Furioso*, where the tournament field, Swiss 'hut', lake, glade, grotto and Moorish tower and greenhouse could all be keyed to scenes in the epic, still a source of inspiration fifty years after the Picenardi quoted it throughout their garden in Torri.[40] The drawing clearly shows how Jappelli's responsibilities were focused on everything behind the villa. The front, with its own collection of mock ruins, had been

---

[39] See Olaussen, 'Freemasonry, occultism', pp. 420–1.
[40] Alberta Campitelli, 'Il Parco di Villa Torlonia da Valadier agli interventi novecenteschi', in Tagliolini (ed), *Il Giardino Italiano dell'Ottocento*, p. 218.

Fig. 10.8 Giardino Giacomini (now Romiati). View from the tower towards Il Santo

completed decades before, while the villa and its sculptural programme (by Thorvaldsen) were entirely out of Jappelli's hands. Throughout the rest of the villa and grounds, the prince had to work around the leavings of his predecessors, but in the back, in his nominally private realm, he asked Jappelli to design a new, romantic landscape, based on the woods and grottoes he had seen at Saonara.

Yet the gap between the privacy and intimacy integral to Saonara and the prince's intentions is apparent even in the first sketch, where instead of a walking path to the grotto complex in the lower right corner, Jappelli has inserted a carriageway. As the design was executed, the pomp and scale of the villa further invaded the landscape garden; the tournament field has the hard symmetries and large scale necessary for fully-staged re-enactments—at Treves Jappelli had only offered the symbols of a tournament field, just enough for literary reflection. Torlonia was more interested in a train of action than a train of thought.

Like most of Jappelli's garden commissions, the Torlonia garden was soon given a public accounting, explaining the mysteries. Giuseppe Checchetelli wrote the description, *Una giornata di osservazione nel palazzo e nella villa di S. E. il sig. Principe D. Alessandro Torlonia* (Rome, 1847).[41] While it is hard to imagine today, when all that

---

[41] Cited at length in Alessandro Tagliolini, *Storia del giardino Italia* (Florence, 1988), p. 354.

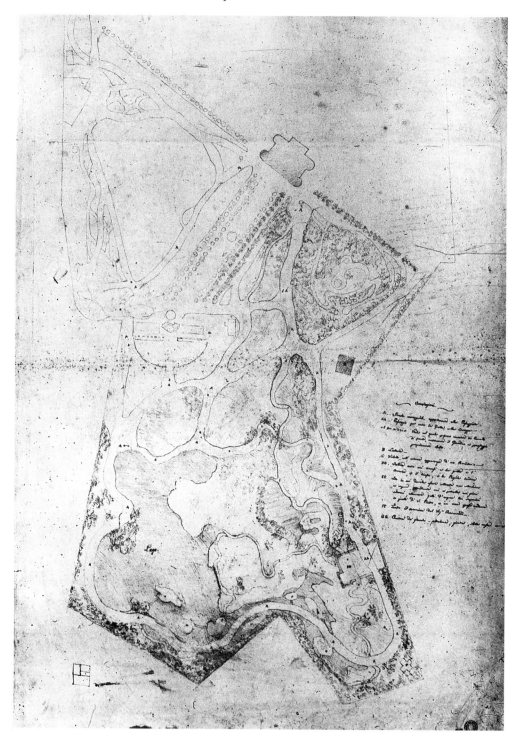

Fig. 10.9 Study for the Giardino Torlonia at Roma

remains is the ruined hulk of the Moorish greenhouse, Checchetelli's description
makes the grotto and Moorish tower above it sound magnificent. It contained two
small lakes, mysterious lighting from above, and led to a room of oriental splendour, at
the base of the hexagonal tower. This interior retreat, which fitted into the
Freemasonic progression from darkness to light typical of Jappelli's earlier garden
designs, domesticated the scenario in a new way – through luxury, from the stained
glass windows above, to the pools full of fish, to the columns decorated in arabesques of
silver and gold. And, as at the end of the Freemasonic sequence, the room could serve
for a banquet, thanks to the engineering of its moving parts: 'Cosa da stupire! esso
innalzasi sino alla cupola della stanza formanco un baldacchino, e una tavola sorge ad
occupare il suo luogo, la quale può essere preparata per un banchetto nella sottoposta
cucina: novella e gaia prova di magnificenza e d'ingegno.'[42]

The pattern here seems almost a direct evocation of the Freemasonic lodge, where
from the lonely darkness and trials, one ascends to the light of wisdom and the convivial
banquet. Furthermore, attached to the tower was the literal proof that mature trees could
be planted in new soil, the exotic plants in the iron and glass and masonry greenhouse (at
the Jardin Monceau, a Freemasonic lodge had been attached to a greenhouse). The
façade of the Torlonia greenhouse is intact, covered in Arabic calligraphy, defining the
greenhouse not as a lucid, scientific container, but as yet another initiatory temple.

One might assume that Jappelli would have been pleased with the opportunity to
demonstrate his skills: architectural, scenographic, engineering (the table rising from
below, bearing the secret feast), and even botanical, offering to the connoisseur
surprise, wonder, and naturalness and the chance to admire the technical skill of their
construction. Jappelli, however, was not satisfied. He had created a complex
topography (especially the convincingly wild *montagnola* adjacent to the villa),
interjected bold architectural moves into a dull landscape; yet nothing was in tune with
his overall programme. He had provided a stunning exposition on the dream – the
dream of Italian epic poetry, of chivalric tournaments, of orientalist mystery, of
progressions through frightening darkness to bright banquet rooms. Yet he complained
that his client did not understand the concomitant responsibility.

Torlonia and his friends, in Jappelli's view, were unable to live up to the implications
of the English landscape garden. (One also wonders whether Torlonia and company
did much to live up to the inevitably heroic sculptural programme of Thorvaldsen at
the villa itself.) Torlonia, a great anglophile, had seen far more of England than Jappelli,
but by 1839 Jappelli had been to England himself (in 1836 and 1837), which must have
affirmed rather than disillusioned his idealised vision of the relationship between the
ruling class and their gardens, a relationship that he found sorely lacking in Torlonia.

In a letter to a Paduan friend, Jappelli characterised Roman princes, presumably
including his client Torlonia: 'I principi non trovano in casa che la noja prodotta

---

[42] Giuseppe Checchetelli, *Una giornata*, p. 94; in Tagliolini, ibid., p. 354.

dall'ozio, e sbucano dalle lora case dorate per abbagliare il volgo, e fuggire da loro stessi.' The Roman princes had no self-definition other than that provided by spectacle, which allowed them to forget their own bored selves. The English aristocracy, on the other hand, in Jappelli's vision had both a more genuine public and private life: 'l'aristocrazia inglesi sorte di casa e per amor di guardagno, e per trattare gl'interessi della Nazione, e vi ritorna per godere i conforti della vita, e le dolcezze della tranquillità dopo le ore operose.'[43]

Thus, the English gentry, raised to lead rather than to show off, also knew when to retire into a pastoral 'gentleness of tranquillity'. They had cultivated themselves, as well as their gardens. Looking at the programme of the Treves Garden, or the Citadella Vigodarzere, or even the Giacomini, one might argue that these each offered spectacle much as the Nomentana villa did, rather than a demonstration of the pastoral. Yet these earlier projects demonstrate a far subtler spectacle, one which, for Jappelli, could be contained within his ideal vision of a life in harmony with the English landscape garden. Giacomini's garden, small as it was, offered (and still does offer) an extraordinary retreat from public life, but the tower is a symbolic tie back to public life. The patron, even in retreat, was ready to lead. The Templars Chapel at Saonara carried the same message; even Treves, too.

In addition, each of these earlier gardens offered up their effects, optical and otherwise, at a small, contemplative scale. By contrast, the garden at the Villa Nomentana was all spectacle. The prince might go through the initiatory motions, but his appetite for spectacle blinded him. Jappelli wrote to his friend: 'Quelle stradelle che tu vedi a Saonara di un metra e mezzo qui sono larghe sei metri almeno e fino a dieci metri ... Entro la grotta si deve girare in carrozza etc. etc. Tu vedi adunque che la grandezza, anziche ajutare, spesse volte toglie o diminuisce l'Effetto ottico...per queste abitudini, ci vogliono i Giardini di Versailles, i giardini di Le Notre.'[44]

Jappelli returned to Padua, back to a culture in which visitors to his gardens were pictured in pairs and trios, admiring the subtle 'optical effects', reflecting on both the spectacular and the delicate relationships, perhaps understanding the message that these gardens indicated a programme in which visitors and patrons could reinvent or reaffirm their relationship and responsibilities in the world.

CONCLUSION

This chapter has focused on Jappelli's designs of gardens, their fabrics, and the Caffè Pedrocchi, because these commissions are taut with moral tension absent in his other

---

[43] Jappelli, letter from Rome to Giuseppe Bernardi, 24 June 1840, in Ms. Biblioteca Civica. Padua, 2592/IV; cited in Marcello Fagiolo, 'Ideologie di Villa Torlonia. Un mecenate e due architetti nella Roma dell'Ottocento', *Giuseppe Jappelli e il suo tempo*, pp. 549–86, p. 585, n. 81.

[44] Jappelli, letter from Rome to Giuseppe Bernardi, 24 June 1840, cited in Azzi Visentini, 'Il giardino Citadella Vigodarzere', p. 192.

executed work. In part, these works are charged with meaning because there was not a great deal of other work: despite a successful career ranging from engineering to scenography, Jappelli never had Schinkel's chance to prove himself, he never realised the great public architecture such as the prison and university that he drew in his studio. Besides the Caffè, his most important commission in Padua was the Macello, where the cattle were slaughtered in a severe Doric rotunda, sacrifices to a hygienic deity.

The stress in these projects comes from the need for the designs to unite Jappelli's extraordinary gift for spectacle – whether in fantastic architecture, hydraulic prowess or natural wonder – with a sober ideal of the moral universe in which the architect saw himself engaged. The spectacle had to serve a purpose; it might shock, creating an initiatory state of mind, but then the train or chain of associations had to lead to a vision of a better life.

The tension broke with the Torlonia project: Jappelli realised that he had provided spectacle, but no train of thought after, just a carriage ride to another show. One wonders whether he entertained similar doubts regarding the moral train of the Caffè Pedrocchi, even as his former pupil Selvatico touted *l'importanza morale* of the modern caffè.

None the less, if Jappelli had come to recognise his work's imperfect utopian effects, his overall project was neither naive nor played out by the early 1840s. His is an extraordinary exercise in containing spectacle – immediate effects – within the imagination of contemplative citizens bound by a common goal of the public good. Frederick Law Olmsted and his European peers would extend this suffrage to the general public, although Olmsted was extremely wary of picturesque drama, avoiding spectacle for the pastoral. Today, spectacle seems so much more enormous and at the same time so much more contained than in nineteenth-century Padua. Jappelli's gardens may demonstrate how to harness more rather than less meaning from landscape, as opposed to a culture where, as at Torlonia, the redemptive walk has been replaced by a redemptive run, right over the grounds' spectacularly grim twentieth-century past.

INDEX